A History of Rock Music in 500 Songs
Volume 1: From Savoy Stompers to Clock Rockers

Andrew Hickey

BY THE SAME AUTHOR:

Non-Fiction

Sci-Ence! Justice Leak!

The Beach Boys On CD: vol 1 - 1961-1969

The Beach Boys On CD: vol 2 - 1970-1984

The Beach Boys On CD: vol 3 - 1985-2015

An Incomprehensible Condition:An Unauthorised Guide To Grant Morrison's Seven Soldiers

Preservation: The Kinks' Music 1964-1974

California Dreaming: The LA Pop Music Scene and the 1960s

The Black Archive: The Mind Robber

Fifty Stories for Fifty Years: An Unauthorised Look at Doctor Who

Fiction

Ideas and Entities (short stories)

Faction Paradox: Head of State

Doctor Watson Investigates: The Curse of the Scarlet Neckerchief (ebook only)

Destroyer: A Black Magic Story

The Basilisk Murders: A Sarah Turner Mystery

The Glam Rock Murders: A Sarah Turner Mystery

For Holly

Contents

CONTENTS

Introduction

Rock and roll as a cultural force is, it is safe to say, dead.

This is not necessarily a bad thing, and nor does it mean that good rock and roll music isn't being made any more. Rather, rock, like jazz, has become a niche musical interest. It's a large niche, and it will be so long as there are people around who grew up in the last half of the last century, but the cultural influence it once had has declined precipitously in the last decade or so. These days, various flavours of hip-hop, electronic dance music, manufactured pop, and half a dozen genres that a middle-aged man like myself couldn't even name are having the cultural and commercial impact that in previous decades was mostly made by guitar bands.

And this means that for the first time, it's possible to assess rock music (or rock and roll – the two terms are not quite interchangeable, but this is not the place for a discussion of the terminology, which will come later) in a historical context. In fact this may be the best time for it, when it's still interesting to a wide audience, and still fresh in the memory, but it's not still an ongoing story that will necessarily change. Almost all of the original generation of rock and roll musicians are now dead (the only prominent exceptions at the moment being Jerry Lee Lewis, Don Everly, and Little Richard, although numerous lesser-known musicians from the time are still working occasionally), but their legacy is still having an impact.

So in this series of books, and the podcasts on which they are based, I will look at the history of rock and roll music, starting with a few pre-rock songs that clearly influenced the burgeoning rock and roll genre, and ending up in 1999 – it makes sense to cut the story off there, in multiple ways. I'll talk about the musicians, and about the music. About how the musicians influenced each other, and about the cultural forces that shaped them. In these pages, you'll read about the impact the Communist Party, a series of strikes, a lack of insect excrement, and a future governor of Texas would all have on rock and roll's prehistory. But more importantly you'll read about the songs and the singers, the instrumentalists and the record producers.

I shall be using a somewhat expansive definition of rock or rock and roll in this series, including genres like soul and disco, because those genres grew up alongside rock, were prominent at the same time as it, and both influenced and were influenced by the rock music of the time. In a future volume in this series, we'll look at the way the words "rock and roll" were slowly redefined, from originally meaning a form of music made almost entirely by black people to later pretty much explicitly excluding all black musicians from their definition, but my own history will include black genres and musicians as much as possible.

But the most important thing I'll be doing is looking at the history of rock in terms of the music. I'll be looking at the records, and at the songs. How they were made and by whom.

I've chosen five hundred songs in total, roughly a hundred per decade from the fifties through the nineties, though our story actually starts in 1938. Some of these songs are obvious choices, which have been written about many times before, but which need to be dealt with in any history of rock music. Others are more obscure tracks which nonetheless point to interesting things about how the music world was developing at the time they were recorded. I say "I've chosen", but this is going to be a project that takes nearly ten years, and no doubt my list will change.

Those of you who have read my earlier work *California Dreaming: The LA Pop Music Scene and the 60s* will be familiar with this narrative technique I'm using here, and this series is in many ways an expansion of that book's approach, but it's important to note that the two works aren't looking at precisely the same thing – that book was dealing with a particular scene, and with people who all knew each other, in a limited geographic and temporal space. Here, on the other hand, the threads we'll be following are more cultural than social. There isn't a direct connection between Little Richard and Talking Heads, for example, but hopefully over the course of this series we will find a narrative thread that still connects them.

If you've listened to the podcast, you'll notice one slight change. The first fifty songs I chose for the podcast included "Honky Tonk" by Bill Doggett, and didn't include "Cry" by Johnnie Ray. The Doggett song was put in as a way of getting new listeners up to speed, as Doggett played on so many records by other musicians the podcast covered. I've incorporated that material into the relevant entries here, and replaced it with "Cry", which I originally did as a Patreon bonus episode.

Now, this is a history of rock and roll, and so I am going to have to deal with a lot of abusers, sex criminals, and even a few murderers. You simply can't tell the history of rock and roll without talking about Ike Turner, Chuck Berry, Jerry Lee Lewis, Phil Spector, Jimmy Page. . . I could go on. But suffice to say that I think the assumption one should make when talking about rock music history is that any man discussed in it is a monster unless proved otherwise.

I'm going to have to talk about those men's work, and how it affected other things, because it's so influential. And I admire a lot of that work. But I never, ever, want to give the impression that I think the work in any way mitigates their monstrosity, or do that thing that so many people do of excusing them because "it was a different time".

But in order for this to be a history of rock music, and not a prurient history of misogynistic crime, I'm probably not going to mention every awful thing these people do. I'm going to deal with it on a case by case basis, and I *will* make wrong calls. If I don't mention something when I get to one of those men, and you think it needed mentioning, by all means contact me about it, and I may update the information in future episodes of the podcast and books in the series. But please don't take that lack of mention as being endorsement of those people.

Obviously, just as there's no definitive end to the time when rock had cultural prominence, there's no definitive beginning either. The quest for a "first rock and roll record" is a futile one – rock and roll didn't spring fully formed into existence in Sam Phillips' studio in 1951 (when he recorded "Rocket "88"") or 1954 (when he recorded "That's

All Right, Mama") – music evolved, and there are clear connections to much earlier works.

And so as these books go on we'll look at R&B and country, at Merseybeat and punk, and try to find the throughlines. But to start with, we want to take a trip back to the swing era.

"Flying Home"

We have to start somewhere, of course, and there's no demarcation line for what is and isn't rock and roll, so we're starting well before rock and roll itself, in 1938.

We're starting, in fact, with swing.

Swing was a form of music that had its roots in 1920s jazz. It's hard to believe now, but when Dixieland jazz was first popularised, in the early 1920s, the reaction to it from "polite society" was essentially the same as to every other black musical form – it was going to be the end of the world, it was evil "jungle music", it was causing our children to engage in acts of lewdness and intoxication, it was inciting violence... it was, in short, everything that was later said about rock and roll, about hip-hop, and... you get the idea. This might sound ridiculous to modern ears, as we don't normally think of the cornet, the trombone, and the banjo as the most lascivious of instruments, but back in the 1920s this kind of music was considered seriously arousing.

And so, as with all of the moral panics around black music, some white people made the music more appetising for other white people, by taking the rough edges off, cleaning it up, and putting it into a suit. In this case, this was done by the aptly-named Paul Whiteman.

Whiteman was a violin player and conductor, and he became known as "the King of Jazz" for being the bandleader of an all-white band of musicians. Where most jazz bands of the time consisted of eight to ten musicians, all improvising based on head arrangements and interacting with each other, Whiteman's band was thirty-five musicians, playing from pre-written charts. It was polite, clean, and massively popular.

Whiteman's band wasn't bad, by any means – at various times he had musicians like Bix Beiderbecke and Joe Venuti playing for him –

and they could play some quite exciting jazz at times. But they were playing something fundamentally different. Something tamer, more arranged, and with the individual players subsumed into the unit.

Whiteman still called the music he made jazz, but when other people started playing with similarly big bands, the music became known as "swing". And so from Whiteman, we move to Goodman.

Benny Goodman, the "King of Swing", was the leader of the most popular of the pre-war swing bands, as well as being an excellent clarinet player. His band hired arranger Fletcher Henderson (a black musician who led his own excellent band, and who had provided arrangements for Whiteman) to provide most of their arrangements, and managed to create music that had a lot of the excitement of less-formalised jazz. It was still highly arranged, but it allowed for soloists to show off slightly more than many of the other bands of the time.

This is partly because Goodman himself was a soloist. While Whiteman was a bandleader first and foremost – someone whose talent was in organising a group of other people, a manager rather than a musician (though he was a perfectly serviceable player), Goodman was a serious player, someone who would later premiere pieces by Bartók, Poulenc, Copland and others, and who had, before becoming a band leader, been one of the most in-demand players on small group jazz recording sessions. Goodman's band was still a big band, but it allowed the soloists far more freedom than many of his competitors did – and many of Goodman's band members, like trumpeter Harry James and drummer Gene Krupa, became well known enough individually to go off and form their own big bands.

And because Goodman's band had a lot of great soloists in, along with the thirty-plus-person big band he ran, he also had a number of smaller groups which were made up of musicians from the big band. These would play sets during the same shows as the big band, allowing the best soloists to show off while also giving most of the band a rest. Their performances would be proper jazz, rather than swing – they would be three, or four, or six musicians, improvising together the way the old Dixieland players had.

And importantly, Goodman was one of the first band leaders to lead an integrated band during the segregation era. While his big band was all white, his small groups started with a trio of Goodman himself (white and Jewish) on clarinet, white drummer Gene Krupa, and black pianist Teddy Wilson.

This integration, like the recruitment of Fletcher Henderson for the arrangements, was the idea of John Hammond, Goodman's brother-in-law. Hammond was an immensely privileged and wealthy man – his mother was a Vanderbilt, and his uncle on his father's side was the US Ambassador to Spain – who had decided to use his immense wealth in the service of two goals. The first of those was racial integration, and the second of them was to promote what would now be called roots or Americana music – pre-bop jazz, folk, blues, and gospel. Hammond would continue making an impact on music well into the 1980s, but at this point he was at the start of his career; a DJ, music journalist, and record producer, who used his wealth to get records made and aired that otherwise wouldn't have been made.

Goodman wasn't the first white bandleader in America to hire black musicians – there had been three in the 1920s – but when he hired Teddy Wilson, no-one had led an integrated group for seven years, and Goodman was hiring him for the most popular band in the USA.

And this was a far more radical thing than it seems in retrospect, because Goodman was pushing in two radically different directions – on the one hand, he was one of the first people to push for mainstream acceptance of jazz music in the classical music world, which would suggest trying to be as conservative as possible, but on the other he was pushing for integration of musicians. Lionel Hampton later quoted him as saying "we need both the black keys and the white keys to play music", which is the sort of facile comparison well-meaning white liberals make now, in 2019, so Goodman saying it eighty years ago is a genuinely progressive statement for the times.

Lionel Hampton was another black musician, who joined the trio and turned it into a quartet. He was a virtuoso vibraphonist who more or less defined how that instrument was incorporated into jazz. He appears to have been the first person to use the vibraphone on a jazz record, on a recording by Louis Armstrong of the song "Memories of You" from 1930. Before that, the vibraphone had only ever been used as a novelty instrument – it was mostly used for radio intermission signals, playing a couple of chimes.

In fact, the vibraphone was so new as an instrument that its name had never been settled – "vibraphone" was just one of a number of trademarks used by different companies making the instrument. The instrument Hampton played was put out under another brand name – Vibraharp – and that was what he called it for the rest of his life.

Hampton had trained as a drummer before becoming a vibraphone player, and was often billed as "the fastest drummer in the world", but he had a unique melodic sensibility which allowed him to become the premiere soloist on this new instrument. Indeed, to this day Hampton is probably the most respected musician ever to play the vibes.

By 1938 Goodman actually reached the point where he was able to bring an integrated band, featuring Count Basie, Lester Young, Teddy Wilson, and Lionel Hampton, plus other black musicians along with white musicians such as Goodman and Krupa, on to the stage of Carnegie Hall, at the time the US' most prestigious music venue. Like many of Goodman's biggest moments, this was the work of Hammond, who after the success of Goodman's show put together a series of other concerts at Carnegie, the "Spirituals to Swing" concerts, which are some of the most important concerts ever in bringing black American music to a white audience.

Goodman's Carnegie Hall concert is still one of the greatest live jazz albums ever recorded, and shows that it was entirely possible to create truly exciting music using the swing band template. One particularly impressive performance was the twelve-minute long version of "Sing Sing Sing".[1]

For US cultural context it would be another nine years before Jackie Robinson was able to break the colour bar in baseball, to give some idea of how extraordinary this actually was. In fact Lionel Hampton would often later claim that it was Goodman hiring him and Wilson (and,

---

[1]You can hear the full performance of that song, along with many of the other songs I discuss in these entries, at http://mixcloud.com/AndrewHickey, where I have produced playlists for most chapters of this book (though some are blocked in some countries due to copyright laws).

later, other black musicians) that paved the way for Robinson's more well-known achievement.

The original Benny Goodman Quartet were an extraordinary set of musicians, but by 1939 both Wilson and Krupa had departed for other bands. There would be reunions over the years, but the classic lineup of the quartet had stopped performing together on a regular basis. Various other pianists (notably Count Basie and Fletcher Henderson) sat in with the Goodman small groups, but Goodman also realised the need to make up for the loss of two such exceptional musicians by incorporating more, and so the Benny Goodman Sextets were formed.

Those sextets featured a rotating lineup of musicians, sometimes including the great trumpet player Cootie Williams, but revolved around three soloists – Goodman himself on clarinet, Hampton on vibraphone, and a new musician, the guitarist Charlie Christian, who would only have a very short career, but who would come to be better known than any of them.

Christian is sometimes erroneously called the first electric guitarist, or the first person to play electric guitar on record, or even the inventor of the electric guitar. He was none of those things, but he was a pioneer in the instrument, and the first person to really bring it to prominence as a solo instrument. The electric guitar allowed a fundamentally different style of guitar playing – before, the guitar had only really worked either as accompaniment for a single vocalist, or at best as a barely-audible rhythm instrument drowned out by the louder pianos and horns of jazz bands. Now the guitar could play single melody lines as loudly as any trumpet or saxophone, and could be used as a solo instrument in an ensemble in the same way as those instruments. This changed the whole approach to the guitar in popular music.

While Goodman claimed responsibility for the head arrangements[2] the small groups used, a lot of people think that Christian was responsible for these, too, and certainly the sextet's music has a much more exhilarating feel than the early quartet or trio work.

---

[2]A musicians' term – a "head arrangement" is an informal arrangement where musicians will agree on things like keys and where solos will come and who will play the riff, before they start playing.

The first song the new Goodman Sextet recorded, on October 2 1939, was a piece called "Flying Home".

"Flying Home" is a great example of the early work of the sextet, and quickly became in many ways their signature song. The band were on a plane from LA to Atlantic City – the first time many of the band members had flown at all – and Hampton started humming the riff to himself. Goodman asked, "What's that you're singing?"

Hampton said, "I don't know, we can call it 'Flying Home' I guess".

Goodman and Hampton were credited as the writers, although John Hammond later claimed that he'd heard Christian improvising the riff before it was picked up by the other two men.

It's hard to emphasise just how strange this record must have sounded then, nearly eighty years ago, when you consider that electronic amplification was a new thing, that only one electric guitar had ever been recorded before the Sextet sessions, and that the record contained two separate electronically amplified instruments – Christian's guitar and Hampton's vibraphone.

Other than the vibraphone and clarinet, though, this small group was almost the prototypical rock band – piano, electric guitar, double bass and drums would be the hallmark instruments of the genre a full twenty years after this record – and the record seems to anticipate many aspects of the rock genre in many details, especially when Charlie Christian starts his soloing. His playing now sounds fairly tame, but at the time it was astonishingly advanced both in technique (he was a huge influence on bop, which wouldn't come along for many more years) and in just the sound of it. No-one else was making music that was amplified in that way, with that timbre.

The song starts with a simple stride piano intro played by Fletcher Henderson, with Artie Bernstein on the bass and Nick Fatool on the drums. This intro is basically just setting out the harmonic structure of the verses before the introduction of the main riff. It does a common thing where you have the chords at the top end stay as close to being the same as they can while you have a descending bass, and the bass includes a few notes that aren't in the same key that the melody is in when it comes in, setting up a little bit of harmonic tension.

Once it does come in, the riff sounds *really odd*. This is a vibraphone, a clarinet, and an electric guitar, all playing the same riff in unison. That's a sound that had never been recorded before.

We then have a very straightforward swing-style clarinet solo by Goodman. I like Goodman's clarinet style a great deal – he is, in fact, one of the musicians who shaped my sense of melodic structure – but there's nothing particularly notable about this solo, which could be on any record from about 1925 through about 1945. After another run through of the riff, we get Charlie Christian's solo, which is where things get even more interesting.

Punctuated by bursts from the clarinet and vibraphone, this longer solo (which includes a whole section that effectively acts as a middle eight for the song) is unlike pretty much anything ever played on guitar in the studio before. Christian's short bursts of single-note guitar line are, to all intents and purposes, rockabilly. It's the same kind of guitar playing we'll hear from Scotty Moore sixteen years later. It doesn't sound like anything revolutionary now, but remember, up to this point the guitar had essentially only been a rhythm instrument in jazz, with a very small handful of exceptions like Django Reinhardt. You simply couldn't play single-note lead lines on the guitar and have it heard over saxes or trumpets until the advent of electrification.

After Christian's solo, we have one from Lionel Hampton. This solo is just a typical example of Hampton's playing – he was a stunning jazz vibraphone player, and at the time was on top of his game – but it's not as astonishing as the one from Christian.

And then at the end, we get a whole new riff coming in. This kind of riff had been common in Goodman's work before – you can hear something similar in his hit version of "King Porter Stomp", for example – but it would become the hallmark of the jump band style a few years later. This call and response, repetitive riffing, would be the sound that would dominate dance music in the next decades.

The song would go on to have a long life after this recording. A couple of years later, Lionel Hampton left Goodman's band to form his own big band, and "Flying Home" became their signature song. That band would be one of the first bands to perform a new type of music – jump band music – which was rooted in swing but had more emphasis on riffs and amplified instruments. That jump band music is the same music that later became known as rhythm and blues, and musicians such as Louis Jordan were clearly inspired by Hampton's band.

Hampton recorded the song multiple times, starting in 1940, but the most famous example is the version he recorded in 1942 for Decca (with "instrumental foxtrot" on the label). That version features Illinois Jacquet on saxophone, and like the Benny Goodman version, it would introduce a whole new sound to people.

This time, it's Jacquet's tenor sax playing, which has a honk and skronk to it that was unlike anything people had heard before. There are predecessors to it of course – as I said earlier, there's no "earliest example" of anything in music – but this saxophone solo became the one that defined a whole new genre, a genre called rhythm and blues. Jacquet's solo was so exceptional that when he left the band, every tenor sax player who replaced him would copy his solo note-for-note rather than improvising their own versions as would usually be the case.

There's another person involved in Hampton's recording of "Flying Home" who probably needs mentioning here – Milt Gabler, the producer. Like John Hammond, he's someone we'll be hearing a lot more about.

Hampton himself remained a respected and popular musician for many more decades. In the late 1940s and early 1950s, the big bands lost a lot of their popularity, and Hampton started playing yet another style of music – he became one of the greats of bebop music, and played in small groups much like the Goodman ones, just playing more harmonically and melodically complex variations of what he had played earlier. But he was also recognised by the rock musicians as a pioneer – you can see him in the 1957 Alan Freed film *Mr. Rock and Roll*, playing his vibraphone as the only jazz musician in a film which otherwise features Little Richard, Clyde McPhatter, and other rock and R&B stars of the time.

Charlie Christian, on the other hand, never even lived to see the influence he had. He was one of the most influential musicians on both jazz and rock music – Chuck Berry later said that Christian was one of the biggest influences on his guitar playing (though he wrongly said that

Christian played with Tommy Dorsey's band, a rival to Goodman's) while Christian was responsible for the name "bebop" being given to the form of music he helped create in jam sessions after his regular work. But he was already suffering from tuberculosis in 1939, when "Flying Home" was recorded. And on March the second, 1941, aged only twenty-five, Charlie Christian died. He was buried in an unmarked grave, which was later concreted over. A memorial was placed for him fifty-three years later, but it was later discovered to be in the wrong place.

"Roll 'Em Pete"

"It's got a backbeat, you can't lose it" – in Chuck Berry's classic song "Rock and Roll Music", that's the only line that actually talks about what the music *is*. The backbeat is, to all intents and purposes, the thing that differentiates early rock and roll from the music that preceded it. And like all of early rock and roll, it's something that had predecessors in rock's pre-history.

If you don't know what a backbeat is... well, in the days of swing, and even on a lot of very early rock and roll records, the typical beat you'd have is one called a shuffle, which sounds like you'd expect from the name, a sort of shuffling sound.

The shuffle rhythm *was* the swing rhythm – so much so that often you'll see "shuffle rhythm" and "swing time" used interchangeably. It can be heard, for example, in the introduction to "In the Mood" by the Glenn Miller Orchestra, the biggest-selling swing record of all time.

The shuffle rhythm was the basis of almost all pre-war popular music, one way or the other. It's a good, strong, sound– there's a reason why it was popular – but... it's a little bit polite. A little bit tame.

A backbeat, on the other hand, gives you a straight, simple, pulse. You stress the second and fourth beats in a bar – boom **BAP** boom **BAP** boom **BAP** boom **BAP**. It's a simpler rhythm, but a more exciting one. That's the rhythm that made rock and roll.

Players in blues and jazz music had been using that rhythm, off and on, since the 1920s. Lionel Hampton, in his autobiography, talking about his earliest work as a drummer before switching to vibraphone, says "I had a different style on drums. I was already playing with a heavy afterbeat, getting that rock-and-roll beat that wouldn't even get popular until the 1950s. I wanted people to dance, have a good time, clap their hands, and they would do it to my drumming."

And that's what a backbeat does – it gives people somewhere to clap their hands, a very clear signal, you clap on TWO and FOUR.

But while Hampton was playing like that, he was never recorded doing that, and nor were any other drummers at the time. In fact, the first recording in the prehistory of rock generally credited as having a backbeat doesn't even have a drummer on it at all. Rather, it features just a vocalist, Big Joe Turner, and a piano player, Pete Johnson. The song, which was recorded in December 1938, is called "Roll 'Em Pete".

Now, before we go any further, I want to say something about that "generally credited". There are two problems with it. The first is that "Roll 'Em Pete", at least in the version recorded under that name, doesn't have a particularly pronounced backbeat at all, and the second is that there *were* other records being made, long before 1938, which do. But that's the way of these things, as we'll see over and over again. The first anything is messy.

But "Roll 'Em Pete" is still a hugely important record, in ways that are more important than whether it has a backbeat on it. So let's have a look at it.

Pete Johnson was a boogie woogie player. Boogie woogie was a style of piano playing that became popular in the 1930s, where the left hand would play a strong bassline – you almost certainly know the generic boogie bassline style, but if you don't know the name, think of the melody of "Rock Around the Clock" where Bill Haley sings "I'm going strong and so are you," for example. That's a boogie bassline. While the left hand played this, the right hand would play decorative melodic stuff over it. That bassline and melody combination was the most popular style of playing for a time, and it became the cornerstone of rock piano playing, as well as of country music and much else. The bassline would have eight notes in a typical bar, and "eight to the bar" was another term some used for boogie woogie at the time.

But boogie woogie was, for the most part, based on that shuffle rhythm. Listen to "Pinetop's Boogie Woogie" by Pinetop Smith, the first real boogie record, from 1928, and you'll hear a rhythm which isn't so different to that Glenn Miller record from a decade or so later. "Roll 'Em Pete" changed that.

Pete Johnson was considered one of the greatest exponents of the boogie-woogie style, and in 1938 when John Hammond was putting together his "Spirituals to Swing" concerts, it was natural that Hammond would choose Johnson to perform. These concerts – one in 1938 and one in 1939 – were probably the most important concerts in popular music history. That's not an exaggeration, by any means, it's just a fact.

As we discussed in the last chapter, at the beginning of 1938, Hammond had promoted a concert by the Benny Goodman band at Carnegie Hall, and that concert itself had been an impressive event. It was the first time an integrated band had played Carnegie Hall, and the first time that popular music had been treated as seriously as classical music.

For a follow-up, at Christmas 1938, Hammond wanted to present only black musicians, but to an integrated audience. He wanted, in fact, to present a history of black music, from "primitive" folk forms to big band swing. This was, to say the least, a controversial choice, and in the end the event was sponsored by *The New Masses*, a magazine published by the Communist Party USA.

And the lineup for that show was pretty much a who's who of black American music at the time. Hammond had wanted to get Robert Johnson, but he discovered that Johnson had recently died – Johnson's place was taken by a then-obscure folk musician called Big Bill Broonzy, who became popular largely on the basis of that appearance. Sonny Terry, Sister Rosetta Tharpe, Meade Lux Lewis, Albert Ammons, the Count Basie Orchestra, and more all appeared, and the show was successful enough that the next year there was a follow-up, with many of the same musicians, which also featured the Benny Goodman Sextet.

For this show, as well as playing on his own, Pete Johnson was backing a blues shouter called Big Joe Turner. And "shouter" *was* the word for what Turner did. If you don't know about blues shouters, that's unsurprising – it's a style of music that went out of fashion with the big bands. But a blues shouter was a singer – usually a man – who could sing loudly and powerfully enough that he could be heard over a band, without amplification. In the early twentieth century, microphones were unknown at first, and singers had to be able to be heard over the musicians simply by the force of their voices. Some singers used megaphones as a crude form of amplification, but many more simply had to belt out their vocals as loud as they could.

Even after microphones were introduced, they were unreliable and amplification wasn't very powerful. And at the same time bands were getting bigger and louder – blues shouters like Big Joe Turner could compete with that power, and get a crowd excited by the sheer volume of their voice, even over bands like Count Basie's.

But for the Carnegie Hall show, Turner and Pete Johnson were playing together, just the two of them. And while they were in New York, they had a recording session, and recorded a track that some say is the first rock and roll record ever.

"Roll 'Em Pete" has the first recorded example – as far as anyone has been able to discover – of a boogie song which uses a backbeat rather than a shuffle beat. All the musical elements of early rock and roll are there in Pete Johnson's piano part. In particular, the right-hand melody lines he's playing, if you transfer them to guitar, are basically the whole of Chuck Berry's guitar style, but you can also hear Jerry Lee Lewis in there.

Now on the studio recording, there's not that much of an audible backbeat, but there's a version of this song with a much clearer backbeat, and that's the live recording of Turner and Johnson performing the song at Carnegie Hall the week earlier. That performance is titled "It's Alright Baby" rather than "Roll 'Em Pete" on the official recordings, but it's the same song. There, Turner is clapping along on the backbeat, and you can hear the claps clearly.

Now this isn't a clearcut differentiation – you can play music in such a way that you can have a shuffle beat going up against a backbeat, and that's a lot of what's going on in boogie music of this period, and the two rhythms rubbing up against each other is a lot of what drives early rock and roll. Talking about a "first backbeat record" is almost as ridiculous as talking about a "first rock and roll record" or a "first soul record". And the more I've listened to this song and the other music of its time, the less convinced I am that this specific song has something altogether new. But still, it's a great example of boogie, of blues, and of the music that would become rock and roll, and it's one you can clearly point to and say "that has all the elements that will later go into rock and roll music". Perhaps not in exactly the same proportions, perhaps not in a way that's massively different from its predecessors, but like "Flying Home", it's as good a place to start as any.

And this is, have no doubt about it, a record of important performers.

Before we go into why, we'll talk briefly about the song, and particularly about the lyrics – or, more precisely, the way that they aren't really coherent lyrics at all. Rather, they fit in a blues tradition called "floating lyrics". A song like "Roll 'Em Pete", you see, isn't really a song in the conventional sense. There's a melodic structure there, and over that melodic structure the singer would improvise. And when blues singers improvised, they'd tend to pull out lyrics from a set of pre-existing phrases that they knew worked. "Well, I got a gal, she lives up on the hill/Well, this woman's tryin' to quit me, Lord, but I love her still" is the opening line, and that is one of those floating lyrics – though sometimes, depending on the singer, the women says she loves me but I don't believe she will, or doesn't love me but her sister will.

Most of Turner's songs were made up of these floating lyrics, and this is something we'll see happening more in the early years of rock and roll, as we look at those. The whole idea of floating lyrics, sadly, makes authorship claims for songs somewhat difficult, and rock and roll, like blues and country before it, was essentially a folk artform to start with. We'll see several examples of people taking credit as "songwriters" for things that are put together from a bunch of pre-existing elements, striking it lucky, and becoming millionaires as a result.

Turner and Johnson could stretch "Roll 'Em Pete" out to an hour sometimes, with Turner just singing new lyrics as needed, and no recording can really capture what they were doing in live performance. And this is the problem with much of the prehistory of rock and roll, as so much of it was created by musicians who were live performers first and recording artists a distant second, if at all.

But those live performances mattered. In 1938, when Pete Johnson and Albert Ammons made their appearances in the Spirituals to Swing shows, boogie woogie was something of a minority form – it was something that had had a brief popularity a decade earlier and which was largely forgotten. That show changed that, and suddenly boogie woogie was the biggest thing in music. Every big band started playing boogie woogie music, adapted to the big band style. The Andrews Sisters sang about "The Boogie Woogie Bugle Boy of Company B" and wanted you to "Beat Me Daddy, Eight to the Bar" (and then, presumably feeling dirty after that, wanted you to "Scrub Me Mama to a Boogie Beat"). Tommy Dorsey recorded "Pinetop's Boogie Woogie" (renamed as "TD's Boogie Woogie"), and you got diabolical novelties like "The Booglie Wooglie Piggy", where the Glenn Miller Orchestra regaled us with the information that "This little piggy had roast beef, this little piggy had none/But this little piggy was a booglie wooglie piggy and he did the Lindy all the way home".

Most of this music was still using that swing beat, but it was clearly boogie woogie music, and that became the biggest style of music in late-period big band music, the music that was popular in the early 1940s. Even in songs that aren't directly about being boogie-woogie – like, say, Glenn Miller's "Chattanooga Choo Choo" – you still get that boogie rhythm, and nods to the generic boogie bassline; and you get lines like, "When you hear that whistle blowing eight to the bar/Then you know that Tennessee is not very far".

And that influence had a bigger impact than it might otherwise have done, and became something bigger than just a fad, because between 1941 and 1943 a whole host of events conspired to change the music industry forever.

Most importantly, of course, the Second World War reached America, and that caused a lot of problems for the big band industry – men who would otherwise have been playing in those bands were being drafted, as were men who would otherwise have been going out dancing to those bands.

But there were two smaller events that, if anything, made even more impact. The first of these was the ASCAP boycott.

The American Society of Composers and Publishers was, and still is, an organisation that represented most of the most important songwriters and music publishers in the USA, the people who had been writing the most successful songs. They collected royalties for live performances and radio plays, and distributed them to the composers and publishers who made up their membership. And they only dealt with the respectable Tin Pan Alley composers, but that covered enough songs – in the early forties they had a repertoire of one and a quarter million songs, including all the most popular songs that the big bands were playing.

And then for ten months in 1941, they banned all the radio stations in the USA from playing any of their songs, over a royalty dispute.

This should have been catastrophic for the radio stations, and would have been if there hadn't been another organisation, BMI, set up as a rival to ASCAP a couple of years earlier. BMI dealt with only the low-class music – the blues, and country songs, and gospel songs, and hillbilly music, and boogie. The stuff ASCAP didn't think was important.

Except that now all that music became *very* important, because that was all you could play on the radio. Well, that and public domain songs, but pretty soon everyone was bored of hearing "I Dream of Jeannie With The Light Brown Hair". And so there was suddenly a much bigger audience for all the hillbilly and blues performers, all of whom had incorporated the boogie style into their own styles.

And then, just as the music industry was getting back on its feet after that, there was what is still the biggest entertainment strike in US history, the AFM[3] strike of 1942-44. This time, the strike didn't affect anyone playing on the radio, so long as it was a live performance. But because of a dispute over royalties, no instrumentalist was allowed to record for the major record labels for two years.

This had several effects, all of them profound.

Firstly, the big bands all recorded a *lot* of music to stockpile in the last weeks before the strike, and this meant that the styles that were current in July 1942 effectively stayed current, at least as far as the record-buying public was concerned. For two years, the only big band music that could be released was from that stockpile, so the music recorded during the boogie fad stayed around longer than it otherwise might have, and remained a major part of the culture.

[3] American Federation of Musicians

Secondly, the ban only affected the major labels. Guess who was on the minor labels, the ones that could keep making music and putting it out? That's right, those blues and hillbilly musicians, and those boogie piano players. The same ones whose songs had just spent a year being the only ones the famous bands could play, and now after being given that free publicity by the famous bands, they had no competition from them.

Third – and this is a real negative effect of the strike, one which is an immense historical tragedy for music lovers – there was a new form of jazz being invented in New York between 1942 and 1944 by musicians like Dizzy Gillespie and Charlie Parker, people who played in the big bands but were also doing something new in their side gigs. That form later became known as bebop, or just bop, and is some of the most important music of the twentieth century, but we have no recordings of its birth

And fourth – the strike didn't affect singers. So Tommy Dorsey's band couldn't record anything, but Dorsey's old vocalist, Frank Sinatra, could, backed by a vocal group instead of instrumentalists. And so could lots of other singers.

The end result of all this was that, at the end of 1944, swing was effectively dead, as was the tradition of instrumentalists being the stars in American music. From that time on, the stars would stop being trombone players like Glenn Miller or clarinettists like Benny Goodman, or piano players like Pete Johnson. Instead they were singers, like Frank Sinatra, and like Joe Turner. The swing musicians either went into bebop, and thus more or less vanish from this story (though their own story is always worth following up), or they went into playing the new forms of music that had sprung up, in particular one form which was inspired by swing bands like Lionel Hampton's and Count Basie's, but also by the boogie music that had influenced them, and by the blues. That form was called rhythm and blues, and Joe Turner became one of its biggest stars.

Seventeen years after "Roll 'Em Pete", Joe Turner recorded another song, which became his most well-known contribution to popular music. That song was written by the songwriter Jesse Stone – though he was using the name "Charles Calhoun", because he was a member of ASCAP under his real name, and this was a BMI song if ever there was one – but there's a very, very clear line to "Roll 'Em Pete". The main difference here is that the backbeat is now stressed, almost to the point of parody, because "Shake, Rattle, and Roll" is a rock and roll song.

We'll be hearing more about Jesse Stone, but for now we'll just talk about this song. Connie Kay, the drummer from the Modern Jazz Quartet, plays on it, emphasising the backbeat with a "whap, whap" on the snare drum. It's safe to say that's not the subtlest piece of drumming he ever did, but it may well be the most influential.

"Shake, Rattle, and Roll" is definitely the same kind of thing as "Roll 'Em Pete". The piano playing is similar, Turner's blues shouting is the same kind of thing, the vocal melody is similar, both are structured around the twelve-bar blues, and both songs are made up largely of floating lyrics. But "Shake, Rattle, and Roll" is rock and roll, and it was covered by both Bill Haley and Elvis Presley, the two biggest white rock and roll singers of the time, and Turner would perform it on shows promoted by Alan Freed, the man who claimed to have coined the term "rock and roll".

So what makes the difference? Well, firstly that backbeat from Connie Kay, that gives it a much bigger forward momentum. But there's a few other things as well – influences from other genres that fed into rock and roll.

First, "Shake, Rattle, and Roll" features prominent saxophone. That's from rhythm and blues, and it's something that rhythm and blues got from swing. Illinois Jacquet's solo on Lionel Hampton's "Flying Home" is a very clear progenitor for this.

But there's also the influence of another type of song; one most people who talk about the origins of rock and roll don't even think of as being a separate type of music, as it just gets rolled up into "blues".

The hokum song is a type of music with a long history, which can trace its origins through vaudeville back to minstrel songs. It was originally for comedy performances more than anything else, but later a whole subgenre of them started being just songs about sex. Some of the more euphemistic of them are songs like "Fishing Pole Blues", which has lines like, "Want to go fishing in my fishing hole/If you want to fish with me you'd better have a great big pole", or songs called things like "Banana in my Fruit Basket", "I Want a Hot-Dog in my Roll", "It's Tight Like That," and "Warm My Weiner".

There were less euphemistic songs, too, called things like "Bull Dyke Blues". Suffice to say, there was plenty of very, very obscene music as well as the comedy songs and the more euphemistic material. And "Shake, Rattle, and Roll", while it's not the dirtiest song in history or anything, is certainly fairly blatant about its subject matter.

(Hilariously, Bill Haley's cover version is famously "cleaned up". They took out lines like "the way you wear those dresses, the sun comes shining through" and "I believe to my soul you're the devil in nylon hose" in case they were too dirty. But they left in "I'm like a one-eyed cat peeping in a sea-food store"...)

So that's what rock and roll was, in its early stages; a blues shouter, singing over a boogie-inspired piano part, with a backbeat on the snare drum, a structure and lyrics patterned after the hokum song, and horns coming out of swing music. And there is a very, very clear line to that from "Roll 'Em Pete", and the boogie-woogie revival of 1938, and the "Spirituals to Swing" concerts.

But wait... isn't the cliché that rock and roll comes from R&B mixed with country music? Where's all the country music in this?

Well, that cliché is slightly wrong. Rock doesn't have much influence from the country music, but it has a lot of influence from Western music...

"Ida Red"

"Rock and Roll? Why, man, that's the same kind of music we've been playin' since 1928!...We didn't call it rock and roll back when we introduced it as our style back in 1928, and we don't call it rock and roll the way we play it now. But it's just basic rhythm and has gone by a lot of different names in my time. It's the same, whether you just follow a drum beat like in Africa or surround it with a lot of instruments. The rhythm's what's important."

Bob Wills said that in 1957, and it brings up an interesting question. What's in a name?

Genre names are a strange thing, aren't they? In particular, did you ever notice how many of them had the word "and" in them? Rock *and* roll, rhythm *and* blues, country *and* western? There's sort of a reason for that.

Rock and roll is a special case, but the other two were names that were coined by *Billboard*, and they weren't originally meant to be descriptors of a single genre, but of collections of genres – they were titles for its different charts. Rhythm and blues is a name that was used to replace the earlier name, "race records", because that was thought a bit demeaning. It was for the chart of music made by black people, whatever music those black people were making, so they could be making rhythm records, or they could be making blues records.

Only once you give a collection of things a name, the way people's minds work, they start thinking that because those things share a name they're the same kind of thing. And people start thinking about "rhythm and blues" records as being a particular kind of thing. And then they start making "rhythm and blues" records, and suddenly it *is* a thing.

The same thing goes for country and western. That was, again, two different genres. Country music was the music made by white people who lived in the rural areas, of the Eastern US basically. People like the Carter Family, for example, who are widely credited as having invented modern country music. Not *country and western*, just country. Country was the music made in Appalachia, especially Kentucky and Tennessee, and *especially* especially Nashville.

Western music was a bit different. That was the music being made in Texas, Oklahoma, and California, and it tended to use similar instrumentation to country music – violins and guitars and so on – but it had different subject matter. A lot of Western songs were about cowboys and outlaws and so on; and at the time we're talking about, the thirties and forties, Western music was a little bit slicker than country music.

This is odd in retrospect, because not many years later the Western musicians influenced people like Johnny Cash, Buck Owens, and Merle Haggard, who made very gritty, raw, unpolished music compared to the country music coming out of Nashville, but the thirties and forties were the heyday of singing cowboy films, with people like Gene Autry and Roy Rogers becoming massive, massive stars, and so there was a lot of Hollywoodisation of the music, lots of crooning and orchestras and so on.

Western music was big, big business. And so was swing music, so it's perhaps not surprising that there was a new genre that emerged around that time. Western swing.

Western swing is, to simplify it ridiculously, swing music made in the West of the USA, largely in places like California. But it's music that was made by the same kinds of people who in the East were making country music, and with a lot of the same influences.

It took the rhythms of swing music, but played them with the same instrumentation as the country musicians were using, so you'd get hot jazz style performances, but they'd be played on fiddle, banjo, guitar, and stand-up bass. There were a few other instruments that you'd usually get included as well, such as the steel guitar and later the pedal steel.

Western swing usually also included a drum kit, which was one of the big ways it differed from country music as it was then. The drum kit was, in the early decades of the twentieth century, primarily a jazz instrument, and it was only because Western swing was a hybrid of jazz and Western music that it got included in those bands – and for a long time drum kits were banned from country music shows like the Grand Ole Opry, and when they did finally relent and let Western swing bands play there, they made the drummers hide behind a curtain.

They would also include other instruments that weren't normally included in country or Western music at the time, like the piano. Less often, you'd have a saxophone or a trumpet, but basically the typical Western swing lineup would be a guitar, a steel guitar, a violin or two, a piano, a bass, and drums.

As with the small-group swing we've already talked about, you can see the rock band lineup starting to form. It was a gradual process though.

Take Bob Wills, the musician whose drummer had to hide behind a curtain.

Wills originally performed as a blackface comedian. Sadly, blackface performances were very, very common in the US in the 1930s (but then, they were common in the UK well into my lifetime. I'm not judging the US in particular here), but he soon became more well known as a fiddle player and occasional singer.

In 1929 Wills, the singer Milton Brown, and guitarist Herman Arn-spiger, got together to perform a song at a Christmas dance party. They soon added Brown's brother Derwood on guitar, and fiddle player John Dunnam, and became the Light Crust Doughboys.

That might seem like a strange name for a band, and it would be if that had been the name they chose themselves, but it wasn't. Their name was originally The Aladdin Laddies, as they got sponsored by the Aladdin Lamp Company to perform on WBAP radio under that name, but when that sponsorship fell through, they performed for a while as the Wills Fiddle Band, before they found a new sponsor – Pappy O'Daniel.

You may know that name, as the name of the governor of Mississippi in the film *O Brother, Where Art Thou?*, and that was... not an *entirely* inaccurate portrayal, though the character in that film definitely wasn't the real man. The real Pappy O'Daniel didn't actually become governor of Mississippi, but he did become the governor of Texas, in the 1940s.

But in the late 1920s and early thirties he was the head of advertising for Burrus Mill and Elevator Company, who made Light Crust Flour, and he started to sponsor the show.

The band became immensely successful, but they were not particularly well paid. In fact, O'Daniel insisted that everyone in the band would have to actually work a day job at the mill as well. Bob Wills was a truck driver as well as being a fiddle player, and the others had different jobs in the factory.

Pappy O'Daniel at first didn't like this hillbilly music being played on the radio show he was paying for. In fact he wanted to cancel the show after two weeks. But Wills invited him down to the radio station to be involved in the broadcasts, and O'Daniel became the show's MC, as well as being the band's manager and the writer of their original material. O'Daniel even got his own theme song, "Pass the Biscuits, Pappy".

Now the music the Light Crust Doughboys were playing wasn't yet what we'd call Western swing, but they were definitely as influenced by jazz music as they were by Western music. In fact, the original lineup of the Light Crust Doughboys can be seen as the prototypical example of the singer-guitarist creative tension in rock music, except here it was a tension between the singer and the fiddle player. Milton Brown was, by all accounts, wanting to experiment more with a jazz style, while Bob Wills wanted to stick with a more traditional hillbilly string band sound. That creative tension led them to create a totally new form of music.

Listening to some of the 1930s recordings of the Light Crust Doughboys, there's a *remarkable* similarity there to the music that would be made a couple of years later by Stephane Grappelli and Django Reinhardt. They share a repertoire, arrangements, and instrumentation. There's a recording of the band performing live in 1936, after Wills left, where they play versions of "Limehouse Blues" and "Dinah" that are almost identical to the versions that Grappelli and Reinhardt played years later, even though we would now think of the Light Crust Doughboys as being "a country band", while Grappelli and Reinhardt are absolutely in the jazz category.

A version of the Light Crust Doughboys continues today, and one member, Smoky Montgomery, who joined the band in 1935, continued with them until his death in 2001. Bob Wills and Milton Brown, however, both left after only a couple of years, because Pappy O'Daniel was apparently not a very good person to work for.

In particular, O'Daniel wouldn't let the Doughboys play any venues where alcohol was served, or play dances generally. O'Daniel was only paying the band members $15 a week, and they could get $40 a night playing gigs, and so Brown left in 1932 to form his own band, the Musical Brownies.

The Musical Brownies are now largely forgotten, but they're considered the first band ever to play proper Western Swing, and they introduced a lot of things that defined the genre. In particular, they introduced electric steel guitar to the Western music genre, with the great steel player Bob Dunn. For a while, they were massively popular, but sadly Brown died in a car crash in 1936.

Bob Wills stayed in the Doughboys for a while longer, as the band's leader, as O'Daniel gave him a raise to thirty-eight dollars a week. And he continued to make the kind of music he'd made when Brown was in the band, because both Brown and Wills clearly recognised that what they'd come up with together was something better and more interesting than just jazz or just Western.

Wills recruited a new singer, Tommy Duncan, but in 1933 Wills was fired by O'Daniel, partly because of rows over Wills wanting his brother in the band, and partly because Wills' drinking was already starting to affect his professionalism. He formed his own band and took Duncan and bass player Kermit Whalen with him. The Doughboys' steel guitar player, Leon McAuliffe, soon followed, and they became Bob Wills and his Texas Playboys. They advertised themselves as "formerly the Light Crust Doughboys", although that wasn't entirely true, as they weren't the whole band, though they were the core of it, and Pappy O'Daniel sued them, unsuccessfully.

And the Texas Playboys then became the first Western swing band to add a drum kit, and become a more obviously rhythm-oriented band.

The Texas Playboys were the first massively, massively successful Western swing band, and their style was one that involved taking elements from everywhere and putting them together. They had the drums and horns that a jazz band would have, the guitars and fiddles that country or Western bands would have, the steel guitar that a Hawaiian band would have, and that meant they could play all of those styles of music if they wanted to.

This was music for dancing, and as music for dancing it had a lot of aspects that would later make their way into rock and roll. In particular it had that backbeat we talked about in the last chapter, although here it was swung less. When you listen to them play with a heavy backbeat but with the fiddle as the main instrument, you can hear the influence of polka music, which was a big influence on all the Western swing musicians, and through them on rock and roll. Polka music is performed in 2/4 time, and there's a very, *very* strong connection between the polka beat and the backbeat[4].

By looking at the lineup of the Texas Playboys, we can see how the rock band lineup evolved. In 1938 the Texas Playboys had a singer, two guitars (one doubling on fiddle), three fiddlers, a banjo player, steel guitar, bass, drums, piano, trumpet, trombone, and two saxes. A *huge* band, and one at least as swing as it was Western. But around that time, Wills started to use electric guitars. Electric guitars only really became popular in 1938, and a lot of people started using them at the same time. Wills' band was one of the first to use them, and Western musicians generally were more likely to use them, as they were already using amplified steel guitars, and so were used to the idea of amplification.

We've already seen how the big bands died between 1942 and 1944, and Wills was able to make his band considerably smaller with the aid of amplification, so by 1944 he'd got rid of most of his horn section

---

[4]If you want to know more about the development of the rock backbeat, and how things like polka music affected it, there's a PhD thesis on the subject currently available at https://www.tagg.org/xpdfs/TamlynPhD1.pdf

apart from a single trumpet, having his electric guitars play what would previously have been horn lines.

So by 1944 the band would consist of two fiddles, two basses, two electric guitars, steel guitar, drums, and a trumpet. A smaller band, an electrified band, and one which, other than the fiddles and the trumpet, was much closer to the kind of lineups that you would get in the 50s and 60s. A smaller, tighter, band.

Now, Wills' band quickly became the most popular band in its genre, and he became widely known as "the king of Western swing[5]", but Wills' music was more than just swing. He was pulling together elements from country, from the blues, from jazz, from anything that could make him popular.

And, sadly, that would sometimes include plagiarism.

Now, the question of black influence on white music is a fraught one, and one that will come up a lot in the course of this history. And a lot of the time people will get things wrong. There were, of course, white people who made their living by taking black people's music and watering it down. There were also, though, plenty of more complicated examples, and examples of mutual influence.

There was a constant bouncing of ideas back and forth between country, western, blues, jazz, swing... all of these genres were coded as belonging to one or other race, but all of them had musicians who were listening to one another. This is not to say that racism was not a factor in who was successful. Of course it was, and after all we are talking about someone who started out as a blackface performer. Race was a *massive* factor, and sadly still is, but the general culture among musicians at the time was that good musicians of whatever genre respected good musicians of any other genre, and there were songs that everyone, or almost everyone, played, in their own styles, simply because a good song was a good song.

In the 1930s, 40s, and 50s there wasn't the same tight association of performer and song that there is now – you'd sometimes have five or six people in the charts with hit versions of the same song. You'd have

---

[5] A title that was also used by Spade Cooley, a famous musician who was also a misogynist murderer and abuser who was irrelevant to subsequent musical history, but who might come up if one Googles that phrase, so needs to be mentioned here.

a country version and a blues version and a swing version of a song, not because anyone was stealing anyone else's music, but because it was just accepted that everyone would record a hit song in their own style.

And certainly, in the case of Bob Wills, he was admired by, and admired, musicians across racial boundaries. As an example the white jazz guitarist Les Paul used to tell a story. Paul was so amazed by Bob Wills' music that in 1938 he travelled from Waukesha, Wisconsin, where he was visiting his mother, to Tulsa, Oklahoma, to hear Wills' band play, after his mother made him listen to Bob Wills on the radio. Paul was himself a famous guitarist at the time, and he got drawn on stage to jam with the band.

And then, in an interval, a black man in the audience – presumably this must have been an integrated audience, which would have been very unusual in 1938 in Oklahoma, but this is how Les Paul told the story, and other parts of it check out so we should probably take his word for it absent better evidence – came up and asked for Les Paul's autograph. He told Paul that he played guitar, and Paul said for the young man to show him what he could do. The young man did, and Paul said "Jesus, you *are* good. You want to come up and sit in with us?"

And that was the first time that Les Paul met his friend Charlie Christian, shortly before Christian got the offer from Benny Goodman. Hanging out and jamming at a Bob Wills gig.

So we can, for the most part, safely put Bob Wills into the mutual respect and influence category. He was someone who had the respect of his peers, and was part of a chain of influences crossing racial and stylistic boundaries.

It gets more difficult when you get to someone like Pat Boone, a few years later, who would record soundalike versions of black musicians' hits specifically to sell to people who wouldn't buy music by black people and act as a spoiler for their records. That's ethically very, very dodgy, plus Boone was a terrible musician.

But what I think we can all agree on is that just outright stealing a black musician's song, crediting it to a white musician, and making it a massive hit is just wrong. And sadly that happened with Bob Wills' band at least once.

Leon McAuliffe, the Texas Playboys' steel guitar player, is the credited composer of "Steel Guitar Rag", which is the instrumental which really made the steel guitar a permanent fixture in country and western music. Without this instrumental, country music would be totally different. He "wrote" it in 1936. Now, in 1927, the guitarist Sylvester Weaver made a pioneering recording, which is now often called the first recorded country blues, the first recorded blues instrumental, and the first slide guitar recording (as I've said before, there is never a first, but Weaver's recording is definitely important). That track is called "Guitar Rag" and. . . well. . . it's identical. Leon McAuliffe always claimed he'd never heard Sylvester Weaver's song, and came up with "Steel Guitar Rag" independently, but given that the melodies are the same and even the titles are nearly identical. . . well, what do you think?

So, the Texas Playboys were not averse to a bit of plagiarism. But the song we're going to talk about for the rest of this chapter is one that would end up plagiarised itself, very famously.

"Ida Red" is an old folk song, first recorded in 1924. As is often the case with this kind of song, it's part of a massive family tree of other songs. There are blues and country songs with the same melody, songs with different melodies but mentions of Ida Red, songs which contain different lines from the song. . . many folk songs aren't so much songs in themselves as they are labels you can put on a whole family. There's no one song "Ida Red", there's a whole bunch of songs which are, to a greater or lesser extent, "Ida Red". "Ida Red" is just a name you can slap on that family, something you can point to.

Most versions of "Ida Red" had the same chorus – "Ida Red, Ida Red, I'm plum fool about Ida Red" – but different lyrics, often joking improvised ones. In the first version of "Ida Red" to be recorded, by Fiddlin' Powers and Family, they sing about Ida Red weighing three hundred and fifty pounds. Oddly, that version doesn't even have the chorus, but it does have the chorus melody played on the fiddle.

Wills' version is very differently structured. It has the familiar chorus, but the verses are totally different and have nothing to do with the character of Ida Red: "Light's in the parlour, fire's in the grate/Clock on the mantle says it's a'gettin' late/Curtains on the window, snowy white/The parlour's pleasant on Sunday night"

Those lyrics, and all the other lyrics in Wills' version except the chorus, were taken from an 1878 parlour song called "Sunday Night" by George Frederick Root, a Civil War-era songwriter who is now best known as the writer of the melody we now know as "Jesus Loves the Little Children". They're cut down to fit into the fast-patter do-si-do style of the song, but they're still definitely the same lyrics as Root's.

"Ida Red" was one of many massive hits for Wills and the Texas Playboys, who continued to be hugely successful through the 1940s, at one point becoming a bigger live draw than Benny Goodman or Tommy Dorsey, although the band's success started to decline when Tommy Duncan quit in 1948 over Wills' drinking. Wills would often miss shows because of his binge drinking, and Duncan was the one who had to deal with the angry fans. Wills replaced Duncan with various other singers, but never found anyone who would have the same success with him.

Bob Wills and the Texas Playboys had a couple of hits in the very early 1950s – one of them, indeed, was a sequel to Ida Red – "Ida Red Likes The Boogie", a novelty boogie song. "Ida Red Likes The Boogie" was recorded in 1949 and went top ten in 1950, a full decade after the boogie fad peaked.

But even as his kind of music was getting more into fashion under the name rock and roll, Wills himself became less popular. The band were still a popular live attraction through most of the 1950s, but they never again reached the heights of the 30s and 40s, and Wills' deteriorating health and the band's lack of success made them split up in 1965.

But before they'd split, Wills' music had had a lasting influence on rock and roll, and not just on the people you might expect. Remember how I talked about plagiarism? Well, in 1955, a musician went into Chess studios with a slight rewrite of "Ida Red" that he called "Ida May". Leonard Chess persuaded him to change the name because otherwise it would be too obvious where he stole the tune... and we will talk about "Maybellene" by Chuck Berry much later.

"Choo Choo Ch'Boogie"

We've spent a lot of time in 1938 so far, haven't we? First there was "Flying Home", first recorded in 1939, but where we had to talk about events from 1938. Then we had "Roll 'Em Pete", recorded in 1938. And "Ida Red", recorded in 1938. 1938 is apparently the real year zero for rock and roll – whether you come at it from the direction of blues and boogie, or jazz, or country and western music, 1938 ends up being the place where you start.

And 1938 is also the year that one man, who would influence rock and roll more than any single other individual, made his solo debut.

If you've seen the Marx Brothers film *A Day at the Races* – well, OK, if you've *not* seen *A Day at the Races*, you really should, because while it's not the best film the Marx Brothers ever made, it's still a good Marx Brothers film, and it'll brighten up your day immensely to watch it, so go and watch that, and then come back and read the rest of this. And if you haven't watched all their earlier films, watch those too. Except *The Cocoanuts*, you can skip that one. Go on. I can wait.

OK, now you've definitely seen the Marx Brothers film *A Day at the Races*, so you'll remember the dance sequence where Ivie Anderson sings "All God's Chillun Got Rhythm", and the amazing dancers in that scene.

That's a dance called the Lindy Hop – you might remember the "booglie wooglie piggy" doing the Lindy back in chapter two. The Lindy Hop was named after Charles Lindbergh, the famous airman and Nazi sympathiser, and the people dancing it in the film are Whitey's Lindy Hoppers. And they were responsible for a controversy, on the night of Benny Goodman's first Carnegie Hall concert, that is still talked about in jazz eighty years later.

One of the most famous swing records ever is "Stompin' at the Savoy" by Benny Goodman. Goodman's version was a cover version of an earlier recording by Chick Webb, and it later inspired the name of Savoy Records, a label we're going to be hearing a lot about later. The Savoy Ballroom was where Whitey's Lindy Hoppers used to dance, and there was an entire corner of the ballroom set off for them, even though the rest of the floor was for the other dancers. The Savoy was where the Lindy Hop was invented, and it was *the* place to dance, because it was where Chick Webb, the real king of swing, played.

We've seen a few kings of swing so far. Benny Goodman was the person most associated with the name, and he had the name longest. A few people called Bob Wills that, too, though he mostly billed himself as the king of *Western* swing. But Chick Webb was the person who deserved the title more than anyone else. He was a small man, who'd contracted tuberculosis of the spine as a child, and he'd taken up the drums as a kind of therapy. He'd been playing professionally since he was eleven, and by the time he was thirty he was leading what was, bar none, the best swing band in New York for dancing. People called him the King of Swing before Goodman, and his band was an absolute force of nature when it came to getting people to do the Lindy Hop. Benny Goodman admired Webb's band enough that he bought the band's arrangements and used them himself. All of the Goodman band's biggest crowd-pleasers, at least the ones that weren't arrangements he'd bought off Fletcher Henderson, he bought from Edgar Sampson, the saxophone player who did most of Webb's arrangements. Sampson is the one who wrote "Stompin' at the Savoy" for Webb, and he arranged Goodman's version.

There was a rivalry there – Goodman's band was bigger in every sense, but Webb's band was more popular with those who knew the real deal when they heard it. And in 1937, the Savoy hosted a cutting contest between Webb's Savoy Orchestra and Goodman's band.

A cutting contest was a tradition that came from the world of stride piano players; the same world that boogie woogie music grew out of. One musician would play his best (and it usually was a "his" – this was a very macho musical world) and then a second would try to top him, playing something faster, or more inventive, or more exciting, often a reworking of the song the first one had played. The first would then take another turn and try to get better than the second had. They'd keep going, each trying to outdo the other, until a crowd decided that one or the other was the winner.

And that 1937 cutting contest was a big event. The Savoy had two bandstands, so they would have one band start as soon as the other one finished, so people could dance all night. Chick Webb's band set up on one stage, Goodman's on another. Four thousand dancers crowded the inside of the ballroom, and despite a police cordon outside to keep trouble down, another five thousand people outside tried to hear what was happening.

And Chick Webb's band won, absolutely. Gene Krupa, Goodman's drummer (one of the true greats of jazz drumming himself) later said "I'll never forget that night. Webb cut me to ribbons!"

And that just was the most famous of many, many cutting contests that Chick Webb's band won. The only time Chick Webb ever definitely lost a cutting contest was against Duke Ellington, but everyone knew that Chick Webb and Duke Ellington weren't really trying to do the same kind of thing, and anyway, there's no shame at all in losing to Duke Ellington.

Count Basie, though, was a different matter. He *was* trying to do the same kind of thing as Chick Webb, and he was doing it well. And on the night of Benny Goodman's Carnegie Hall concert, Webb and Basie were going to engage in their own cutting contest after hours. For all that the Goodman Carnegie Hall show was important – and it was – the real jazz fans knew that this after-show party was going to be the place to be. Basie had already played the Carnegie Hall show, guesting with Goodman's band, as had Basie's tenor sax player Lester Young, but here they were going to get to show off what they could do with their own band.

Basie's band was on top form at that time, with his new vocalists Jimmy Rushing, a great blues shouter, and Billie Holiday, who was just then becoming a star. Chick Webb had a couple of good vocalists too, though . His new teenage singer, Ella Fitzgerald, in particular, was already one of the great singers.

And *everyone* was in the audience. Goodman's band, Mildred Bailey, Ivie Anderson (the singer with Duke Ellington's band, who appeared with the Marx Brothers in that scene I mentioned earlier), Red Norvo the vibraphone player, Duke Ellington. Every musician who mattered in the jazz scene was there to see if Basie could beat Chick Webb.

And... there was a dispute about it, one which was never really resolved in Webb's lifetime.

Because Webb won. Everyone agreed, when it came to a vote of the audience, Webb's band did win, though it was a fairly close decision. Again, the only band to ever beat Chick Webb was Duke Ellington.

But everyone also agreed that Basie's band had got people dancing more. A *lot* more.

What nobody realised at the time was that Whitey's Lindy Hoppers had gone on strike. Chick Webb had misheard a discussion between a couple of the dancers about how good the Basie band was going to be that night, assumed that they were saying Basie was going to be better than him, and got into a huff. Webb said, "I don't give a good Goddam what those raggedy Lindy Hoppers think or say. Who needs 'em? As far as I'm concerned they can all go to hell. And their Mammies too."

After this provocation, Whitey issued an ultimatum to his Lindy Hoppers. That night, they were only going to dance to Basie, and not to Webb. So even though most of the audience preferred Webb's band, every time they played a song all the best dancers, the ones who had an entire quarter or so of the ballroom to themselves to do their most exciting and visual dances, all sat down, and it looked like the Webb band just weren't exciting the crowd as much as the Basie band.

Of course, the Basie band *were* good that night, as well. When you've got the 1938 Count Basie band, with Jimmy Rushing and Billie Holiday singing, you're going to get a good show. Oh, and they persuaded Duke Ellington to come up and play a piano solo – and then all the band joined in with him, unrehearsed and unprompted.

But despite all that, Webb's band still beat them in the audience vote.

That's how good Webb's band were, and it's also how good his two big stars were. One of those stars, Ella Fitzgerald, we've already mentioned, but the other one was an alto sax player who also took the male lead vocals. This sax player did a lot of the frontman job for Webb's band and was so important to the band in those years that, allegedly, some people thought *he* was Chick Webb. That man was Louis Jordan.

Louis Jordan was a good sax player, but what he really was was a performer. He was someone who could absolutely sell a song, with wit and humour and a general sense of hipness that could possibly be matched at that time only by Cab Calloway and Slim Gaillard, and Jordan was a better musician than either of them. He was charming, and funny, and tuneful, and good looking, and he knew it.

He knew it so well, in fact, that shortly after that 1938 show, he started making plans. He thought that he and Ella were the two important ones in the Webb band, and he planned to form his own band, and take her, and much of the rest of the band with him. Webb found out and fired Jordan, and Ella and most of the band remained loyal to Webb.

In fact, sadly, Jordan would have had what he wanted sooner rather than later anyway. Chick Webb's disability had been affecting him more, and he was only continuing to perform because he felt he owed it to his musicians. He would often pass out after a show, literally unable to do anything else. He died, aged thirty-four, in June 1939, and Ella Fitzgerald became the leader of his band, though like many big bands it eventually broke up in the mid-forties.

So if Jordan had held on for another few months, he would have had a good chance at being the leader of the Louis Jordan and Ella Fitzgerald band, and history would have been very different. As it was, instead, he formed a much smaller group, the Elks Rendez-vous Band, made up of members of Jesse Stone's band, apparently with Stone's blessing. And on December 20, 1938, ten days before "Roll 'Em Pete", Louis Jordan and his Elks Rendez-vous Band went into the studio for the first time, to record "Honey in the Bee Ball" and "Barnacle Bill the Sailor". Shortly after that, they changed their name to Louis Jordan and his Tympany Five.

Before we talk about them more, I want to briefly talk about some-one else who worked with Jordan. I want to talk about Milt Gabler. Gabler is someone we'll be seeing a lot of in this story, and he's someone who already had an influence on it, but here's where he becomes important.

You see, even before his influence on rock and roll, Gabler had made one important contribution to music. He had started out as the owner of a little record shop, and he had a massive passion for good jazz music. And so did his customers. And many of those customers had wanted to get hold of old records, now out of print. So in 1935 Gabler started his own record label, and licensed those out of print recordings by people like Bix Beiderbecke and Bessie Smith, becoming the owner of the very first ever reissue record label. His labels pioneered things like putting a full list of all the musicians on a record on the label – the kind of thing that real music obsessives cared far more about than executives who only wanted to make money.

After he had some success with that, he branched out into making new records, on a new label, Commodore. That would have stayed a minor label, but for one thing.

In 1939, one of his regular customers, Billie Holiday, had a problem. She'd been performing a new song which she really wanted to record, but her current label, Columbia, wasn't interested. That song was too political even for her producer, John Hammond – the man who, you will remember, persuaded Benny Goodman to integrate his band and who put on shows that same year sponsored by the Communist Party. But the song was too political, and too inflammatory, even for him. The song, which became Billie Holiday's best-known performance, was "Strange Fruit", and it was about lynching.

"Strange Fruit" is a short song – so short that it's difficult to quote just *some* of the lyrics. If you haven't heard it, I urge you to check it out. But be warned, it is *very* explicit in its descriptions of racist murder, and might be disturbing even for 2019 listeners. For eighty years ago, it was potentially incendiary.

Billie Holiday could not get her label to put that track out, under any circumstances. But she knew Milt Gabler might do it, as he'd been recording several small group tracks with Lester Young, who was Holiday's colleague and friend in the Basie band. As Gabler was a friend of hers, and as he was politically left-leaning himself, he eventually negotiated a special deal with Columbia, that he could produce her for one session and put out a single recording by her, on Commodore.

That recording sold over a million copies, and became arguably the most important recording in music history. In December 1999, *Time* magazine called it the "song of the century". And in 2017, when the black singer Rebecca Ferguson was invited to play at Donald Trump's inauguration, she agreed on one condition – that the song she performed could be "Strange Fruit". She was disinvited.

As a result of "Strange Fruit"'s success, Milt Gabler was headhunted away from his own label, and became a staff producer at Decca records in 1941. There he was responsible for producing many of the greatest records of the forties, not least the Lionel Hampton band's proto-R&B version of "Flying Home," and he began a long collaboration with Louis Jordan.

Jordan's new band had a sound unlike anything else of the time. Clarence "Gatemouth" Brown later claimed that Jordan had most of the responsibility for the decline of the big bands, saying "He could play just as good and just as loud with five as seventeen. And it was cheaper."

And while we've talked before about a whole raft of economic and social reasons for the decline of the big bands, there was a lot of truth in that statement. While there were sometimes actually as many as seven or eight members of the Tympany Five, the original lineup was just Jordan plus one trumpet, one sax, piano, bass, and drums, and yet their recordings did sound almost as full as many of the bigger bands.

The style they were playing in was a style that later became known as jump band music, and it was a style that owed a lot to Lionel Hampton's band, and to Count Basie. This is a style of music that's based on simple chord changes, usually blues changes. And it's based on the concept of the riff.

We haven't really talked much about the idea of riffs yet, but they're absolutely crucial to almost all popular music from the twentieth century. A riff is, in its conception, fairly straight forward. It's an instrumental phrase that gets repeated over and over. It can act as the backbone to a song, but it can also be the basis for variation and improvisation – when you "riff on" something, you're coming up with endless variations and permutations of it.

Riffs were important in swing music, where they generally used in a sort of back-and-forth manner. You'd have the saxophones play the riff, and then the trumpets and trombones repeat it after them. But swing wasn't just about riffs – with a big orchestra, you had to have layers, and sophisticated orchestrations.

In jump band music, on the other hand, you strip everything back. The track becomes about the riff, the solos, and the vocal if there is one, and that's it. You play that riff over the simplest possible changes, you play it to a rhythm that will get everyone dancing – often a boogie rhythm with a backbeat – and you make everything about the energy of the performance.

Jordan's band did that, and they combined it with Jordan's own unique stage personality. Jordan, remember, had been the male singer in a band whose female singer was Ella Fitzgerald. You don't keep a job like that very long if you're not good.

Now, Jordan wasn't good in the same way as Ella was – no-one was good in the same way as Ella Fitzgerald – but what he was very good at was putting personality into his vocals. He belonged to a whole tradition of jive singing which dates back at least to the 1920s and Cab Calloway.

Jive singers weren't usually technically great, but they had *personality*. They were hip, and they often used made up words of their own. They were clever, and funny, and sophisticated, and they were often singing about the underworld or drug use or prostitution or other such disreputable concepts – when they weren't just singing nonsense words like Slim Gaillard anyway.

And Louis Jordan was very much in the mould of singers like Gaillard or Calloway or Fats Waller, all of whom would deserve looking at if we were going far enough back into rock's prehistory. But Jordan is the way that that stream became part of the makeup of rock music.

Most of Jordan's songs were written by Jordan himself, although he's not the credited writer on many of them. Rather, his then-wife, Fleecie Moore, is credited for contractual reasons. Jordan and Moore later split up after multiple separate occasions where she stabbed him, but she retained credit on the songs.

"Choo Choo Ch'Boogie," Jordan's biggest hit, was slightly different. From early 1943, just after Gabler started producing his records, Jordan had been having occasional crossover hits on the country charts. These days, his music sounds to us clearly like it's blues or R&B – in fact he's basically the archetype of a jump blues musician – but remember that Western swing used a large number of swing and boogie elements. If you were making boogie music then, you were likely to appeal to the same audience that was listening to Bob Wills, just as much as you were to the audience that was listening to Big Joe Turner.

And because of this crossover success, Jordan started recording occasional songs that were originally aimed at the white country market. "Choo Choo Ch'Boogie" was co-written by Gabler, but the other songwriters were pure country and western writers. Denver Darling, one of the writers, was a hillbilly singer who recorded songs such as "My Little Buckaroo", "I've Just Gotta Be A Cowboy" and "Ding Dong Polka", while the other writer, Vaughn Horton, wrote "Dixie Cannonball" and "Muleskinner Blues".

So "Choo Choo Ch'Boogie" was, in conception, a hillbilly boogie, but in Louis Jordan's hands, it was almost the archetypal rhythm and blues song. A lot of it resembles music Bob Wills was making, and the song itself would fit absolutely into the genre of Western swing. But Jordan's arrangement has the horn-driven pulse, and the hip vocals, that characterise rhythm and blues. The internal rhymes and slangy lyrics in the song – "take me right back to the track, Jack" – come straight from the jive school of vocals, even though it's a country and western song.

If there's any truth at all to the claim that rock and roll was the mixing of country and western music with rhythm and blues, this is as good a point as any to say, "*this* is where rock and roll really started". Essentially every musician in the early rock and roll period was, to a greater or lesser extent, copying the style of Louis Jordan's 1940s records. And indeed "Choo Choo Ch'Boogie" was later covered by another act Milt Gabler produced – an act who, more than any other, based their style on Jordan's. But we'll come to Bill Haley and his Comets later.

For now, "Choo Choo Ch'Boogie" is a great illustration of the way that jump band music sounds. This is not music that sounds like it's a small band. The record sounds like it has a full horn section, but during the sax solo the other horns just punch in a little, rather than playing a full pad under it as they would with a big band. The arrangement is stripped back to the basics, to what's necessary. This is a punchy track, and it's a track that makes you want to dance.

And it's music that, because it's so stripped down, relies on vocal personality. This is why Louis Jordan was able to make a success of this – his jive singing style gives the music all the character that in the larger bands would be conveyed by other instruments.

It's also worth noting that the lyrics talk about "the rhythm of the clickety clack". It's that backbeat again, the one we've been talking about. And the lyrics here are all about that rhythm, but also about the rhythm of the steam trains.

That mechanical steam train rhythm is one of the key influences in blues, rhythm and blues, and rock and roll. Rock and roll started at almost exactly the point that America changed from being a train culture to being a car culture. By the 1960s people would be singing "Nobody cares about the railroads any more" or about "the last of the good old fashioned steam powered trains", but in the 1940s and early fifties the train still meant freedom, still meant escape, and even once that had vanished from people's minds, it was still enshrined in the chug of the backbeat, in the choo choo ch'boogie.

And speaking of trains...

"This Train"

One of the problems when dealing with the history of rock and roll is the way it's dominated by men. Indeed, the story of rock and roll is the story of men crowding out women, and white men crowding out black men, and finally of rich white men crowding out poorer white men, until it eventually becomes a dull, conservative genre. Sorry if that's a spoiler, but don't say I didn't warn you when I get to the nineties.

But one black woman is as responsible as anyone for the style of rock and roll, and in particular, for its focus on the guitar.

To find out why, we're going to be making our final trip back to 1938 and Carnegie Hall.

We've talked before about John Hammond's legendary Spirituals to Swing concerts. These were tremendously important, but also tremendously problematic. I know that's a word that gets overused these days, but I mean it literally. They had problems, but weren't all bad. Far from it.

One of the most problematic aspects of them, indeed, is encoded in the name. "From Spirituals to Swing". It gives you a nice, simple, linear narrative, which was still being pushed in books I read in the 1980s. You start with the spirituals – or, as we *still* occasionally see people call them, "Negro spirituals" – and you end with swing. It's like those diagrams of the evolution of man, with the crawling monkey on one side and the tall, oddly hairless, white man with his genitals carefully concealed on the other.

The fact is, most of the narrative about "primitive" music – a narrative that was put forward by very progressive white men like John Hammond or the Lomaxes – is deeply mistaken. The forms of music made largely by black people could sound less sophisticated in the

1930s, but that wasn't because they were atavistic survivals of more primitive forms, musical coelacanths dredged up from the depths. It was because the people making the music often couldn't afford expensive instruments, and were recorded on cheaper equipment, and all the other myriad ways society makes the lives of black people, and underprivileged people in other ways, just that bit more difficult.

But this was, nonetheless, the narrative that was current in the 1930s. And so the Spirituals to Swing concerts featured a bisexual black woman who basically invented much of what would become rock guitar, an innovator if ever there was one, but portrayed her as somehow less sophisticated than the big band music on the same bill. And they did that because that innovative black woman was playing religious music.

In fact, black gospel music had grown up around the same time as the big bands. Black people had, of course, been singing in churches since their ancestors were forcibly converted to Christianity, but gospel music as we talk about it now was largely the creation of one man, Thomas Dorsey.

(This is not the same man as the white bandleader Tommy Dorsey who we've mentioned a couple of times earlier).

Dorsey was a blues and jazz musician, who had led the band for Ma Rainey, one of the great early blues singers, and under the name "Georgia Tom" he'd collaborated with Tampa Red on a series of singles. Their song "It's Tight Like That", from 1928, is one of the earliest hokum records, and is largely responsible for a lot of the clichés of the form, and it sold seven million copies.

"It's Tight Like That" is one of the most important records that has ever been made. You can trace from that song, through hokum blues, through R&B, and find its influence in basically every record made by a black American, or by anyone who's ever listened to a record made by a black American, since then. If Dorsey had only made that one record, he would have been one of the most important figures in music history.

But some time around 1930, he also started writing a whole new style of music. It combined the themes, and some of the melody, of traditional Christian hymns, with the feel of the blues and jazz music he'd been playing. It's rare that you can talk about a single person inventing a whole field of music, but gospel music as we know it basically *was* invented by Thomas Dorsey.

Other people had performed gospel music before, of course, but the style was very different from anything we now think of as gospel. Dorsey was the one who pulled all the popular music idioms into it and made it into something that powered and inspired all the popular music since.

He did this because he was so torn between his faith and his work as a blues musician that he had multiple breakdowns, at one point finding himself on stage with Ma Rainey and completely unable to move his fingers to play the piano. While he continued parallel careers for a while, eventually he settled on making religious music. And the songs he wrote include some of the most well-known songs of all time, like "Peace in the Valley" and "Take My Hand, Precious Lord".

That's a song he wrote in 1932, after his wife died in childbirth and his newborn son died a couple of days later. He was feeling a grief that most of us could never imagine, a pain that must have been more unbearable than anything anyone should have to suffer, and the pain came out in unimaginable heartbreaking beauty.

"Take My Hand, Precious Lord" is not "primitive" music, not music that is unsophisticated. It's not some form of folk art. It's one man, a man who personally revolutionised music multiple times over, writing about his own personal grief and creating something that stands as great art without having to be patronised or given special consideration.

And that goes for the gospel singer at the Spirituals to Swing show, Sister Rosetta Tharpe, who, like Dorsey, is someone who doesn't need to be given special treatment or be thought of as good considering her disadvantages or any of that patronising nonsense. Sister Rosetta Tharpe was one of the great singers of her generation, and one of the great guitar players of all time. And she was making music that was as modern and cutting-edge as anything else made in the 1930s and 40s. She wasn't making music that was a remnant of something that would evolve into swing, no matter what John Hammond thought. She was making important music, and music that would in the long run be seen as far more important than most of the swing bands.

Obviously, one should not judge Hammond too harshly. He was from another time. A primitive.

Sister Rosetta was brought up in, and spent her life singing for, the Church of God in Christ. As much of my readership is outside the US, as I am myself, it's probably worth explaining what this church is, because while it does have branches outside the US, that's where it's based, and that's where most of its membership is.

The Church of God in Christ is a Pentecostal church, and it's the largest Pentecostal church in the US, and the fifth-largest church full stop. I mention that it's a Pentecostal church, because that's something you need to understand to understand Rosetta Tharpe. Pentecostals believe in something slightly different to what most other Christian denominations believe.

Before I go any further, I should point out that I am *not* an expert in theology by any means, and that what I'm going to say may well be a mischaracterisation. If you're a Pentecostal and disagree with my characterisation of your religion here, I apologise, and if you let me know I'll do my best to fix my errors in future editions. No disrespect is intended.

While most Christians believe that humanity is always tainted by original sin, Pentecostals believe that it is possible for some people, if they truly believe – if they're "born again" to use a term that's a little more widespread than just Pentecostalism – to become truly holy. Those people will have all their past sins forgiven, and will then be sinless on Earth. To do this, you have to be "baptised in the Holy Ghost". This is different from normal baptism, what Pentecostals call "water baptism" – though most Pentecostals think you should be water baptised anyway, as a precursor to the main event. Rather, this is the Holy Spirit descending from Heaven and entering you, filling you with joy and a sense of sanctity. This can often cause speaking in tongues and other strange behaviours, as people are enthused (a word which, in the original Greek, actually meant a god entering into you), and once this has happened you have the tendency to sin removed from you altogether.

This is all based on the Acts of the Apostles, specifically Acts 2:4, which describes how at the Pentecost (which is the seventh Sunday after Easter), "All were filled with the Holy Spirit. They began to express themselves in foreign tongues and make bold proclamation as the Spirit prompted them".

Unlike the many Protestant denominations which adhere to Calvinist beliefs that nobody can know if they're going to Heaven or Hell, and that only God can ever know this, and that nothing you do can make a difference to your chances, most Pentecostals believe that you can definitely tell whether you're going to Heaven. You're going to Heaven once you're sanctified by the Holy Spirit, and that's an end of it.

At least, it's an end of it so long as you continue with what's called "outward holiness", and so you have to dress conservatively, to avoid swearing, to avoid drinking or gambling or smoking, or dancing suggestively, or wearing makeup. If you do that, once the spirit's entered into you, you're going to remain holy and free from temptation. If you don't do that, well, then the Devil might get you after all.

This is a very real fear for many Pentecostals, who have a belief in a literal heaven and hell. And it's a fear that has inspired a *lot* of the most important musicians in rock and roll. But Pentecostalism isn't just about fear and living right, it's also about that feeling of elation and exhilaration when the holy spirit enters you. And music helps bring that feeling about.

It's no surprise that a lot of the early rock and rollers went to Pentecostal churches – at many of them, especially in the South of the US, there's a culture of absolutely wild, unrestrained, passionate music and dancing, to get people into the mood to have the spirit enter them. And Sister Rosetta Tharpe is probably the greatest performer to come out of those churches.

But while most of the performers we'll be looking at started playing secular music, Sister Rosetta never did, or at least very rarely. But she was, nonetheless, an example of something that we'll see a lot in the history of rock – the pull between the spiritual and the worldly.

From the very start of her career, Sister Rosetta was slightly different from the other gospel performers. While she lived in Chicago at the same time as Thomas Dorsey and Mahalia Jackson, she isn't generally considered part of the gospel scene that they were at the centre of, because she was travelling round the country playing at revival meetings, rather than staying in one place. When her first marriage – to a fellow evangelist, who apparently abused her – broke up, she moved on to New York, and there she started playing to audiences that were very different from the churches she was used to.

Where people like Jackson were playing church music for church people, Rosetta Tharpe was taking the gospel to the sinners. Throughout her career, she played in nightclubs and theatres, playing for any audience that would have her, and playing music that got them excited and dancing, even as she was singing about holiness.

She started playing the Cotton Club in 1938. The Cotton Club was the most famous club in New York, though in 1938 it was on its last days of relevance. It had been located in Harlem until 1936, but after riots in Harlem, it had moved to a more respectable area, and was now on Broadway.

In the twenties and early thirties, the Cotton Club had been responsible for the success of both Duke Ellington and Cab Calloway, though only Calloway was still playing there regularly by the time Rosetta Tharpe started performing there. It was still, though, the place to be seen – at least if you were white. The Cotton Club was strictly segregated – only black people on stage, but only white people in the audience. The black performers were there to be leered at, in the case of the showgirls, or to play up to black stereotypes. Even Duke Ellington, possibly the most sophisticated musician ever to come out of the United States, had been presented as a "jungle musician". The name itself – the Cotton Club – was trading on associations with slavery and cotton picking, and the feel of the new venue could probably be summed up by the fact that it had, on its walls, pictures of famous white bandleaders in blackface.

So it's not surprising that the performances that Sister Rosetta did at the Cotton Club were very different from the ones she'd been doing when she was travelling the country with her mother performing to church crowds. She was still playing the same music, of course – in fact, over her career, she mostly stuck to the same quite small repertoire, rerecording the same material in new arrangements and with new emphases as she grew as an artist – but now she was doing it as part of a parody of the very kind of church service she had grown up in and devoted her life to, with dancers pretending to be "Holy Rollers", mocking her religion even as her music itself was still devoted to it.

Originally, she was only taken on at the Cotton Club as a sort of trial, on a two-week engagement – and apparently she thought the manager was joking when she was offered five hundred dollars a week, not believing she could be making that much money – and her role was simply to be one of many acts who'd come on and do a song or two between the bigger acts who were given star billing. But she soon became a hit, and she soon got signed to Decca to make records.

Her first record was, of course, a song by Thomas Dorsey, originally titled "Hide Me in Thy Bosom" but given the newer title "Rock Me" by Tharpe. Her arrangement largely stuck to Dorsey's original, with one important exception – where he had written "Now hear me singing/Hear the words that I'm saying/Wash my soul with water from on high", Tharpe sang "Won't you hear me *swinging*/Hear the words that I'm singing".

Many people also claimed to hear a double entendre in the lyrics to "Rock Me", and to think the song was about more worldly matters than Dorsey had intended. Whether Tharpe thought that or not, it almost certainly factored into the decision to make it her first single.

When she was booked to perform at the Spirituals to Swing concerts, she performed both that song and "That's All", backed by Albert Ammons, one of the boogie woogie players who also appeared on the bill, and in the recording of that we can hear, rather better than in the studio recording, the raw power of Tharpe's performance.

Tharpe's performances at the Cotton Club drew a great deal of attention, and *Time* magazine even did a feature on her, and how she "Swings Same Songs in Church and Night Club." When the Cotton Club shut down she moved on to the Cafe Society, a venue booked by John Hammond, which was an integrated club and which fit her rather better.

While she was working there, she came to the attention of Lucky Millinder, the big band leader. Different people have different ideas as to how the two started working together – Moe Gale, Millinder's manager, was also Chick Webb's manager, and claimed that it was his idea and that he'd seen Tharpe as being an Ella Fitzgerald to Millinder's

Chick Webb, but Bill Doggett, the piano player with Millinder's band, said that it was Millinder's idea, not Gale's, to get Tharpe on board.

Either way, the combination worked well enough at first, as Tharpe got to sing the same songs she'd been performing earlier – her gospel repertoire – but with a big band backing her. She'd also switched to playing an electric guitar rather than an acoustic, and the effect on her guitar playing was extraordinary. Where before she'd had to be a busy accompanist, constantly playing new notes due to the lack of sustain from an acoustic guitar, now she was able to play single-note lead lines and rely on the orchestra to provide the chordal pad.

Her remake of "Rock Me" with Millinder's band, from 1941, shows just how much her artistry had improved in just three years. With that record, she more or less invented the guitar style that T-Bone Walker, B.B. King, and others would adapt for themselves. That's just how you play electric blues now, but it wasn't how anyone played before Rosetta Tharpe.

Soon after she joined Millinder's band they moved to a residency at the Savoy Ballroom, and became one of the most popular bands for dancers in New York. Regulars there included a young man known as Detroit Red, who later changed his name to Malcolm X. The Savoy Ballroom was closed down not long after – allegedly for prostitution, but more likely because it allowed white women to dance with black men, and the city of New York wouldn't allow that. Although as Malcolm X said, it wasn't as if they were dragging the white women in there.

However, Millinder's band was an odd fit for Rosetta Tharpe, and she was increasingly forced to sing secular numbers along with the gospel music she loved. There were plenty of good things about the band, of course – she became lifelong friends with its young trumpet player, Dizzy Gillespie, for example, and she enjoyed a tour where they were on the same bill as a young vocal group, The Four Ink Spots – but she was a little bit uncomfortable singing songs like "Tall Skinny Papa", which wasn't particularly gospel-like, with lyrics like "I want a tall skinny papa/That's all I'll ever need... He's got to do what he's told/And bring sweet mama that gold".

And it's not particularly likely that she was keen on the follow-up, "Big Fat Mama", although she didn't sing on that one.

So eventually, she quit the Millinder band, without giving notice, and went back to performing entirely solo, at least at first.

This was in the middle of the AFM strike, but when that ended, Tharpe was back in the studio, and in September 1944 she began one of the two most important musical collaborations of her career, when she recorded "Strange Things Happening Every Day", with Sam Price on piano.

Sam Price did *not* get along with Tharpe. He insisted on her playing with a capo, because she was playing in an open tuning and wasn't playing in a normal jazz key. He didn't like the idea of combining gospel music with his boogie woogie style (eventually he was persuaded by Tharpe's mother, a gospel star in her own right who was by all accounts a fearsome and intimidating presence, that this was OK), and when the result became a massive hit, he resented that he got a flat fee.

But nonetheless, "Strange Things Happening Every Day" marks out the start of yet another new style for Tharpe, and it's yet another song often credited as "the first rock and roll record".

Shortly after this, Tharpe started working with another gospel singer, Marie Knight. Their partnership may have been a partnership in more than one sense. Knight denied the relationship to the end of her days, and it's entirely understandable that she would, given that she was a gospel singer who was devoted to a particularly conservative church, and whose career also depended on that church, but their relationship was regarded as an open secret within the gospel music community, which had a rather more relaxed attitude to homosexuality and bisexuality than the rest of the church. Some of Tharpe's friends have described her as a secret lesbian, but given her multiple marriages to men it seems more likely that she was bi, although of course we will never know for sure.

Either way, Tharpe and Knight were a successful double act for many years, with their voices combining perfectly to provide a gospel vocal sound that was unlike anything ever recorded. They stopped working together in 1950, but remained close enough that Knight was in charge of Tharpe's funeral in 1973.

The two of them toured together – and Tharpe toured later on her own – in their own bus, which was driven by a white man. This gave them a number of advantages in a deeply segregated and racist country. It was considered acceptable for them to go into some public places where they otherwise wouldn't have been allowed, because they were with a white man. If a black woman was with a white man, it was just assumed that she was sleeping with him, and unlike a white woman sleeping with a black man, this was considered absolutely acceptable, a sexual double-standard that dated back to slavery. If they needed food and the restaurant in a town was whites-only, they could send the white driver in to get them takeout. And if it came to it, if there was no hotel in town that would take black people, they could sleep on the bus.

And segregation was so accepted at the time by so many people that even when Tharpe toured with a white vocal group, the Jordanaires (who would later find more fame backing up some country singer named Elvis something) they just thought her having her own bus was cool, and didn't even make the connection to how necessary it was for her.

While Tharpe and Knight made many great records together, probably Tharpe's most important recording was a solo B-side to one of their singles, a 1947 remake of a song she'd first recorded in 1938, "This Train", again featuring Sam Price on piano.

That song sets out the theology of the Pentecostal church as well as you'll ever hear it. This train is a *clean* train. You want to ride it you better get redeemed. No tobacco chewers or cigar smokers. No crap shooters. If you want to be bound for glory, you need to act holy.

There was no-one bigger than Tharpe in her genre. She is probably the first person to ever play rock and roll guitar in stadiums. And not only that, she played rock and roll guitar in a stadium *at her wedding*. Her third wedding, to be precise, which took place at Griffith Stadium, the home of the Washington Senators and the Homestead Grays. Twenty thousand people came to see her get married and perform a gospel show afterwards, concluding with fireworks that first exploded in the shape of Tharpe playing her guitar before taking on other shapes like two hearts pierced with Cupid's arrow. Even Tharpe's half-sister had to pay for her ticket to the show. Apparently Tharpe signed the contract for her wedding seven months earlier, and then went out to find herself a husband.

Rosetta Tharpe's popularity started to wane in the 1950s, at least in her home country, but she retained a following in Europe. There's fascinating footage of her in 1964 filmed by Granada TV, playing at the abandoned Wilbraham Road railway station in Manchester. If you live in Manchester, as I do, that piece of track, which is now part of the Fallowfield cycle loop, was the place where some of the greats of black American music were filmed for what may have been the greatest blues TV programme of all time – along with Tharpe, there was Muddy Waters, Otis Spann, Reverend Gary Davis, and Sonny Terry and Brownie McGhee, all performing in the open air in Manchester in front of an extremely earnest audience of young white British people. Fittingly for an open-air show in Manchester, Tharpe opened her short set with "Didn't It Rain".

By that time, Tharpe had become primarily known as a blues musician, even though she was still doing the same thing she'd always been doing, simply because music had moved on and recategorised her. But she'd had an influence on blues, R&B, and rock and roll music that most people didn't even realise. "This Train" was not written by Tharpe, exactly – it dates back to the 1920s – but it was definitely her version, and her rewrite, that inspired one of the most important blues records of all time, "My Babe", by Little Walter, which has an identical melody and feel.

Indeed, only a few months after Rosetta Tharpe's UK performances, Gerry and the Pacemakers, one of the biggest bands of the new Merseybeat sound, who'd had three number one records that year in the UK, were recording their own version of "My Babe". Gerry and the Pacemakers were, in most respects, as far as you could imagine from gospel music, and yet the connection is there, closer than you'd think.

Rosetta Tharpe died in 1973, and never really got the recognition she deserved. She was only inducted into the Rock and Roll Hall of Fame in 2017. But if you've ever liked rock guitar, you've got her to thank. Shout, Sister, Shout!

"That's When Your Heartaches Begin"

OK, so we've covered the Carnegie Hall concerts of 1938 and 39 and the performers around them *quite* exhaustively now. We had a bit of a diversion into Western swing, but mostly we've stayed around there.

Now, we're still looking at New York in the late 1930s and early forties, but we're moving away from those shows, and we're going to look at the most popular vocal group of the era, and possibly the most important vocal group of all time.

We've already covered almost all the major elements of what we now think of as rock and roll – the backbeat, the arrangements that focus on a rhythm section, the riffs, the electric guitar and the amplification generally. We've seen, quite clearly, how most of these elements were being pulled together, in different proportions and by different people, in the late 1930s, almost but not quite coalescing into what we now call rock and roll.

There's one aspect which might be quite easy to overlook, though, which we've not covered yet, and that's the vocal group. Vocal harmonies have become much less prominent in rock music in the last forty years or so, and so today they might not be thought of as an essential element of the genre, but vocal groups played a massive role in the fifties and sixties, and were a huge element of the stew of genres that made up rock and roll when it started.

And the vocal group that had the most influence on the groups that became rock and roll was a band whose basis was not as a vocal group, but in coffee pot groups.

Coffee-pot groups were groups of poor black teenagers, who performed on street corners and tried to reproduce the sounds of the lush records they heard on the radio, using... well, using the equipment they had to hand. For string parts, you'd play ukuleles or guitars or banjos, but for the horns you'd play the kazoo. But of course, kazoos were not particularly pleasant instruments, and they certainly didn't sound much like a saxophone or clarinet. But it turned out you could make them sound a lot more impressive than they otherwise would if you blew them into something that resonated. Different sizes of container would resonate differently, and so you could get a pretty fair approximation of a horn section by having a teapot, a small coffee pot, and a large coffee pot, and having three of your band members play kazoos into them. The large coffee pot you could also pass around to the crowd afterward, to collect the money in – though, as Deek Watson said about his coffee-pot group the Percolating Puppies "all of us had to keep our eyes on the cat who passed the collection for the evening, or else some of the money found its way from the pot to his pocket before dividing time arrived".

Other instrumental parts, of course, would be replaced with simple mouth noises. You can make quite an impressive collection of instrumental sounds with just your voice, if you try hard enough.

The Ink Spots formed out of people who'd started their careers in these groups. Charlie Fuqua was in one with Jerry Daniels before they became the imaginatively-named duo "Charlie and Jerry", while Deek Watson was in another. Those three, plus Hoppy Jones, performed in a variety of combinations under a variety of names before they settled on calling themselves "King, Jack, and Jester" or sometimes "King, Jack, and Jesters".

In the early years of their career, they actually got themselves a radio show on a local station, where they were a fill-in for another band, the Four Mills Brothers. And the Four Mills Brothers were the people who influenced them the most.

The Mills Brothers had actually started out not so differently from the coffee pot groups – they entered a talent contest, and John Mills had lost the kazoo he was going to play. He cupped his hands in front of his mouth and imitated a trumpet, and the brothers decided that they were going to start imitating brass instruments with their voices. And they got good at it.

On most of the Mills Brothers' records, there is no instrument other than a single acoustic guitar, but listening to them – especially given the primitive recording and playback equipment at the time – many people were convinced there was a full band on there. They imitated trumpets, a tuba, and a trombone with their voices, and they'd listen to instrumental musicians and copy their voicings. This is something that a lot of vocal groups have continued to do, but no-one has done it better than the Mills Brothers.

The Mills Brothers became massively successful, and from 1930 through 1939 they were far and away the biggest black act in the US, making multiple appearances on Bing Crosby's radio show, appearing in films, and touring the world. It was the touring the world that caused their eventual downfall – they went to play the UK in 1939, and discovered that with World War II imminent, the only ship away from the UK they could get at the end of their tour was one that went to Australia.

Between that massive transport disruption, and then the further disruption caused by the war itself, it took them two years to get back into the US, by which time their popularity had faded somewhat (although they went on to have a massive hit with "Paper Moon" when they got back – their career was far from over). They carried on having occasional hits into the late sixties, and carried on performing together into the late eighties – and the last surviving Mills Brother carried on performing until his death in 1999, with one of his sons who carries on the family band to this day.

But they'd lost their place as the top of the entertainment tree, and they'd lost it to people who'd been imitating them, to the band who'd been performing as "King, Jack, and Jesters".

By the mid 1930s, those four men were in New York and performing as the Riff Brothers, but not getting very far. They were doing a mix of Mills Brothers inspired stuff and more jive music, and were earning decent money but not yet massive successes.

In his autobiography, Deek Watson talks about how the Riff Brothers decided to change their name. There were too many brother and cousin acts for the Riff Brothers to stand out, and the band eventually ended up in their booking agent's office, arguing for hours over what name they should choose and getting nowhere. Finally, as their agent toyed with a pen, a few drops of ink fell out. The next few paragraphs are a quote from Watson's autobiography:

> To me, it seemed like inspiration. "That's it!" I shouted. "How about calling us the Ink Spots?"
> The boys really yelled this time. "There you go again Deek!" Charlie exclaimed. "That's right!" agreed Hoppy, "always wanting us to be something colored. Black Dots, Ink Spots, next thing you know he'll be wanting us to call ourselves the Old Black Joes"
> They all talked at once. "Man, you know ain't nobody wants to be no Ink Spot".

Now, Watson in his book does seem to take credit for absolutely every good idea anyone involved in the band had (and for other things which had nothing to do with them, like writing "Your Feet's Too Big", which was written by Fred Fisher and Ada Benson). He also makes up some quite outrageous lies, like that this original lineup of the Ink Spots played at the coronation of King Edward VIII (anyone who knows anything about inter-war British history will know why that is impossible), but this does have the ring of truth about it. When he was in the Percolating Puppies, Watson used to work under the name "four-dice Rastus", and many early reviews of the Ink Spots criticised him for eye-rolling, hand-waving, and other minstrelly behaviours, which many black reviewers of the time considered brought black people into disrepute. It's entirely possible that his bandmates would be irritated by his emphasis on their race.

That said, I'm not going to criticise Watson for this, or repeat some of the insulting names he was called by other black people. Everyone has a different response to the experience of oppression, and I'm not, as a white man, going to sit here and moralise or pontificate about how black people "should" have behaved in the 1930s. A lot of much better artists than Deek Watson did a lot more to play along with those stereotypes.

Either way, and whatever they thought about it, Charlie Fuqua, Deek Watson, Jerry Daniels and Hoppy Jones became the Ink Spots, and that was the name under which their group would eventually become even more famous than the Mills Brothers.

But there was a problem. Jerry Daniels, their main jive singer, was getting seriously ill from the stress of the band's performing schedule, and eventually ended up hospitalised. He couldn't continue touring with them, and so for a little while the Four Ink Spots were down to three. They had to change, and in changing their lineup, they became the band that would change music.

In 1936 Bill Kenny, a twenty-one year old high tenor singer, won an amateur night contest at the Savoy Ballroom. Moe Gale, the Ink Spots' manager, was the co-owner of the Savoy, and Charles Buchanan, the club's manager, knew his boss' band wanted a new singer and suggested Kenny. Kenny was, by any standards, an extraordinary singer, and his vocals would become the defining characteristic of the Ink Spots' records from that point on. When you think of the Ink Spots, it's Kenny's voice you think of. Or at least, it's Kenny and Hoppy Jones.

Because as well as being an utterly astonishing singer, Bill Kenny was an inspired arranger, and he came up with an idea that changed the whole style and sound of the Ink Spots' music, and would later indirectly change all of popular music. The idea he came up with was called "top and bottom".

(Note that Deek Watson also claimed credit for this idea in his autobiography, but the story as he tells it there is inconsistent with the known facts, so I'm happy to believe the consensus view that it was Kenny).

Up until Bill Kenny joined the band, and for a while afterward, the Ink Spots had been a jive band, performing songs in the style of Cab Calloway or Fats Waller. They were performing uptempo comedy numbers, and they were doing it very well indeed.

Sometimes in those performances Hoppy Jones would speak-sing a line or two in his bass voice, but it was mostly fairly straightforward vocal group singing. They were still basically doing the Mills Brothers sound. And that was fine, because the Mills Brothers were, after all, the most popular black vocal group ever up to that point. But if the Ink Spots were going to be really big, they needed their own sound, and Bill Kenny came up with it.

He refined the idea of Hoppy's spoken vocals and came up with a hit formula, which they would use over and over again. They first did it in the studio with their massive hit "If I Didn't Care", but the one that probably had the most impact in the medium term is their 1941 minor hit "That's When Your Heartaches Begin". But really, it doesn't matter which song we talk about, because they stuck so closely to the same formula.

Their hits were ballads, and they would all be introduced by an acoustic guitar playing what would become a familiar figure, four bars of arpeggiated chords in the kind of clip-clop Western rhythm you get in songs like "Tumbling Tumbleweeds". We'd then get the whole song sung through by Bill Kenny in his high tenor, with the others singing backing vocals. Then Kenny would join in with the backing vocals, as Hoppy Jones repeated the whole song, speak-singing it in his deep bass voice. And finally there'd be a final line with Kenny singing lead again.

When I say this was a formula, I mean it *really* was a formula. They'd found a sound and they were going to absolutely stick with it. If you visit the MixCloud playlist I put together of the songs mentioned in this chapter[6], you can hear how rigidly they stuck to it.

But the thing is, they kept having hits. Between 1939, when they released "If I Didn't Care," and 1951 when they split up, they had *forty-seven* top thirty hits, and six of them hit number one. This was a formula that absolutely, undoubtedly, worked.

And when I say "number one" or "top thirty", I don't mean on the R&B charts. I mean number one on the *pop* charts. They did sometimes deviate from the formula slightly – and when they did, they didn't have hits that were quite so big (unless the deviation was to have Ella Fitzgerald sing the second verse instead of Kenny). The public knew what it liked, and what it liked was a guitar going dun-dun-dun-dun, then Bill Kenny singing a song in a high voice, then Hoppy Jones

---

[6]https://bit.ly/2loDrSx

saying the same words that Bill Kenny had just sung, in a much lower voice. And the Ink Spots were happy to give that to them.

That may sound like I'm being dismissive of the Ink Spots' music. I'm not. I absolutely love it. One of the great things about popular music before about 1970 is it had a lot of space for people who could do one thing really really well, and who just did their one thing. Artists like Duane Eddy and John Lee Hooker just kept making basically the same record over and over, and it was a great record, so why not?

The Ink Spots sold tens of millions of records over the decade or so when they were at their peak – roughly from 1939, when they started making "top and bottom" records, until the late forties. Their manager Moe Gale was also the manager of most of the bands who played the Savoy, and so could put on package tours combining, say, Ella Fitzgerald and the Ink Spots and Lucky Millinder's band, all of whom often played on the same bill together. This also meant that, for example, when Deek Watson took ill with pneumonia in 1943, Trevor Bacon from Millinder's band could fill in for him. Or when the Ink Spots needed a new pianist to back them in 1942, Bill Doggett, who had been in Millinder's band, was easily available.

But Gale was taking the majority of the money – Gale took sixty percent while the Ink Spots got the other forty between them, split four ways. But forty percent of multiple millions of 1940s dollars is still a lot of money, and with a lot of money come the kind of problems you only get when you've got a big pile of money and think you could get a bigger pile of money if you didn't have to share it.

The Ink Spots' period in the spotlight was eventually brought to an end by personality conflicts, lineup changes, legal squabbles, and deaths. Four years after their career took off, in 1942, Charlie Fuqua was drafted, and that began a whole series of lineup shifts, as replacements were brought in to cover his parts for the three years he was away. But then, two years later, in 1944, everything started falling apart.

Deek Watson and Bill Kenny never got on very well. Watson thought of himself as the leader, on the grounds that he was the one who'd put the band together, named it, and been the on-stage leader until Kenny came along. Meanwhile Kenny thought of himself as the leader, on account of being the lead singer and arranger. Hoppy Jones was the peacemaker between the two of them – he'd worked with Watson for years before Kenny came along, but he also had an assured place in the band because of his spoken bits, so he took it on himself to keep the peace.

But Hoppy Jones was growing ill, and started missing more and more dates because of what turned out to be a series of brain haemorrhages. Meanwhile, Moe Gale allegedly gave Bill Kenny a pay rise, but not Watson or Jones. Deek Watson quit the band as a result of this and went off to form his own "Ink Spots". Kenny and Hoppy Jones carried on for a month – but then, tragically, Hoppy Jones collapsed on stage and died.

After this, Deek Watson tried to rejoin the band, but Kenny wouldn't let him.

The result was a complicated four-way legal battle. Deek Watson wanted the right to rejoin the band, or failing that to form his own Ink Spots. Bill Kenny wanted to continue touring with his current Ink Spots lineup, Charlie Fuqua wanted to make sure that once the war was over he was allowed back into the band – unlike Watson he hadn't quit, but he was worried that with Jones and Watson out, Kenny would see no reason to let him back in. And Moe Gale wanted to be able to continue taking sixty percent of what any of them was making. There was a whole flurry of lawsuits and counter-suits.

In the end, Bill Kenny more or less won. The courts ruled that no club could book an act called "the Ink Spots" which didn't have Bill Kenny in it, but also that Deek Watson and Charlie Fuqua continued to have a financial interest in the band, that Moe Gale was still everyone's manager, and that Charlie Fuqua would be paid a regular salary as an Ink Spot while he was in the army. The only real loser was Deek Watson. He continued to get some money for his share of the Ink Spots name – although I've seen some claims that Bill Kenny bought him out totally. But he wasn't allowed to tour as the Ink Spots, or to rejoin the band he'd founded.

Fuqua came back, and for a few years a new lineup of Bill Kenny and his brother Herb, Fuqua, and Billy Bowen toured and recorded. Deek Watson, meanwhile, had been performing with his own Ink Spots before the lawsuits, but once they were settled, and not in his favour, he said he was going to form a new vocal group based on "a completely new idea".

This completely new idea was to have a vocal group made up of four people, which would start their songs off with a guitar playing four bars of arpeggiated chords, have a bloke sing the song in a high tenor, then have someone recite the same song lyrics in a lower voice, then finish the song off with the high tenor again. And called The Brown Dots.

The Brown Dots actually made a record that would itself go on to be hugely influential – "I Love You For Sentimental Reasons", written by two of their members (and not by Watson, despite what he claims in his book). That song has been covered by almost everyone who ever sang a ballad, from Nat "King" Cole to Ella Fitzgerald to Sam Cooke to the Righteous Brothers to Rod Stewart.

It looked like Deek Watson had found himself a second great band to be with. But then the other band members realised that it was hard to get on with Deek Watson, and left him to form their own band without him. The Four Tunes, their new name, would have several big hits in the 1950s, without Watson.

Meanwhile, back in the Ink Spots, in 1952 Fuqua and Bill Kenny decided to part ways. The lawsuit from eight years earlier had said that both of them had an equal share in the band name, but had *also* said that only bands with Bill Kenny in could legally be presented as "The Ink Spots". Rather than reopen that can of worms, they eventually came to an agreement that Kenny and his band could carry on calling themselves "The Ink Spots" and Fuqua would tour as "Charlie Fuqua's New Ink Spots".

Except that Fuqua soon ended up breaking this agreement, and just touring and recording as "The Ink Spots". He even got Deek Watson back into his band for a while. There's one recording of that version of the band – Jimmy Holmes, Charlie Fuqua, Deek Watson, and Harold Jackson – live at the Apollo before Watson was kicked out. It *sort of* sounds like the Ink Spots, but without the two most prominent vocalists it doesn't really. Meanwhile Bill Kenny was still making records as the

Ink Spots, which still sounded like the old Ink Spots minus Hoppy's bass vocal.

So there was one version of "The Ink Spots" touring with two original members, and another with no original members, but with the bloke who'd sung lead on all their hits and had the memorable voice that everyone wanted to hear when they heard the Ink Spots.

That wasn't a situation that was sustainable, so they went to court again. Most people would have expected the court to make the same ruling it had before, that they owned the band name equally but that Bill Kenny was the only one who could tour as the Ink Spots.

Instead, the ruling was one that no-one had expected, and that no-one wanted.

You see, it turns out that the Ink Spots weren't a corporation, they were a partnership. And the judge ruled that, when Hoppy Jones had died, ten years earlier, that partnership had been dissolved. Since then, there had been *no* legitimate group called the Ink Spots, and no-one owned the name. Neither the surviving original members of the band, nor the man whose arrangement ideas and lead vocals had brought the band their success, had any claim over it. Anyone at all could go out and call themselves The Ink Spots and go on tour, and there was nothing anyone could do about it.

And they did. Every surviving member of the band – not just the three surviving members of the classic lineup, but anyone who had filled in in a later version of the band on guitar or backing vocals – went out on tour as "the Ink Spots". At one point there were up to forty different "Ink Spots" groups touring, and many of them were recording too. Usually, at first, these bands would have *some* claim to authenticity, having at least one person who'd been in a proper version of the Ink Spots – and indeed a few times in the fifties and sixties Fuqua and Watson would get together again and tour as "Ink Spots", in between bouts of suing each other. But more and more they'd just be any group of four black men, so long as you could get one old enough that he might plausibly have been in the band with Bill Kenny at some point.

The last actual Ink Spots member, Huey Long, who had been one of the temporary replacements for Charlie Fuqua in 1945 for nine months, died aged 106 in 2009. The last Ink Spots gig I've been able to find details for took place in 2013.

But the Ink Spots' career ending in legal infighting, arguments over credit, and disputes over the band name isn't the only way in which they were a precursor to rock music. Over the next few chapters we'll see how, along with the jump band sound that was coming to dominate rhythm and blues, a new wave of Ink Spots-inspired vocal groups ended up shaping the new music.

And in 1953, shortly after the Ink Spots' final split, a young man walked into a recording studio in Memphis that let you make your own single-copy records. He wanted to make a record of himself singing, as a gift for his mother, and he chose one of his favourite songs, "That's When Your Heartaches Begin", as one of the two tracks he would record.

But we'll get to Elvis Presley in chapter nineteen. . .

"Good Rockin' Tonight"

There's a comic called *Phonogram*, and in it there are people called "phonomancers". These are people who aren't musicians, but who can tap into the power of music other people have made, and use it to do magic.

I think the concept of the phonomancer is actually very useful for dealing with the real world as well. There are people in the music industry who don't themselves play an instrument or sing or any of the normal musician things, but who manage to get great records made – records which are *their* creative work – by moulding and shaping the work of others. Sometimes they're record producers, sometimes they're managers, sometimes they're DJs or journalists. But there are a lot of people out there who've shaped music enormously without being musicians in the normal sense. Brian Eno, Sam Phillips, Joe Meek, Phil Spector, Malcolm McLaren, Simon Napier-Bell... I'm sure you can add more to the list yourself. People – almost always men, to be honest – who have a vision, and a flair for self-publicity, and an idea of how to get musicians to turn that idea into a reality. Men who have the power to take some spotty teenager with a guitar and turn him into a god, at least for the course of a three minute pop song.

And there have always been spaces in the music industry for this sort of person. And in the thirties and forties, that place was often in front of the band.

Most of the big band leaders we remember now were themselves excellent musicians. Count Basie, Duke Ellington, Benny Goodman, you could put those people up against most others on their instruments. They might not have been the best, but they could hold their own.

But plenty of other band leaders were mediocre musicians or couldn't play at all. Glenn Miller was a competent enough trombone player, but no-one listens to the Glenn Miller band and thinks "wow, one of those four trombone players is fantastic!" And other band leaders were much less involved in the music. Kay Kyser, the most successful bandleader of the big band era, who had eleven number one records and thirty-five in the top ten, never played an instrument, didn't write songs, didn't sing. He acted as onstage MC, told jokes, and was the man at the front of the stage. And there were many other bandleaders like that – people who didn't have any active involvement in the music they were credited with. Bob Crosby, Bing's brother, for example, was a bandleader and would sing on some tracks, but his band performed plenty of instrumentals without him having anything to do with them.

Most non-playing bandleaders would sing, like Bob Crosby, but even then they often did so rarely. And yet some of them had an immense influence on the music world.

Because a good bandleader's talent wasn't in playing an instrument or writing songs. It was having an idea for a sound, and getting together the right people who could make that sound, and creating a work environment in which they could make that sound well. It was a management role, or an editorial one. But those roles can be important. And one of the most important people to do that job was Lucky Millinder, who we've talked about a couple of times already in passing.

Lucky Millinder is a largely forgotten figure now, but he was one of the most important figures in black music in the 1940s. He was a fascinating figure – one story about how he got his name is that Al Capone was down ten thousand dollars playing dice, Millinder offered to rub the dice for luck, and Capone ended the night fifty thousand dollars up and called him Lucky from then on.

(I think it's more likely that Lucky was short for his birth name, Lucius, but the story shows the kind of people Millinder was hanging around with).

He didn't play an instrument or read music or sing much. What Millinder could definitely do was recognise talent. He'd worked with Bill Doggett, before Doggett went off to join the Ink Spots' backing band, and the trumpet player on his biggest hit was Dizzy Gillespie, who

Millinder had hired after Gillespie had been sacked from Cab Calloway's band after stabbing Calloway in the leg. He had Rosetta Tharpe as his female singer at the beginning of the forties, and Ruth Brown later on (though not for long).

He'd started out as the leader of the Mills Blue Rhythm Band, the house band in the Cotton Club, before moving on to lead, as his own band, one of the main bands in residence at the Savoy, along with occasionally touring the chitlin circuit – the rather derogatory name for the clubs and theatres that were regular tour stops for almost all major black artists at the time.

Slowly, during the 1940s, Millinder transitioned his band from the kind of swing music that had been popular in the thirties, to the jump band style that was becoming more popular. And if you want to point to one band that you can call the first rhythm and blues band, you probably want to look at Millinder's band, who more than any other band of the era were able to combine all the boogie, jump, and jive sounds with a strong blues feeling and get people dancing.

In 1944, after Rosetta Tharpe had left his band, Millinder needed a new second singer, to take the occasional lead as Tharpe had. And he found one – one who later became the most successful rhythm and blues artist of the late 1940s. Wynonie Harris.

Harris was already known as "Mr. Blues" when Millinder first saw him playing in Chicago and invited him to join the band. He was primarily a blues shouter, inspired by people like Big Joe Turner and Jimmy Rushing, but he could also perform in a subtler style, close to the jive singing of a Cab Calloway or Louis Jordan.

Harris joined the Millinder band and started performing with them in their residency at the Savoy. Shortly after this, the band went into the studio to record "Who Threw the Whiskey in the Well?"

That song has a strong backbeat. As we discussed earlier, the combination of the backbeat and the boogie bass is what really makes rock and roll, and we're now getting to the point that that combination was turning up more and more.

"Who Threw the Whiskey in the Well?" was recorded in May 1944, almost straight after the end of the AFM strike, but it wasn't released straight away. Records, at that time, were released on discs made out of shellac, which is a resin made from insect secretions. Unfortunately, the insects in question were native to Vietnam, which was occupied by Japan, and India, which was going through its own problems at the time, so shellac was strictly rationed. There was a new product, vinylite, being made which seemed promising for making records, but that was also used for lifejackets, which were obviously given a higher priority during a war than making records was. So the record wasn't released until nearly a year after it was recorded. And during that time, Wynonie Harris had become a much more important part of Millinder's band, and was starting to believe that maybe he deserved a bit more credit.

Harris, you see, was an absolutely astonishing stage presence. Lots of people who spoke about Elvis Presley in later years said that his performances, hip thrusts and leg shaking and all, were just a watered-down version of what Wynonie Harris had been doing. Harris thought of himself as a big star straight away,

This belief was made stronger when "Who Threw the Whiskey in the Well?" was finally released. It became a massive hit, and the only money Harris saw from it was a flat $37.50 session fee. Millinder, on the other hand, was getting the royalties. Harris decided that it was his vocal, not anything to do with the rest of the band, that had made the record a success, and that he could make more money on his own.

In case you hadn't realised, yet, Wynonie Harris was never known as the most self-effacing of people, and that confidence gave him a huge amount of success on stage, but didn't win him many friends in his personal life.

Harris went solo, and Lucky Millinder replaced him with a trumpet player and singer called Henry Glover. Harris started making records for various small labels.

His first record as a solo artist was "Around the Clock Blues", with a band led by a session drummer named Johnny Otis. This was one of the most influential records ever made. Arthur Crudup later rewrote part of it into his song "So Glad You're Mine," later covered by Elvis Presley; Chuck Berry rewrote it as "Reelin' and Rockin'"; and of course there was another song with "Around the Clock" in the title, which we'll get to eventually. . .

Even though "Around the Clock Blues" is one of the milestones in the development of rock and roll, it's not the most important record Wynonie Harris made in the late 1940s[7].

Wynonie Harris became a *big* star within the world of rhythm and blues, and that was in large part because of his extremely sexualised performance style, and the way he aimed his performances at women, not at the young girls many other singers would target. As he said himself, the reason he was making fifteen hundred dollars a week when most famous singers were getting fifty or seventy-five dollars a night was, "The crooners star on the Great White Way and get swamped with Coca-Cola-drinking bobby-soxers and other 'jail bait'. I star in Georgia, Texas, Alabama, Tennessee, and Missouri and get those who have money to buy stronger stuff and my records to play while they drink it. I like to sing to women with meat on their bones and that long green stuff in their pocketbook".

And he certainly made enough of that long green stuff, but he spent it just as fast as he made it. When he got a ten thousand dollar royalty cheque, he bought himself two Cadillacs and hired two chauffeurs, and every night at the end of his show they'd both arrive at the venue and he'd pick which one he was riding home in that night.

Now, having talked about Wynonie Harris for a little bit, let's talk about one of his fans. Roy Brown was a big fan of Harris, and was a blues singer himself, in something like the same style. Brown had originally been hired as "a black singer who sounds white", which is odd because he used a lot of melisma in his vocals, which was normally a characteristic of black singing. But other than that, Brown's main vocal influences when he started were people like Bing Crosby and other crooners, rather than blues music.

However, he soon became very fond of jump blues, and started writing songs in the style himself. In particular he thought one, called "Good Rockin' Tonight", might be popular with other audiences, since

---

[7]Another record he made around this time isn't important enough to talk about in the main body of the text, but "Dig This Boogie" is notable for its pianist. Herman "Sonny" Blount later became rather better known as Sun Ra, and while he didn't have enough to do with rock music for me to cover him here, I had to make note of that.

it always went down so well in his own shows. Indeed, he thought it might be suitable for Wynonie Harris, and when Harris came to town, Brown suggested the song to him.

And Harris wasn't interested. But after Brown moved back to New Orleans from Galveston, Texas, where he'd been performing — there was a girl, and a club owner, and these things happen and sometimes you have to move — Brown took his song to Cecil Gant instead. Gant was another blues singer, and if Harris wasn't up for recording the song, maybe Gant would be.

Cecil Gant was riding high off his biggest hit, "I Wonder", which was a ballad, and he might have seemed a strange choice to record "Good Rockin' Tonight". But while Gant's A-sides were ballads, his B-sides were boogie rockers, and very much in the style of Brown's song.

But Gant wasn't the best person for Brown to ask to record a song. According to Jim Bulleit, who produced Gant's records, everything Gant recorded was improvised in one take, and he could never remember what it was he'd just done, and could never repeat a song. So Gant wasn't really in the market for other people's songs.

But he was so impressed by Brown's singing, as well as his song, that he phoned the head of his record company, at 2:30AM, and got Brown to sing down the phone. After hearing the song, the record company head asked to hear it a second time. And then he told Gant "give him fifty dollars and don't let him out of your sight!"

And so Roy Brown ended up recording his song, on Deluxe Records, and having a minor hit with it.

Brown's original version of "Good Rockin' Tonight" doesn't sound all that innovative at all in retrospect. In fact it wears its influences on its sleeve so much that it namechecks Sweet Lorraine, Sioux City Sue, Sweet Georgia Brown, and Caldonia, all of whom were characters who'd appeared in other popular R&B songs around that time.

It might also sound odd to anyone who's familiar with later cover versions by Elvis Presley, or by Paul McCartney and others who followed the pattern of Elvis' version. Brown only sings the opening line once, before singing "I'm gonna hold my baby as tight as I can". Those later versions restructure the song into a fairly conventional sixteen-bar blues form by adding in a repeat of the first line and a chord change along with it.

Roy Brown's original, on the other hand, just holds the first chord, and keeps playing the same riff, for almost the entire verse and chorus. The chord changes are closer to passing chords than to anything else, and the song ends up having some of the one-chord feel that people like John Lee Hooker had, where the groove is all and harmonic change is thrown out of the window. Even though you'd think, from the melody line, that it was a twelve-bar blues, it's something altogether different.

This is something that needs to be pointed out when discussing music for dancing. The more chords something has, in general, the harder it is to dance to. And there will always, always, be a tension between music that's all about the rhythm, and which is there for you to dance to, and music which is all about the melody line, and which treats harmonic interest as an excuse to write more interesting melodies. You can either be Burt Bacharach or you can be Bo Diddley, and the closer you get to one, the further you get from the other. And on that spectrum, "Good Rockin' Tonight" is absolutely in the Diddley corner.

But at the time, this was an absolutely phenomenal record, and it immediately started to take off in the New Orleans market.

And then Wynonie Harris realised that maybe he'd made a mistake. Maybe he should have recorded that song after all. And so he did – cutting his own, almost identical, cover version of Brown's song.

There are a few differences between the two, of course. In particular, Harris introduced a vocal refrain, "hoy hoy", which wasn't part of Roy Brown's original. That's a line which comes from "The Honeydripper", another massively important R&B record. Harris also included a different instrumental introduction, playing "When the Saints Go Marchin' In" at the start, a song whose melody bears a slight resemblance to Brown's song.

Harris also adds a backbeat, which doesn't feature on Brown's version, and it's for that reason that Wynonie Harris' version of the song, not Roy Brown's original, is the one that people call "the first rock and roll record".

Other than those changes, Harris' version is a carbon copy of Roy Brown's version. Except, of course, that Wynonie Harris was one of the biggest stars in R&B, while Roy Brown was an unknown who'd just released his first single. That makes a lot of difference, and Harris had the big hit with the song.

And "Good Rockin' Tonight", in Harris' version, became one of those records that was *everywhere*. Roy Brown's version of the song made number thirteen on the R&B charts, and two years later it would re-enter the charts and go to number eleven – but Harris' was a world-changing hit, at least in the R&B market.

Harris' version, in fact, started off a whole chain of soundalikes and cash-ins, records that were trying to be their own version of "Good Rockin' Tonight". Harris himself recorded a sequel, "All She Wants to Do is Rock", but for the next two years everyone was recording songs with "rock" in the title. There was Roy Brown's own sequel, "Rockin' at Midnight", there was Cecil Gant's "We're Gonna Rock", there was "Rock the Joint" by Jimmy Preston... From 1948 through about 1951, if you listened to rhythm and blues records at all you couldn't escape this new rock craze. Record after record with "rock" in the title, with a boogie woogie bassline, with a backbeat, and with someone singing about how they were going to rock and roll.

This was, in fact, the real start of the rock and roll music fad. We're still six years away from it coming to the notice of the white mainstream audience, but all the pieces are there together, and while we're still three years away even from the canonical "first rock and roll record", Jackie Brenston's "Rocket "88"", 1948 is when rock and roll first became a cohesive, unified, whole; something that was recognisable and popular, a proper movement in music rather than odd individuals making their own separate music.

Of course, it was still missing some of the ingredients that would later be added. First-wave rock and roll is a music that's based on the piano and horn sections rather than guitars, and it wouldn't be until it merged with hillbilly boogie in the early fifties that the electric guitar started to be an important instrument in it. But still, I keep making the point that there's no real "first rock and roll record", but if you insist on looking for one then "Good Rockin' Tonight" is as good a candidate as any.

Neither of its creators did especially well from the rock and roll craze they initiated though. Roy Brown got a reputation for being difficult after he went to the musicians' union to try to get some of the money the record company owed him – in the 1950s, as today, record companies thought it was unreasonable for musicians and singers to actually want them to pay the money that was written in their contract – and so after a period of success in the late forties and very early fifties he spent a couple of decades unable to get a hit. He eventually started selling encyclopaedias door to door, with the unique gimmick that when he was in black neighbourhoods he could offer the people whose doors he was knocking on an autographed photo of himself. He sold a lot of encyclopaedias that way, apparently. He continued making the occasional great R&B record, but he made more money from sales. He died in 1981.

Wynonie Harris wasn't even that lucky. He basically stopped having hits by 1953, and he more or less gave up performing by the early sixties. The new bands couldn't play his kind of boogie, and in his last few performances, by all accounts, he cut a sad and pitiful figure. He died in 1969 after more or less drinking himself to death.

The music business is never friendly towards originals, especially black originals. But we're now finally into the rock era. Much of the rest of this book is taken up with "first rock and roll songs", but if you've ever listened to a rock and roll record and enjoyed it, a tiny part of the pleasure you got is owed to Roy Brown and Wynonie Harris.

"The Fat Man"

In his 1970 book *The Sound of the City*, which was the first attempt at a really serious history of rock and roll, Charlie Gillett also makes the first attempt at a serious typology of the music. He identifies five different styles of music, all of them very different, which loosely got lumped together (in much the same way that country and western or rhythm and blues had) and labelled rock and roll.

The five styles he identifies are Northern band rock and roll – people like Bill Haley, whose music came from Western swing; Memphis country rock – the music we normally talk about as rockabilly; Chicago rhythm and blues – Chuck Berry and Bo Diddley; what he calls "vocal group rock and roll" but which is now better known as doo wop; and New Orleans dance blues. I'd add a sixth genre to go in the mix, which is the coastal jump bands – people like Johnny Otis and Lucky Millinder, based in the big entertainment centres of LA and New York.

So far, we've talked about the coastal jump bands, and about precursors to the Northern bands, doo wop, and rockabilly. We haven't yet talked about New Orleans dance blues though. So let's take a trip down the Mississippi.

We can trace New Orleans' importance in music back at least to the early nineteenth century, and to the first truly great American composer, Louis Moreau Gottschalk.

Gottschalk was considered, in his life, an unimportant composer, just another Romantic. Mark Twain made fun of his style, and he was largely forgotten for decades after his early death. When he was remembered, if at all, it was as a performer – he was considered the greatest pianist of his generation, a flashy showman of the keyboard, who could make it do things no-one else could. But listening now to his music, it sounds staggeringly modern. While Gottschalk knew Chopin and Liszt, and was composing so long ago he *taught someone* who played for Abraham Lincoln, his music sounds like it could easily come from the 1920s or 1930s.

And the reason it sounds so advanced, and so modern, is that Gottschalk was the first person to put New Orleans music into some sort of permanent form.

We don't know – we can't know – how much of later New Orleans music was inspired by Gottschalk, and how much of Gottschalk was him copying the music he heard growing up. Undoubtedly there is an element of both – we know, for example, that Jelly Roll Morton, who was credited (mostly by himself, it has to be said) as the inventor of jazz, knew Gottschalk's work. But we also know that Gottschalk knew and incorporated folk melodies he heard in New Orleans.

And that music had a lot of influences from a lot of different places. There were the slave songs, of course, but also the music that came up from the Caribbean because of New Orleans' status as a port city. And after the Civil War there was also the additional factor of the brass band music – all those brass instruments that had been made for the military, suddenly no longer needed for a war, and available cheap.

Gottschalk himself was almost the epitome of a romantic – he wrote pieces called things like "The Dying Poet", he was first exiled from his home in the South due to his support for the North in the Civil War and then later had to leave the US altogether and move to South America after a scandalous affair with a student, and he eventually contracted yellow fever and collapsed on stage shortly after playing a piece called "Morte!" (with an exclamation mark) which is Portuguese for "death". He never recovered from his collapse, and died three weeks later of a quinine overdose.

So as well as presaging the music of the twentieth century, Gottschalk also presaged the careers of many twentieth-century musicians. Truly ahead of his time.

But by the middle of the twentieth century, time had caught up to him, and New Orleans had repeatedly revolutionised popular music, often with many of the same techniques that Gottschalk had used.

In particular, New Orleans became known for its piano virtuosos. We'll undoubtedly cover several of them over the course of this series, but anyone with a love for the piano in popular music knows about the piano professors of New Orleans, and to an extent of Louisiana more widely. Jelly Roll Morton, Professor Longhair, James Booker, Allen Toussaint, Huey "Piano" Smith... it's in the piano that New Orleans music has always come into its own.

And if there's one song that sums up New Orleans music, more than any other, it's "Junker's Blues". The first known recording of the song is by Champion Jack Dupree, in 1940, and Dupree claims songwriting credit on the label, but it was actually written by a New Orleans piano player, Drive-Em Down Hall, some time in the 1920s. Dupree heard the song from Hall, who also apparently taught Dupree his piano style.

"Junker's Blues" itself never became a well-known song, but its melody was reused over and over again. Most famously there was the Lloyd Price song "Lawdy Miss Clawdy", but there was also "Tipitina" by Professor Longhair, "Tee Nah Nah" by Smiley Lewis, and more. This one melody, by a long-dead unknown New Orleans piano player, has been performed under various names and with different sets of lyrics, by everyone from the Clash to the zydeco accordion player Clifton Chenier, by way of Elvis, Doctor John, and even Hugh Laurie.

But the most important recording of it was in 1949, by a New Orleans piano player called Fats Domino. And in his version, it became one of those songs that is often considered to be "the first rock and roll record".

Fats Domino was not someone who could have become a rock star even a few years later. He was not mean and moody and slim, he was a big cheerful fat man, who spoke Louisiana Creole as his first language. He was never going to be a sex symbol. But he had a way of performing that made people happy, and made them want to dance, and in 1949 that was the most important thing for a musician to do.

He grew up in a kind of poverty that's hard to imagine now. His family *did* have a record player, but it was a wind-up one, not an electrical one, and eventually the winding string broke. But young Antoine Domino loved music so much that he would sit at the record player and manually turn the records using his finger so he could still listen to them.

By 1949, Domino had become a minor celebrity among black music fans in New Orleans, more for his piano playing than for his singing. He was known as one of the best boogie woogie players around, with a unique style based on triplets rather than the more straightforward rhythms many boogie pianists used. He'd played, for example, with Roy Brown, although Domino and his entire band got dropped by Brown after Domino sang a few numbers on stage himself during a show – Brown said he was only paying Domino to play piano, not to sing and upstage him.

But minor celebrities in local music scenes are still only minor celebrities – and at aged twenty-one Fats Domino already had a family, and was living in a room in his in-laws' house with his wife and kids, working a day job at a mattress factory, and working a second job selling crushed ice with syrup to kids, to try to make ends meet. Piano playing wasn't exactly a way to make it rich, unless you got to make records.

Someone who *had* made records, and was the biggest musician in New Orleans at the time, was Dave Bartholomew; and Bartholomew, who was working for Imperial Records, suggested that the label sign Domino.

Like many musicians in New Orleans in the late forties, Dave Bartholomew learned his musical skills while he was in the Army during World War II. He'd already been able to play the trumpet, having been taught by the same man who taught Louis Armstrong, but once he was put into a military brass band he had to learn more formal musical skills, including writing and arranging.

After getting out of the army, he got work as an A&R man for Imperial Records, and he also formed his own band, the Dave Bartholomew Orchestra, who had a hit with "Country Boy".

Now, "Country Boy" is most notable for its horn part, a "dah, *dah-dah*" sound that came to typify New Orleans R&B, but which had never been played on a rhythm and blues record before. And we can link that horn part back to Gottschalk pieces like "Danza", by its use of a rhythm called the tresillo.

The tresillo is one of a variety of related rhythms that are all known as habanera rhythms. That word means "from Havana", and was used to describe any music that was influenced by the dance music – Danzas, like the title of the Gottschalk piece – coming out of Cuba in the mid nineteenth century.

It's difficult to explain the tresillo rhythm in text, without musical notation, in a way that can be understood by the casual reader, but imagine that in a bar of music you have the beats broken down one-and, two-and, three-and, four-and. In a tresillo rhythm, you play the first beat, the "and" of the second beat, and the four, so it goes *one*-and-two-*and*-three-and-*four*-and-*one*-and-two-*and*-three-and-*four*-and.

These rhythms were the basis of the original tango – which didn't have the beat that we now associate with the tango, but instead had that "dan, *dah*-dah" tresillo rhythm (or rhythms like it, like the cinquillo). And through Gottschalk and people like him – French-speaking Creole people living in New Orleans – that rhythm entered New Orleans music generally. Jelly Roll Morton called it the "Spanish tinge", and most of his early compositions use it. The tresillo rhythm *is* the sound of New Orleans.

But what really made that rhythm interesting was when you put that rhythm up against something else. In the work of Gottschalk or Morton, you have the habanera rhythm as the main pulse, but by the time Dave Bartholomew was doing it – and he seems to have been the first one to do this – that rhythm was put against drums playing a shuffle or a backbeat. The combination of these pulses rubbing up against each other is what gave New Orleans R&B its special flavour.

The musicians on "Country Boy" were ones that Bartholomew would continue to employ for many years on all the sessions he produced, and in particular they included the drummer Earl Palmer, who was bar none the greatest drummer working in America at that time.

Earl Palmer has been claimed as the first person to use the word "funky" to describe music, and he was certainly a funky player. He was also an *extraordinarily* precise timekeeper. There's a legend told about him at multiple sessions that in the studio, after a take that lasted, say, three minutes twenty, the producer might say to the band "can we have it a little faster, say two seconds shorter?"

Palmer would then pretend to "wind up" his leg, like a clock, count out the new tempo, and the next take would come in at three minutes eighteen, dead on. That's the kind of story that's hard to believe, but it's been told about him by multiple people, so it might just be true.

Either way, Earl Palmer was the tightest, funkiest, just plain best drummer working in the US in 1949, and for many years afterwards. And he was the drummer in the band of session musicians who Dave Bartholomew put together. That band were centred around Cosimo Matassa's studio, J&M, in Louisiana, which would become one of the most important places in the history of this new music.

Cosimo Matassa was one of many Italian-American or Jewish people who got in at the very early stages of rock and roll, when it was still a predominantly black music, and acted as a connection between the black and white communities, usually in some back-room capacity. In Matassa's case, it was as an engineer and studio owner. We've actually already looked at one record he was involved in – Roy Brown's "Good Rockin' Tonight", which he recorded with Matassa in 1947. "Good Rockin' Tonight" was made in New Orleans, and engineered by the man most responsible for recording the New Orleans sound, but in other respects it doesn't have that New Orleans sound to it – it's of the type we're referring to as coastal jump band music. It's music recorded *in* New Orleans, but not music *of* New Orleans. But the records that Matassa would go on to engineer with Dave Bartholomew and his band, and with other musicians of their type, would be the quintessential New Orleans records that still, seventy years on, sum up the sound of that city.

Matassa's studio was tiny – it was in the back room of his family's appliance store, which also had a bookmaker's upstairs and a shoeshine boy operating outside the studio door. Matassa himself had no training in record production – he'd been a chemistry student until he dropped out of university, aged eighteen, and set up the studio, which was laughably rudimentary by today's standards. He had a three-channel mixer, and they didn't record to tape but directly to disc. They had *two* disc cutters plugged into the mixer.

To explain why this is, I should probably explain how records were actually made, at least back then. A disc cutter is essentially a record player in reverse. It uses a stylus to cut a groove into a disc made of some soft material, which is called the master – the groove is cut by the vibrations of the stylus as the music goes through it. Then, a mould, called the mother, is made of the master – it's a pure negative copy, so that instead of a groove, it has a ridge. That mother is then used to stamp out as many copies as possible of the record before it wears out, at which point, you create a new mother from the original master.

J&M had two disc cutters, and during a recording session someone's job would be to stand by them and catch the wax they cut out of the discs before it dropped on to the floor. By this point, most professional studios, if they were using disc cutters at all, were using acetate discs, which are slightly more robust, but apparently J&M were still using wax.

A wax master couldn't be played without the needle causing so much damage it couldn't be used as a master, so you had two choices. You could either get the master made into a mother, and then use the mother to stamp out copies, and just hope they sounded OK, or you could run two disc cutters simultaneously. Then you'd be able to play one of them, destroying it in the process, to check that it sounded OK, and be pretty confident that the other disc, which had been cut from the same signal, would sound the same.

To record like this, mixing directly onto wax with no tape effects or any way to change anything, you needed a great engineer with a great feel for music, a great room with a wonderful room sound, and fantastic musicians.

Truth be told, the J&M studio didn't have a great room sound at all. It was too small and acoustically dead, and the record companies who received the masters and released them would often end up adding echo after the fact.

But what they did have was a great engineer in Matassa, and a great bandleader in Dave Bartholomew, and the band he put together for Fats Domino's first record would largely work together for the next few years, creating some of the greatest rock and roll music ever made.

Domino had a few tunes that would always get the audiences going, and one of them was "Junker's Blues". Dave Bartholomew wanted him to record that, but it was felt that the lyrics weren't quite suitable for the radio, what with them being pretty much entirely about heroin and cocaine.

But then Bartholomew got inspired, by a radio show. "The Fat Man" was a spinoff from "The Thin Man", a radio series based on the Dashiel Hammet novel. (Hammet was credited as the creator of "The Fat Man", too, but he seems to have had almost nothing to do with it). The series featured a detective who weighed two hundred and thirty seven pounds, and was popular enough that it got its own film version in 1951. But back in 1949 Dave Bartholomew heard the show and realised that he could capitalise on the popular title, and tie it in to his fat singer. So instead of "they call me a junker, because I'm loaded all the time", Domino sang "they call me the fat man, 'cos I weigh two hundred pounds".

Now, "The Fat Man" actually doesn't have that tresillo rhythm in much of the record. There are odd parts where the bass plays it, but the bass player (who it's *really* difficult to hear anyway, because of the poor sound quality of the recording) seems to switch between playing a tresillo, playing normal boogie basslines, and playing just four root notes as crotchets. But it does, definitely, have that "Spanish tinge" that Jelly Roll Morton talked about. You listen to "The Fat Man", and you have no doubt whatsoever that this is a New Orleans musician. It's music that absolutely couldn't come from anywhere else.

And while this recording doesn't have the rhythmic sophistication of the later records that Domino and Bartholomew would make, it's definitely a step towards what would become their eventual sound. You'd have Earl Palmer on drums playing a simple backbeat, and then over that you'd lay the bass playing a tresillo rhythm, and then over *that* you'd lay a horn riff, going across both those other rhythms, and then over *that* you'd lay Domino's piano, playing fast triplets. You can dance to all of the beats, all of them are keeping time with each other and going in the same $\frac{4}{4}$ bars, but what they're not doing is playing the same thing. There's an astonishing complexity there.

Bartholomew's lyrics, to the extent they're about anything at all, follow a standard blues trope of being fat but having the ability to attract women anyway – the same kind of thing as Howlin' Wolf's later

"Three Hundred Pounds of Joy" or "Built for Comfort" – but what really matters with the vocal part is Domino's obvious cheeriness.

Domino was known as one of the nicest men in the music industry, to the extent that it's difficult to find much biographical information about him compared to any of his contemporaries, because people tend to have more anecdotes about musicians who shoot their bass player on stage, get married eight times, and end up accidentally suing themselves than they do about people like Fats Domino. He remained married to the same woman for sixty-one years, and while he got himself a nice big house when he became rich, it was still in the same neighbourhood he'd lived in all his life, and he stayed there until Hurricane Katrina drove him out in 2005.

By all accounts he was just an absolutely, thoroughly, nice person – I have read a lot about forties rhythm and blues artists, and far more about fifties rock and rollers, and I don't recall anyone ever saying a single negative word about him. He was shy, friendly, humble, gracious, and cheerful, and that all comes across in his vocals. While other rhythm and blues vocalists of the era were aggressive – remember, this was the era of the blues shouter – Domino comes across as friendly. Even when, as in a song like this, he's bragging sexually, he doesn't actually sound like he means it.

"The Fat Man" went on to sell a million copies within four years, and was the start of what became a monster success for Domino – and as a result, Fats Domino is the first artist we've seen who's going to have more chapters devoted to him in this book. We've now reached the point where we're seeing the very first rock star, and this is the point beyond which it's indisputable that rock and roll has started.

Fats Domino, usually with Dave Bartholomew, carried on making records that sounded just like this throughout the fifties. Everyone called them rock and roll, and they sold in massive numbers. He outsold every other rock and roll artist of the fifties other than Elvis, and had *thirty-nine* charting hit singles in a row in the fifties and early sixties. Estimates of his sales vary between sixty-five million and a hundred and ten million, but as late as the early eighties it was being seriously claimed that the only people who'd sold more records than him in the rock era were Elvis, the Beatles, and Michael Jackson. Quite a few others have now overtaken him, but still, if anyone can claim to be the first rock star, it's Fats Domino.

And as the music he was making was all in the same style as "The Fat Man", it's safe to say that while we still have many records that have been claimed as "the first rock and roll record" to go, we're now definitely in the rock and roll era.

"How High the Moon"

To be a truly great guitarist, you need to have an imagination. You need to be inventive. And you need to have a sense of musicality. Some would also say that you need to have a lot of dexterity, and to be able to move your fingers lightning fast. Maybe also have long fingers, so you could reach further down the neck.

But let's talk about Django Reinhardt for a bit.

We mentioned Django a little bit in the chapter on Bob Wills and "Ida Red". We talked, in particular, about how he was making music that sounded very, very similar to what the early Western swing musicians were doing.

We're not going to talk much about Django in this book, because he was a jazz musician, but he *was* very influential on a few of the people who went on to influence rock, so we're going to touch on him briefly here. He never played an electric guitar, but he still influenced pretty much every guitarist since, either directly or indirectly.

And this was despite having disadvantages that would have stopped almost anyone. One point we haven't made very much yet, but which needs to be made repeatedly, is that the people in most of these early chapters were crushingly, hellishly, poor by today's standards. Poverty still exists of course, to far too great an extent, but the people we're talking about here lived in conditions that would be unimaginable to almost anyone reading this.

And Reinhardt had it worse than most. He was a Romani traveller, and while growing up his greatest skill was stealing chickens. But he became a professional musician, and it looked like he might actually become well off. And then his bad luck got worse. His caravan caught on fire, and in trying to rescue his wife and child, he suffered such extreme burns that one of his legs became paralysed – and more importantly for Reinhardt as a musician, he lost the use of two of his fingers on his left hand. He had to re-teach himself to play the guitar, and to use only two fingers and a thumb on his left hand to play.

Remarkably, he managed well enough to become one of the greatest guitarists who ever lived.

Reinhardt influenced many guitarists, and one American guitarist in particular became a friend of Reinhardt and said that he and Reinhardt were the only two guitarists in the world at that time who were actually serious about their instrument. He was another jazzman, with a similar style to Reinhardt but one who had a more direct influence on rock and roll.

Waukesha, Wisconsin, is not the most rock and roll town in the world. It was a spa town, before the water started to dry up, and about the most exciting thing that ever happened there is that Mr Sears, the founder of Sears & Roebuck, retired there when he got too ill to work any more. It's a bland, whitebread, midwestern town in a state that's most notable for dairy farming.

Yet it's also the birthplace of the only man who is in the Rock and Roll Hall of Fame *and* the National Inventors Hall of Fame, and who probably did more than any other individual to make the guitar a respected lead instrument.

Almost every moderately-known guitarist eventually gets a "signature" model named after them, and most of these sell a small number of instruments before being discontinued. But one man has a signature model that's so popular that other guitarists get their signatures *alongside his*. When you buy a Jimmy Page or Mark Knopfler or Slash or Eric Clapton signature guitar, there are two names on there – the name of Page or Clapton or whoever, and the name Les Paul.

Les Paul was a remarkable man, whose inventions are far more widely known even than his name. You'll almost certainly have seen musicians playing guitar and harmonica at the same time, using a harmonica holder. Les Paul invented that, as a teenager, making the first one out of a coathanger. I guess if you were a teenager in Waukesha in the 1920s, you'd have little better to do with yourself than invent coathanger harmonica holders too.

But Les Paul was, first and foremost, a guitar player, and he became a semi-professional musician by the time he was thirteen. The choice of the guitar was one that was actually made by his mother. She explained to him, "If you play the piano you got your back turned to the audience. If you play the drums, you gotta carry all that stuff around, it's not musical. If you play a saxophone, you can't sing and talk at the same time." In his own words, she "whittled it down to guitar in a hurry". His mother, indeed, seems to have been a remarkable woman in many ways. If you read any interviews with Les, he barely ever goes a few sentences without saying something about how much she did for him.

Les Paul's admiration for his mother was one of the defining characteristics of his life. There were two more things that characterised him though. The first was that pretty much dead on, every ten years, he would have some major health crisis that would put him out of commission for a year. The other was his lifelong devotion to learning, which meant that he used those health crises as an opportunity to learn something new.

This love of learning could be seen from his very early days. When he was just learning the guitar, the singing cowboy star Gene Autry came to town. Gene Autry was a star of Western music – the very biggest star in the country – and his music was a cleaned-up, politer, version of the kind of music Bob Wills played.

Les and his friend went to every show in the residency, and after a couple of nights, Autry stopped the show in the middle of the set and said, "Something strange has been happening here. Every time I play an F chord, and *only* when I play an F chord, there's a flash of light. What's going on, how is this happening?"

It turned out that Les had been wanting to learn how Autry made that chord shape, so he'd been there with a pencil and paper, and his friend had a torch, and every time he played the chord Les Paul wanted to learn, the torch would come on and Les would be trying to sketch the shape of Autry's fingers. Autry invited Les Paul onto the stage, showed him how to make the chord, and had him play a couple of songs. A few years later, when Autry moved from radio to films, he suggested Les Paul take over his radio show.

So Les Paul was always fascinated by learning, and always trying to improve himself and his equipment. And once he decided to be a guitarist, he also decided to electrify his guitar, a full decade before electric guitars became a widespread instrument.

He explained that when he was starting out, he was playing at a hotdog stand, using a homemade microphone for his voice and harmonica. The microphone was made out of bits of an old telephone, and it was plugged in to his mother's radio.

People who were listening liked his performances, but they said they wished the guitar was as loud as his voice. So he took his *dad's* radio, too, and connected it to a record player needle, which he jammed into the body of his guitar.

Once electric guitars started being manufactured, Paul started playing them, but he never liked them. The electric guitars of the late 1930s were what we'd now call electro-acoustics – they were acoustic guitars, playable as such, but with pickups. There were two main problems with them. Firstly, they were very prone to feedback, because the hollow body of the guitar would resonate. And secondly, most of the sonic energy from the strings was going into the guitar itself, so there was no sustain. Paul came up with a simple solution to this problem, which he called "the log".

The log was almost exactly what the name would suggest. It was a plank, to which were nailed some pickups, strings, and tuning pegs. On the front was attached the front of a normal guitar – not anything that would actually resonate, just to make it look like a proper guitar. But basically it was just a lump of wood.

Les Paul wasn't the first person to build a solid-body electric guitar – but as he put it himself later "there may be some guy out there in Iowa says he built the guitar in 1925, for all I know, and he may have. I only know what I was doing and I was out there weaving my own basket, and there wasn't anybody else around and it had to be done".

He perfected the solid-body guitar during the first of his years of illness. He'd been running an illegal radio station, accidentally stuck his hand in the transmitter, and not only got an electric shock but had a load of equipment fall on him. By the time he was well enough to work again, he had the idea perfected.

He took his solid-body guitar idea to Gibson in 1941, but they weren't interested – no-one was going to want to buy a solid guitar. It wasn't until Leo Fender started selling *his* guitars in 1950 that Gibson realised that it might be worth doing.

But by then Les Paul had become one of the most famous guitarists in the country. Even before he became hugely famous, though, he'd been one of the *best* guitarists in the country. In 1944, when the guitarist Oscar Moore was unable at the last minute to play at Jazz at the Philharmonic – the first of what would eventually become the most famous series of jazz concerts ever – Les Paul was drafted in at short notice, and the live recordings of that show are some of the greatest instrumental jazz you'll hear, at a time when the borders between jazz, R&B, and pop music were more fluid than they became.

The group he played with that night included Illinois Jacquet, and a pianist who was already regarded as one of the best in the business, even before he started to sing, and who later had two further, separate careers under his more familiar name – one in R&B in which he inspired a generation of singers like Charles Brown and Ray Charles, and one in pop, where he became one of the great ballad singers of all time. He's credited on the recordings of the show as "Shorty Nadine" for contractual reasons, but you probably know him better as Nat "King" Cole.

Listening to the *Jazz at the Philharmonic* live album, you can hear musicians performing at a time when jazz and R&B and rock and roll were all still sort of the same thing, before they all went off in their different directions, and it's hard not to wish that that cross-fertilisation had continued a while longer.

But it didn't, and it would be easy to imagine that as a result Les Paul, who was absolutely a jazz musician, would make no further contributions to rock and roll after his popularising the solid-body electric guitar. But we haven't even got to his real importance yet. Yes, something he did that was even more important than the Les Paul guitar.

It started when his mother told him she'd enjoyed something she heard him play on the radio. He'd replied that it wasn't him she'd heard, and she'd said, "Well, all those electric guitar players sound the same. If you want to be a real success, you want to sound different from everyone else – at least different enough that your own mother can recognise you". And over the years, Les Paul had learned to listen to his mother – she'd been the one who'd got him playing guitar, and she'd been the one who had told him to go and see Bob Wills, the day he'd ended up meeting Charlie Christian for the first time.

So he went and spent a lot of time working on a sound that was totally different from anything else, spending days and weeks alone. He stopped working with his trio, and started working with a young country singer who renamed herself Mary Ford, who Gene Autry had introduced him to and who he soon married. And he eventually came up with a whole new idea.

This chapter is primarily about Les Paul, because he was such an astonishing force of nature, but it's worth making clear that Mary Ford was very much an equal partner in their sixteen years together. She was an excellent singer – *far* better than Les Paul was – and also a pretty good guitarist herself. On their live dates she would play rhythm guitar, and often the two would do a comedy guitar duel, with her copying everything Les Paul played. She was a vital part of the sound, and of the sonic innovations the records contained, because one of the things they did for the first time was to have her sing very close to the mic – a totally different technique than had been used before, which gave her vocals a different tone which almost everyone imitated.

But that wasn't the only odd sound on the records. It sounded like Les Paul was playing two or three guitars at the same time, playing the same part. And sometimes he was playing notes that were higher than any guitar could play.

And sometimes, when Mary Ford was singing... it sounded as if there were two or more of her!

This was such an unusual sound that on the duo's radio and TV appearances they made a joke of it. They pretended that Paul had invented a "Les Paulveriser", which could duplicate everything, and that for example he could use the Les Paulveriser on Mary, so there'd be multiple Marys and she could get the vacuum cleaning done quicker.

It was the fifties.

But of course, what Paul was actually doing was overdubbing – recording one guitar part, and then going back and recording a second over it. He'd been fascinated by the idea for decades and he'd first done it as an experiment when he was still with the trio. He'd wanted to rehearse a song on his own, but with the arrangement the rest of the band played, so he'd recorded himself playing all the parts, using a disc cutter and playing along with previous takes.

This didn't give good results until the introduction of magnetic tape recording in the very late forties. When you recorded directly to a disc there was so much surface noise, and recording quality was so poor, that no-one would even think of recording overdubs.

But in 1945, American soldiers brought back a new technology from Germany as spoils of war – high fidelity tape recording. With magnetic tape you could record sound with orders of magnitude less noise than by cutting to disc.

And Bing Crosby, who often worked with Les Paul, was the first person to see the possibilities of this new technology (in his case, for pre-recording his radio shows so they didn't have to go out live, which meant he could record them in batches and have more time to spend on the golf course).

Les Paul was far more technical than Crosby, though, and far more aware of what could happen if, for example, you had two tape recorders. Or if you ran one slow so that when you played it back at normal speed everything sounded sped up. Or a dozen other obvious tricks that occurred to him, but had never occurred to anyone else.

So on those Les Paul and Mary Ford records, literally every instrument was Les Paul on the guitar. The bass was Les Paul's guitar slowed down to half speed, the percussion was his guitar, *everything* was his guitar.

So now we come to "How High the Moon" itself. This is a song that originally dated back to 1940. The Benny Goodman band had the first hit with it, and indeed Les Paul had recorded a version of it in 1945, with his trio, right before his experiments with tape recording started.

Shortly after the first recording experiments were released, in 1948, there was another one of those every-decade health problems. In this case, Mary Ford was driving the two of them from Wisconsin to LA. She was from California, and not used to driving in winter weather. She hit a patch of ice and the two of them went off the road. Les

Paul spent hours in ice water with multiple bones broken before anyone could get him to a hospital. For a while, it was believed it would not be possible to save his right arm, and then for a while after that the doctors believed they could save it, but it would permanently be fixed in a single position if they did, as his elbow would be unfixable. He told them to try their best, and to set it in a position with his hand over his navel, because if it was in that position he could still play guitar.

As a precaution, he spent his time in hospital drawing up plans for a synthesiser, ten years before Robert Moog invented his, because he figured he could play the synth with one arm.

When he got better, he and Mary Ford recorded a new version of "How High The Moon", but at first the record label didn't want to release it. It sat unreleased for eighteen months, until 1951, because Jim Conkling at Capitol said that there'd been seventy-five recordings of the song before and none of them had been a hit. Conkling thought this was because the lyrics don't make sense, but Les Paul was insistent that no-one was going to listen to the lyrics anyway. "It doesn't matter what Mary sang or if it was done by the Four Nosebleeds. It didn't make any difference, because that wasn't what made the record. It was the arrangement and the performance."

And he was right – the version by Les Paul and Mary Ford was an absolute phenomenon. It spent twenty-five weeks in the *Billboard* pop charts, nine of them at number one, and while it was at number one another Paul and Ford track was at number two. Even more astonishingly, it also made number two on the rhythm and blues charts. Remember, that was a chart that was specifically aimed at the black audience, and between 1950 and 1955 only five records by white performers made the R&B charts at all, mostly very early rock and roll records.

"How High the Moon" might easily seem an odd fit for the R&B charts. To twenty-first century ears, it's hard to imagine anything more white-sounding.

But what it does, absolutely, share with the music that was charting on the R&B charts at the time, and the reason it appealed to the R&B audience, is a delight in finding totally new sounds. The R&B charts at the time were where you looked for experimentation, for people trying new things.

And also, it's entirely a record that's driven by the rhythm. It's not quite dance music, not like the jump bands – and there's only guitar and vocals on it, something which would be absolutely out of the ordinary for rhythm and blues records at the time with their emphasis on piano and saxophone – but what there is in that guitar playing is personal expression.

And R&B was all about individual expression.

Les Paul was doing something which was qualitatively different both from jazz and from R&B, and so it's not surprising that he ended up crossing over from one market to another.

But in doing so, he also invented the way the guitar was to be used in rock and roll music. There's a lot of Western swing about what he's doing on "How High the Moon", unsurprisingly. But while the rhythm guitar is keeping to the same kind of rhythms that the Western swing people would use, the lead guitar is much more aggressive and forceful than anything you got in country or western music at the time. It's playing jazz and R&B lines – it's playing, in fact, the kind of thing that a saxophone player like Illinois Jacquet might play, full of aggressive stabs and skronks.

And more than that, Les Paul invented the way the recording studio would be used in rock and roll. Before Les Paul and Mary Ford's early records, the recording studio was used solely as a way of reproducing the sound of live instruments as accurately as possible. After them, it became a way to create new sounds that could not be made live.

One thing we're going to see over and again in this series is the way technological change, artistic change and social change all feed back into each other. The 1950s was a time of absolutely unprecedented technological change in America, and people went from, in the beginning of the decade, listening to recordings played at 78RPM, often on wind-up gramophones, made of breakable shellac, to listening to high fidelity forty-five RPM singles and long-playing records which could – shockingly – last more than four minutes a side. Radio went from being something that had to be listened to as a family because of the size of the radiogram to something a teenager could listen to in bed under the blankets on a transistor radio, or something that you could even have on in your car!

The combination of these changes made music into something that could be personal as well as communal. Teenagers didn't have to share the music with their parents.

All of that was still to come, of course, and we'll look at those things as they happen during our history. But "How High the Moon" was the first and best sign of what was to come, as the 1940s gave way to the 1950s, and music entered a totally new age.

Les Paul kept playing the guitar into his nineties. Interviewed in his late seventies, when his arthritis was so bad he only had movement in two fingers, with all the others so stiff they just had to stay where he put them, he said he played better than he had when he had ten fingers, because he'd had to learn more about the instrument to do it this way. In the end, his arthritis got to the point that he could no longer move any fingers on either hand – so he just let his fingers stay where they were, but would move his whole hand to play single notes and bar chords. He could lift his fingers up and down, just not move the knuckles.

But he could still play. There's a video available of him playing on his ninetieth birthday, with an excellent small jazz band. He's not as fluid as he had been in his prime, but he was playing solid jazz guitar.

So it turns out you don't even need the two fingers Django had left, not if you have the kind of mind that gets you into the rock and roll hall of fame *and* the inventors' hall of fame.

Les Paul died, aged ninety-four, in 2009.

"Double-Crossin' Blues"

To keep with the theme of the loss of fingers, we're now going to talk about how a great musician losing the use of a couple of fingers led directly to several of the biggest careers in rhythm and blues.

When we think of the blues now, we mostly think of guitar-based music – people like Robert Johnson and Muddy Waters – rather than piano-based musicians and the more vaudeville style of what's called "classic blues", people like Ma Rainey or Bessie Smith. And that tends to give a rather ahistorical perspective on the development of rock and roll.

Rock and roll when it started – the music of the mid fifties – is not really a guitar-based music. It's dominated by the piano and the saxophone, and that domination it takes from jump band rhythm and blues. We've already heard how blues shouters in jump bands were massively influential for the style, but of course the blues, along with the jump bands, fed into what was just becoming known as "rhythm and blues", and that in turn fed into rock and roll.

There were two real links in the chain between the blues and rock and roll. And we'll talk about the Chess label later. But to the extent that there was any influence at all from what we now think of as the blues, it was mostly down to one man, Johnny Otis. It's probably safe to say that if Johnny Otis had never lived, the whole of 1950s music would be totally different.

To put it as simply as possible, Johnny Otis was responsible for basically every good record that came from the West Coast of the US between about 1947 and 1956. He's a name that will continue coming up in this book and the next, and that's for a very good reason.

Johnny Otis had his first hit in 1945, with "Harlem Nocturne", which featured his friend Bill Doggett on piano. After "Harlem Nocturne" became a hit, and partly through the connection with Doggett, he got the opportunity to tour backing the Ink Spots, which exposed him to a wider audience. He was on his way to being a big star.

At that time, he was a drummer and vibraphone player. And he was one of the great drummers of the period. He played, for example, on Illinois Jacquet's version of "Flying Home", and on "Jamming With Lester" by Lester Young.

He was leading a big band, and had been trying to sound like Count Basie, as you can hear if you listen to the records he made at that time, but that soon changed when the jump bands came in. Instead, Otis slimmed down his band to a much smaller one and started playing this new R&B music, but he still wanted to give the people a show. And so he started the Johnny Otis Show, and rather than devote the show to his own performances, he would tour with a variety of singers and groups, who'd all play with his band as well as perform in different combinations. These singers and groups would be backed by the Johnny Otis band, but would be able to put out their own records and put on their own shows. He was going to use his fame to boost others – while also giving himself more stars for his show, which meant more people coming to the shows.

One thing that's very important to note here is that Otis was a white man who chose to live and work only with black people. We'll be talking more about his relationship with race as we go forward, but Johnny Otis was *not* the typical white man in the music industry, in that he actually respected his black colleagues as friends and equals, rather than just exploiting them financially.

He also lived in the Watts area of LA, the black area, and did all sorts of things in the community, from having his own radio show (which was listened to by a lot of the white kids in the LA area as well as its intended black audience – both Frank Zappa and Brian Wilson talked about listening to Johnny Otis' show as children) to running a pigeon-breeding club for the local children. One of the kids who went along to learn how to breed pigeons with Johnny Otis was Arthur Lee, who later went on to be the leader of the band Love.

Otis was always a bit of an entrepreneur, and someone who was doing twenty different things at the same time. For example, he kept chickens in coops outside his house in Watts, running The Progressive Poultry company with a friend of his, Mario Delagarde, who was a bass player who worked with Johnny "Guitar" Watson and who died fighting in Cuba with Castro against Batista. Apparently, the chickens they sold were too popular, as Otis lost the use of a couple of fingers on his right hand in a chainsaw accident while trying to build more chicken coops – though as he said later, he was still able to play piano and vibraphone with only eight fingers. After a doctor botched an operation on his hand, though, he couldn't play drums easily.

But it was because of his damaged hand that he eventually discovered Little Esther. Otis prided himself on his ability at discovering artists, and in this case it was more or less by accident. One night he couldn't sleep from the pain in his hand, and he was scared of taking painkillers and becoming addicted, so he went for a walk.

He walked past a club, and saw that Big Jay McNeely was playing. McNeely, who died in 2018, was one of the great saxophone honkers and skronkers of rhythm and blues, and was a friend of Otis who'd played on several records with him. Otis went inside, and before the show started there was a talent show. These talent shows were often major parts of the show in black entertainment at this time, and were sometimes *hugely* impressive. Otis would later talk about one show he saw in Detroit, where he discovered Hank Ballard, Little Willie John, and Jackie Wilson all in the same night, and none of them were even the winner.

On this night, one girl was impressive, but didn't win, and went and cried in the back of the theatre. Johnny Otis went over to comfort her, and offered her a job with his band.

That girl was only fourteen when she became a professional blues singer after Otis discovered her. She was born Esther Mae Washington, but later took the surname of her stepfather and became Esther Mae Jones. A few years from the time we're talking about, she took the name of a petrol station company and became Esther Phillips.

At first, Otis had trouble getting her a record deal, because of the similarity of her sound to that of Dinah Washington, who was Esther's biggest inspiration, and was the biggest female R&B star of the period. Anyone listening to her was instantly struck by the similarity, and so she was dismissed as a soundalike.

But Otis had a little more success with a vocal group he knew called the Robins.

We haven't talked much about doo wop yet, but we're at the point where it starts to be a major factor. doo wop is a genre that mostly came from the East Coast of the US. Like many of the genres we've discussed so far, it was a primarily black genre, but it would soon also be taken up by Italian-American singers living in the same areas as black people. This was a time when Italian-Americans weren't considered fully "white" according to the racial standards then prevalent in the US. (As an example, in the early 1960s, the great jazz bass player Charles Mingus was asked why, if he was so angry at white people, he played with Charlie Mariano. Mingus looked surprised and said "Charlie's not white, he's Italian!")

But at this point doo wop was very much on the fringes of the music business. It was music that was made by people who were too poor to even afford instruments, standing around on street corners and singing with each other. Usually the lead singer would try to sound like Bill Kenny of the Ink Spots, though increasingly as the genre matured the lead vocalists would take on more and more aspects of gospel singing as well. The backing vocalists – usually three or four of them – would do the same kind of thing as the Mills Brothers had, and imitate instrumental parts.

And in the tradition of the Ink Spots' "top and bottom", these bands would also feature a very prominent bass vocal, though the bass singer wouldn't speak the words like Hoppy Jones, but would instead sing wordless nonsense syllables. This is where the name "doo wop", which was only applied later, comes from, as the bass singer would sing things like "doo wop a-doo bom".

The first and most successful of the new vocal groups that came along was called the Ravens. We're not going to talk much about them directly, but they caused a huge explosion of black vocal groups in the late forties and early fifties – and you can tell how influential they were just by looking at the names of many of these bands, which included the Orioles, the Penguins, the Flamingos and more.

And the Robins were another of these "bird groups". They started out as a vocal group called the A-Sharp Trio, who entered a talent contest at a nightclub owned by Johnny Otis and came second (the performer who came first, the guitarist Pete Lewis, Otis got into his band straight away). Otis gave the A-Sharp Trio a regular gig at his club, and soon decided to pair them with another singer who sang there solo, turning them into a quartet. They were originally called the Four Bluebirds, and under that name they recorded a single with Otis, "My Baby Done Told Me". However, they didn't like the name, and soon settled on the Robins.

The Robins recorded with Otis on various labels. Their first single, "Around About Midnight"[8], was a remake of Roy Brown's earlier "Long About Midnight". That was recorded on the Aladdin label, an independent record label that also had recordings by Illinois Jacquet, Louis Jordan, Wynonie Harris, and many, many more early R&B people. But soon after this Otis and the Robins – and Esther Mae Washington – would all go on to another label, Savoy.

Ralph Bass, the A&R[9] man who signed Johnny Otis to Savoy, is another of those white back-room people who devoted their life to black music who keep showing up at this stage of the story, and he's another one we'll be seeing a lot of. Born Ralph Basso, he'd been an amateur musician and had also worked for Shell. When he was working for Shell, one of his jobs had been to organise corporate events, and because of the war there was a lack of musicians to play them, and he'd taken to playing records through an amplifier, becoming one of the very first live DJs.

---

[8] That's noted as their first single on some discographies I've seen. Others, however, say that these original tracks weren't released until a few months after they were recorded. It's definitely from their first session under the name The Robins though.

[9] Artists and Repertoire – an industry term for a label executive in charge of signing performers and choosing the songs they would perform. In the period from the forties through the early sixties, the A&R man (they were almost always men) would also be responsible for most of the functions that later became the responsibility of the producer.

He'd always had a love of music – he used to sneak into the Savoy Ballroom to watch Chick Webb as a teenager – and when he was playing these records, he realised that many of them sounded awful. He was convinced he could make records that sounded better than the ones he was playing, and so he decided to write to every record company he could find, offering his services. Only one record company answered – Black and White Records in Los Angeles. They weren't certain that they could use him, but they'd give him an interview in a few weeks if he flew to LA.

Bass flew to LA two weeks before his interview, and started preparing. He asked the musicians unions for a list of who they thought their most talented local musicians were, and went to see them all live, and chat to some of them. Then, when he went into the actual interview and was asked who he would record, he had an answer – he was going to record Sammy Franklin and his Atomics doing "The Honeydripper".

But he still didn't actually know anything at all about how to make a record. He had a solution to that too. He booked the band and the studio, then got to the studio early and told the engineers that he didn't have a clue about how to record sound, but that his boss would be expecting him to, and to just go along with everything he said when the boss got there, and that the engineers would really be in charge.

The boss of Black and White Records did get there, shortly afterward, and Bass spent the next half hour tweaking settings on the board, changing mic placements, and a thousand other tiny technical differences. The boss decided he knew what he was doing and left him to it. The engineers then put everything back the way it was originally. The record came out, and it didn't do wonderfully (for reasons we'll discuss in the next chapter) but it was enough to get Bass firmly in place in Black and White Records.

Over the next few years, he produced dozens of classics of jazz and blues, including "Stormy Monday" by T-Bone Walker and "Open the Door, Richard" by Jack McVea.

That record was based on an old routine by the black comedian Dusty Fletcher, and it was Bass who suggested that the old routine be set to music by McVea, who had previously been a saxophone player with Lionel Hampton's band. It became a massive hit, and was covered by Count Basie and Louis Jordan, among others. Six different versions of the song made the R&B top ten more or less simultaneously in the first few months of 1947.

But the problem with "Open the Door, Richard" was that it was actually too successful – the record label just assumed that any of its records would sell that well. And when they didn't, Bass had to find another label to work with.

Bass had proved his ability enough that he ended up working for Savoy. For most of its time, Savoy was a jazz label, but while Ralph Bass was in charge of A&R it was, instead, an R&B label, and one that put out some of the greatest R&B of its time. He had an eye for talent and a real love for good rhythm and blues music.

And so when Ralph Bass saw the Johnny Otis revue performing live, he decided that Savoy needed to sign all of them – Otis and his band, Esther, the Robins, everyone. He got in touch with Herman Lubinsky, who was the owner of Savoy Records, and got Lubinsky to come down to see Otis' band. During intermission, Lubinsky met up with Otis, and got him to sign a record contact. The contract only specified a one percent royalty, but Lubinsky promised he'd triple the royalty rate after Otis' first hit with Savoy. Like many of Lubinsky's promises, this proved to be false.

When the Otis band, Esther, and the Robins went into the studio together, Esther was so intimidated by the studio that she started giggling, and while they did manage to cut a few songs, they didn't get as much done as they wanted to in the session. But at almost literally the last minute, twenty minutes before the end of the session, Otis came up with a song that was, like "Open the Door Richard", based around a comedy routine from a well-known black comedy act. In this case, it was based on a double act called Apus and Estrellita, and Esther and Bobby Nunn of the Robins engaged in some good-spirited comedy back and forth, copied from their routines.

The jokes that they copied include things like "How come you ain't in the forest?" "I'm a lady", "they got lady bears out there!" And they take on a bit of a different colour when you realise that "lady bear" was, at the time, slang for an ugly, sexually aggressive woman.

Lubinsky was not impressed with the record or with Esther Phillips, and according to Bass "I sent the record to Lubinsky and asked for five dollars to pay for the kid's expenses – lunch and all that, coming to Hollywood from Watts. He shouted, 'Whaddaya mean five bucks? For what?' He wouldn't give me the five bucks".

Lubinsky put the recording aside until a DJ in Newark asked him if he could look through the new recordings he had to see if there was anything that might be a hit. The DJ loved the record, and even ran a competition on his radio station to pick the song's name, which is where the title "Double-Crossin' Blues" comes from. Although as Bass said "Everybody who was involved with the record got double-crossed. The songwriter, Johnny and I, the Robins, everybody connected with it."

Lubinsky was suddenly so sure that the record was going to be a success that he phoned Bass at five in the morning, Bass' time, waking him up, and getting Bass to go and wake Johnny Otis up so they could both go and track down Esther and her mother, and get them to sign a contract immediately. It was around this point that Esther's stage name was decided upon. Lubinsky said to Otis, "You need a stage name for that girl," to which Otis replied, "Which girl? Little Esther?" And Lubinsky said, "That's perfect!"

And so for the next few years, Esther Washington, who would later be Esther Phillips, was Little Esther, and that was the name under which she became a phenomenon.

The record went to number one on the R&B charts, and was the biggest thing in the genre in years. In July 1950, *Billboard* published its annual listing of best-selling R&B acts. Johnny Otis came first, Little Esther second, and the Robins came fourth.

But the record's success caused friction between Otis and the Robins, who he later described as the people "who hummed behind Little Esther". They decided that *they* were the big stars, not Little Esther, and that they were going to go on tour on their own. Otis had to find another male singer to sing the parts that Bobby Nunn had sung, and so he found his new singer Mel Walker, who would be the main lead vocalist on Otis' future records, and would duet with Little Esther on more than a few of them. The Robins offered Otis a job as musical director for twenty dollars a night, but Otis refused.

The Robins would go on to have many, many successes themselves, some of which we'll talk about later, but Otis, Mel Walker, and Little Esther went on to have a string of hits in various combinations as well – "Mistrustin' Blues", "Deceivin' Blues", "Dreamin' Blues", "Wedding Boogie", "Rockin' Blues" and more.

We'll be seeing much more of Johnny Otis, and of the Robins, as the story goes on, but this is the only time we'll be talking about Little Esther. In her first year, she had an amazing seven records make the R&B top ten, three of them (including "Double-Crossin' Blues") going to number one. She was regarded as one of the finest R&B vocalists of her generation, and had a promising future.

She decided, after a year on Savoy with Johnny Otis, to go solo and to move with Ralph Bass to Federal Records, a new label Bass had joined after falling out with Herman Lubinsky. According to Bass, Lubinsky often blackmailed his employees, in order to get leverage over them. But he was unable to find any dirty secrets about Bass – not that Bass didn't have them (and not necessarily that he did, either – I don't know) – but that he didn't mix his business and personal lives. He didn't hang out with the musicians he worked with or with his colleagues, and so there was no vector for Lubinsky to get any kind of leverage over him.

So Lubinsky sent Bass to a party for a distributor at the last minute, which ran until three or four AM, and then when Bass' wife phoned up to ask where he was, Lubinsky claimed not to know, causing Bass and his wife to have a row.

Bass instantly realised that Lubinsky was trying to mess with his marriage in order to get some leverage over him, and decided he was simply not going to go back to work the next day. Instead, he went to King Records, who set up a subsidiary, Federal, for Bass to run. Bass took Little Esther with him, but Johnny Otis and the Robins were both still on Savoy.

Over the next few years, Bass would produce a lot of records which would change the course of rhythm and blues and rock and roll music, but sadly his further collaborations with Little Esther simply weren't as successful as the work they'd done together with Johnny Otis. She stopped having hits, and started doing heroin.Eventually her career got a second wind, and she had a few minor hits in the 1960s and 70s under her new name Esther Phillips.

Most impressive of these was "Home is Where the Hatred is", a song by about addiction by Gil Scott-Heron that she recorded in 1972. That song clearly meant a lot to her, given her own history with drugs, and the album it came from, *From a Whisper to a Scream*, was nominated for a Grammy for Best R&B Vocal Performance (Female). Aretha Franklin won the award, as she did every year from 1968 through 1975 inclusive. And to be fair, that's one of the few examples of the Grammies actually recognising talent when they saw it, because if it's possible to give Aretha Franklin an award between 1968 and 1975, you give Aretha Franklin that award. But this time, Aretha said publicly that she didn't deserve the award, and gave it to Phillips.

Sadly, Esther Phillips never won the award in her own right – she was nominated four times, but all during that period of Aretha dominance. She continued having minor hits into the 1980s, but she never recaptured that brief period when she was the biggest female star in R&B, back in 1950. She died in 1984, aged only 48. Johnny Otis, who by that time was ordained as a minister, performed her funeral.

"Rocket "88""

There is, of course, no actual "first rock and roll record", and if there is, it's not "Rocket "88"". But nonetheless, "Rocket "88"" has been officially anointed "the first rock and roll record ever made" by generations of white male music journalists, and so we need to talk about it. And it is, actually, quite a good record of its type, even if not especially innovative.

Before we go any further, please recall the disclaimer in the introduction about my attitudes towards misogynistic abusers who happen also to have played on some great records. I don't want to repeat all that here, but at the same time I definitely want to go on record that I'm not an admirer of Ike Turner. Because as it is, here at the official "beginning of rock" according to thousands of attempts to set a canon, we also have the beginning of rock being created by abusive men. Literally at the beginning in this case – Ike Turner plays the opening piano part. And here we see how impossible it is to untangle the work of people like him from this history, as that piano part is one that would echo down the ages, becoming part of the bloodstream of popular music.

Anyway, enough about that.

To talk about "Rocket "88"" we first have to talk about the Honeydrippers, and about the Liggins brothers.

Joe Liggins was a piano player, with a small-time band called Sammy Franklin and the California Rhythm Rascals. In 1942, Liggins wrote a song called "The Honeydripper", which the California Rhythm Rascals used to perform quite regularly. It's a pleasant, enjoyable, boogie-flavoured jump band piece, which had a very catchy, unusual, riff, based loosely around the riff from "Shortenin' Bread". It was mostly just an excuse for soloing and extended improvisation – sometimes it could last for fifteen minutes or more when performed live – but it was surprisingly catchy nonetheless.

Liggins believed it had some commercial potential, so he went to his boss, Franklin, with a deal. He said he thought it could be a big hit, and they should make a record of it. If Sammy Franklin would pay $500 towards the cost of making the record, Liggins would give Franklin half the composer rights for the song.

Sammy Franklin turned him down, and Liggins believed in his song so much that he quit the band and formed his own jump band, which he named after the song. Eventually, three years later, Joe Liggins and the Honeydrippers went into the studio and recorded "The Honeydripper Parts 1 & 2" for a small indie label, Exclusive Records, and it was released in April 1945.

It went to number thirteen on the pop charts, which is a remarkable feat for an R&B record in itself, but its performance on the R&B charts was just ludicrous. It went to number one on the race charts (later the R&B charts) for eighteen weeks straight, from September 1945 through January 1946. The only reason it didn't stay at the top for longer was because the record label simply couldn't keep up with the demand, and it was replaced at number one by Louis Jordan, but at number two was Jimmie Lunceford playing. . . "The Honeydripper".

At number three, meanwhile, was Roosevelt Sykes playing. . . "The Honeydripper". Later in 1946, Cab Calloway also had a number three hit with the song.

Joe Liggins and the Honeydrippers' version, alone, sold over two million copies in 1945 and 46, and it still, seventy-three years later, is joint holder of the title for longest stay at number one in the race or R&B charts ("Choo Choo Ch'Boogie" is the other joint holder, and that came a few months later). It's likely that nobody will ever beat that record. "The Honeydripper" was a sensation.

Meanwhile the California Rhythm Rascals had renamed themselves Sammy Franklin and his Atomics, in an attempt to sound more up to date and modern, with the atomic bomb having so recently gone off. They recorded their own version of "The Honeydripper". It sank without trace, but you'll remember from the last chapter that that record launched the production career of Ralph Bass. "The Honeydripper" made money and careers for everyone in the music industry, except for Sammy Franklin.

Sammy Franklin may not have been the single most unwise person in the history of rock and roll – he didn't turn down Elvis or quit the Beatles or anything like that – but still, one has to imagine that he spent the whole rest of his life regretting that he hadn't just spent that five hundred dollars.

Joe Liggins never had another success as big as "The Honeydripper", but he had a few minor successes to go along with it, and that was enough for him to give his brother Jimmy a job as the band's driver. At that time, it was *very* rare for bands to have actual employees, rather than doing their own driving and carrying their own instruments, and for Jimmy it was certainly an improvement on his previous career as a boxer under the name Kid Zulu.

But Jimmy also played a bit of guitar, and so he decided, inspired by his brother's success, to try his hand at his own music career, and he formed his own jump band, the Drops of Joy.

The Drops of Joy signed up to Specialty Records. But the Drops of Joy would normally not be a band that we'd be talking about. They weren't the most imaginative or innovative band by a long way, and they only had minor hits. Their songs were mostly generic boogies, called things like "Saturday Night Boogie Woogie Man" or "Night Life Boogie" – all perfectly good music of its type, but nothing that set the world on fire.

But one B-side, "Cadillac Boogie" was, indirectly, responsible for a great deal of the music that would follow...

To see why "Cadillac Boogie" was a big influence, we now need to turn to Sam Phillips. It's safe to say that he's one of the two or three most important people in the history of rock and roll music – and it's also safe to say that even if rock and roll had never happened at all, we'd still be talking about Sam Phillips because of his influence on country and blues music. He may well have been the single most important record producer of the 1950s, and he's as important to the history of American music as anyone who ever lived.

Phillips had started out as a DJ, but had moved sideways from there into recording bands for radio sessions. He had very strong opinions about the way things should sound, and he was willing to work hard to get the sound the way he wanted it. In particular, when he recorded big bands for sessions, he would mic the rhythm section far more than was traditional. When you heard a big band recorded by Sam Phillips, you could hear the guitar and the bass in a way you couldn't when you heard that band on the records.

He had a real ear for sound, but he also had an ear for *performance*.

Like a lot of the men we're dealing with at this point, Sam Phillips was a white man who was motivated by a deeply-felt anger at racial injustice, which expressed itself as a belief that if other white people could just see the humanity, and the talent, in black people the way he could, the world would be a much better place. The racial attitudes of people like him can seem a little patronising these days, as if the problems in America were just down to a few people's feelings, and if those feelings could be changed everything would be better, but given the utterly horrendous attitudes expressed by the people around him, Phillips was at least partly right. If he could get his fellow white people to just stop being vicious towards black people, well, that wouldn't fix all the problems by any means, but it would have been a good start.

And what Sam Phillips thought he could do to stop the evil of racism – and also to improve the world in other ways – was to capture the music that the black people he saw around him in Memphis were making. The world seemed to him to be full of talented, idiosyncratic, people who were making music like nothing else he had heard.

And so he started Memphis Recording Services, with the help of his mistress Marion Keisker, who acted as his assistant and was herself a popular radio presenter. Both kept their jobs at the radio station while starting the business, and they tried to get the business on a sound financial footing by recording things like weddings and funerals (yes, funerals, they'd mic up the funeral home and get a recording of the service which they'd put on an acetate disc – apparently this was a popular service).

But the real purpose of the business was to be somewhere where real musicians could come and record. Phillips didn't have a record label, but he had arrangements with a couple of small labels to send them recordings, and sometimes those labels would put the recordings out.

Musicians of all kinds would come into Memphis Recording Services, and Phillips would spend hours trying to get their sound onto disc and, later, tape. Not trying to perfect it, but trying to get the most authentic version of that person's artistry onto the tape.

In 1951 Memphis Recording Services hadn't been open that long, and Phillips had barely recorded anything worth a listen – but he *had* made some recordings with a local DJ called Riley King, who had recently started going by the name "Blues Boy", or just "B.B." for short. To my mind they're actually some of King's best material – much more my kind of thing than the later recordings that made his name.

A couple of years earlier, King had met a young musician in Clarksdale, Mississippi called Ike Turner, who led a big band called the Top Hatters. Turner had sat in with King on the piano and had impressed King with his ability, and King had even stopped over a couple of nights at Turner's house. The two hadn't stayed in touch, but they both liked each other.

The Top Hatters had later split up into two bands – there was the Dukes of Swing, who played classy big band music, and the Kings of Rhythm, who were a jump band after the Louis Jordan fashion, led by Turner. One day, the Kings of Rhythm were coming back from a gig when they noticed a large number of cars parked outside a venue which had a poster advertising one "B.B. King". Ike Turner had noticed that name on posters before, but didn't know who it was, but thought he should check out why there were so many people wanting to see him.

The band stopped and went inside, and discovered that B.B. King was Ike Turner's old acquaintance Riley. Turner asked King if his band could get up and play a number, and King let him, and was hugely impressed, telling Turner that he should make records. Turner said he'd like to, but he had no idea how one actually went about making a record.

King said that the way he did it was there was a guy in Memphis called Sam who recorded him. King would call Sam up and tell him to give Turner a call on Monday. Monday came around, and indeed Sam Phillips did call Ike Turner on the telephone, and asked when they could come up to record. "Straight away", Ike replied, and they set off

– five men, two saxes, a guitar, and a drum kit in a single car, with the guitar amp and bass drum strapped to the roof.

The drive from Mississippi to Memphis was not without incident. They got arrested and fined, ostensibly for a traffic violation but actually for being black in the deep South, and they also got a flat tyre, and when they changed it the guitar amp fell on the road.

At least, that's one story as to what happened to the guitar amp – like everything when it comes to this music, there are three or four different stories told by different people, but that's definitely one of them.

Anyway, when they got to the studio, and got their gear set up, the amplifier made a strange sound. The band were horrified. Their big break, and it was all going to be destroyed because their amp was making this horrible dirty sound. The speaker cone had been damaged.

Sam Phillips, however, was very much not horrified. He was delighted. He got some brown paper from the restaurant next door to stuff inside as a temporary repair, but said that the damaged amp would sound different, and different, to Sam Phillips at least, was always good.

The song they chose to record that day was one that was written by the saxophone player, Jackie Brenston.

Well, I say written by... as with so many of the songs we've seen here, the song was not so much written as remembered[10]. Specifically, he was remembering "Cadillac Boogie", and the song they played was nearly identical to that earlier record.

Now the main difference in the songwriting is simply the car that's being talked about – the 88 was a new, exciting, model, and Brenston made the song more hip and current as a result. But musically there are a few things of note here.

Firstly, there's the piano part, written and played by Ike Turner – Little Richard admired it so much that he used it, almost note for note, as the intro to "Good Golly Miss Molly", and you can tell that a lot of his piano style came from Ike Turner.

---

[10]As indeed that line is – I remembered it from Leslie Halliwell, talking about Talbot Rothwell's scripts for the *Carry On* films, so I thought I should give it credit here.

There's another difference as well – the guitar sound. There's distortion all over it, thanks to that cone.

Now, this probably won't even have been something that anyone listening at the time noticed. If you're listening in the context of early fifties R&B, on the poor-quality 78 RPM discs that the music was released on, you'd probably think that buzzing boogie line was a baritone sax – the line it's playing is the kind of thing that a horn would normally play, and the distortion sounds the same way as many of the distorted sax lines at the time did. But that was enough that when white music critics in the seventies were looking for a "first rock and roll record", they latched on to this one, because in the seventies rock and roll *meant* distorted guitar.

When the record came out, Ike Turner was horrified, because he'd assumed it would be released as by Ike Turner and his Kings of Rhythm, but instead it was under the name "Jackie Brenston and his Delta Cats". And the record was successful enough to make Jackie Brenston decide to quit the Kings of Rhythm and go solo. He released a few more singles, mostly along the same lines as "Rocket "88"", but they did nothing.

Brenston's solo career fizzled out quite quickly, and he joined the backing band for Lowell Fulson, the blues star. After a couple of years with Fulson, he returned to play with Ike Turner's band. He stayed with Turner from 1955 through 1962, a sideman once more, and Turner wouldn't let Brenston sing his hit on stage – he was never going to be upstaged by his sax player again.

Eventually Jackie Brenston became an alcoholic, and from 1963 until his death in 1979, he worked as a part-time truck driver, never seeing any recognition for his part in starting rock and roll.

But "Rocket "88"" had repercussions for a lot of other people, even if it was only a one-off hit for Brenston. For Ike Turner, after "Rocket "88"" was released, half of his band quit and stayed with Brenston, so for a long time he was without a full band. He started to work for Phillips as a talent scout and musician, and it was Turner who brought Phillips several artists, including the artist who Phillips later claimed was the greatest artist and greatest human being he ever worked with, Howlin' Wolf.

Phillips licensed several singles by Howlin' Wolf and others to Chess Records, but then the Chess brothers, the owners of that label, used contractual shenanigans to cut Phillips out of the loop and record the Wolf directly. So Phillips made a resolution to start his own record label, where no-one would steal his artists. Sun Records was born out of this frustration.

Meanwhile, Ike Turner resolved that he would never again see his name removed from the credits for a record he was on. When he got a new Kings of Rhythm together, he switched from playing piano, where you're sat at the side of the stage, to playing guitar, where you can be up front and in the spotlight And when the Kings of Rhythm got a new singer, Annie-Mae Bullock, Turner made sure he would always have equal billing, by giving her his surname as a stage name, so any records she made would be by the new act, "Ike and Tina Turner".

And finally, "Rocket "88"" was going to have a profound effect on the career of one man who would later make a big difference to rock and roll. The lead singer of the country band the Saddlemen, a singer who was best known as a champion yodeller, was also working as a DJ for a small Pennsylvania station, and he noticed that Louis Jordan records were popular among the country audience, and he decided to start incorporating a Louis Jordan style in his own music.

But Jordan's records were so popular with a crossover audience that when the Saddlemen came to make their first records in this new style, they chose to cover something by someone other than Jordan – someone that hadn't crossed over into the country market yet. And so they chose to record "Rocket "88"", which had been a big R&B hit but hadn't broken through into the white audience. Their version of the song is *also* credited by some as the first rock and roll record. But Bill Haley is for another chapter...

"Lawdy Miss Clawdy"

We talked about Dave Bartholomew a bit in the chapter about "The Fat Man" by Fats Domino, but he needs to be discussed in more detail, as he was one of the most important musicians of the fifties. As we saw, he brought the "Spanish tinge" to rhythm and blues records and collaborated with Fats Domino on almost all of Domino's big hits. But he did a lot more. Not only did he produce classic records by Frankie Ford and T-Bone Walker, not only did he write "One Night", which became a big hit for Smiley Lewis and a bigger one for Elvis, but he also wrote Chuck Berry's only number one hit, "My Ding-A-Ling".

OK, that may not be Berry's finest moment as a performer, but it shows just how wide Bartholomew's influence was.

Despite that, rather astonishingly, there's never been a biography written of Bartholomew, and even *Honkers and Shouters*, the classic book on the history of rhythm and blues which contains almost the only in-depth interviews with many of the musicians and record producers who made this music, only devotes a handful of paragraphs to Bartholomew's work. I've barely been able to even find any in-depth interviews with Bartholomew, and so my knowledge of him is built up from lots of offhand mentions and casual connections in books on other people.

But he worked with so *many* other people that that still amounts to quite a lot. So let's talk about "Lawdy Miss Clawdy", and let's do it by picking up the story of Dave Bartholomew and Fats Domino after "The Fat Man".

"The Fat Man" was a massive hit, but it caused some strain between its producer and its performer. Domino had gone on tour to support the record, as part of a larger package with Bartholomew's band as the headliners. Domino would only perform a few songs at a time, and most of the show was Bartholomew's band.

Domino resented Bartholomew for getting most of the money, while Bartholomew resented Domino for his popularity – Domino was starting to overshadow the nominal star of the show. But more than that, Domino just didn't seem to be getting on well with the rest of the band.

This wasn't because he was unfriendly – although Domino was always someone who seemed a little socially awkward – just that Domino was a homebody who absolutely resented ever having to go away from home, and especially as he had a newborn baby son he wanted to be home for. Indeed, when the tour had started, Domino had missed the first few days by the simple expedient of hiding for several days, and it was only when a union official had come knocking at his door explaining what happened to people who broke their contracts that he relented and went on the tour. And even then, he packed a suitcase full of foods like pickled pig's feet, in case he couldn't get his favourite foods anywhere else.

Domino was a sheltered, nervous, shy, person – someone who had been so unworldly that when his first record came out he didn't have a record player to play it on and had to listen to it on jukeboxes – and this exasperated Bartholomew, who was a far more well-travelled and socially aware person. But the two of them still continued to collaborate, and to make records together, including some great ones like a version of the traditional New Orleans song "Eh La Bas!", which Bartholomew rewrote with the great boogie pianist Professor Longhair and titled "Hey! La Bas Boogie".

The collaborations caused other problems, too. Both Bartholomew and Domino thought, with good reason, of themselves as the true talent in their collaborations. Domino believed that his piano playing and singing were the important things on the records, and that since he was bringing in most of the ideas fully-formed Bartholomew wasn't doing much to make the records successful. Bartholomew, on the other hand, thought that the song ideas Domino was bringing in were basically nursery rhymes, while his own songs were more sophisticated. Domino had little formal musical knowledge and usually used only a couple of chords, while Bartholomew was far more musically knowledgeable; and Domino wasn't a native English speaker, and tended to use very simple lyrics while when Bartholomew brought in ideas he would come up with strong narratives and punning lyrics. Bartholomew thought that when the songs Domino brought in became successful, it was because of Bartholomew's patching up of them and his arrangements.

Bartholomew resented that Domino was becoming a big star, and Domino resented that Bartholomew patronised him in the studio, treating him as an employee, not an equal partner.

Of course, both were right. Bartholomew was by far the better songwriter, but Domino had great instincts for a hook. Bartholomew was a great arranger, and Domino was a great performer. As so often in musical collaborations, the sum was much greater than its parts, and it was the tension between the two of them that drove the collaboration.

But while Bartholomew had problems with Fats, his real problems were with Al Young, a white New Orleans record store owner who was an associate of Lew Chudd, Imperial Records' owner. He didn't like Young's habit of trying to make it look like it was Young, rather than Bartholomew, who was producing the records, and he especially didn't like when Young cut himself in on the songwriting royalties for songs Bartholomew wrote.

This problem came to a head when Bartholomew got back home from a particularly stressful tour with Domino over Thanksgiving. It had been far too cold for the Louisiana musicians in the Midwest, and they'd been ripped off by the tour promoters – they'd received only something like two hundred dollars between them, rather than the two thousand they'd been promised. Domino actually had to call home and ask his family to wire him his bus fare back from Missouri to New Orleans.

And when Bartholomew got back, he popped into Al Young's record shop... and Young showed him the fifteen hundred dollar Christmas bonus cheque he'd just received from Imperial Records for all his hard work that year. Bartholomew had received no bonus, despite having done far more for the company than Young had, and he assumed that the reason was because Bartholomew was black and Young was white.

He decided right then to quit Imperial, and to become a freelancer working for whoever had work.

Domino continued making records in the same style, and even continued to have hits with songs that followed the formula he'd established with Bartholomew, some of them even bigger than the ones they'd made together, like "Goin' Home". But Al Young was the producer on that record, and while Domino did his usual great performance and it had that tresillo rhythm, Young knew nothing about music, and so the arrangement was haphazard and the sax solo was off-key at points, to the point where once you notice it the record becomes almost unlistenable.

But it was still a big hit, and Al Young got his name stuck on the credits as a co-writer, which is what mattered to him at least, even if everyone was unhappy with the recordings. That song went to number one on the R&B charts, and made its way into the top thirty on the pop charts, and you can hear its influence all over the place, in records like Faye Adams' "Shake a Hand", as well as in the work of a young piano player and arranger named Ray Charles. But the fact remains, it's not as good as the stuff Domino was doing with Bartholomew. It has the power and the catchiness, but it doesn't have the depth and the sophistication.

Lew Chudd, around this time, tried to get Art Young to get Dave Bartholomew back working with Domino again, but Bartholomew just slammed the phone down on Young. He didn't need Imperial Records, he didn't need Fats Domino, and he *certainly* didn't need Art Young. He was working with other people now. In particular, he was working with Specialty Records.

Specialty Records was an LA-based record label, like most of the labels that worked with New Orleans musicians were. For whatever reason, even though LA and New Orleans are thousands of miles away from each other, it was the Los Angeles companies rather than anywhere closer that seemed to pick up on the sound coming from New Orleans.

Specialty was run by Art Rupe. Art Rupe is, amazingly, still alive at the time of writing – he turned 102 in September 2019 – and he's one of the most important figures in the development of rhythm and blues in the 1950s. Indeed, he was the producer of yet another record occasionally labelled "the first rock and roll record", "R.M.'s Blues" by Roy Milton, which was one of the early records to combine a boogie piano and a backbeat.

And in his case, it's no coincidence that he ended up working with New Orleans musicians – he was impressed by Fats Domino's Imperial Records releases, Imperial being another Los Angeles based label, and so he came to New Orleans to see if there were other people like Domino about. Rupe put out an ad for people to come to Cosimo Matassa's studio to audition, but it wasn't until he was packing up to leave and fly back to Los Angeles without any success, that a singer called Lloyd Price walked into the studio and sang his song "Lawdy Miss Clawdy". Rupe cancelled his flight – this was someone worth recording.

Price was, at the time, a jingle creator for a local radio station, providing music for the DJs to use while they were advertising various products. At the time, radio advertising in the US was much like podcast advertising is now, and in the same way that a podcast host might interrupt what they're doing and try to tell you about the benefits of a new mattress, so, then, might DJs – and in the same way that some podcast hosts will vary their set texts, so would the DJs. And one of the DJs for whom Lloyd Price created jingles had a catchphrase , "Lawdy Miss Clawdy".

Price had come up with a melody to go along with those words – or, rather, he'd adapted a pre-existing melody to it – and the result had been popular enough that he had decided to turn it into a full song.

And Price had sat in with Dave Bartholomew and his band in Kenner, his home town, singing a few songs with them. Bartholomew had told him "I'm not working with Lew Chudd any more, I'm just hanging around Cosimo Matassa's studio catching the odd bit of arrangement work there. Why don't you come down and see if we can get you recorded?" But Price was so unfamiliar with New Orleans that he didn't even know how to get to Rampart Street, which is why he'd arrived so late. Luckily for everyone concerned, he managed to find the most famous street in New Orleans eventually.

When they started recording the song, Bartholomew started to get annoyed with the guitarist on the session, Ernest McLean. "I wanted to get some sort of a rhythm going and he de dum de dum, de dum de dum [Laurel and Hardy rhythm]. I say, man, that's, that's, that ain't nothing. What the hell you get that thing from?"

That's from one of the few interviews I've seen with Bartholomew. Other sources say it was his piano player, Salvador Doucette, who was the problem. Whichever musician it was was apparently a jazz musician who had no real love or feel for rhythm and blues, and Bartholomew was getting exasperated, but at the same time he had no option but to go with what he had. But then fate intervened.

Fats Domino happened to be passing the studio, and he decided to just call in and say hello, since it was the studio he recorded in regularly, and he found Dave Bartholomew there. Domino and Bartholomew hadn't worked together in over a year at this point – March 1952 – and things were tense at first, but Bartholomew decided he'd be the one to ease the tension, and asked Domino to sit in.

At first Domino refused, saying "Man, you know I can't sit in! I'm under contract!", but he sat around in the session, having a few drinks and watching the band work. Eventually, he said "Well, I'm gonna have me some fun, I'm gonna sit in anyway!" The resulting record was the one that knocked "Goin' Home" off the top of the R&B charts, and it would become one of the defining records of the rock and roll era.

"Lawdy Miss Clawdy" is, in many ways, an attempt to recapture the success of "The Fat Man". It has many of the same musicians, the same arranger, and the same basic melody that the earlier record did. But being recorded three years later on meant it was also recorded after three years more advancement in the rock and roll style, and "Lawdy Miss Clawdy" is notably more rhythmically complex than the earlier record. And that's largely down to Dave Bartholomew's arrangement.

Domino is mostly playing triplets, which is the way that he played most of the time; but on the drums there's the great Earl Palmer, making the transition between his early shuffle style and his later backbeat emphasis. He's trying to do two things at once on the drums, he's trying to swing it *and* produce a backbeat, so you've essentially got him doing polyrhythms. Over that the bass plays a different rhythm again, and then the horns, just doing long, sustained, "blaaaat" parts. And on top of all that you've got Lloyd Price, singing in a Roy Brown imitation, but with a teenager's style – Price had just turned nineteen. And then there's the sax solo by Herb Hardesty, the prototype for the solos he would provide for all Domino's hits from this point on. It's an amazing combination; this is the record that crystallised the New Orleans sound and became the template all the others would follow. "The Fat Man" had been the prototype, with some rough edges still there. This was a slicker, more assured, version of the same thing.

Art Rupe was certainly pleased, but they were lucky to have been working with Rupe himself. Soon after this recording, Rupe decided to expand his operations in New Orleans, and put Johnny Vincent in charge. While Rupe has a reputation as a decent businessman by 1950s record company standards, Johnny Vincent does *not*. When Vincent later owned his own record company, Ace, he was so bad at paying the musicians that Huey "Piano" Smith and Mac Rebennack had to go and hold Vincent at gunpoint while they searched his office – and his person – for the money he owed them. And then, a few months later, they had to do the same thing again, because being held up at gunpoint just the once wasn't enough for him to think better of ripping them off.

Vincent was also not a particularly skilled record producer, at least according to Rebennack, who said "Johnny Vincent was a very good con artist. For instance, if the session was with Huey Smith, he'd say 'Hu-ree, put some *shit* into it'. And everyone would respond and, sure enough, put some shit into it. That was the compiled wisdom of Johnny Vincent's approach to making records."

It's probably not a massive coincidence that Dave Bartholomew stopped working for Specialty very shortly after the recording of "Lawdy Miss Clawdy". I've not seen a precise enough timeline to know for sure that it was Johnny Vincent's arrival at the label that persuaded Bartholomew he didn't want to work for them any more, but it seems likely to me. What I do know, though is that Lew Chudd heard "Lawdy Miss Clawdy", compared it to the records Al Young was producing for Fats Domino, and realised that he could be doing a hell of a lot better than he was. He eventually, through an intermediary, managed to persuade Bartholomew to talk to him again, and Bartholomew was hired back to work at Imperial. The same month, April 1952, that "Lawdy Miss Clawdy" came out, Domino and Bartholomew were back in

Matassa's studio, working together again, and recording a collaboration which sounds like a true combination of both men's styles, "Poor Me". Domino and Bartholomew would work together regularly in the studio until at least 1967, and live off and on for decades after that.

But Lloyd Price wasn't hampered by the fact that his producer had gone off to another label either. His follow-up single, cut at the same session as "Lawdy Miss Clawdy" with the same musicians, was a double-sided hit, both sides making the top ten on the R&B charts. And the same happened with the single after that, cut with different musicians – a song called "Ain't it a Shame", which may just have given Domino and Bartholomew an idea. After that he hit a bit of a dry spell in his career, and by 1956 he was reduced to recording a sequel to "Lawdy Miss Clawdy", "Forgive me Clawdy".

But then "Lawdy Miss Clawdy" itself got a second wind, and was covered in 1956 by both Elvis and Little Richard. This seems to have jump-started Price's career, and we'll pick up his story in later volumes of this series.

"Lawdy Miss Clawdy" had a long life – it's been recorded over the years by everyone from Paul McCartney to the Replacements, and happily most of the major figures involved in the record did too, which makes a very pleasant change from the bit of the chapter where I usually tell you that the singer died in poverty and obscurity of alcoholism. Sadly Dave Bartholomew died during the production of this book, at the age of one hundred, but he kept making music well into his nineties. Lloyd Price is still going strong, still performing aged eighty-six, and he released his most recent album in 2016. Art Rupe is still alive aged 102, and while I'm sad to say Fats Domino is now dead, he died only in 2017, aged 89, an extremely wealthy man who had received every award his peers could bestow and had been given medals by multiple Presidents.

"Cry"

Here we get to a song which I debated putting in this history at all. Put simply, I don't think that "Cry" is part of the story of rock and roll at all, but almost all the histories of the genre disagree with me, and it's an important enough record that it's worth discussing here regardless.

That's not to say I think it's a bad record, or an uninteresting one – far from it. I think it's a very interesting record, and Ray has a very interesting story. I just think it's a story about the dying days of the pre-rock showbiz world, not about rock and roll itself.

Before I start, though, I just want to say that my sources on this story are rather more unreliable than normal. There have only been, to my knowledge, two books about Johnnie Ray written. One is a self-published book by a friend of his who got to know him in his later life, full of personal anecdotes, and from what I can tell everything in it is also in the other book, an actual biography. But that other book is full of fairly basic factual errors that any competent fact-checker could have fixed. As one example, the book talks about how in the late sixties Ray worked with a songwriter named Jack Newman, and it talks about him recording some of Newman's songs, and has quotes from an associate of Ray about how after shopping their demos around "Jack could never get it going".

It then talks about how one of those songs was later recorded by Jack Jones – a song called "I Think It's Going to Rain Today".

Now, that is a famous song, and it's in Ray's style, but it was famously written by *Randy* Newman. There *is* a songwriter called Jack Newman, who was a country singer in the early sixties. It's possible that Ray worked with him, it's possible that the author of the book conflated Ray working with two different songwriters called Newman and Ray also worked with Randy, it's possible that the whole thing is made up out of whole cloth. With nothing to fact-check against, because no-one's been interested in Johnnie Ray for sixty years, it's impossible for me to tell how much of the story I'm about to tell is accurate. Johnnie Ray did exist, and did record the songs I'm going to talk about, but other than that, don't take my word for anything that follows.

These days, if Johnnie Ray is known at all, it's as as someone mentioned in the opening to "Come on Eileen" by Dexy's Midnight Runners – "Poor old Johnnie Ray sounded sad upon the radio/Moved a million hearts in mono". The only other way most people of my generation will know of Ray is because of Morrissey. Morrissey admired, or claimed to admire, Johnnie Ray, to the extent that he wore a hearing aid on stage and in TV performances to emulate Ray, despite the fact that he had perfectly good hearing. I hope I don't need to explain to anyone how contemptible that is.

But back in the early 1950s, Johnnie Ray was a massive star. He was so big that at one point he started only wearing the cheapest clothes he could find, because literally every time he went outside his clothes would get torn at by screaming fans. So how come these days he's only known as a trivia question answer for people who can parse Kevin Rowland's inscrutable lyrics?

Johnnie Ray is always pointed to as a precursor of rock and roll, and in particular to the work of Elvis Presley, and barely a book about 1950s rock and roll doesn't discuss him. Yet none of them mention any actual influence he had on any of the artists who came up after him, there's no stylistic similarity to rock and roll, and he seems to have had no influence on any musicians before the late seventies and early eighties, when a handful of British acts half-ironically took inspiration from him.

Just judging purely on the music, there's really no link between Ray's work and that of the later rock and rollers. To my ears, Ray is a little bit of an evolutionary dead end – he's what the next stage of the Sinatra type crooner would have been, if the Sinatra-style crooners had continued being teen idols as Sinatra himself was. Ray was the last example of something, rather than the first example of something else.

But that doesn't mean he – and his career – wasn't interesting in its own right.

Ray was very much a part of the old showbiz rather than the new rock and roll – to the extent that he appeared with Ethel Merman and Marilyn Monroe in *There's No Business Like Showbusiness* and was best man at Judy Garland's last wedding.

There is, however, one way in which Ray had some commonality with the early rock musicians. We've talked before about how rock and roll was the music of the marginalised, and while Ray was a relatively well-off white man, he was bisexual at a time when same-sex relationships were still illegal, and he was also disabled. He was deaf in one ear at the start of his career, and by 1958 he was almost completely deaf in both ears thanks to a botched surgery.

And while it's difficult now to see any connection between Ray's music and early rock and roll, he was one of the first white people ever to get to number one on the R&B charts. So what was it that the R&B audience saw in Ray that it didn't see in Tony Bennett or Frank Sinatra? It's hard to say now, but I believe the answer may lie in what Ray himself identified as the secret of his success – his sincerity.

One of the big differences between R&B and the pop music of the time is that R&B singers – and country singers, too – were attempting to express emotion in their vocal performances, by straining at notes, using melisma, shrieking, whatever it would take to get the audience to believe that the singer meant what they were singing. The pop crooners, on the other hand, were extremely restrained. This is not to say that the crooners' music couldn't be emotionally moving, but the experience of listening to a great crooner was like reading a book – you'd get moved by the words (and in the case of the crooner, by the melody), and the crooner's job was to let the song move you.

Johnnie Ray, on the other hand, wanted to move you himself. He became known as "the nabob of sob", for his overly-emoted delivery. And listening to his sobbing vocals on tracks like "The Little White Cloud That Cried", it's hard not to think of Clyde McPhatter's similarly emotional, over the top, singing on "The Bells" by Billy Ward and his Dominoes.

Ray's odd, emotive, style can possibly be explained in part by his social isolation growing up. He had always been regarded as an eccentric child, but when he lost the hearing in one ear in an accident, that became much worse. For whatever reason, some confusion of perception led him to not realise what was wrong for a long time afterward, even though he knew straight away that something was different. He didn't know he was deaf, and so nobody else did. He couldn't hear them, they thought he was stupid or ignoring them, and he didn't know what it was that was making them stop talking to him.

This went on for a long time, and it wasn't until several years later that Ray's parents saw him pressing his ear up against the radio to listen to it and realised that he was actually deaf. They got him a hearing aid, and this changed his life – but in the meantime, he'd become alienated from all his peers at school, and the fact that this seemed to happen around the same time he went through puberty and discovered his own attraction to other men just made that worse. At a crucial point in his life, he'd become isolated from the world around him.

But Ray had always had a talent for music. He'd tried taking piano lessons, but the piano teacher had given up trying to teach him, because he could just play anything he heard after hearing it once, so didn't bother with practising. There are stories about him, as a teenager, seeking out famous singers who came to play near the small town he lived in, and them telling him things like "You have to become a singer, with a God-given talent like yours". Of course, those stories all always attach themselves to any famous musician after they become well-known, but they seem to surround Ray so much that one has to presume there's a grain of truth in some of them.

But when he tried for a career in music, at first it was as a songwriter rather than a singer. At the time we're talking about, the role of singer-songwriter didn't really exist in the pop world. Singers performed songs, and songwriters wrote them, and the two jobs were separate. Things were different in country and R&B – while it was perfectly OK to be a non-writing singer, it was still normal in those genres for the singer to also write their own material. But in pop there was a demarcation, and Johnnie Ray wanted to become a songwriter.

Early in his career, he tried to pitch songs he'd written to Frankie Laine – a big star who was something of a precursor for Ray's own style. Both were crooners but with an influence from black R&B – Laine was a big fan of Jimmy Rushing and Big Joe Turner, and he was the one who'd given Ruth Brown the nickname "Little Miss Rhythm". Ray pitched many songs to Laine, and to Laine's representatives (whose other major client at the time was Liberace), but they weren't interested, and so he turned to performing as a singer.

In fact, he turned to performing in R&B clubs, where he would sing the blues in the handful of integrated clubs that were around, playing on otherwise-black bills. And many of these clubs were run and owned by gangsters – and there would be Mafia connections with Ray for several years to come, with several prominent gangsters claiming, some of them even legitimately, that he was contracted to work for them.

While working at one of these clubs, he became very friendly with the R&B singer LaVern Baker, who would later become a big star herself – in fact, there were rumours that the two of them were more than just friends. He was good enough that singers like Jimmy Witherspoon respected him as a blues singer, as did Baker. And Baker was a huge part of developing Ray's stage style. In particular – and this is going to sound very odd – she introduced him to the work of Al Jolson.

Now, for those of you who don't know, Jolson was the biggest performer of the 1920s and early thirties, and he was one of the few white men to sing with emotion and have success in the pop field before the fifties. But Jolson was also a blackface performer, and it's been argued that he used blackface as a way to give himself the freedom to sing more emotionally. And if I had an entire lifetime rather than a mere half hour that would not be enough time to unpack the cultural dynamics of a black female blues singer who performed in ragged clothes to play up to an image she hated, teaching a white man who was in the closet and who wanted to sing the blues, how to give a more authentic performance, by introducing him to the work of a blackface performer.

And even if I could parse that particular interaction, that would be so far out of my lane that I wouldn't want to touch it with someone else's bargepole.

Ray took on several of Jolson's mannerisms, and he loosened up his performance extraordinarily. He would start banging on the piano, climbing over things, dropping to his knees – every night the manager of the club had to send someone out into the audience to collect Ray's cufflinks, because they would shoot twenty or thirty feet out of his cuffs while he was performing.

Baker was a huge influence, and most of Ray's vocal style was influenced by women, and especially black women. While the white pop star Kay Starr was his single biggest influence, his other major influence was Billie Holiday, and he was obsessed in particular with her recording of "Lover Man".

But the artist to whom he was most often compared was Dinah Washington, the most prominent female rhythm and blues singer of the immediate pre-rock era, and a big influence on singers like Esther Phillips and Ruth Brown. If you compare the versions Washington and Ray performed of the Drifters' "Such a Night" you can see an immediate similarity in their vocal techniques.

Ray sounded so much like Washington that when the record company executive dealing with Ray's work played his early recordings to the company sales force, their unanimous response was "We don't think she's going to make it". They had assumed that Ray was a black woman copying the style of Dinah Washington, rather than the white man he was.

The other singer to whom Ray was often compared was Jimmy Scott, who like Washington had sung with Lionel Hampton's band, and who bore a vocal resemblance to her. In Scott's case, the feminine quality of his voice was because he had a hormonal condition that prevented him ever hitting puberty – but Scott had a great musical brain, as well, and Ray copied his phrasing extensively.

Ray also added his own twist, finding a workaround to turn his disability to his advantage. He would often not be able to hear the band, and so found it difficult to stay in tempo with them, especially after he stopped accompanying himself on the piano. So he learned to play with his phrasing, learning to drag and rush the tempo so he could slow down or speed up to get back in synch with the band and have it sound intentional. In his early years he didn't wear his hearing aid on stage, and so he had to rely on these sorts of workarounds in order to perform with the band.

Ray's first record was a rhythm and blues record, although on the polite end of the R&B spectrum, and listening to it you can see exactly why those sales people thought Ray was a black woman. The record, "Whiskey and Gin", was banned from the radio for its lyrics, though it seems tame today.

Ray was signed to Okeh, which was a subsidiary of Columbia, a major label. At this point there was a big split between the major labels and the indies, in terms of how they were distributed. One of the results of this was that when the major labels did put out R&B acts, they didn't get many sales, because the R&B customers didn't think that the major labels had anything to say to them – and they didn't even get sold in the same shops that sold the R&B records.

But Okeh was a special case. It was originally an independent label, before Columbia bought it and largely shut it down, and in the thirties and forties it had built up a reputation in the blues market. The Columbia executives were banking on the idea that if R&B customers saw a record on Okeh rather than on Columbia, they would remember it and not have the negative associations they had with Columbia.

But whatever the label, Okeh was still, in reality, part of Columbia, and Ray's recordings for Okeh were produced, not by a blues producer, but by Mitch Miller.

Miller is a paradoxical, perplexing figure in music history. He worked with some of the greatest singers of his time, and produced hugely crafted, astonishingly produced records... of terrible novelty songs.

Now, I want to make clear that this series of books will never take a purist approach to rock and roll music. There is a place for the novelty song, and a place for pure pop music. I can't say enough good things about, for example, "Sugar Sugar" by the Archies. You will never hear me say a bad thing about that record.

And I can have respect for the craft even of records I don't like. Indeed, one of the things I'm trying my hardest to do in this series is keep my own personal tastes out of this. We haven't covered any music I dislike so far, but we will, and I hope to still talk about how it was important and influential and innovative in just the same way that I have with music that I adore.

But Miller's music was something a little different from this. Miller was an infuriating figure. He had an unerring ear for a hit, but used it to create monstrosities like "Come on-a My House" by Rosemary Clooney. That's a record with an absolutely phenomenal sound, and you can draw a very direct line from Miller to people like Phil Spector, Joe Meek, or Lee Hazelwood. But it's also clearly a dreadful song on multiple levels, and Rosemary Clooney always said you could hear the gritted teeth in her performance.

And the thing is, Miller didn't even like the records he was producing himself. "I wouldn't buy that stuff for myself," he said. "There's no real artistic satisfaction in this job. I satisfy my musical ego elsewhere." He forced his singers to perform songs they hated, songs that he didn't even like himself, because he had contempt for the audience. The fact that his low assessment of the audience's taste often proved correct didn't help matters.

But Miller did produce hit after hit, and once he took over producing Ray's records, Ray became massive. "Cry", a song Miller picked for him, and Ray's own "The Little White Cloud That Cried" went to the number one and two positions in the charts, and became two of the biggest successes of the 1950s – a remarkable feat for the A and B sides of a single.

Ray was soon the biggest star in the country, and newspaper columns talked about how this exciting young performer was scandalising America. He entered into a very public feud with Frank Sinatra, who was also produced by Miller and was going through a downward slump in his own career, which he blamed on Miller's poor choice of material. Sinatra felt threatened by Ray as a musician, and also as a man – Sinatra's then-wife, Ava Gardner, made no secret of lusting after Ray.

But the followups to Ray's initial hit increasingly ignored the emotional core of Ray's performances which had made him a success, and Ray stopped writing songs altogether, sticking to songs by other writers. While he had quite a few more hits for the rest of the decade, some of them really big (though never as big as his first hit) he soon lost his cultural relevance, and only returned to the news in a negative way.

He had been pegged as undesirable by the police in Detroit, and they had arrested him for soliciting in 1951, just before he hit stardom. That had more or less been hushed up by Ray's mob connections, although a few of the scandal sheets had dug it up around 1955. But in 1959 he was visiting Detroit again, and entrapped by the police in a not-particularly-subtle sting operation, which involved getting Ray drunk (not a difficult task) and him stopping to urinate in the street in the dark and then immediately afterwards putting his arm round his new friend, who turned out to be an undercover cop. Penis out in public, plus arm around another man, meant instant arrest.

That particular problem was dealt with – Johnnie Ray's then-girlfriend, the columnist Dorothy Kilgallen, had contacts at every level of government, and Ray was acquitted thanks in large part to her work behind the scenes. But there was enough publicity around this that Ray's career as a recording artist was over. His last single for Columbia came out in 1960. He moved to Decca for a couple of records, and then entered obscurity. He'd lost the support of his Mafia friends – and Ray would later claim that that had been part of the idea, that he'd been set up by Frank Sinatra.

He continued to get work, playing showrooms and the nostalgia circuit and occasionally making the odd TV appearance singing his old hits, but his musical career was gone, and he ended up dying of drink-induced liver failure in 1990, aged sixty-three.

"Mama, He Treats Your Daughter Mean"

While I've often made the point that fifties rhythm and blues is not the same thing as "the blues" as most people now think of it, there was still an obvious connection (as you'd expect from the name if nothing else) and sometimes the two would be more connected than you might think. So Ruth Brown, who was almost the epitome of a rhythm and blues singer, had her first hit on the pop charts with a song that couldn't have been more blues inspired.

For the story of "Mama, He Treats Your Daughter Mean", we have to go all the way back to Blind Lemon Jefferson in the 1920s. Jefferson was a country-blues picker who was one of the most remarkable guitarists of his generation – he was a blues man first and foremost, but his guitar playing influenced almost every country player who came later. Unfortunately, he recorded for Paramount Records, notoriously the label with the worst sound quality in the 20s and thirties (which, given the general sound quality of those early recordings, is saying something).

One of his songs was "One Dime Blues", which is a very typical example of his style, and contained the line "Mama, don't treat your daughter mean." That song was later picked up by another great blind bluesman, Blind Willie McTell.

McTell is an example of how white lovers of black music would manage to miss the point of the musicians they loved and try to turn them into something they're not. A substantial proportion of McTell's recordings were made by John and Alan Lomax, for the Library of Congress, but if you listen to those recordings you can hear the Lomaxes persuading McTell to play music that's very different from the songs he normally played – while he was a commercial blues singer, they wanted him to perform traditional folk songs and to sing political protest material, and basically to be another Lead Belly (a singer he did resemble slightly as a musician, largely because they both played the twelve-string guitar). He said he didn't know any protest songs, but he did play various folk songs for them, even though they weren't in his normal repertoire.

And this is a very important thing to realise about the way the white collectors of black music distorted it – and it's something you should also pay attention to when I talk about this stuff. I am, after all, a white man who loves a lot of black music but is disconnected from the culture that created it, just like the Lomaxes. There's a reason why I call this series "A History of Rock Music..." rather than "The History of Rock Music..." – the very last thing I want to do is give the impression that my opinion is the definitive one and that I should have the final word about these things.

But what the Lomaxes were doing, when they were collecting their recordings, was taking sophisticated entertainers, who made their living from playing to rather demanding crowds, and getting them to play music that the Lomaxes *thought* was typical black music, rather than the music that those musicians would normally play and that their audiences would normally listen to. So they got McTell to perform songs he knew, like "The Boll Weevil" and "Amazing Grace", because they thought that those songs were what they should be collecting, rather than having him perform his own material.

To put this into a context which may seem a little more obvious to current readers, imagine you're a singer-songwriter in Britain in the present day. You've been playing the clubs for several years, you've got a repertoire of songs you've written which the audiences love. You get your big break with a record company, you go into the studio, and the producer insists on you singing "Itsy-Bitsy Spider" and a hymn you had to sing in school assembly like "All Things Bright and Beautiful". You probably could perform those, but you'd be wondering why they wouldn't let you sing your own songs, and what the audiences would think of you singing this kind of stuff, and who exactly was going to buy it.

But on the other hand, money is money, and you give the people paying you what they want.

This was the experience of a *lot* of black musicians in the thirties, forties, and fifties, having rich white men pay them to play music that they saw as unsophisticated. It's something we'll see particularly in the late fifties as musicians travel from the US to the UK, and people like Muddy Waters discovered that their English audiences didn't want to see anyone playing electric guitars and doing solos – they thought of the blues as a kind of folk music, and so wanted to see a poor black sharecropper playing an acoustic guitar, and so that's what he gave those audiences.

But McTell's version of "One Dime Blues", retitled "Last Dime Blues", wasn't like that. That was the music he played normally, and it was a minor hit, and it inspired one of the most important records in early rock and roll.

Ruth Brown had run away from home when she was seventeen. She'd wanted to become a singer, and she eloped with a trumpet player, Jimmy Brown, who she married and whose name she kept even though the marriage didn't last long.

She quickly joined Lucky Millinder's band, as so many early R&B stars we've discussed did, but that too didn't last long. Millinder's band, at the time, had two singers already, and the original plan was for Brown to travel with the band for a month and learn how they did things, and then to join them on stage. She did the travelling for a month part, but soon found herself kicked out when she got on stage.

She did two songs with the band on her first night performing live with them, and apparently went down well with the audience, but that was all she was meant to do on that show, so one of the other musicians asked her to go and get the band members drinks from the bar, as they were still performing. She brought them all sodas on to the stage... and Millinder said "I hired a singer, not a waitress – you're fired. And besides, you don't sing well anyway".

She was fired that day, and she had no money. Millinder refused to pay her, arguing that she'd had free room and board from him for a month, so if anything *she* owed *him* money. She had no way to make her way home from Washington. She was stuck.

But what should have been a terrible situation for her turned out to be the thing that changed her life. She got an audition with Blanche Calloway, Cab's sister, who was running a club at the time.

Well, I say Blanche Calloway was Cab's sister, and that's probably how most people today would think of her if they thought of her at all, but it would really be more appropriate to say Cab Calloway happened to be her brother.

Blanche Calloway had herself had a successful singing career, starting before her brother's career, and she'd recorded songs like "Just a Crazy Song", which contained a chorus going "Hi de hi, ho de ho", several months *before* her brother recorded "Minnie The Moocher". Blanche Calloway wasn't the first person to sing "Just a Crazy Song" – Bill "Bojangles" Robinson recorded it a month before, though in a very different style – but she's clearly the one who gave Cab the idea. She was a successful bandleader before her brother, and her band, the Joy Boys, featured musicians like Cozy Cole and Ben Webster, who later became some of the most famous names in jazz.

She was the first woman to lead an otherwise all-male band, and her band was regularly listed as one of the ten or so most influential bands of the early thirties. And that wasn't her only achievement by any means – in later years she became prominent in the Democratic Party and as a civil rights activist; she started Afram, a cosmetic company that made makeup for black women and was one of the most popular brand names of the seventies, and she was the first black woman to vote in Florida, in 1958.

But while her band was popular in the thirties, it eventually broke up. There are two stories about how her band split, and possibly both are true. One story is that the Mafia, who controlled live music in the thirties, decided that there wasn't room for two bands led by a Calloway, and put their weight behind her brother, leaving her unable to get gigs. The other story is that while on tour in Mississippi, she used a public toilet that was designated whites-only, and while she was in jail for that one of the band members ran off with all the band's money and so she couldn't afford to pay them.

Either way, Calloway had gone into club management instead, and that was what she was doing when Ruth Brown walked into her club, desperate for a job.

Calloway said that the club didn't really need any new singers at the time, but she was sympathetic enough with Brown's plight, and impressed enough by her talent, that she agreed that Brown could continue to sing at her club until she'd earned her fare home.

And it was at that club that Willis Conover came to see her. Conover was a fascinating figure. He presented the jazz programme on Voice of America, the radio station that broadcast propaganda to the Eastern bloc during the Cold War, but by doing so he managed to raise the profile of many of the greatest jazz musicians of the time. He was also a major figure in early science fiction fandom – a book of his correspondence with H.P. Lovecraft is now available.

Conover was visiting the nightclub along with his friend Duke Ellington, and he was immediately impressed by Ruth Brown's performance – impressed enough that he ran out to call Ahmet Ertegun and Herb Abramson and tell them to sign her.

Ertegun and Abramson were the founders of Atlantic Records, a new record label which had started up only a couple of years earlier. We've talked a bit about how the white backroom people in early R&B were usually those who were in some ways on the borderline between American conceptions of race, and this is something that will become even more important as the story goes on, but that was certainly true of Ahmet Ertegun. Ertegun was considered white by the then-prevailing standards in the US, but he was a Turkish Muslim, and so not part of what the white culture considered the default.

He was also, though, extremely well off. His father had been the Turkish ambassador to the United States, and while young Ahmet had ostensibly been studying Medieval Philosophy at Georgetown University, in reality he was spending much of his time in Milt Gabler's Commodore Music Shop. He and his brother Neshui had over fifteen thousand jazz records between them, and would travel to places like New Orleans and Harlem to see musicians. And so Ahmet decided he was going to set up his own record company, making jazz records. He got funding from his dentist, and took on Herb Abramson, one of the dentist's protégés, as his partner in the firm. They soon switched from their initial plan of making jazz records to a new one of making blues and R&B, following the market.

Atlantic's first few records, while they were good ones, featuring people like Professor Longhair, weren't especially successful, but then in 1949 they released "Drinking Wine Spo-De-O-Dee" by Sticks McGhee.

That record is another of those which people refer to as "the first rock and roll record", and it was pure good luck for Atlantic. McGhee had recorded an almost identical version two years earlier, for a label called Harlem Records. The song had originally been rather different – before McGhee recorded it for Harlem Records, instead of "Drinking wine spo-de-o-dee/Drinking wine mop mop", the lyrics had been "Drinking wine motherfucker/Drinking wine goddamn!"

Wisely, Harlem Records had got him to tone down the lyrics, but the record had started to take off only after the original label had gone out of business. Ertegun knew McGhee's brother, the more famous blues musician Brownie McGhee, and called him up to get in touch with Sticks. They got Sticks to recut the record, sticking as closely as possible to his original, and rushed it out. The result was a massive success, and had cover versions by Lionel Hampton, Wynonie Harris, and many more musicians we've talked about here. Atlantic Records was on the map, and even though Sticks McGhee never had another hit, Atlantic now knew that the proto-rock-and-roll style of rhythm and blues was where its fortunes lay.

So when Herb Abramson and Ahmet Ertegun saw Ruth Brown, they knew two things – firstly, this was a singer who had massive commercial potential, and secondly that if she was going to record for them, she'd have to change her style, from the torch songs she was singing to something more... spo-de-o-dee.

Ruth Brown very nearly never made it to her first recording session at all. On her way to New York, with Blanche Calloway, who had become her manager, she ended up in a car crash and was in hospital for a year, turning twenty-one in hospital. She thought for a time that her chance had passed, but when she got well enough to use crutches she was invited along to a recording session.

It wasn't meant to be a session for her, it was just a way to ease her back into her career – Atlantic were going to show her what went on in a recording studio, so she would feel comfortable when it came to be time for her to actually make a record. The session was to record a few tracks for *Cavalcade of Music*, a radio show that profiled American composers. Eddie Condon's band were recording the tracks, and all Brown was meant to do was watch.

But then Ahmet Ertegun decided that while she was there, they might as well do a test recording of Brown, just to see whether her voice sounded decent when recorded. Herb Abramson, who would produce most of Brown's early records, listed a handful of songs that she might know that they could do, and she said she knew Russ Morgan's "So Long". The band worked out a rough head arrangement of it, and they started recording. After a few bars, though, Sid Catlett, the drummer – one of the great jazz drummers, who had worked with Louis Armstrong, Dizzy Gillespie, Duke Ellington and Benny Goodman, among others – stopped the session and said "Wait a minute. Let's go back and do this right. The kid can *sing*!"

And she certainly could. The record, which had originally been intended just as a test or, at best, as a track to stick in the package of tracks they were recording for *Cavalcade of Music*, was instead released as a single, by "Ruth Brown as heard with Eddie Condon's NBC Television Orchestra".

"So Long" became a hit, and the followup "Teardrops From My Eyes" was a bigger hit, reaching number one on the R&B charts and staying there for eleven weeks. "Teardrops From My Eyes" was an uptempo song, and not really the kind of thing Brown liked – she thought of herself primarily as a torch singer – but it can't be denied that she had a skill with that kind of material, even if it wasn't what she'd have been singing by choice.

While the song was picked for her by Abramson, who continued to be in charge of Brown's recordings until he was drafted into the Korean War, the strategy behind it was one that Ertegun had always advocated – to take black musicians who played or sang the more "sophisticated" styles and to get them instead to record in funkier, more rhythm-oriented styles. It was a strategy Atlantic would use later with many of the artists that would become popular on the label in the 1950s.

In the case of "Teardrops From My Eyes", this required a lot of work. Brown spent a week rehearsing the song with Louis Toombs, the song's writer, and working out the arrangement – and this was in a time when most hit records were either head arrangements worked out in half an hour in the studio or songs that had been honed by months of live performance. Spending a week working out a song for a recording was extremely unusual, but it was part of Atlantic's ethos, making sure the musicians were totally comfortable with the song and with each other before recording. It was the same reason that for the next few decades vocalists on Atlantic also played instruments on their own recordings, even if they weren't the best instrumentalists. The idea was that the singer should be intimately involved in the rhythm of the record.

But it worked even better for Ruth Brown than for most of those artists. "Teardrops From My Eyes" became a million seller, Atlantic's first. Or at least, it was promoted as having sold a million copies. Herb Abramson would later claim that all the record labels were vastly exaggerating their sales. But then, he had a motive to claim that, just as they had a motive to exaggerate – if the artists believed they sold a million copies, then they'd want a million copies' worth of royalties.

But Brown's biggest hit was her third number one, "Mama He Treats Your Daughter Mean", which was also one of the few records she made to cross over to the pop charts, reaching number twenty-three. This was not a record that Brown thought at the time was particularly one of her best, but twenty years later in interviews she would talk about how she couldn't do a show without playing it and that when she said her name people would ask "the Ruth Brown who sings 'Mama He Treats Your Daughter Mean'?"

The song also made a difference to Brown because it meant she had to join the musicians' union. Vocalists, unlike instrumentalists, didn't have to be union members. But "Mama, He Treats Your Daughter Mean" had a prominent tambourine part, which Brown played live. That made her an instrumentalist, not just a vocalist, and so Brown became a union member.

Johnny Wallace and Herbert Lance wrote that song after hearing a blues singer playing out on the street in Atlanta. The song the blues singer was playing was almost certainly "Last Dime Blues", and contained a line which they heard as "Mama, he treats your daughter mean".

Brown didn't want to record the song originally. The way the song was originally presented to her was as a much slower blues, but Herb Abramson raised the tempo to something closer to that of "Teardrops From My Eyes", turning it into a clear example of early rock and roll. You can hear the song's influence, for example, in "Work With Me Annie" by Hank Ballard and the Midnighters from two years later.

But Brown always claimed that the reason for the song's greater success than her other records was down to that tambourine – or more precisely because of the way she played the tambourine live, because she used a fluorescent painted tambourine which would shine when she hit it. That apparently got the audiences worked up and made it her most popular live song.

Brown continued to have hit records into the sixties, though she never became one of the most well-known artists. In the seventies she used to talk about adults telling their children "she was our Aretha Franklin", and this was probably true. Certainly she was the most successful female rhythm and blues artist of the fifties, and was popular enough that for a while Atlantic Records became known as "the house that Ruth Brown built", but like many of the pioneers of the rock and roll era, she was largely (though far from completely) erased from the cultural memory in favour of a view that has prehistory start in 1954 with Elvis and history proper only arrive in 1962 with the Beatles.

Partly, this was because in the mid fifties, just as rock and roll was becoming huge, she had children and scaled down her touring activities to take care of them, but it was also in part because Atlantic Records was expanding. When they only had one or two big stars, it was easy for them to give each of them the attention they needed, but as the label got bigger, their star acts would have the best material divided among themselves, and their hit rate – at least for those who didn't write their own material – got lower.

So by the early sixties, Ruth Brown was something of a has-been. But she got a second wind from the late seventies onwards, after she appeared in the stage musical *Selma*, playing the part of Mahalia Jackson. She became a star again. Not a pop star as she had been in her first career, but a star of the musical stage, and of films and TV. And she used that fame to do something remarkable.

She had been unhappy for years with Atlantic Records not paying her the money she was owed for royalties on her records – like most independent labels of the fifties, Atlantic had seemed to regard honouring its contracts with its artists and actually giving them money as a sort of optional extra. But unlike those other independent labels, Atlantic had remained successful, and indeed by the eighties it was a major label itself. It had been bought in 1967 by Warner Brothers and had become one of the biggest record labels in the world. And Ruth Brown wanted the money to which she was entitled, and began a campaign to get the royalties she was owed.

But she didn't just campaign for herself. As part of the agreement she eventually reached with Atlantic, not only did she get her own money back, but dozens of other rhythm and blues artists also got their money – and the Rhythm and Blues Foundation was founded with money donated by Atlantic as compensation for them. The Rhythm and Blues Foundation now provides grants to up-and-coming black musicians and gives cash awards to older musicians who've fallen on hard times, often because of the way labels like Atlantic have treated them.

Now of course that's not to say that the Rhythm and Blues Foundation fixed everything. It's very clear that Atlantic continued (and continues) to underpay the artists on whose work they built a billion-dollar business, and that the Foundation is one of those organisations that exists as much to forestall litigation as anything else, but it's still notable that when she had the opportunity to do something just for herself, Ruth Brown chose instead to also help her friends and colleagues. Maybe her time in the union paid off. . .

Brown spent her last decades as an elder stateswoman of the rhythm and blues field, She died in 2006.

"Jambalaya"

The music that became rock and roll had many different progenitors. The cliché – which we've already established as being very wrong – is that it was a mixture of the blues and country music.

While that's very far from being the actual truth, we've also seen that country and western did have a substantial influence on the development of rock and roll. And yet so far we've only looked at one country and western star, Bob Wills.

Now, this is probably the correct balance – early rock and roll grew primarily out of rhythm and blues records. But it would be ahistorical in the extreme if we were to completely ignore the growth of the hillbilly boogie, which is the branch of music that eventually led to much of what we now think of as rock and roll and rockabilly. Obviously, even from its name you can tell that hillbilly boogie was hugely influenced by boogie and R&B, but it was its own unique thing as well.

If you haven't heard of it, hillbilly boogie is a type of music that grew out of Western swing, and which itself later turned into honky-tonk music. It's music that combined country music instruments – guitars, fiddles, and steel guitars, primarily – with the rhythms of boogie music, and it was a big, big, genre in the late forties and fifties. It was less subtle than Western swing was, with most of its subjects being drinking, fighting, sex, and boogie-woogie, in approximately that order of importance. This was party music, for working-class white men who wanted to get drunk, hit something, and have sex with something.

But as is often the case with music that appeals to such primal emotions, much of the music had a power to it that was far greater than one might expect from the description, and some of it rises to the status of actual great art. And in the right hands, some of the hillbilly boogie music could be as powerful as any music around.

So in this chapter we're going to talk about a song that was, as far as we can tell, a collaboration between two greats of the country field: Hank Williams, who is pretty much the epitome of the 1950s country musician, a man who could perform in many country and western sub-genres; and Moon Mullican, who was a far less versatile musician, one who pretty much only played hillbilly boogie, but who managed to be a massive influence on early rock and roll as a result.

You've probably heard of Hank Williams, but you've probably *not* heard of Moon Mullican, yet Mullican was massively important to the development of both country and rock music. He was a hillbilly boogie piano player who could play faster than almost anyone around, and who could keep a pounding left hand going while playing lightning-fast trills with his right. If you listen to his piano playing, you can see in particular exactly where the other great Louisiana piano player Jerry Lee Lewis takes his style from.

Mullican was, like many of the hillbilly boogie players, equally in-fluenced both by country and blues music. You can hear the influence of people like Bob Wills very clearly in his music, but you can also hear people like Bessie Smith or, especially, Big Joe Turner, in his style. Most of his early influences were blues singers, although he didn't sound very blues. He would record cover versions of old blues songs by people like Memphis Minnie, but they would become absolutely country and western in Mullican's performance. We're again looking at one of those musicians who would take influences from everywhere, but transmute them into his own style. And this is something we need to talk about more when we talk about influence.

There are, roughly, three things you can do when you hear some-thing you like from outside your genre. One is to completely ignore it and continue ploughing your own field. Another is to switch over completely and copy it totally, either for one song (like the white peo-ple who would record knock-offs of black hits) or for the rest of your career.

But the third thing you can do —the one that tends to lead to the most interesting music, and to the best art in any medium and genre, is to take what appeals to you about the other work, see what about it you can get to work with your own style, and incorporate it. Cover your inspiration's song, but do it in your own style and arrangement. Borrow that rhythm, but put your own melody line and lyrics over it. That's the way most truly interesting creative artists work, and it's what Mullican did. You hear any of his records, and you can hear a whole host of different influences in there, but he's not directly copying any of them.

People like that are the most important vectors for different musical ideas and the creation of new genres, and the most important influence that Mullican brought into country music, and which through him became a major influence on rock and roll, was Cajun music.

Cajun music is music made by the Cajun people in Louisiana. There's a whole lot of stuff around Cajun people that involves social class and racial stuff that, frankly, I'm not the best person to talk about. I'm likely to say something that is very offensive while trying to be well-meaning, because I simply don't know enough to talk sensibly. But the main thing you need to know here is that Cajun people are, or certainly were at this point, looked down upon by other residents of Louisiana, and by other Americans, and they have their own culture. They have their own cooking, largely involving things that many other cultures would discard as inedible, very heavily spiced; and they have their own language, Cajun French, rather than speaking English as so many other people in the US do.

It's Cajun and Creole culture which makes New Orleans, and Louisiana more generally, such a unique place, and which makes its music so different from the rest of the US. That's not the only factor, of course, but it's a big one.

We've talked a little bit already about New Orleans music, and Cajun music definitely plays a part in that style. But Cajun music has its own unique traditions, which we can only briefly touch upon here. If you're interested in hearing more about Cajun music as it applies to country music, as opposed to its influence on rock and roll, I'd recommend the episode of the great country music podcast Cocaine and Rhinestones[11] on Doug and Rusty Kershaw.

But this is, of course, a book about rock and roll music, and so I'm going to talk about the influence that Cajun music had on rock and roll, and that mostly came through zydeco, which is a genre that mostly grew up among Creole people – black and mixed race people in Louisiana who speak the same Cajun French as the white Cajuns.

The name "zydeco" itself tells you quite a bit about Cajun and Creole culture generally. There are a few plausible explanations for the word's origins, but the one I prefer is that it's a mispronunciation of the phrase "les haricots" – French for "the beans" – as used in the Cajun French phrase "Les haricots ne sont pas salés". That translates as "the beans aren't salty", a phrase which idiomatically meant "things are difficult" or "I'm tired". "Zydeco ne sont pas salés" was the title of a song recorded by the great zydeco accordion player Clifton Chenier, among others.

Zydeco is very closely related to another genre – fais dos dos music. This is music that's mostly played by white Cajun people, and it features the accordion and fiddle as the main instruments. Fais dos dos music has a strong Western Swing influence too, and Moon Mullican brought that fais dos dos music right into the mainstream of country music. You can hear it best on his hit "New Jole Blon" which went to number two on the country charts in 1951.

"New Jole Blon" is a really strange mixture of fais dos dos music and Western Swing. It has the high "ahh" sound that Bob Wills would make, and traditional country instrumentation, without the prominent accordion of fais dos dos music, but you've also got a thoroughly Louisiana melody, and you've got lyrics in an odd mixture of Cajun French and English, with lots of mentions of typical Cajun foods. It's a really *odd* track, frankly, not least because of the way he'll sometimes just depart totally from any conventional idea of melody and start singing random notes, trying to get as much lyric as he can into a space.

---

[11]http://cocaineandrhinestones.com

There were other Cajun musicians who played country music, of course, and vice versa, but if you listen to Mullican's records you get a real sense of someone who is equally at home with both kinds of music.

Now let's talk some more about Hank Williams.

I try to assume that the people reading this have absolutely no idea about any of the music I'm talking about. For everyone who knows far more details about the career of Benny Goodman or Bob Wills than I could ever fit into a four thousand word essay, there's someone who has literally never heard of those people, and I try to make these pieces readable for both.

I'm going to try that with Hank Williams as well, but that means I'll possibly be sounding patronising to some of you. Hank Williams is, by far, the most famous person I've dealt with so far in this book, and so you might think that I could just skip over the basics. But in my experience, there will be someone reading this who has never heard of Hank Williams and will appreciate the background.

So, Hank Williams was, as you may have guessed from that preamble, the most important single figure in country music, possibly ever and certainly after the death of Jimmie Rodgers. He had thirty-five hits in the country top ten, of which eleven went to number one in the country chart, and he wrote dozens upon dozens of country and gospel classics — "I Saw the Light", "I'm So Lonesome I Could Cry", "Lovesick Blues", "Your Cheatin' Heart", "Cold Cold Heart", "Hey Good Lookin'" and far more than I could name here. He was, in short, the most important songwriter alive during his very short career.

And it *was* a very short career. His career as a recording artist started in 1946, though he'd been a live performer for quite a few years already by then, and ended in 1952. In that six-year period, he basically redefined country and western music.

Unlike Moon Mullican, who basically did his one thing very, very well, but didn't do anything else, Hank Williams varied his style enormously. Where Mullican would pull different genres into his own style and incorporate them, Williams would somehow make the definitive records in a whole slew of different subgenres, while still always sounding like himself.

He started out, as so many musicians in the 1940s did, basically as a Jimmie Rodgers tribute act. Jimmie Rodgers the Singing Brakeman – not to be confused with the similarly-named blues musician – was one of those people who, if this book was going just a little further back in time, we would definitely be covering. His yodelling country blues was the most popular country music of his time, and massively influential on everyone.

Every country and western performer in the late thirties and forties was working in the margins of what Jimmie Rodgers did, but by the time Hank Williams finally got a record contract, he was very much his own man.

His first big hit, "Move it on Over" in 1947, is a fun example of hillbilly boogie. But that wasn't the only style that Williams could do. He made gospel records, heartbreaking ballads, and uptempo dance music, and he was good at all of it. He wrote a catalogue of songs that still gets covered, a lot, to this day, and he was popular enough that his name has given his son and grandson successful careers in the country music world, though neither of them has one millionth his talent.

And like Jimmie Rodgers, Hank Williams' appeal crossed racial boundaries. Johnny Otis used to tell a story about his tour bus stopping at a truck stop somewhere in the middle of the US, and getting out and seeing Williams there. Otis was a fan of Williams, and struck up a conversation, introducing him to Little Esther, and it turned out that Hank was a Johnny Otis fan. They all chatted and got back on the bus, and it drove off. Little Esther's mother asked Esther who she'd been speaking to, and she said, "Just some cowboy", but when Otis said it was Hank Williams, Esther's mother screamed, "You turn this bus round right now!" She was a fan and she desperately wanted to meet him.

Fats Domino, too, was a fan of Hank Williams, and so were many other rhythm and blues musicians. Williams was listening to rhythm and blues, and rhythm and blues musicians were listening to him. Don't let the cowboy hat fool you – everyone was listening to Hank Williams, except for the pop audience – and even they were listening to Williams' songs when, for example, Tony Bennett recorded them.

At the time we're talking about his career was on the way down. He was twenty-eight years old, but he was often in agony with back pain, and he was drinking too much and taking too many pills to numb the pain. He was getting divorced from his first wife, who was also his manager, and he was missing so many shows due to alcoholism that he was about to get fired from the Grand Ole Opry, the popular country radio show which was responsible more than anything else for making him a star. His life was, frankly, in a mess.

But he was still the most popular singer in country and western music, and he was still making great records – and one of the records he made, in June 1952, was a song he probably co-wrote with Moon Mullican, called "Jambalaya (On the Bayou)".

I say "probably", because no-one knows for sure, but it seems likely that Mullican co-wrote it, but wasn't given songwriting credit because he was contracted to a different publisher than Williams. Mullican recorded his own version of the song the same month, and Mullican's version had slightly different lyrics.

The two versions have a lot of basic similarities, but they both bear the unmistakeable stamp of their creators' sound on them. Mullican's has a far more hillbilly boogie or Cajun sound to it, while Williams has far more of a straight-ahead honky-tonk country sound.

But both tracks still have the same basic attraction to them. This is a celebration of Cajun culture, and in particular a celebration of the way Cajun people celebrated – their food, their music, and their dancing. "Jambalaya, crawfish pie and fillet gumbo", "pick guitar, fill fruit jar, we're gonna be gay-o". And this is at a time when Cajun people were, as far as the wider audience was concerned, about the lowest of the low if they were thought of at all. There's a defiance to the song that may not be audible to modern listeners, but is definitely there.

The guitar player on Williams' record, incidentally, is the great Chet Atkins. Like Hank, he was far more influential in country music than in rock and roll – though he always denied that he was a country guitarist, saying rather that he was "a guitarist, period" – but he was one of the great guitarists of all time, and also produced a handful of early rock and roll classics.

But what we can see from both versions of "Jambalaya" is that there was an appetite in country music for a kind of music that was rather broader than the styles that the major labels were interested in. If you just looked at the history of Nashville pop-country, you'd think that country music was as bland and whitebread as the crooners who were dominating popular music at the time, but country music was a stranger, and more eclectic, music than the media impression of it would have you think. It was a music that had as much to do with the blues as rhythm and blues did, and which had an audience that was far happier with experiment and new ideas than you might think.

In the 1950s, this tendency in country music would lead to a number of subgenres of its own, many of which would be major influences on rock and roll. There was bluegrass, which started in the late forties and which we'll be talking about a lot later, and there was rockabilly, and the Bakersfield sound.

But "Jambalaya" is a record which had the same kind of crossover appeal as "Choo Choo Ch'Boogie" had in the opposite direction. Like the stew from which it takes its name, it takes elements from a variety of different areas and throws them together, creating something that had a much greater appeal than you might imagine.

"Jambalaya" would go on to be a staple of early rock and roll music. It was especially loved by musicians from Louisiana, like Fats Domino and Jerry Lee Lewis, both of whom made great piano-driven records of the song. Williams is remembered now as a country musician, but that's largely because he died before the rock and roll craze. Had he lived, it's entirely possible we'd now be thinking of him as a rockabilly star.

Sadly, Hank Williams would not live to see the immense influence he was having on a generation of young musicians who would go on to revolutionise not only country music, but also rock and roll. Barely six months after recording "Jambalaya" he was dead. His back pain had led him to drink even more heavily, he'd developed even more of a dependency on pills, he'd developed a reputation for unreliability and missing shows – he was a mess. And on New Year's Eve, 1952, while he was being driven from Tennessee to Ohio, for a show he had to play on New Year's Day, he fell asleep in the back of the car and never woke up.

When his death was announced at the show he'd been driving to, the audience laughed at first – they thought it was just another excuse for him not turning up. His last single, released a month earlier, was titled "I'll Never Get Out of This World Alive". He was twenty-nine years old.

"Hound Dog"

One of the things that is easy to miss when talking about early rock and roll is that much of the development of the genre is about the liminal spaces in race in America.

(Before I start talking about this, a disclaimer I have to make: I'm a white person, from a different country, born decades after the events I'm talking about. I'm trying to be as accurate as I can here, and as sensitive as I can, but I apologise if I mess up, and nothing I say here should be taken as more accurate or authoritative than the words of the people who were actually affected).

"Black" and "white" are two categories imposed by culture, and like all culturally-imposed binaries, they're essentially arbitrary and don't really map very well onto really existing people. There have always been people who don't fit neatly into the boxes that a racist society insists everyone fits into, and part of the reason that rock and roll happened when it did was that in the 1950s America was in the process of redefining those boxes, and moving some people who would have previously fit into one category into the other. The lines were being redrawn, and that led to some interesting art happening at the borders.

(That sounds like I'm doing the "at least some good art came from this terrible event" thing. I'm really, really, not. Racism in all its forms is nothing but negative, and its distortions of culture are all negative too. But they do exist, and need noting when talking about culture subject to those distortions).

There were a lot of groups who would now be regarded as white in the USA but which back in the 1940s and 1950s weren't, quite. Jewish people, for example, were still legally discriminated against in a lot of places (unlike now, when they're merely *illegally* discriminated

163

against). They weren't black, but they weren't quite white either. The same went for several other ethnic minorities, like Greek people.

So it's perhaps not all that surprising that one of the most successful blues records of all time, which later inspired an even more successful rock and roll record, was the result of a collaboration between a black singer, a Greek-American producer who said "As a kid I decided that if our society dictated that one had to be black or white, I would be black", and two Jewish songwriters.

Willie Mae Thornton was big in every sense. She weighed three hundred and fifty pounds, or about twenty-five stone, and she had a voice to match it – she would often claim that she didn't need a microphone, because she was louder than any microphone anyway.

She became a blues singer when she was fourteen, thanks to her mentor, a singer called "Diamond Teeth Mary". Diamond Teeth Mary kept performing until the 1990s, when she was *in* her nineties. She performed constantly until her death aged ninety-seven, but she only made her first record when she was ninety-two.

Diamond Teeth Mary was the half-sister of the great blues singer Bessie Smith – Mary had four stepmothers, one of whom was Smith's mother – and she was a powerful singer herself, singing with the Hot Harlem Revue around Alabama. She was called "Diamond Teeth Mary" because she had diamonds embedded in her front teeth, so she'd be more imposing on stage.

Diamond Teeth Mary heard the young Willie Mae Thornton singing while she was working on a garbage truck, got her to get off the garbage truck, and got her a job with the revue. Mary probably felt a kinship with the fourteen-year-old Willie Mae, a girl who only wore boys' clothes – Mary had, herself, become a performer when she was only thirteen, having run away from her abusive family, dressed in boy's clothes, and joined the circus.

Willie Mae Thornton stayed with that revue for most of the next decade, playing with musicians like Richard Penniman, who would later become known as Little Richard, playing to audiences that were mostly black and also (according to Little Richard) exclusively gay. The Hot Harlem Revue was not exactly respectable – Sammy Green, who managed it, made most of his money from owning several brothels – but it was somewhere that a young singer could very quickly learn how to be an entertainer.

You had to be impressive as a female blues singer in the 1940s, especially if, as with Willie Mae Thornton, you were also not conventionally attractive and not of a societally-approved sexuality or gender identity. I've seen suggestions from people who would know that Thornton was bisexual, but from others like Johnny Otis that she showed no interest in men or women (though she did have a child in her teens), and I've also seen suggestions that she may have been trans (though I'm going to refer to her using she and her pronouns here as that's what she used throughout her life).

She was a remarkable figure in many ways. One of her favourite drinks was embalming fluid and grape juice (just in case anyone was considering doing this, please don't. It's really not a good idea, at all, even a little bit. Don't drink embalming fluid.) According to Jerry Leiber she had razor scars all over her face. She was a very, very, intimidating person.

At the very least, she didn't fit into neat boxes.

But you see, all that stuff I just said... *that* is putting her into a box – the caricature angry, aggressive, black woman. And that was a box she never liked to be put in either, but which she was put in by other people. What I just said, you'll notice, is all about what other people thought of her, and that's not always what she thought of herself. She would get very upset that people would say she used to fight promoters, saying "I never did fight the promoters. All I ever did was ask them for my money. Pay me and there won't be no hard feelings."

And while she is uniformly described as "masculine-looking" (whatever *that* means), she put it rather differently, saying "I don't go out on stage trying to look pretty. I was *born* pretty."

Thornton is someone who didn't get to tell her own story much. Much of what we know about her is from other people's impressions of her, and usually the impressions of men. People who knew her well described her as intelligent, kind, charming, funny, and hugely talented, while people who only spent a brief time around her tend to have talked about the razor scars on her face or how aggressive she seemed. Depending on which narrative you choose, you can make a very good case for her being either a loud, swaggering, vulgar, aggressive stereotype of unfeminine black femininity, or a rather sweet, vulnerable, person who intimidated men simply by her physical size, her race, and her loud voice, and who may have played up to their expectations at times, but who never liked that, and who used alcohol and other substances to cope with what wasn't a very happy life, while remaining outwardly happy.

But because we as a society value black women so little, most of this story is filtered through the white men who told it, so be aware that in what follows, you may find yourself picturing a caricature figure, seeing Big Mama as the angry sassy black woman you've seen in a million films. She was a real person, and I wish we had more of her own words to set against this.

While the Hot Harlem Revue was a good place to learn to be an entertainer, it wasn't necessarily the best place to work if you actually wanted to earn a living, and Willie Mae had to supplement her income by shining shoes. She often had to sleep in all-night restaurants and bars, because she couldn't afford to pay rent, and go begging door to door for food. But she would pretend to everyone she knew that everything was all right, and smile for everyone. She became pregnant in her teens, and tried to be a good mother to the child, but she was deemed an unfit mother due to poverty and the child was taken away from her.

After several years with the Harlem Revue, she quit them because she was being cheated out of money, and decided to stay in Houston, Texas, which is where she really started to build an audience. Around this time she recorded her first single, "All Right Baby", credited to "The Harlem Stars" – it's a song she wrote herself, and it's a boogie track very much in the vein of Big Joe Turner.

Shortly after moving to Houston, she began working for Don Robey, who ran Peacock Records and the Bronze Peacock Club. Robey had a mixed reputation – most singers and musicians he worked with thought highly of him, but most songwriters he worked with were less enamoured of his penchant for stealing their money and credit.

Robey had a reputation as a thug, too, but according to Little Richard he was too scared of Thornton to beat her up like he would his other acts.

She recorded several singles for Peacock, but her talents weren't really suited to the slick Texas blues backing she was given. The kind of music Peacock put out was in the smoother style that was becoming prominent in the south-western US – the kind of music that people like Lightnin' Hopkins made – and that wasn't really suited to Thornton's louder, more emotional style. But after a run of unsuccessful singles, things started to change.

Peacock Records was in the process of expanding. Don Robey acquired another label, Duke Records of Memphis, and merged them, and he got distributors working with him in different areas of the country. And he started working with Johnny Otis.

Otis came to Texas, and he and Robey made a deal. Otis would audition several of the acts that were on Duke and Peacock records, people like Thornton who had not had much success but clearly had talent, and he would incorporate them into his Johnny Otis Revue. Otis would take charge of producing their records, which would be cut in Los Angeles with Otis' band, and he would let Robey release the results.

Some of the artists still couldn't find their commercial potential even with Otis producing. For example, Little Richard's recordings with Otis, while interesting, are an artistic dead-end for him. Though of course, Little Richard went on to do quite well for himself later. . .

But in the case of Willie Mae Thornton, something clicked. The two became lifelong friends, and also began a remarkable collaboration, with Otis being the first person to encourage Thornton to play harmonica as well as sing. On her first show with the Johnny Otis Revue, Willie Mae Thornton sang "Have Mercy Baby", the then-current hit by Billy Ward and the Dominoes, and the audience went so wild that they had to stop the show. After that point, they had to put Thornton at the top of the bill, after even Little Esther, so the audience would allow the other performers to come on.

And with the top billing came a change of name. Johnny Otis had a knack for giving artists new names – as well as Little Esther, he also gave Etta James and Sugar Pie DeSanto their stage names – and in the case of Willie Mae Thornton, for the rest of her career she was known as "Big Mama" Thornton.

At the time we're talking about, Otis was, as much as a musician, a fixer, a wheeler-dealer, a person who brought people together. And this was a role that those people on the margins of whiteness – like Otis, a son of Greek immigrants who chose to live among black culture – excelled in. The people who were on the borderline between the two different conceptions of race often ended up as backroom facilitators, bringing white money to black artists – people like Milt Gabler or Ahmet Ertegun or Cosimo Matassa, people of ethnicities that didn't quite fit into the black/white binary, people who were white enough to use white privilege to get financing, but not so white they identified with the majority culture.

And in 1952, the people Otis brought together were Big Mama Thornton and two young songwriters who would change the world of music.

Jerry Leiber and Mike Stoller were Jewish teenagers, both of whom had moved to California from elsewhere – Stoller from New York and Leiber from Maryland. Mike Stoller was a musician, who was into modern jazz and modern art music – he loved Bartók and Thelonius Monk – but he also had a background in stride and boogie woogie. After he found normal piano lessons uncongenial, he'd been offered lessons by the great James P Johnson, who had taught him how to play boogie. James P Johnson was essentially the inventor of jazz piano. He'd started out playing ragtime, and had invented the stride piano style, and taught it to Fats Waller. He'd been one of the performers at the Spirituals to Swing concerts, and was also a major composer of serious music, but what he taught young Mike Stoller was how to play a boogie bassline, how to understand twelve-bar blues structure and other rudiments of the blues pianist's art. As Stoller later put it, "It was as if Beethoven were about to give me a lesson—except that, unlike James P. Johnson, Beethoven had never given a piano lesson to Fats Waller".

After moving to LA, Stoller started studying with Arthur Lange, a composer of film soundtracks, and playing piano for jazz bands, jamming with people like Chet Baker.

Meanwhile, Jerry Leiber was a blues fanatic, who had had a minor epiphany after hearing Jimmy Witherspoon's "Ain't Nobody's Business if I Do". Leiber had heard Witherspoon's song, and realised that he could do that, and he decided he was going to. He was going to become a songwriter, and he started working on song lyrics immediately, although he had no idea how to go about getting anyone to perform them.

The first song he wrote was called "Real Ugly Woman". The lyrics went "She's a real ugly woman, don't see how she got that way/Every time she comes 'round, she runs all my friends away".

He didn't have much knowledge of the music business, but luckily that knowledge walked right through the door. Leiber was working at a small record store, and one day Lester Sill, who was the national sales manager for Modern Records, walked into the shop.

Modern Records was one of the dozens of tiny blues labels that were springing up across the country, usually run by Jewish and Italian entrepreneurs who could see the potential in black music even if the owners of the major labels couldn't, and Sill was a real enthusiast for the music he was selling. He started pitching records to Jerry Leiber, telling him he'd love them, acting as if Leiber was the most important person in the world, even though Leiber kept explaining he didn't make the buying decisions for the shop, he was only a shop assistant.

Eventually, after playing a record called "Boogie Chillen", by a new artist called John Lee Hooker, which excited Leiber enormously, Sill asked Leiber what he was going to do when he grew up. Leiber replied that he was already grown up, but he planned to become a songwriter. Sill asked to hear one of the songs, and Leiber sang "Real Ugly Woman" to him. Sill liked it, and asked for copies of his songs. When Leiber explained that he didn't know how to write music, Sill told him to find a partner who did.

Leiber found Stoller through a mutual friend, who told Leiber that Stoller knew about music. Leiber phoned Stoller, who was unimpressed by the idea of writing songs together, because to his mind "songs" were the kind of thing that was dominating the pop charts at the time, the kind of thing that Patti Page or someone would record, not something someone who was into hard bop music would like. But Leiber eventually persuaded him to at least take a look at the lyrics he'd been writing.

Stoller looked at the lyrics to "Real Ugly Woman", and said "These are blues! You didn't tell me you were writing blues. I love the blues."

They started collaborating together that day, in 1950, and worked together for the rest of their lives. Soon Jimmy Witherspoon himself was singing "Real Ugly Woman", just like Leiber had hoped when he'd started writing.

Soon after, Ralph Bass moved to LA from New York. He'd got to know Leiber and Stoller on their trips East and when he moved west he introduced them to Johnny Otis, who Bass had kept in touch with after leaving Savoy Records. Through the connection with Otis and Bass, they wrote many songs for Little Esther, and they also started a partnership with Little Esther's former backing vocalists the Robins, who put out the very first single with a Leiber and Stoller writing credit, "That's What the Good Book Says". The partnership between the Leiber and Stoller team and the Robins would end up defining all their careers.

But right now, Leiber and Stoller were a couple of teenagers who were working with their heroes. And at least one of those heroes was not very impressed. Johnny Otis had introduced them to Big Mama Thornton and asked if they had a song for her. They said, "We don't, but we will have in a few minutes", ran back to Stoller's house, and quickly knocked out "Hound Dog" in a style that they thought would suit Thornton.

"Hound dog" was, at the time, black slang for a gigolo, and what Leiber and Stoller wanted to do was have a song that was as aggressive as possible, with their singer demeaning the man she was singing to, while also including sexual undertones. (Those undertones were strengthened in the follow-up Thornton recorded, "Tom Cat", where she told a "tom cat" "I ain't going to feed you fish no more").

Leiber and Stoller had very strong ideas about how their new song should be performed, and they made the mistake of telling her about them. Big Mama Thornton was not about to let two white teenagers teach her how to sing the blues.

In truth, Big Mama Thornton was only a few years older than those kids – they were in their late teens, and she was in her mid twenties – but that kind of gap can seem like a big difference, and it might well also be that Thornton was offended by the fact that these white men were telling her, a black woman, how to do her job. So when Jerry Leiber insisted that rather than croon the song as she had been doing, she should "attack it", her response was to point to her crotch and say, "Attack this!"

Johnny Otis didn't help by playing a rimshot right after Thornton said that. But he then suggested that Leiber sing it for Thornton, and she did listen, and agreed to try it that way. Once the communication problem had been sorted, Thornton turned in the definitive performance of the song.

"Hound Dog" is also notable as being one of the last times Johnny Otis played drums on a record. While he could still play the vibraphone, he could no longer hold his drumsticks properly, and so he'd largely given up drumming.

But when they were working out the arrangement for the recording session, Otis played the drums in the rehearsals, playing with a style of his own, turning the snare off on his snare drum so it sounded more like a tom-tom. When it came to the actual recording, though, Otis was in the control room, while a session drummer was playing in the studio. But Leiber and Stoller both agreed that he simply wasn't playing the part properly, and enticed Otis into the studio and got him to play the part as he'd been playing it in rehearsal.

What happened next is a subject of much debate. What everyone is agreed on is that Otis was credited as a co-writer early on, but that he wasn't credited later. The story as Otis told it is that he did actually help Leiber and Stoller pull the song together, rewriting it with them, as well as doing the arrangement in the studio (which no-one disputes him doing). He claimed specifically that he'd come up with the lines "You made me feel so blue, you make me weep and moan/You ain't looking for a woman, you're just looking for a home", because Leiber and Stoller had had, "some derogatory crap" in there; that he'd had to remove references to chicken and watermelon, and that he constantly had to edit their songs.

He said that Leiber and Stoller acknowledged he was a co-writer right up until the point where Elvis Presley wanted to record the song a few years later.

Leiber and Stoller, on the other hand, claimed that Otis had no involvement with the songwriting, and that he'd misrepresented himself to Don Robey. They claimed that Otis had falsely claimed he had power of attorney for them, as well as falsely claiming to have co-written the song, and deliberately defrauded them.

On the other hand, it's only because of Otis that Leiber and Stoller got credit at all. Don Robey, who as I've mentioned was a notorious thief of writing credits, originally put himself and Thornton down as the writers, and it was Otis who got the credits amended.

Either way, Leiber and Stoller have, for more than sixty years, had the sole songwriting credits for the track, and Otis never bothered to dispute their claim in court. Indeed, they don't appear to have had any particular animosity, and they all repeatedly praised the others' abilities.

Although as Otis put it "I could have sent my kids to college, like they sent theirs. But, oh well, if I dwell on that I get quite unhappy, so we try to move on."

What's most ridiculous about the whole credit mess is that Elvis' version bore almost no resemblance to the song Leiber and Stoller wrote. Elvis' version was a cover of a version by the white Vegas lounge band Freddie Bell and the Bellboys, which was more or less a parody of the original.

But still, Elvis came later, as did the money. In 1953, all Leiber and Stoller got for a record that sold over a million copies was a cheque for one thousand two hundred dollars. A cheque which bounced. As a result of their experience getting ripped off by Robey, Leiber and Stoller formed their own record label with Lester Sill.

Big Mama Thornton did actually get paid for her million-seller – a whole five hundred dollars – but she never had the success she deserved. She later wrote the song "Ball and Chain", which Janis Joplin later had a hit with, and you can hear from Thornton's version just how much Joplin took from Thornton's vocal style. But due to a bad contract Thornton never made a penny in royalties from the song she wrote (which is a far more egregious injustice than the one people complain about, that Elvis had a hit with "Hound Dog" – she didn't write that one, and Elvis did pay the writers).

She continued performing until a few days before she died, in July 1984, despite getting so sick and losing so much weight (she was under a hundred pounds at the end) that she was almost unrecognisable. She died two weeks before Little Esther, and like Esther, she had asked Johnny Otis, now the Reverend Johnny Otis, to give her eulogy.

Otis said, in part "Mama always told me that the blues were more important than having money. She told me: Artists are artists and businessmen are businessmen. But the trouble is the artist's money stays in the businessmen's hands... Don't waste your sorrow on Big Mama. She's free. Don't feel sorry for Big Mama. There's no more pain. No more suffering in a society where the color of skin was more important than the quality of your talent."

"Crazy Man Crazy"

We talked back in the chapter on "The Fat Man" about how there were multiple different musics that got lumped together in the mid-fifties under the name "rock and roll". There's rockabilly, Chicago rhythm and blues, doo wop, New Orleans R&B, the coastal jump bands, and Northern band rock and roll. We've looked at most of these – and the ones we haven't we'll be looking at over the next few weeks – but what we haven't looked at so far is Northern band rock and roll.

And in many ways that's the most interesting of all the rock and roll musics, because it's the one that at first glance has had almost no obvious impact on anything that followed, but it's also the one that first came to the attention of the white American public as rock and roll – the one that made the newspapers and got the headlines. And it's the one that had only one real example. While the other styles of music had dozens of people making them, Northern band rock and roll really only had Bill Haley and the Comets. A whole pillar of rock and roll – a whole massive strand of the contemporary view of this music – was down to the work of one band who had no peers and left no real legacy.

Or at least, they *seem* to have left no legacy, until you look a bit closer. But before we look at where the Comets' music led, we should look at where they were coming from.

Bill Haley didn't set out to be a rock and roll star, because when he started there was no such thing. He set out to be a country and western singer.

He played with various country bands over the years – bands with names like the Down Homers and the Texas Range Riders – before he decided to become a band leader himself, and started his own band, the Four Aces of Western Swing. Obviously this wasn't a full Western swing band in the style of Bob Wills' band, but they played a stripped-down version which captured much of the appeal of the music – and which had a secret weapon in Haley himself, the Indiana State Yodelling Champion. Yes, yodelling. At the time, Jimmie Rodgers was a huge, huge, star, and his gimmick was his yodelling.

Every country singer in the 1940s wanted to sound like Jimmie Rodgers – at least until Ernest Tubb and Hank Williams came along and everyone wanted to sound like them instead. And that's the sound that Bill Haley was going for when he started the Four Aces of Western Swing.

That's how Bill Haley started out – as a Jimmie Rodgers imitator whose greatest strength was his yodelling. Listening to, say, "Yodel Your Blues Away", it definitely doesn't sound like the work of someone who would change music forever. You'd expect, without knowing the rest of his history, that the Four Aces of Western Swing would become a footnote to a footnote; a band who, if they were remembered at all, would be remembered for one or two singles included on some big box set compilation of vintage country music.

Without Bill Haley's future career, it's unlikely there'd be any more attention paid to the Four Aces than that. They don't really make a dent in country music history, and didn't have the kind of career that suggested they would ever do so. Most of their records didn't even get a proper release – Haley was signed to a label called Cowboy Records, which was a Mafia-run organisation. The first five thousand copies of every Cowboy release went to Mafia-owned jukeboxes, for free, and artists would only get royalties on any records sold after that. Since jukeboxes accounted for the majority of the money in the record business at this point, that didn't leave much for the artists – especially as Haley had to pay his own recording and production costs, and he had to do any promotion himself – buying boxes of records at $62.50 for two hundred and fifty copies, and sending them out to DJs through the post at his own expense.

It was basically a glorified vanity label, and the only reason Haley got any airplay at all was because he was himself a DJ. And after a few unsuccessful singles, he decided to give up on performance and become just a DJ.

But soon Haley had a new band, which would become far more successful – Bill Haley and his... Saddlemen.

Yes, the Saddlemen.

By all accounts, the Saddlemen weren't Haley's idea. One day two musicians turned up at the radio station, saying they wanted to join his band. Billy Williamson and Johnny Grande were unhappy with the band they were performing in, and had heard Haley performing with his band on the radio. They had decided that Haley's band would be a perfect showcase for their talents on steel guitar and accordion, and had travelled from Newark New Jersey to Chester Pennsylvania to see him. But they'd showed up to discover that he didn't have a band any more.

They eventually persuaded him that it would be worth his while going back into music, and Haley arranged for the band to get a show once a week on the station he was DJing on.

While Haley was the leader on stage, they were an equal partnership – the Saddlemen, and later the Comets, split money four ways between Haley, Williamson, Grande, and the band's manager; with any other band members who were later hired, such as drummers and bass players, being on a fixed salary paid out by the partnership.

The band didn't make much money at first. They all had other jobs, with Williamson and Grande working all sorts of odd jobs, while Haley was doing so much work at the radio station that he often ended up sleeping there. Haley worked so hard that his marriage disintegrated, but the Saddlemen had one big advantage – they had the radio station's recording studio to use for their rehearsals, and they were able to use the studio's recording equipment to play back their rehearsals and learn, something that very few bands had at the time. They spent two whole years rehearsing every day, and taking whatever gigs they could, and that eventually started to pay off.

The Saddlemen started out making the same kind of music that the Four Aces had made. They put out decent, but not massively impressive, records on all sorts of tiny labels. Most of these recordings were called things like "Ten Gallon Stetson", and in one case the single wasn't even released as the Saddlemen but as Reno Browne and Her Buckaroos. This was about as generic as country and western music could get.

But Bill Haley had bigger plans, inspired by the show that was on right before his.

The radio had changed enormously in a very short period of time. Before the Second World War, playing records on the radio had been almost unknown, until in 1935 the first recognised DJ, Martin Block, started his radio show *Make Believe Ballroom*, in which he would pretend to be introducing all sorts of different bands. The record labels spent much of the next few years fighting the same kind of copyright actions they would later fight against the Internet, in this case aided by the AFM, but harmed by the fact that there was no federal copyright protection for sound recordings until the 1970s.

Indeed a lot of the musicians' strikes of the 1940s were, in part, about the issue of playing records on the radio. But eventually, the record labels – especially the ones, like RCA and Columbia, which were also radio network owners – realised that being played on the radio was great advertising for their records, and stopped fighting it.

And at the same time, there was a massive expansion in radio stations, and a drop in advertising money. After the war, restrictions on broadcasting were lifted, and within four years there were more than twice as many radio stations as there had been in 1946. But at the same time, the networks were no longer making as much money from advertising, which started going to TV instead. The solution was to go for cheap, local, programming – and there was little programming that was cheaper than getting a man to sit in the studio and play records.

And in 1948 and 49, Columbia and RCA introduced "high fidelity" records; the 33RPM album from Columbia, and the 45RPM single from RCA. These didn't have the problems that 78s had, of poor sound quality and quick degradation, and so the final barrier to radio stations becoming devoted to recorded music was lifted.

This is, incidentally, why the earlier musicians we've talked about in this series are largely forgotten compared to musicians from even a few years later – their records came out on 78s. Radio stations threw out all their old 78s when they could start playing 45s, and so you'd never hear a Wynonie Harris or Louis Jordan played even as a golden oldie, because the radio stations didn't have those records any more. They disappeared from the cultural memory, in a way the fifties acts didn't.

And the time we're talking about now is right when that growth in the radio was at its height, and all the new radio stations were turning to recorded music.

But in the early fifties, only a handful of stations were playing black music, only for an hour or two a day at most. And when they did, the DJ was always a white man, but usually a white man who could "sound black", and thought himself part of black culture. Zenas Sears in Atlanta, Dewey Phillips in Memphis, Alan Freed in Cleveland, Johnny Otis in LA – all of these were people who even many of their black listeners presumed were black, playing black records, speaking in black slang.

All of them, of course, used their privilege as white men to get jobs that black people simply weren't given. But that was the closest that black people came to representation on the radio at the time, and those radio shows were precious to many of them. People would tune in from hundreds of miles away to hear those few DJs who for one hour a day were playing their music.

And the show that was on before Bill Haley's country and western show was one of those handful of R&B shows. *Judge Rhythm's Court* was presented by a white man in his forties named Jim Reeves (not the singer of the same name) under the name of "Shorty the Bailiff". Reeves' theme song was "Rock the Joint" by Jimmy Preston and the Prestonians.

Haley liked the music that Reeves was playing – in particular, he became a big fan of Big Joe Turner and Ruth Brown – and he started adding some of the R&B songs to the Saddlemen's setlists, and noticed they went down especially well with the younger audiences. But they didn't record those songs in their rare recording sessions for small labels.

Until, that is, the Saddlemen signed up to Holiday Records. As soon as they started with Holiday, their style changed completely.

Holiday, and its sister label Essex which also released Saddlemen records, were owned by Dave Miller, who also owned the pressing plant that had pressed Haley's earlier records for the Cowboy label, and Miller had similar mob connections. Haley would later claim that while Miller always said the money to start the record labels had come from a government subsidy, in fact it had been paid by the Mafia. His labels had started up during the musicians' union strikes of the 1940s, to put out records by non-union musicians, and Miller wasn't too concerned about bothering to pay royalties or other such niceties.

Haley also later claimed that Miller invented payola – the practice of paying DJs to play records. This was something that a lot of independent labels did in the early fifties, and was one of the ways they managed to get heard, even as many of the big labels were still cautious about the radio.

Miller wanted to have big hits, and in particular he wanted to find ways to get both the white and black markets with the same records, and here he had an ally in Haley, who took a scientific approach to maximising his band's success. Haley would try things like turning up the band's amplifiers, on the theory that if customers couldn't hear themselves talking, they'd be more likely to dance – and then turning the amps back down when the bar owners would complain that if the customers danced too much they wouldn't buy as many drinks.

Haley was willing to work hard and try literally anything in order to make his band a success, and wasn't afraid to try new ideas and then throw them away if they didn't work. This makes his discography frustrating for listeners now – it's a long record of failed experiments, dead ends, and stylistic aberrations unlike almost any other successful artist's. This is someone not blessed with a huge abundance of natural talent, but willing to work much harder in order to make a success of things anyway.

Miller was a natural ally in this, and they hit on a formula which would be independently reinvented a couple of years later by Sam Phillips for Elvis' records – putting out singles with a country song on one side and an R&B song on the other, to try to appeal to both white and black markets.

And one song that Dave Miller heard and thought that might suit Haley's band was "Rocket "88"".

This might have seemed an odd decision – after all, "Rocket "88"" was a horn-driven rhythm and blues song, while the Saddlemen at this point consisted of Haley on acoustic guitar, double-bass player Al Rex, Billy Williamson on steel guitar, and Johnny Grande, an accordion player who could double on piano.

This doesn't sound the most propitious lineup for an R&B song, but along with ace session guitarist Danny Cedrone they actually managed to come up with something rather impressive. It's not a patch on the original, but translating that R&B song into a western swing style had ended up with something a little different to the hillbilly boogie one might expect. In particular, there's the drum sound... or at least, what the casual listener might think was a drum sound. But there are no drums there. It's what's called slapback bass.

Now, before we go any further, I'd better explain that there's some terminological confusion, because "slap bass" is a similar but not identical electric bass technique, while the word "slapback" is also used for the echo used on some rockabilly records, so talking about "rockabilly slapback bass" can end up a bit like "Who's on first?"

But what I mean when I talk about slapback bass is a style of bass playing used on many rockabilly records. It's used in other genres, too, but it basically came to rockabilly because of Bill Haley's band, and because of the playing style Haley's bass players Al Rex and Marshall Lytle used.

With slapback bass, you're playing a double bass, and you play it pizzicato, plucking the strings. But you don't just pluck them, you pull them forward and let them slap right back onto the bridge of the instrument, which makes a sort of clicking sound. At the same time, you might also hit the strings to mute them – which also makes a clicking sound as well. And you might also hit the body of the instrument, making a loud thumping noise.

Given the recording techniques in use at the time, slapback bass could often sound a lot like drums on a recording, though you'd never mistake one for the other in a live performance.

And at a time when country music wasn't particularly keen on the whole idea of a drum kit – which was seen as a dangerous innovation from the jazz world, not something that country and western musicians should be playing, though by this time Bob Wills had been using one in his band for a decade – having something else that could keep the beat and act as a percussion instrument was vital, and slapback bass was one of the big innovations that Haley's band popularised.

So yes, Bill Haley and the Saddlemen's version of "Rocket "88"" had no drum kit on it. Despite this, some people still cite this, rather than Jackie Brenston's original, as "the first rock and roll record". As we've said many times, though, there is no such thing. But Haley's recording makes an attractive candidate – it's the mythical "merging of black R&B with white country music", which of course was something that had been happening since the very start, but which people seem to regard as something that marked out rock and roll, and it's the first recording in this style by the person who went on to have the first really massive rock and roll hit to cross over into the pop charts.

"Rocket "88"" wasn't that big hit. But Haley and Miller felt like they were on to something, and they kept trying to come up with something that would work in that style. They put out quite a few singles that were almost, but not quite, what they were after, things like a remake of "Wabash Cannonball" retitled "Jukebox Cannonball", and then they finally hit on the perfect formula with "Rock the Joint", which had been in Haley's setlist off and on since he heard it on Jim Reeves' programme.

The original "Rock the Joint" had been one of the many, many, records that attempted to cash in on the rock craze ignited by Wynonie Harris' version of "Good Rockin' Tonight", but it hadn't done much out- side of the Philadelphia area. Haley and the band went into the studio to record their own version, which had a very different arrangement – and in particular had an astonishing guitar solo.

That solo is played by the session musician, Danny Cedrone, who played the lead guitar on almost all of Haley's early records. He wasn't a member of the band – Haley kept costs low in these early years by having as small a band as possible, but hiring extra musicians for the recordings to beef up the sound – but he was someone that Haley trusted to always play the right parts on his records.

Haley and Cedrone were close enough that in 1952 – after "Rocket "88"" but before "Rock the Joint" – Haley gave Cedrone a song for his own band, The Esquire Boys. That song, "Rock-A-Beatin' Boogie", would probably have been a hit for Haley, had he recorded it at the time – instead, he didn't record it for another three years. But that song, too, shows that he was on the right track. He was searching for something, and finding it occasionally, but not always recognising it when he had it.

"Rock the Joint" was a massive success, by the standards of a small indie country label, reportedly selling as much as four hundred thousand copies. But even after "Rock the Joint", the problems continued. Haley's next two records were "Dance With a Dolly (With a Hole in Her Stockin')" – which was to the tune of "Buffalo Gals Won't You Come Out Tonight?" – and "Stop Beatin' Around the Mulberry Bush", which was a rewrite of "Here We Go Round the Mulberry Bush" as a hillbilly boogie.

But "Stop Beatin' Around the Mulberry Bush" was notable for one reason – it was the first record by "Bill Haley and Haley's Comets", rather than by the Saddlemen. The pun on Halley's comet was obvious, but the real importance of the name change is that it marked a definitive moment when the band stopped thinking of themselves as a country and western band and started thinking of themselves as something else – Haley didn't pick up on the term "rock and roll" til fairly late, but it was clear that that was what he thought he should be doing now. They now had a drummer, too – Dick Richards – and a sax player. Al Rex was temporarily gone, replaced by Marshall Lytle, but Rex would be back in 1955.

They were still veering wildly between rhythm and blues covers, country songs, and outright novelty records, but they were slowly narrowing down what they were trying to do, and hitting a target more and more often – they were making records about rhythm, using slang catchphrases and trying to appeal to a younger audience.

And there was a genuine excitement in some of their stage performances. Haley would never be the most exciting vocalist when working in this new rock and roll idiom – he was someone who was a natural country singer and wasn't familiar with the idioms he was incorporating into his new music, so there was a sense of distance there – but the band would make up for that on stage, with the bass player riding his bass (a common technique for getting an audience going at this point) and the saxophone player lying on his back to play solos.

And that excitement shone through in "Crazy Man Crazy", which became the Comets' first real big hit.

This was another example of the way that Haley would take a scientific approach to his band's success. He and his band members had realised that the key to success in the record business was going to be appealing to teenagers, who were a fast-growing demographic and who, for the first time in American history, had some real buying power. But teenagers couldn't go to the bars where country musicians played, and at the time there were very few entertainment venues of any type that catered to teenagers.

So Bill Haley and the Comets played, by Johnny Grande's count, one hundred and eighty-three school assemblies, for free. And at every show they would make note of what songs the kids liked, which ones got them dancing, which ones they were less impressed by, and they would hone their act to appeal to these kids.

And one thing Haley noted was that the teenagers' favourite slang expression was "crazy", and so he wrote a song based around the word. That went to number fifteen on the pop charts, a truly massive success for a country and western band.

Marshall Lytle, the Comets' bass player, later claimed that he had co-written the song and not got the credit, but the other Comets disputed his claims.

This is another of those records that is cited as the first rock and roll record, or the first rock and roll hit, and certainly it's the first example of a *white* band playing this kind of music to make the charts. And, more fairly to Haley, it's the first example of a band using guitars as their primary instruments to get onto the charts playing something that resembles jump band music. "Crazy Man Crazy" is very clearly patterned after Louis Jordan, but they play guitar fills for parts which would be played by a horn section on Jordan's records.

With Danny Cedrone's solos, Bill Haley and the Comets were responsible for making the guitar the standard lead instrument for rock and roll, although it took a while for that to become the standard, and we will see plenty of piano and saxophone, including on later records by Haley himself.

So why was Haley doing something so different from what everyone else did? In part, I think that can be linked to the reason he didn't stay successful very long – he wasn't part of a scene at all.

When we look at almost all the other musicians we're talking about in this series, you'll see that they're all connected to other musicians. The myth of the lone genius is just that – a myth. What actually tends to happen is that the "lone genius" is someone who uses the abilities of others and then pretends it was all himself – and it almost always is a him. There's a whole peer group there, who get conveniently erased.

But the fact remains that Haley and the Comets, as a group, didn't have any kind of peer group or community. They weren't part of a scene, and really had no peers doing what they were doing. There was no-one to tell them what to do, or what not to do.

So Bill Haley and the Comets had started something unique. But it was that very uniqueness that was to cause them problems. . .

"Money Honey"

There's a thought experiment, popular with the kind of people for whom philosophical thought experiments are popular, called the Ship of Theseus. It asks if you have a ship, and you replace every plank of wood in it as each plank rots away, so eventually you have a ship which doesn't share a single plank with the original – is that still the same ship that you had at the start, or is it a totally new ship?

A little while ago, I saw a Tweet from a venue I follow on Twitter, advertising The Drifters, singing "all their great hits".

There's only one problem with this, which is that no-one currently in the Drifters has ever had a hit, and none of them have even ever been in a band with anyone who had a hit as a member of the Drifters. Indeed, I believe that none of them have even been in a band with someone who has been in a band with someone who was in a version of the Drifters that had a hit.

This kind of thing is actually quite common these days, as old band members die off. I've seen a version of The Fourmost which had no members of the Fourmost, a version of the Searchers with none of the original members (though it did have the bass player who joined in 1964, and it would have had an original member had he not been sick that day), The New Amen Corner (with no members of the old Amen Corner), all on package tours with other, more "authentic", bands.

And of course we talked back in the chapter on the Ink Spots about the way that some old bands lose control of their name and end up being replaced on stage by random people who have no connection with the original act. It's sad, but we expect that kind of thing with bands of a certain age. A band like the Drifters, who started nearly seventy years ago now, should be expected to have had some personnel changes.

But what's odd about the Drifters is that this kind of thing has been the case right from the beginning of their career. The Drifters formed in May 1953. By July 1955, the band that was touring as the Drifters had no original members left. And by June 1958, the band touring as the Drifters had no members of the July 1955 version. An old version of the band's website, before someone realised that it might be counterproductive to show how little connection there was between the people on stage and the people on their famous records, lists fifty-two different lineups between 1953 and 2004. In the future, everyone will have been lead singer of the Drifters for fifteen minutes.

Indeed, the Rock and Roll Hall of Fame (for what this is worth – I value their opinion fairly low, but in this case it's an interesting indicator) actually inducted the Drifters as *two separate groups*. They're in as "The Drifters" and as "Ben E. King and the Drifters", because the Hall of Fame didn't consider them as being the same group.

For now, we're mostly going to talk about the second lineup of the Drifters, the one that was together from July through October 1953, and which had only one member in common with the May 1953 lineup of the band.

That member was Clyde McPhatter, and he was already something of a star before the Drifters formed, as the lead singer of Billy Ward and his Dominoes.

Billy Ward was an exceptional man in many ways. He was one of the first black people to graduate from the Juilliard School of Music, and he was a hugely talented pianist and arranger. And while he wasn't a particularly strong singer, he was a great vocal coach, and so when he noticed that vocal groups were becoming the new big thing in rhythm and blues, he hit upon a surefire way to make money. He'd form a group, featuring his best students, and pay them a salary. He and his agent would own the band name, and they could hire and fire people as they wished. And the students would all work for cheap, because... well, that's what young people do.

Indeed, it would go further than them working for low pay. If you were a member of Billy Ward and his Dominoes, and you messed up, you got fined, and of course the money went straight into Ward's pocket.

The Dominoes started out as an integrated group; their name was because they were black and white, like the spots on a domino. But soon Ward had fired all of the white members, and put together a group that was entirely made up of black people.

The music they were performing was in the style that would later become known as doo wop, but that wasn't a term that anyone used at the time. Back then, this new vocal group sound was just one of the many things that were lumped together under the rhythm and blues label. And as this was still the early stages of the music's development, it was a little different from the music that would later characterise the genre.

doo wop started as a style that was strongly influenced by the Ink Spots – and by acts before them like the Mills Brothers. It was music made by impromptu groups on street corners, sung by people who had no instruments to accompany them, and so it relied on the techniques that had been used by the coffee-pot groups of the twenties and thirties – imitating musical instruments with one's mouth.

These days, thanks largely to its late-fifties and early-sixties iteration in which it was sung by Italian-American men in sharp suits, there's a slight aura of sophistication and class around doo wop music. It's associated in a very general sort of way with the kind of music that the Rat Pack and their ilk made, though in reality there's little connection other than the ethnicity of some of its more famous performers.

But doo wop in its early years was the music of the most under-privileged groups. It was music made by people who couldn't afford any other kind of entertainment, who couldn't afford instruments, who had nothing else they could do. It was the music of the streets, in a very literal way. People, usually black people but also Latino and Italian-Americans, would stand on street corners and sing.

doo wop would later become a very formalised genre, and thus of less interest, but early on some of the music in the genre was genuinely innovative. Precisely because it was made by untutored teenagers, it was often astoundingly inventive in its harmonies and rhythms.

And the particular innovation that the Dominoes introduced was bringing in far more gospel flavour than had previously been used in vocal group music. The earlier vocal groups, like the Ravens or the

Orioles, had had very little in the way of gospel or blues influence. They mostly followed the style set by the Ink Spots, of singing very clean, straight, melody lines with no ornamentation or melisma.

The Dominoes, on the other hand, were a far more gospel-tinged band, and that was mostly down to Clyde McPhatter.

Clyde McPhatter was the lead singer on most of the band's biggest records; although he was billed as Clyde Ward, with the claim that he was Ward's brother, in order to stop him from becoming too much of a star in his own right, and possibly deserting the Dominoes.

McPhatter was actually a church singer first and foremost, and had expressed extreme reluctance to move into secular music, but eventually he agreed, and became the Dominoes' star performer.

Their biggest hit, though, didn't have McPhatter singing lead, and was very different from their other records. "Sixty Minute Man" was, for the time, absolutely filthy, with lyrics like "There'll be fifteen minutes of kissing/Then you'll holler 'Please don't stop'/There'll be fifteen minutes of teasing/And fifteen minutes of squeezing/And fifteen minutes of blowing my top."

Now, that doesn't sound like anything particularly offensive to our ears, but in the early 1950s, that was absolutely incendiary stuff. And again, along with the fact that radio stations were more restrained in the early fifties than they are these days, there is cultural context that it's easy to miss. For example, the line "they call me loving Dan" – Dan was often the name of the "back door man" in blues or R&B songs, the man who'd be going out of the back door when the husband was coming in the front. (And "back door man" itself was a phrase that could be taken to have more meanings than the obvious. . .)

The song was popular enough in the R&B field that it inspired other artists to change their songs. Ruth Brown's big hit "Five-Ten-Fifteen Hours" was originally written to have her asking for "five-ten-fifteen minutes of loving" until someone pointed out that in the era of "Sixty Minute Man" fifteen minutes of loving didn't seem very much.

"Sixty Minute Man" was remarkable in another way – it crossed over from the rhythm and blues charts to the pop charts, which was something that basically *never* happened in 1951. I've seen claims that it was the first rock and roll record to do so, and I suppose that depends on what you count as a rock and roll record – Louis Jordan had had several crossover hits over the previous few years – but if you're counting rock and roll musicians as only being people who started recording around 1948 or later, then it may well be. If it's not the first, it was certainly one of the first, and like all big hits at the time it inspired a wave of imitators. However, Bill Brown, the lead singer on the song, quit in 1952 to form his own band, the Checkers. He took with him Charlie White, who had sung lead on an early Dominoes duet with Little Esther.

With both the other main singers having left the band more or less simultaneously, Clyde McPhatter was left as the default star of the show. There was no-one else who was even slightly challenging him for the role by this point, and the Dominoes' records became a showcase for his vocals.

Once McPhatter was the star, the band moved away from the more uptempo rock style to a more ballad-based style which suited McPhatter's voice better.

What's obvious from the Dominoes' records is that McPhatter was clearly a remarkable singer. He was the star of the show, and the reason that people came to see Billy Ward and the Dominoes, and soon he decided that it was unfair that he was making $100 a week, minus costs, while Ward was becoming rich. He didn't want to be an interchangeable Domino any more, he was going to make his own career and become a star himself. He stayed in the band for long enough to train his replacement, a new young singer named Jackie Wilson who had been discovered by Johnny Otis, and then left.

(At the same time a couple of other band members left. One of their replacements was Cliff Givens, who had previously been a temporary Ink Spot for five months between Hoppy Jones dying and Herb Kenny replacing him).

The Dominoes continued on for quite some time after McPhatter left them, but while they scored a few more hits, the way the band's career progressed can probably best be summed up by their sequel to "Sixty Minute Man" from 1955, "Can't Do Sixty No More".

Jackie Wilson, of course, was a fantastic singer and if you had to replace Clyde McPhatter with anyone he was as good a choice as you could make, but McPhatter was sorely missed in their shows.

Shortly after the lineup change – indeed, some have claimed on the very first day after McPhatter left – Ahmet Ertegun of Atlantic Records went to see the Dominoes live, and saw that McPhatter wasn't there. When he discovered that the lead singer of the biggest vocal group in the North-East was no longer with them, he left the venue immediately and went running from bar to bar looking for McPhatter. As soon as he found him, he signed him that night to Atlantic Records, and it was agreed that McPhatter would put together his own backing group – which became the first lineup of the Drifters.

That first lineup was made up of people from McPhatter's church singing group; one of whom, incidentally, was the brother of the author James Baldwin. That lineup – Clyde McPhatter, David Baughan, William Anderson, David Baldwin, and James Johnson – recorded four tracks together, but only one was ever released, "Lucille", which came out on a B-side.

From that one release, it doesn't sound like there was anything wrong with the band, but clearly Atlantic disagreed – I've heard it claimed by some of the later members of the group that Atlantic thought this first version of the Drifters had voices that were too light for backing McPhatter. Either way, there was a new lineup in place by a few weeks later, with only McPhatter of the original band, and that lineup would last a whole four months and get a hit record out.

Their first session included versions of five songs, including the other three that were recorded but never released by the initial lineup. But one of the two new songs was the one that would make the band stars.

That song, "Money Honey", was written by Jesse Stone, or Charles Calhoun to give him his pen-name. We talked about him in the chapters on "Roll 'Em Pete", talking about his song "Shake, Rattle, and Roll", and "Choo Choo Ch'Boogie", talking about how Louis Jordan ended up taking Stone's entire band and making them into the Tympany Five.

Stone was a fascinating man, who lived a long, long, life that spanned the twentieth century almost completely. He was born in 1901 and died in 1999, and his entertainment career lasted almost as long.

He'd started performing professionally in 1905, at the age of four, in a trained dog act – he'd sing and the dogs would perform. Apparently the dogs were so well trained that they could perform the act without him, but that's the kind of thing that passed for entertainment in 1905; a singing four-year-old and some dogs.

By 1920 he was the best piano player in Kansas City - and that was the opinion of Count Basie, a man who knew a thing or two about piano playing – and he was making a living as a professional arranger. He later claimed that he'd written a large number of classical pieces but that no-one was interested in playing them, but he could make money off the music that became rock and roll. It's been claimed by some jazz historians that he was the first person ever to write out proper horn charts for a jazz band's horn section, rather than having them play head arrangements, and while I don't think the timeline works for that, I'm not enough of an expert in early jazz to be confident he wasn't.

If he was, then that makes him responsible for the birth of swing, and specifically for the kind of swing that later ended up becoming rhythm and blues – the kind with an emphasis on rhythm and groove, with slickly arranged horn parts, which came out of Kansas.

Stone worked as an arranger in the thirties and forties with Chick Webb, Louis Jordan, and others, and also started dabbling in songwriting.

It was a discussion with Cole Porter that he later credited as the impetus for him becoming a serious songwriter. Porter had discovered that Stone was writing some songs, and he asked what tools Stone used. Stone didn't even understand the question. He later said "I didn't know what he was talking about. I had never even heard of a rhyming dictionary. I didn't know what a homonym was. I didn't know the difference between assonance and alliteration. 'Tools?' I said. 'Hell', he said, 'if you're gonna dig a ditch you use a shovel, don't you?' I began to approach songwriting more professionally".

And the results paid off. His first big hit was "Idaho", recorded by among others Guy Lombardo and Benny Goodman, but unlike most of the successful songwriters of the 1940s, he managed to continue his career into the rock and roll era. Stone wrote a huge number of early rock and roll classics, such as "Shake, Rattle, and Roll", "Flip, Flop and

Fly", "Smack Dab in the Middle", "Razzle Dazzle" and "Your Cash Ain't Nothin' But Trash", many of them recorded by Atlantic Records artists such as Ray Charles and Big Joe Turner.

This was because Stone was one of the founders of Atlantic. He'd worked with Herb Abramson before the formation of Atlantic Records, and moved with Abramson to Atlantic when the label started, and he was the only black person on the label's payroll at first.

Stone was credited by Ahmet Ertegun as having been the arranger who had most to do with the early rock and roll sound, and it certainly seems likely that it was Jesse Stone, more than all the other staff producers and writers at Atlantic, who pushed Atlantic Records in a rock and roll direction. According to Stone himself, he took a trip down to the Southern states to see why Atlantic's records weren't selling there as well as they were in the coastal states, and he realised that the bands playing in bars were playing with far more emphasis on rhythm than the bands Atlantic had.

At first, he wasn't impressed with this music – as he put it later "I considered it backward, musically, and I didn't like it until I started to learn that the rhythm content was the important thing. Then I started to like it and began writing tunes."

He adapted the rhythms that those bands were playing, especially the bassline – he later said "I designed a bass pattern, and it sort of became identified with rock 'n' roll - doo, da-DOO, DUM; doo, da-DOO, DUM - that thing. I'm the guilty person that started that."

But, other than "Shake, Rattle, and Roll", the most well-known song Stone wrote, under his Calhoun pseudonym, was "Money Honey". It's a song and arrangement owes a lot to the work that Leiber and Stoller had been doing with the Robins, and like those records the song is very, very funny. And this is something I've not emphasised enough so far – the sense of humour that so many R&B records had. From Louis Jordan on, the R&B genre wasn't just about rhythm, though it was of course about that, but it was often uproariously funny.

And it was funny in a very particular way – it was funny about the experience of black people living in poverty in cities. Almost all the R&B acts we've discussed so far, especially the ones around Johnny Otis, had a very earthy sense of humour, which was expressed in all their recordings. Songs would be about infidelity, being out of work, being drunk, or, as in this case, being desperate for money to pay the landlord and having your girlfriend leave you for someone who had more money.

This is something that was largely lost in the transition from R&B to rock and roll, as the music became more escapist and more focused on the frustrations and longings of horny adolescents, but even where rhythm and blues records were about dancing and escapism, they were from a notably more adult and witty perspective than those that followed only a few years later.

While Stone was the most important figure in the musical side of Atlantic Records, however, he quit by 1956. Atlantic's bosses wouldn't agree to make their first black employee and co-founder of the company an equal partner. In July 1953, though, he was working with the Drifters.

The lineup on "Money Honey" was a six-piece group – McPhatter, backing singers Bill Pinkney, Andrew and Gerhardt Thrasher, and Willie Ferbee, and guitarist Walter Adams, who was the third guitarist the group had had. They signed to a management contract with George Treadwell, who was at the time also the manager of another Atlantic Records star, Ruth Brown. They also signed to Moe Gale's booking agency, but by the time of their first show, on October 9 1953, at the Apollo Theater supporting Lucky Millinder, there'd already been another lineup change – Ferbee had been in an accident and could no longer perform, and the group decided to carry on with just four voices. And by the end of October, tragedy had struck again, as Walter Adams died of a heart attack. So by the time "Money Honey" started to get noticed and went to number one on the R&B charts, the band was already very different from the one that had recorded the song.

This new lineup still had McPhatter, though, and quickly followed up their first hit with another, "Such a Night", which wasn't as funny as "Money Honey", but was raunchy and controversial enough that it got banned from the radio, which made people rush to buy it. That one went to number two on the R&B charts.

Things were going well for the Drifters... but then McPhatter got drafted. He could still record with the band – he was stationed in the US – and the band continued to tour without him. They got David Baughan from the original lineup to rejoin, as he could sound enough like McPhatter that he could sing his parts on stage, and when McPhatter's armed services commitments meant that he couldn't make a recording session, they'd record duets with other famous acts, like Ruth Brown.

But eventually the band's management and Atlantic Records decided that they didn't need McPhatter to be the lead singer, and it might be more profitable to have the band not be reliant on any particular star; and McPhatter, for his part, was quite keen to start a solo career on his discharge. The Drifters and Clyde McPhatter were going to part.

While McPhatter had formed his own group because he didn't want to be an employee and wanted to have the rights over his own work, he had decided to set things up so that he owned fifty percent of the band's name, while George Treadwell owned the other fifty percent. When he left the group, he decided to sell his fifty percent stake in the band's name to Treadwell, which of course meant that the other Drifters were now in precisely the same position as McPhatter had been with the Dominoes, except that there at least the name's owner had been a band member. Bill Pinkney did later manage to get ownership of the name "The Original Drifters" and many of the fifties members would tour with him under that name in the sixties, but the band name "The Drifters" now belonged not to any of the performers, but to their management.

The Drifters went through many, many, lineup changes, and we'll be picking up their story later, but sadly we won't be picking up McPhatter's.

McPhatter's solo career started well, with a duet with Ruth Brown, "Love Has Joined Us Together", and something certainly had joined them together, as Ruth Brown later revealed that McPhatter was the father of her son, Ronald, who now tours as "Clyde McPhatter's Drifters". And for a while, McPhatter looked like he would continue being a major star. He had a string of hits between 1955 and 1958, but then the hits started to dry up. He changed labels a few times and would have the occasional one-off hit, but had far more flops than successes. By the early 70s, he was an alcoholic, and Marv Goldberg describes him telling someone introduced to him as a fan "I have no fans", and seeing a show with a drunk McPhatter sitting on the edge of the stage and saying "I'm not used to coming on third; I used to be a star."

He died in 1972, aged thirty-nine, completely unaware of how important his music had been to millions. I said near the start of this chapter that I don't consider the rock and roll hall of fame important, and that's true, but McPhatter was the first person to be inducted into the hall of fame twice, once as a Drifter and once as a solo artist. Anyone since him who's been inducted multiple times – people like John Lennon, Eric Clapton, Neil Young, and Michael Jackson – are referred to as members of "the Clyde McPhatter club".

A club I suspect none of the current Drifters will be joining. . .

"Sh-Boom"

Let's talk about one-hit wonders for a while. One-hit wonders have an unusual place in the realm of music history, and one which it's never easy to decide whether to envy or to pity. After all, a one-hit wonder has had a hit, which is more than the vast majority of musicians ever do. And depending on how big the hit is and how good it is, that one hit might be enough to keep them going through a whole career. There are musicians to this day who can go out and perform in front of a crowd of a few thousand people, every night, who've come there just to hear that one song they recorded nearly sixty years ago – and if the musician is good enough they can get that crowd enjoying their other songs as well.

But there are other musicians who can never capitalise on that one record, and who never get another shot. What initially looked like it might be a massive career turns into a fluke. Sometimes they take it well and it just becomes a story to tell the grandkids, but other times it messes up everyone's life.

There are people out there who've spent thirty or forty years of their life chasing a second hit, who will never be truly happy because they expected more from their brief success than it brought them.

There are a lot of one-hit wonders in the world of rock and roll, and a lot of people who end up unlucky, but few have been as unlucky as the Chords, who wrote and recorded one of the biggest hits of all time, but who through a combination of bad luck in choosing a name, and more than a little racism, never managed to have a follow-up. Amazingly, they seem to have handled it far better than most.

"Sh-Boom", the Chords' only hit, was the first rhythm and blues record by a black artist or group to make the top ten in the Billboard pop charts, so I suppose this is as good a time as any to talk about how the Billboard charts worked in the 1950s, and how they differ from charts in the UK and some other countries.

While the UK's singles charts are based only on record sales (and, these days, streams, but that doesn't really apply to this pre-digital era), the Billboard charts have always been an industry-specific thing rather than aimed at the public, and so they were based on many different metrics. As well as charts for record sales, they had (or have) charts for jukebox plays, for radio plays, and various other things. These would be combined into different genre-specific charts first, and those genres would be based on what the radio stations were playing. This means that the country charts would include all the songs played by country stations, the R&B charts all those played by R&B stations, and so on, rather than Billboard deciding themselves what counted as what genre. Then all of these charts would be combined to make the "Hot 100", which is sort of a chart of charts.

This would sometimes lead to anomalous results, when more than one type of station started playing a song, and some songs would end up on the country chart *and* the rhythm and blues chart *and* the pop chart.

Pop is here a separate type of music in itself, and in the early 1950s what got played on "pop" radio was, essentially, the music that was made by white people in the suburbs *for* white people in the suburbs. In 1954, the year we're talking about, the big hits were "O Mein Papa" by Eddie Fisher, "Secret Love" by Doris Day, and records by Perry Como, Rosemary Clooney, Jo Stafford, and Tony Bennett. Polite, white, middle-class music for polite white middle-class people. None of that hillbilly nonsense, and certainly nothing by any black people.

Some of it, like the Tony Bennett tracks, was pretty good, but much of it was the kind of horrible pap which made rock and roll, when it finally broke on to the pop charts, seem like such a breath of fresh air. And even the Tony Bennett records weren't in any way exciting – they were good, but they'd relax you after a hard day, not make you want to get up and dance.

What's noticeable here is that the pop music charts were dominated by music aimed at adults. There was no music for teenagers or younger adults hitting the pop charts, and no music for dancing. During the height of the swing era, the big bands had of course been making dance music, but now every last bit of black or lower-class influence was being eradicated, in order to appeal to the "return to normalcy".

You see, by the end of the Second World War, America had been through a lot – so much so that the first call for a "return to normalcy" had been from Warren G. Harding in the 1920 election, nearly thirty years earlier. In the previous forty-five years, the country had been involved in two world wars, suffered through the depression and the dust-bowl, and simultaneously seen an unprecedented growth in technology which had brought the car, the plane and now the jet, the cinema and then the talkies, the radio and the TV, and now the atomic bomb, into people's lives. People had undergone the greatest disruption in history, and several generations had now grown up with an idea of what was "normal" that didn't match their reality at all.

And so the white, semi-prosperous, middle and upper-working class in America made a collective decision around 1946 that they were going to reconstruct that normality for themselves, and to try to pretend as much as possible that nothing had really changed. And that meant pretending that all the black people who'd moved to the Northern cities from the south in that time, and all the poor white people from Oklahoma and Texas who'd moved west to avoid the dustbowl, simply didn't exist.

Obviously those other people had some ideas of their own about that, and about how they fit into the world. And those people had a little more of a voice now than they'd had previously. The black people living in the cities had enjoyed something of a war boom – there had been so much work in the factories that many black people had pulled themselves up into something approaching affluence. That was quickly snatched away when the war ended and those jobs were "needed by the returning heroes", but a small number of them had managed to get themselves into economically secure positions, and a larger number now knew that it was *possible* for them to make money, and were more motivated than ever for social change that would let them return to their previous status.

(This is a recurring pattern in the American economy, incidentally. Every time there's an economic boom, black people are the last to benefit from it and then the first to be damaged in the downturn that follows. White America is like Lucy, putting the football of the American Dream in front of black people and then taking it away again, over and over.)

And so the pop chart was for the people who were working in advertising, having three-martini lunches, and driving home to their new suburban picket-fence houses. And the other charts were for everyone else.

And this is why it was the music on the other charts that was so interesting. There's an argument that what made rock and roll something new and interesting wasn't any one feature of the genre, but an attitude towards creation. Early rock and roll was very much what we would now think of as "mash ups" – collages or montages of wildly different elements being brought together – and this is what really distinguishes between the innovative musicians and the copycats. If you were bringing together half a dozen elements from different styles, then you were doing rock and roll. But if you were just copying one other record – even if that other record was itself a rock and roll record – and not bringing anything new to it, then you weren't doing rock and roll, you were doing pop.

And it was the people at the margins who would do rock and roll. Because they were the ones who weren't sealing themselves off and trying to deny reality.

We talked a little bit about doo wop previously, but the songs we talked about there probably wouldn't be called doo wop by most listeners, though there are clear stylistic similarities. It's probably time for me to explain what doo wop actually is, musically. It's a style you don't get now, except in conscious pastiches, but it was basically an extension of the Ink Spots' style. You have at least four singers, one of whom is a very prominent bass vocalist who sings nonsense words like "doo wop" or "bom bom ba dom", another of whom is a high tenor who takes most of the leads, and the rest sing harmonies in the middle.

While the jump bands and Western swing were both music that dominated on the West Coast – the early jump bands were often based in New York, but LA was really the base of the music – doo wop was a music of the North-East. It sometimes got as far west as Detroit, but it was mostly New York, Washington DC, and a bit later New Jersey, that produced doo wop singers.

And it was doo wop that would really take off as a musical style. While the jump bands remained mildly successful, the early fifties saw them decline in popularity as far as the R&B charts went, because the new vocal groups were becoming the dominant form in R&B – and this was especially true of the "bird groups".

The first "bird group" was the Ravens, and they might be considered the first doo wop group full stop. They took the Ink Spots' "top and bottom" format and extended it, so that on their ballads there'd be more interplay between the high and low vocals. And the Ravens became massively influential. They'd found a way to get the catchiest parts of the Ink Spots sound, but without having to stick so closely to the formula. It could work for all kinds of songs, and soon there were a whole host of bands named after birds and singing in the Ravens' style – the Orioles, the Flamingos, the Penguins, the Wrens, and many more. We've already talked about one of the bands they influenced, the Robins.

The other major influential bird group was the Orioles, whose "It's Too Soon to Know" is another record that's often considered by some to be "the first rock and roll record" – though to my ears it just sounds like a derivative of the Ink Spots rather than anything new.

So there's a clear stylistic progression there, but we're not looking at anything radically different from what came before.

The first real doo wop record to really have a major impact was "Gee", by the Crows, another bird group, which was recorded and released in 1953, but became a hit in 1954, charting a month after "Sh-Boom" was recorded, but before Sh-Boom itself became a hit. "Gee" is doo wop absolutely fully formed, and it's a record which had a massive influence, particularly on young California teenagers who were growing up listening to Johnny Otis' radio show – both Frank Zappa and the Beach Boys would later record their own strange takes on the song, emphasising how odd the record actually sounded.

It's also widely credited as the first R&B record to become a hit with a large part of its audience being white teenagers. More than any other form of R&B, doo wop traded in the concerns of the adolescent, and so it was the first subgenre to become accessible to that huge demographic of white kids who wanted something new they could appropriate and call their own.

"Gee" is a record that deserves a chapter to itself, frankly, in terms of importance, but there's not much to say about it. The Crows had one hit, never had another, split up soon after, and there's no real biographical information out there about them. The record just stands on its own.

That's also true for "Sh-Boom", and the Chords were another one-hit wonder, but there's a difference there. While "Gee" was the first doo wop record to make money from white people, "Sh-Boom" was the first doo wop record to lose money to white people.

The Chords were not actually a bird group – they were too individual for that – but in other respects they're very much in the typical mould of the early doo wop groups, and "Sh-Boom" is, in many ways, an absolutely typical doo wop song.

"Sh-Boom" was not meant to be a hit. It was released on Cat Records, a subsidiary of Atlantic Records, but apparently everyone at Atlantic hated the song – it was only recorded at the Chords' insistence, and it was originally only a B-side until the song started to hit with the DJs.

"Sh-Boom" was arranged by Jesse Stone, but presumably his contribution was the instrumental, rather than the vocal arrangement, as the song was written by the Chords themselves, originally while sitting together in a car. At the time, according to Buddy McCrea of the group, "When they talked to each other, they'd say 'boom.' They'd say 'Hey, man, boom, how ya doin'." Jimmy Keyes, another Chord, said "'Boom' was the slang word. If you were standing on this block for five minutes, you'd hear that slang word fifteen times or more. We would take the 'boom' and make it sound like a bomb: 'shhhhhh-BOOM'."

Even the nonsense words in the background were, according to Keyes, meaningful to the band – "'A langala langala lang.' Well, you could hear the church bells over there," while other parts were references to someone called "Bip", the uncle of band members Carl and Claude Feaster. Bip was homeless, and apparently stank, and when Bip would come to visit, according to Keyes, "We could smell Bip as soon as he opened the door." They would cover their noses and sing "here comes Bip, a flip a dooba dip."

And one suspects that this played a big part in the song's success. While the lyrics are genial gibberish, they're genial gibberish that had meaning to the singers, if not to the audience.

That wasn't necessarily appreciated by older people though. The great satirist Stan Freberg recorded a rather mean-spirited parody of the song, combining it with a parody of Marlon Brando who was similarly popular at the time and who Freberg thought comparable in unintelligibility.

But there's an element of racism in the popular reaction to the success of "Sh-Boom". There was a belief among many people that since they couldn't understand the lyrics, they were hiding some secret code. And any secret code sung by black men must, obviously, have to do with sex. We'll see a lot of this kind of thing as the story goes on, unfortunately.

But of course, meaningless lyrics have a long, long, history in popular music – much longer than is usually appreciated. Most people, when they're talking about nonsense lyrics, trace scat singing back as far as Louis Armstrong imitating his own trumpet. But there's a good argument that they go back as far as we have records of songs existing, or almost.

If you look at traditional folk music you'll often find a common pattern, of people singing "As I walked out one bright summer's day/sing too ra la loo ra la loo ra la lay" or similar. That kind of nonsense singing dates back as far as we have records, and no-one knows how it started, but one hypothesis I've seen which makes sense to me is that it comes from Gregorian chant and similar religious forms.

No, seriously. It makes sense when you think about it. One of the places that people in the Middle Ages were most likely to hear music was in church, and many early motets contained Latin texts, usually sung by the tenors, while other people would sing commentary or explanation of the lyrics in the vernacular – English or French or whatever language.

Now, for a peasant hearing this, what do you hear? You hear some of the people singing words that make sense to you, in your own language, but it's mixed in with this other gibberish that you don't understand. If the people you're listening to are singing something that makes sense and they drop into Latin, they might as well be singing "Sh-Boom Sh-Boom sha la la la la la la la la la la la" for all the sense it'll make to you. So you come to the conclusion that that's just how songs *are*. They have bits that make sense and then bits of nonsense that sounds good.

Indeed, one of the bits of lyric of "Sh-Boom" as it's commonly transcribed is "hey nonny", which if that's the lyric would tie directly back into that old folk tradition – that is, sadly, the one bit of nonsense syllabics that the band weren't asked about, and so we can't know if they were thinking of minstrels singing "hey nonny nonny", or if it had some other inspiration as personal as Uncle Bip.

But either way, after "Sh-Boom" doo wop, and R&B in general, became obsessed with nonsense syllabics. We'll be hearing a lot of examples of this in the next few years, and it became so prevalent that by 1961 Barry Mann was asking the musical question, "Who Put the Bomp?"

Doo wop started as a musical style among black teenagers in East Coast cities, but within a few years it became dominated by Italian-American teenagers from the same areas, and we'll see that progression happen over the next few books. But we can also see it happening in miniature in the Chords' career.

Because while they had a big hit with "Sh-Boom", they didn't have the biggest hit with it.

If you vaguely know "Sh-Boom", maybe from hearing it in a film soundtrack, chances are the record you know isn't "Sh-Boom" by the Chords, but "Sh-Boom" by the Crew Cuts.

To explain why, we're first going to have to talk about "A Little Bird Told Me".

"A Little Bird Told Me" was a song originally recorded by Paula Watson on Supreme Records. Watson, and all the musicians on the record, and the record label's owner, were all black. Watson's record went to number two on the R&B charts and number fourteen on the bestseller charts. And then Decca put out a record – "A Little Bird Told Me", sung by Evelyn Knight. That record went to number one on the pop charts. And everyone involved in *that* record – the singer, the backing band, the record label owners – was white.

And Knight's record was a direct copy of Watson's, in tempo, key, arrangement, everything, At times her record gets so close to the original that you can actually play parts of them together and have it sound like a single stereo recording.

As you can imagine, the owners of Supreme Records were more than a little put out by this. This kind of direct copying was *not* the norm in the late 1940s – as we've talked about before, it was perfectly normal for people to rework songs into their own style, and to do different versions for different markets, but just to make a record sounding as close as possible to someone else's hit record of the song, that was unusual.

So Supreme Records took Decca to court, and said that Decca's record was copyright infringement. It was a direct copy of their record and should be treated as such.

Before we go any further, you have to know that there are roughly three different concepts that many people confuse when they're talking about the music industry, all of which are important. There's the song, the recording, and the arrangement.

The song is, to put it simply, just what the singer sings. It's the words and the melody line, and maybe the chord sequence if the chord sequence is sufficiently original. But basically, if you can sing it to yourself unaccompanied, that bit's the song. And the copyright in that is owned by the songwriter or her publisher.

Now, once a song has been published, either as a record or as sheet music, anyone at all can make a recording of it or perform it live. There are certain conditions to that – you can change the song in minor ways, to put it into your own style, or for example to give the protagonist's love interest a different gender if that's something that concerns you, but you can't make major changes to the song's melody or lyrics without the writer or publisher's permission. You also can't use the song in a film or TV show without jumping through some other hoops, just on a record or live performance.

But I could, right now, make and release an album of "Andrew Hickey Sings the Lennon and McCartney Songbook in the Bath" and I wouldn't need anyone's permission to do so, so long as I paid Lennon and McCartney's publishers the legal minimum amount for every copy I sold. I need a songwriter's permission to make the *first* record of their song, but anyone can legally make the second.

The next thing is the recording itself – the specific recording of a specific performance. These days, that too is under copyright. I can put out my own recording of me singing Beatles songs, but I can't just release a CD of one of the Beatles' albums, at least if I don't want to go to prison. A lot of people get confused by this because we talk, for example, about "She Loves You" being "a Beatles song" – in fact, it's a Lennon and McCartney *song* performed on a Beatles *recording*. These days, each individual recording has its own copyright, but at the time we're talking about, in the US, there was no federal legislation giving copyright to sound recordings – that didn't end up happening, in fact, until the 1970s.

Up to that point, the copyright law around sound recordings was based on case law and odd rulings (for example it was ruled that it was illegal to play a record on the radio without permission, not because of copyright, but because of the right to privacy – playing a record which had only been licensed for individual use to a group was considered like opening someone's mail).

But still, there was usually at least state-level copyright law around recordings, and so record labels were fairly safe.

But there's a third aspect, one somewhere between the song and the recording, and that's the arrangement. The arrangement is all the decisions made about how to perform a song – things like how much of a groove you want it to have, whether you're going to back it with guitar or harpsichord or accordion, whether the backing instruments are going to play countermelodies or riffs or just strum the chords, whether you're going to play it as a slow ballad or an uptempo boogie. All that stuff.

Until the "A Little Bird Told Me" case, everyone had assumed that arrangements were copyrightable. It makes sense that they would be – you can write them down in sheet music form, they make a massive difference to how the performance sounds, they're often what we re-member most, and they require a huge amount of creative effort. By every basic principle of copyright law, arrangements should be copy-rightable.

But the court ruled otherwise, and set a precedent that held until very recently – until, in fact, a case that only went through its final appeal in December 2018, the "Blurred Lines" case, which ruled on whether Robin Thicke's "Blurred Lines" plagiarised Marvin Gaye's "Got to Give it Up".

Between "A Little Bird Told Me" and "Blurred Lines", copyright law in the US held that you could copyright an actual recording, and you could copyright a song, but you couldn't copyright an arrangement or groove.

And this had two major effects on the music industry, both of them hugely detrimental to black people.

The first was simply that people could steal a groove – a riff or rhythm or feel – and make a new record with new lyrics and melody but the same groove, without giving credit. As the genres favoured by black musicians were mostly groove-based, while those favoured by white musicians were mostly melody-based, white musicians were more protected from theft than black musicians were. Bo Diddley, for example, invented the "Bo Diddley beat", but didn't receive royalties from Buddy Holly, the Rolling Stones, or George Michael when they used that rhythm.

And secondly, it opened the floodgates to white musicians remaking black musicians' hits in the same style as the black musicians. Up to this point, if a white singer had covered a black musician, or vice versa, it would have been with a different feel and a different arrangement.

But now, all of a sudden, whenever a black musician put out an interesting-sounding record, a white person would put out an identical copy, and the white version would get the radio play and record sales. As the black musicians tended to record for tiny labels while the white ones would be on major labels that wouldn't sign black musicians, the result was that a whole generation of black innovators saw their work stolen from them. And we'll be seeing the results of that play out in a lot of the records we talk about in the future.

But for most of the records we're going to look at, the one that's stood the test of time will be the original – very few people nowadays listen to, say, Pat Boone's versions of "Tutti Frutti" or "Ain't That a Shame", because no-one would do so when the Little Richard or Fats Domino versions are available. But with "Sh-Boom", the version that still has most traction is by the Crew Cuts.

The Crew Cuts were a white, Canadian, vocal group, who specialised in rerecording songs originally performed by black groups, in near-identical arrangements, and scoring bigger hits with them than the black people had. In the case of "Sh-Boom", sadly, the characterless white copy has dominated in popular culture over the version that actually has some life in it.

The Chords never had another hit, although "Sh-Boom" was successful enough that at one point in 1955 there was even a Sh-Boom shampoo on the market, made by a company owned by the Chords themselves. Lawsuits over the band's name which made them have to be known for a time as the Chordcats contributed to their decline, and while there were several reunions over the years, they never replicated the magic of "Sh-Boom".

The Crew Cuts, on the other hand, had many more hits, successfully leeching off sales of records of black artists like the Penguins, Gene and Eunice, Nappy Brown, and Otis Williams and the Charms, and getting more airplay and sales from identical copies. They even had the gall to say that those artists should be grateful to the Crew Cuts, for giving their songs exposure. We'll be talking about several of those songs in the rest of the book. It seems it's not as hard to follow up your first hit if you don't have to have any ideas yourself, just be white.

"That's All Right, Mama"

The Starlite Wranglers were not a band you would expect to end up revolutionising music – and indeed only some of them ever did. But you wouldn't have expected even that from them.

They were based in Memphis, but they were very far from being the sophisticated, urban music that was otherwise coming from big cities like that. Their bass player, Bill Black, would wear a straw hat and go barefoot, looking something like Huckleberry Finn, even as the rest of the band wore their smart Western suits. He'd hop on the bass and ride it, and tell cornpone jokes.

They had pedal steel, and violin, and a singer named Doug Poindexter. Their one record on Sun was a pure Hank Williams soundalike, which came out and did no better or worse than thousands of other singles by obscure country bands. In most circumstances it would be no more remembered now than, say "Cause You're Always On My Mind" by Wiley Barkdull, or "Twice the Loving" by Floyd Huffman.

But then something unprecedented in modern music history happened.

Sun Records was the second record label Sam Phillips had set up – the first one had been a very short-lived label called Phillips, which he'd started up with his friend, the DJ Dewey Phillips (who was not related to Sam). After his experiences selling masters to other labels, like Modern and Duke and Chess, had caused him more problems than he'd initially realised, he'd decided that if he wanted to really see the music he loved become as big as he knew it could be, he'd have to run his own label.

Because Sam Phillips had a mission. He was determined to end racism in the US, and he was convinced he could do so by making white audiences love the music of black people as much as he did. So the success of his new label was a moral imperative, and he wanted to find something that would be as big as "Rocket "88"", the record he'd leased to Chess. Or maybe even a performer as important as Howlin' Wolf, the man who decades later he would still claim was the greatest artist he'd ever recorded.

Howlin' Wolf had recorded several singles at Sam's studio before he'd started Sun records, and these singles had been leased to other labels. But like so many of the people Phillips had recorded, the record labels had decided they could make more money if they cut out the middle-Sam and recorded Wolf themselves. Sam Phillips often claimed later that none of the records Wolf made for Chess without Sam were anything like as good as the music he'd been making at 706 Union Ave, and he may well have been right about that. But still, the fact remained that the Wolf was elsewhere now, and Sam needed someone else as good as that.

But he had a plan to get attention – make an answer record. This was something that happened a lot in blues and R&B in the fifties – if someone had a hit with a record, another record would come along, usually by another artist, that made reference to it. We've already seen this with "Good Rockin' Tonight", where the original version of that referenced half a dozen other records like "Caldonia".

And Sam Phillips had an idea for an answer song to "Hound Dog". There had been several of these, including "Mr Hound Dog's in Town" by Roy Brown. Phillips, though,thought he had a particularly good take. The phrase "hound dog", you see, was always used by women, and in Phillips' view it was always used for a gigolo. And the female equivalent of that, in Phillips' telling, was a bear cat. And so Sam Phillips sat down and "wrote" "Bear Cat".

Well, he was credited as the writer, anyway. In truth, the melody is identical to that of "Hound Dog", and there's not much difference in the lyrics either, but that was the way these answer records always went, in Phillips' experience, and nobody ever kicked up a fuss about it.

He called up a local Memphis DJ, Rufus Thomas, and asked him to sing on the track. Thomas said yes, and the song was put out as one of the very first records on Phillips' new record label, Sun.

What was surprising was how big a hit it became – "Bear Cat" eventually climbed all the way to number three on the R&B charts, which was a phenomenal success for a totally new label with no track record.

What was less phenomenal was when Duke Records and their publishing arm came to sue Sam Phillips over the record. It turned out that if you were going to just take credit for someone else's song and not give them any of the money, it was best not to have a massive hit, and be based in the same city as the people whose copyright you were ripping off. Phillips remained bitter to the end of his life about the amount of money he lost on the record.

But while he'd had a solid hit with "Bear Cat", and Joe Hill Louis was making some pretty great blues records, Sam was still not getting to where he wanted to be.

The problem was the audiences. Sam Phillips knew there was an audience for the kind of music these black men were making, but the white people just wouldn't buy it from a black person. But it was the white audiences that made for proper mainstream success for any musician. White people had more money, and there were more of them.

Maybe, he started to think, he could find a white person with the same kind of feeling in their music that the black people he was working with had? If he could do that – if he could get white people to *just listen* to black people's music, *at all*, even if it was sung by a white person, then eventually they'd start listening to it from black people, too, and he could break down the colour barrier.

(Sam Phillips, it has to be noted, always had big ideas and thought he could persuade the world of the righteousness of his cause if everyone else would just listen. A few years later, during the Cuban missile crisis, Phillips decided that since in his mind Castro was one of the good guys – Phillips was on the left and he knew how bad Batista had been – he would probably be able to negotiate some sort of settlement if he could just talk to him. So he got on the phone and tried to call Castro – and he actually did get through to Raul Castro, Fidel's brother, and talk to him for a while. History does not relate if Phillips' intervention is what prevented nuclear war.)

So Sam Phillips was in the right frame of mind to take advantage when history walked into his studio.

Elvis Aaron Presley was an unlikely name for a teen idol and star, and Elvis had an unlikely background for one as well. The son of a poor sharecropper from Mississippi who had moved to Memphis as a young man, he was working as a truck driver when he first went into Memphis Recording Services to record himself singing a song for his mother.

And when Phillips' assistant, Marion Keisker, heard the young man who'd come in to the studio, she thought she'd found just the man Phillips had been looking for – the white man who could sing like a black man.

Or at least, that's how Keisker told it. Like with so many things in rock music's history, it depends on who you listen to. Sam Phillips always said it had been him, not Keisker, who "discovered" Elvis Presley, but the evidence seems to be on Keisker's side. However, even there, it's hard to see from Elvis' original recording – versions of "My Happiness" and "That's When Your Heartaches Begin" – what she saw in him that sounded so black. While the Ink Spots, who recorded the original version of "That's When Your Heartaches Begin", were black, they always performed in a very smooth, crooner-esque, style, and that's what Presley did too in his recording. He certainly didn't have any particular blues or R&B feel in his vocal on those recordings.

But Keisker or Phillips heard something in those recordings. More importantly, though, what Sam Phillips saw in him was an attitude. And not the attitude you might expect.

You see, Elvis Presley was a quiet country boy. He had been bullied at school. He wore strange clothes and kept to himself, only ever really getting close to his mother. He was horribly introverted, and the few friends he did have mostly didn't know about his interests, other than whichever one he shared with them. He mostly liked to listen to music, read comic books, and fantasise about being in a gospel quartet like the Jordanaires, singing harmony with a group like that.

He'd hang around with some of the other teenagers living in the same housing block – Johnny and Dorsey Burnette, and a guy called

Johnny Black, whose big brother Bill was the bass player with the Starlite Wranglers. They bullied him too, but they sort of allowed him to hang around with them, and they'd all get together and sing, Elvis standing a little off from the rest of them, like he wasn't really part of the group. He'd thought for a while he might become an electrician, but he kept giving himself electric shocks and short-circuiting things – he said later that he was so clumsy it was a miracle that he didn't cause any fires when he worked on people's wiring.

He didn't have many friends – and no close friends at all – and many of those he did have didn't even know he was interested in music. But he was absorbing music from every direction and every source – the country groups his mother liked to listen to on the radio like the Louvin Brothers, the gospel quartets who were massive stars among the religious, poor, people in the area, the music he heard at the Pentecostal church he attended (a white Pentecostal church, but still as much of a Holly Roller church as the black ones that Sister Rosetta Tharpe had learned her music from). He'd go down Beale Street, too, and listen to people like B.B. King – young Elvis bought his clothes from Lansky's on Beale, where the black people bought their clothes, rather than from the places the other white kids got their clothes.

But he wasn't someone like Johnny Otis who fitted in with the black community, either. Rather, he was someone who didn't fit in anywhere. Someone who had nobody, other than his mother, who he felt really close to. He was weird, and unpopular, and shy, and odd-looking.

But that feeling of not fitting in anywhere allowed him to pick up on music from everywhere. He didn't own many records, but he *absorbed* songs from the radio. He'd hear something by the Ink Spots or Arthur Crudup once, and sing it perfectly.

But it was gospel music he wanted to sing – and specifically what is known euphemistically as "Southern Gospel", but which really means "white Gospel". And this is an important distinction that needs to be made as we go forward, because gospel music has had a huge influence on rock and roll music, but that influence has almost all come from black gospel, the music invented by Thomas Dorsey and popularised by people like Sister Rosetta Tharpe or Mahalia Jackson. That's a black genre, and a genre which has many prominent women in it – and it's also a genre which has room for solo stars. When we talk about a gospel influence on Ray Charles or Aretha Franklin or Sam Cooke, that's the gospel music we're talking about.

That black form of gospel became the primary influence on fifties rhythm and blues vocals, and through that on rock and roll. But there's another gospel music as well – "Southern Gospel" or "quartet gospel". That music is, or at least was at the time we're talking about, almost exclusively white, and male, and sung by groups. To ears that aren't attuned to it, it can sound a lot like barbershop music. It shares a lot of its repertoire with black gospel, but it's performed in a very, very different style.

The Blackwood Brothers were young Elvis Presley's favourite group, and he was such a fan that when two of the group died in a plane crash in 1954, Elvis was one of the thousands who attended their funeral. He auditioned for several gospel quartets, but never found a role in any of them. But all his life, that was the music he wanted to sing, the music he would return to. He'd take any excuse he could to make himself just one of a gospel group, not a solo singer.

But since he didn't have a group, he was just a solo singer. Just a teenager with a spotty neck. And *that* is the feature that gets mentioned over and over again in the eyewitness descriptions of the young Elvis, when he was starting out. The fact that his neck was always filthy and covered in acne. He had greasy hair, and would never look anyone in the eye but would look down and mumble. What Sam Phillips saw in that teenage boy was a terrible feeling of insecurity.

It was a feeling he recognised himself. Phillips had already been hospitalised a couple of times with severe depression and had to have electric shock therapy a few years earlier. But it was also something he recognised from the black musicians he'd been working with. In their cases it was because they'd been crushed by a racist system. In Phillips' case it was because his brain was wired slightly differently from everyone else's.

He didn't know quite what it was that made this teenage boy have that attitude, what it was that made him a scared, insecure, outsider. But whatever it was, Elvis Presley was the only white man Sam Phillips had met whose attitudes, bearing, and way of talking reminded him of the great black artists he knew and worked with, like Howlin' Wolf or B.B. King, and he became eager to try him out and see what could happen.

Phillips decided to put Elvis together with Scotty Moore and Bill Black, the guitarist and bass player from the Starlite Wranglers. Neither was an impressive technical musician – in fact at the time they were considered barely competent – but that was a plus in Phillips' book. These were people who played with feeling, rather than with technique, and who wouldn't try to do anything too flashy and showboaty. And he trusted their instincts, especially Scotty's. He wanted to see what Scotty Moore thought, and so he got Elvis to go and rehearse with the two older musicians.

Scotty Moore wasn't impressed... or at least, he *thought* he wasn't impressed. But at the same time... there was *something* there. It was worth giving the kid a shot, even though he didn't quite know why he thought that.

So Sam Phillips arranged for a session, recording a ballad, since that was the kind of thing that Elvis had been singing in his auditions.

The song they thought might be suitable for him turned out not to be, and nor were many other songs they tried, until eventually they hit on "That's All Right, Mama", a song originally recorded by Arthur "Big Boy" Crudup in 1946.

Arthur Crudup was a country-blues singer, and he was another of those people who did the same kind of record over and over. He would sing blues songs with the same melody and often including many of the same lyrics, seemingly improvising songs based around floating lyrics.

The song "That's All Right, Mama" was inspired by a line from Blind Lemon Jefferson's classic "Black Snake Moan". Crudup had first used the line in "If I Get Lucky". He then came up with the melody for what became "That's All Right", but recorded it with different lyrics as "Mean Ol' Frisco Blues". Then he wrote the words to "That's All Right", and sang them with the chorus of an old Charley Patton song, "Dirt Road Blues", and then he recorded "That's All Right, Mama" itself.

Crudup's records were all based on a template – and he recorded several more songs with bits of "That's All Right" in, both before and after writing that one. Elvis, Scotty, and Bill, however, didn't follow that template.

Elvis' version of the song takes the country-blues feel of Crudup and reworks it into hillbilly music. It's taken at a faster pace, and the sound is full of echo. You have Bill Black's slapback bass instead of the drums on Crudup's version. It still doesn't, frankly, sound at all like the black musicians Phillips was working with, and it sounds a hell of a lot like a lot of white ones. If Phillips was, as the oversimplification would have it, looking for "a white man who could sing like a black one", he hadn't found it. Listening now, it's definitely a "rock and roll" record, but at the time it would have been thought of as a "hillbilly" record.

There is, though, an attitude in Presley's singing which is different from most of the country music at the time. There's a playfulness, an air of irreverence, which is very different from most of what was being recorded at the time. Presley seems to be treating the song as a bit of a joke, and to have an attitude which is closer to jazz-pop singers like Ella Fitzgerald than to blues or country music. He wears the song lightly, unafraid to sound a bit silly if it's what's needed for the record. He jumps around in his register and sings with an assurance that is quite astonishing for someone so young, someone who had basically never performed before, except in his own head.

The B-side that they chose was a song from a very different genre – Bill Monroe's bluegrass song "Blue Moon of Kentucky". Elvis, Scotty, and Bill chose to rework that song in much the same style in which they'd reworked "That's All Right, Mama". There's nothing to these tracks but Elvis' strummed acoustic, Black's clicking slapback bass, and Scotty Moore's rudimentary electric guitar fills – and the secret weapon, Sam Phillips' echo.

Phillips had a simple system he'd rigged up himself, and no-one else could figure out how he'd done it. The room he was recording in didn't have a particularly special sound, but when he played back the recordings, there was a ton of echo on them, and it sounded great.

The way he did this was simple. He didn't use just one tape recorder – though tape recorders themselves were a newish invention, remember – he used two. He didn't do multitracking like Les Paul; rather, what he did was use one tape recorder to record what was happening in the studio, while the other tape recorder played the sound back for the first recorder to record as well. This is called slapback echo, and Phillips would use it on everything, but especially on vocals. Nobody knew his secret, and when his artists moved off to other record labels, they often tried to replicate it, with very mixed results.

But on "Blue Moon of Kentucky" it gave the record a totally different sound from Bill Monroe's bluegrass music – a sound which would become known, later, as rockabilly.

Phillips took the record to his friend, the DJ Dewey Phillips, who played it on his R&B show. When Elvis found out that Dewey Phillips was going to be playing his record on the radio, he was so nervous that rather than listen to it, he headed out to the cinema to watch a film so he wouldn't be tempted to turn the radio on. There was such a response to the record, though, that Phillips played the record fourteen times, and Elvis' mother had to go to the cinema and drag him out so he could go on the radio and be interviewed.

On his first media interview he came across well, largely because Phillips didn't tell him the mic was on until the interview was over – and Phillips also asked which school Elvis went to, as a way of cluing his listeners into Elvis' race – most people had assumed, since Phillips' show normally only played records by black people, that Elvis was black.

Elvis Presley had a hit on his hands – at least as much of a hit as you could get from a country record on a blues label. Sadly, Crudup had sold the rights to the song years earlier, and never saw a penny in royalties – when he later sued over the rights, in the seventies, he was meant to get sixty thousand dollars in back payments, which he never received. I've seen claims, though I don't know how true they are, that Crudup's total pay for the song was fifty dollars and a bottle of whisky.

But it was at the band's first live performance that something even more astonishing happened, and it happened because of Presley's stage-fright, at least as Scotty Moore used to tell the story. Presley was, as we've mentioned, a deeply shy young man with unusual body language, and he was also unusually dressed – he wore the large, baggy, trousers that black men favoured. And he was someone who moved *a lot* when he was nervous or energetic – and even when he wasn't, people would talk about how he was always tapping on something or moving in his seat. He was someone who just couldn't keep still.

And when he got on stage he was so scared he started shaking. And so did his pants. And because his pants were so baggy, they started shaking not in a way that looked like he was scared, but in a way that was, frankly, sexual. And the audiences reacted. A lot.

Over the next year or two, Presley would rapidly grow utterly confident on stage, and when you look at footage of him from a few years later it's hard to imagine him ever having stage fright at all, with the utter assurance and cocky smile he has. But all his stage presence developed from him noticing the things that the audience reacted to and doing more of them, and the thing they reacted to first and most was his nervous leg-twitching.

And just like that, the unpopular poor boy with the spotty neck became the biggest male sex symbol the world had ever seen.

"Rock Around the Clock"

Sometimes, the very worst thing that can happen to a musician is for them to have a big hit. A musician who has been doing fine, getting moderate sized hits and making a decent living, suddenly finds themselves selling tens of millions of records. It's what everyone wants, and it's what they've been working up to for their whole career, but what happens then? Is it a fluke? Are they ever going to have another hit as big as the first? How do they top that?

Those problems can be bad enough if your big hit is just a normal big hit. Now imagine that your big hit becomes a marker for a whole generation, that it inspires a musical trend that lasts decades, that it causes actual rioting. Imagine that it's a record that literally everyone in the Western Hemisphere knows, that sixty-five years and counting after its release is still instantly recognisable. When your big hit is that big, where do you go from there? What can you do next?

For a while, before leaving Essex Records, Bill Haley had wanted to record a song called "Rock Around the Clock". It had been passed to him by Jimmy Myers, one of the song's two credited writers, but for some reason Dave Miller, Haley's producer, didn't want Haley to record it – to the extent that Haley claimed that a couple of times he'd brought the sheet music into the studio and Miller had ripped it up rather than let him record the song.

According to John Swenson's biography of Haley, Miller and Myers knew each other and didn't get on, which might be the case, but it might also just be as simple as "Rock Around the Clock" being very derivative. In particular, the lyrics owed more than a little to Wynonie Harris' "Around the Clock Blues". Indeed, even the title "Rock Around the Clock" had already been used, four years earlier, by Hal Singer.

So, "Rock Around the Clock" was an absolutely generic song for its time, and whatever Dave Miller's reasons for not allowing Haley to record it, it wasn't like he was missing out on anything special, was it?

After "Rock the Joint" and "Crazy Man Crazy", Bill Haley was in a position to make a real breakthrough into massive commercial success, but... nothing happened. He released a bunch more singles on Essex, but for some reason they weren't following up on the clear direction he'd set with those singles. Instead he seemed to be flailing around, recording cover versions of recent country hits, or remakes of older songs like "Chattanooga Choo Choo". None of his follow-ups to "Crazy Man Crazy" did anything at all in the charts, and it looked for a while that he was going to be a one-hit wonder, and getting to number fifteen in the charts was going to be his highest achievement.

But then, something happened. Bill Haley quit Essex Records, the label that had led him to become a rockabilly performer in the first place, and signed with Decca. And there his producer was Milt Gabler.

Decca was in an interesting position in 1954, one which readers may not quite appreciate. You might remember that we've mentioned Decca quite a few times. That's because in the 1940s, Decca was the only major label to sign any of the proto-rock artists we've talked about. In the late forties, Decca had Lucky Millinder, Lionel Hampton, Louis Jordan, the Ink Spots, Ella Fitzgerald, Rosetta Tharpe, Marie Knight, and the Mills Brothers on its roster. It also had a number of country artists who contributed a lot to the hillbilly boogie sound – people like Ernest Tubb, Red Foley, and more.

But Decca was the only one of the major labels to sign up acts like this. The major labels were, as we've discussed, going mostly for a white middle-class market that wanted Doris Day and Tony Bennett – not that there's anything wrong with Doris Day or Tony Bennett – and indeed Decca had plenty of its own acts like that too, and mostly dealt in that sort of music.

But any artist that was working in those styles that wasn't signed to Decca had to sign to tiny independent labels. And those independent labels set up their own distribution networks, which went to shops that specialised in the black or hillbilly markets. And so those speciality shops eventually just started buying from the indie distributors, and didn't buy from the major labels at all – since Decca was the only one they'd been buying from anyway, before the indies came along.

And this caused problems for a lot of Decca's artists. The reason that Louis Jordan, say, was so big was that he'd been selling both to the R&B market – since he was, after all, an R&B artist, and one of the best – and to the pop market, because he was on a major label. You sell to both those markets, and you'd sell to a lot of people – the casual record buyer market was much larger than the market for speciality genres, while the speciality genre audience was loyal and would buy everything in the styles it liked.

But if you were only selling to the Doris Day buyers, and not to the people who liked honking saxophones and went out of their way to buy them, then your honking-saxophone records were not going to do wonderfully in sales.

This change in the distribution model of records is one of the two reasons that all the artists we talked about in the first few chapters had a catastrophic drop in their sales in the early fifties. We mentioned the other reason in the chapter on "Crazy Man Crazy", but as a reminder, when the radio stations switched to playing forty-fives, they threw out their old seventy-eights.

That meant that if you were one of those Decca artists, you simultaneously lost all the radio play for your old singles – because the radio stations had chucked out their copies – and stopped having new hits because the distribution model had changed under your feet. And so pretty much all Decca's roster of rhythm and blues or country hitmakers had lost their hit potential, all at the same time.

But Decca still had Milt Gabler.

Milt Gabler, if you remember, was the one who produced Lionel Hampton's version of "Flying Home", the one with the Illinois Jacquet sax solo, and who produced "Strange Fruit" and most of Louis Jordan's records and the Ink Spots' hits. He'd been the one who put Sister Rosetta Tharpe together with pianist Sammy Price. He was largely – almost solely – responsible for the difference between Decca's roster and that of the other major labels, and he still wanted to carry on making records in the styles he loved. But to do that, he had to find a way to sell them to the pop audience.

And Bill Haley seemed like someone who could appeal to that audience. Indeed, Haley already *had* appealed to that audience once, with "Crazy Man Crazy", and if he could do it once he could do it again.

Bill Haley's style was not very like most of the music Milt Gabler had been making – Gabler was, after all, a serious jazz fanatic – but over recent months Haley's style had been drifting closer and closer to the sort of thing Gabler was doing. In fact, Gabler saw a way to make him even more successful, by pushing the similarity to Louis Jordan, which had already been apparent in some of Haley's earlier records.

And so the group were in the studio to record what was intended to be Bill Haley and the Comets' latest hit, "Thirteen Women and Only One Man in Town".

We haven't talked enough about how much nuclear paranoia was fuelling the popular culture of the early 1950s. Remember, when this record was made, the first atomic bombs had only been dropped eight and a half years earlier, and it had been five years since the Russians had revealed that they, too, had an atom bomb. At the time, everyone was absolutely convinced that a nuclear war between America and Russia was not only likely but inevitable – yet at the same time the development of nuclear weapons was also something to be proud of – a great American technological innovation, something that was out of a science fiction film.

Both of these things were true, more or less, as far as the American popular imagination went, and this led to a very odd sort of cognitive dissonance. And while it's not a good idea to put too much weight on the lyrics of "Thirteen Women", which is, after all, just an attempt at having a novelty hit with a Louis Jordan-style song about having thirteen women to oneself, it is notable that it does reflect that ambiguity. The dream the singer has is that the hydrogen bomb has been dropped and left only fourteen people alive in the whole town – thirteen women plus himself.

Now, one might normally think that that was a devastating, horrific, thought, and that it was a prelude to some sort of *Threads*-esque story of post-apocalyptic terror. In this case, however, it merely becomes an excuse for a bit of casual sexism, as the thirteen women become Haley's harem and servants, each with their own specified task.

Obviously, I'm being a little facetious here. For what it is, a comedy hillbilly boogie that plays on Haley's genial likeability, "Thirteen Women" is perfectly pleasant, if a little "of its time". It's very obviously influenced by Louis Jordan, but that makes sense given that Gabler was Jordan's producer.

Indeed, Gabler was also the one who introduced the H-bomb theme – the original version of the song, by the blues guitarist Dickie Thompson, makes no mention of the bomb or the dream, just treats it as something that happened to him. And, frankly, Thompson's version is much, much better than Haley's, and has some truly great guitar playing.

But Thompson's record is absolutely a blues record, in the same style as people like Guitar Slim or Johnny "Guitar" Watson. Haley's record is very different, and while Thompson's sounds better to modern ears – or at least to my ears – Haley's was in a style that was massively popular for the time.

But it would probably make an unlikely massive hit. And you certainly wouldn't expect its B-side to become that massive hit.

For the B-side, Haley decided to cut that "Rock Around the Clock" song that he'd been offered a year earlier. It might have come back into his mind because, two weeks earlier, another group had released their version of it.

Sonny Dae and his Knights were a band from Virginia who had never made a record before, and who never would again, but who had a regular radio spot. "Rock Around the Clock" was their only recorded legacy, and it might have had a chance at being a hit by them with some proper promotion – or maybe not, given the... experimental... nature of the intro, which has the instrumentalists *mostly* playing in something that approximates the same rhythm. Mostly.

So the single did very little, and now Sonny Dae and his Knights are a footnote. But their release may have reminded Haley of the song, and he recorded his new version in two takes.

But the interesting thing is that Haley didn't record the song as it was written, or as the Knights recorded it. What he sang was a totally different melody, changed to one that is essentially the standard boogie bassline. But I think there's a specific reason for that.

Hank Williams' very first big hit, remember, was a comedy Western swing song called "Move it on Over". That song has almost exactly the same melody that Haley is singing for the verse of "Rock Around the Clock". We know that Haley knew the song, because he later cut his own version of it, so it's reasonable to assume that this was a very deliberate decision.

What Haley and the Comets have done is take the utterly generic song "Rock Around the Clock", and they've used it as an excuse to hang every bit of every other song that they know could be a hit on, to create an arrangement that could encapsulate everything about successful music.

They kept the basic arrangement and structure they'd worked out for "Rock the Joint" right down to Danny Cedrone playing the same solo note-for-note. For the beginning, they came up with a stop-start intro that emphasised the word "rock". And then, at the end, they used a variant of the riff ending you'd often get in swing songs like "Flying Home", which one strongly suspects was Gabler's idea. The Knights did something similar, but only for a couple of bars, in their badly-thought-out solo section. With the Comets, it's a far more prominent feature of the arrangement.

This was *wildly* experimental. They were trying this stuff, not with any thought to listenability, but to see what worked. It didn't matter, no-one was going to hear it. It was something they knocked out in two takes – and the finished version had to be edited together from both of them, because they didn't have time in the studio to get a decent take down. This was not a record that was destined to have any great success.

And, indeed, it didn't.

"Rock Around the Clock" made almost no impact on its original release. It charted, but only in the lower reaches of the chart, and didn't really register on the public's consciousness.

But Haley and his band continued making records in that style, and their next one, a cover of Big Joe Turner's "Shake, Rattle, and Roll", did rather better, and started rising up the charts quite well.

Their version of "Shake, Rattle, and Roll" was nowhere near as powerful as Turner's had been. It cleaned up parts of the lyric – though notably not the filthiest lines, presumably because the innuendo in them completely passed both Haley and Gabler by – and imposed a much more conventional structure on it. But while it was a watered-down version of the original song, it was still potent enough that for those who hadn't heard the original, it was working some sort of magic.

Haley was a real fan of Turner, and indeed the two men became close friends in later years, and the Comets were Turner's backing band on one sixties album. But he doesn't have the power or gravitas in his vocals that Turner did, and the result is rather lightweight.

Haley's cover was recorded the same week that Turner's version reached number one on the R&B charts, and it's easy to think of this as another "Sh-Boom" situation, with a white man making a more radio-friendly version of a black musician's hit. But Haley's version is not just a straight copy, and not just because of the changes to remove some of the more obviously filthy lines. It's structured differently, and has a whole different feel to it. This feels to me more like Haley recasting things into his own style than him trying to jump on someone else's bandwagon, though it's a more ambiguous case than some.

"Shake, Rattle, and Roll" became Bill Haley's biggest hit so far, going top ten in the pop charts, and both Haley's version and Turner's sold a million copies. It looked like Haley was on his way to a reasonable career – not, perhaps, a massive stardom, but selling a lot of records, and doing well in shows.

But then everything changed, for Bill Haley and for the world.

It was only when a film, *The Blackboard Jungle*, was being made nearly a year after "Rock Around the Clock" was recorded, that the track became important.

The Blackboard Jungle was absolutely not a rock and roll film. It was a film about teenagers and rebellion and so on, yes, but in a pivotal scene when a teacher brings his old jazz records in, in order to bond with the kids, and they smash them and play their own, it's not rock and roll they're playing but modern jazz. Stan Kenton is the soundtrack to their rebellion, not anything more rock.

But in order to make the film up-to-the-minute, the producers of the film borrowed some records from the record collection of Peter Ford, the teenage son of the film's star. They wanted to find out what kind of records teenagers were listening to, and he happened to have a copy of "Rock Around the Clock".

They made the decision that this was to be the theme tune to the film, and all of a sudden, everything changed. Everything.

Because The Blackboard Jungle was a sensation. Probably the best explanation of what it did, and of what "Rock Around the Clock" did as its theme song, is in this quote from Frank Zappa from 1971.

> "In my days of flaming youth I was extremely suspect of any rock music played by white people. The sincerity and emotional intensity of their performances, when they sang about boyfriends and girlfriends and breaking up et cetera, was nowhere when I compared it to my high school negro[12] R&B heroes like Johnny Otis, Howlin' Wolf and Willie Mae Thornton.
>
> But then I remember going to see Blackboard Jungle. When the titles flashed up there on the screen, Bill Haley and his Comets started blurching 'One, Two, Three O'clock, Four O'clock Rock...' It was the loudest rock sound kids had ever heard at the time. I remember being inspired with awe. In cruddy little teen-age rooms, across America, kids had been huddling around old radios and cheap record players listening to the 'dirty music' of their lifestyle. ("Go in your room if you wanna listen to that crap...and turn the volume all the way down".) But in the theatre watching Blackboard Jungle, they couldn't tell you to turn it down. I didn't care if Bill Haley was white or sincere...he was playing the Teen-Age National Anthem, and it was so LOUD I was jumping up and down."

There were reports of riots in the cinemas, with people slicing up seats with knives in a frenzy as the music played.

12

When Zappa said this, that word was the accepted polite term for black people. Language has evolved since.

"Rock Around the Clock" went to number one on the pop charts, but it did more than that. It sold, in total, well over twenty-five million copies as a vinyl single, becoming the best-selling vinyl single in history. When counting compilation albums on which it has appeared, the number of copies of the song that have sold must total in the hundreds of millions.

Bill Haley and the Comets had become the biggest act in the world, and for the next couple of years, they would tour constantly, playing to hysterical crowds, and appearing in two films – *Rock Around the Clock* and *Don't Knock the Rock*. They were worldwide superstars, famous at a level beyond anything imaginable before.

But at the same time that everything was going right for "Rock Around the Clock"'s sales, things were going horribly wrong for everything else in Haley's life. Ten days after the session for "Shake, Rattle, and Roll", at the end of June 1954, Danny Cedrone, the session guitarist who had played on all Haley's records, and a close friend of Haley, fell down the stairs and broke his neck, dying instantly. At the end of July, Haley's baby daughter died suddenly, of cot death.

And... there was no follow-up to "Rock Around the Clock". You *can't* follow up anything that big – there's nothing to follow it up with. And Haley's normal attitude, of scientifically assessing what the kids liked, didn't work any more either. The kids were screaming at everything, because he was the biggest star in the world. The next few records all hit the pop charts, and all got in the top twenty or thirty – they were big hits by most standards, but they weren't "Rock Around the Clock" big.

And then in 1955, the band's bass player, saxophone player, and drummer quit the band, forming their own group, the Jodimars.

Haley soldiered on, however, and the new lineup of the band had another top ten hit in December 1955 – their first in over a year – with "See You Later Alligator". While that was no "Rock Around the Clock", it did sell a million copies. But it was a false dawn. The singles after that made the lower reaches of the top thirty, and then the lower reaches of the top one hundred, and then stopped charting altogether.

They had one final top thirty hit in 1958, with the rather fabulous "Skinny Minnie". "Skinny Minnie" is an obvious attempt to copy Larry

Williams' "Bony Moronie", but also, it's a really good record. But the follow-up, "Lean Jean", only reached number sixty, and that was it for Bill Haley and the Comets on the US charts.

And that's usually where people leave the story, assuming Haley was a total failure after this, but that shows the America-centric nature of most rock criticism. In fact, Bill Haley moved to Mexico in 1960.

The IRS were after Haley's money, and he found that he could make money from a Mexican record label, and if it stayed in Mexico, he didn't have to give his new income to them. He was going through a divorce, and he'd met a Mexican woman who was to become his third wife, and so it just made sense for him to move.

And in Mexico, Bill Haley became king of the Twist.

"Florida Twist" went to number one in Mexico, as did the album of the same name. Indeed, "Florida Twist", by Bill Haley y sus Cometas, became the biggest-selling single ever up to that point in Mexico. The Comets had their own TV show in Mexico, *Orfeón a Go-Go*, and made three Spanish-language films in the sixties. They had a string of hits there, and Mexico wasn't the only place they were having hits. Their "Chick Safari" went to number one in India.

And even after his success as a recording artist finally dried up, in the late sixties, not the late fifties like most articles on him assume, Haley and the Comets were still a huge live draw across the world. At a rock revival show in the late sixties at Madison Square Garden, Haley got an eight-and-a-half-minute standing ovation before playing a song. He played Wembley Stadium in 1972 and the Royal Variety Performance in 1979.

Haley's last few years weren't happy ones. He started behaving erratically shortly after Rudy Pompilli, his best friend and saxophone player for over twenty years, died in 1976. He gave up performing for a couple of years – he and Pompilli had always said that if one of them died the other one wouldn't carry on – and when he came back, he seemed to be behaving oddly. People usually put this down to his alcoholism, and blame that on his resentment at his so-called lack of success, forgetting that he had a brain tumour, and that just perhaps that might have led to some of the erraticness.

But people let that cast a shadow back over his career, and let his appearance – a bit fat, not in the first flush of youth – convince them that because he didn't fit with later standards of cool, he was "forgotten" and "overlooked".

Bill Haley died in 1981, just over a year after touring Britain and playing the Royal Variety Performance – a televised event which would regularly get upwards of twenty million viewers. I haven't been able to find the figures for the 1979 show, but the Royal Variety Performance regularly hit the top of the ratings for the *year* in the seventies and eighties. Bill Haley was gone, yes, but he hadn't been forgotten. And as long as "Rock Around the Clock" is played, he won't be.

"Rock Island Line"

So far we've only looked at musicians in the US – other than a brief mention of the Crew Cuts, who were from Canada. And this makes sense when it comes to rock and roll history, because up until the 1960s rock and roll was primarily a North American genre, and anyone outside the US was an imitator, and would have little or no influence on the people who were making the more important music.

But this is the point in which Britain really starts to enter our story. And to explain how Britain's rock and roll culture developed, I first have to tell you about the trad jazz boom.

In the fifties, jazz was taking some very strange turns. There's a cycle that all popular genres in any art-forms seem to go through – they start off as super-simplistic, discarding all the frippery of whatever previous genre was currently disappearing up itself, and prizing simplicity, self-expression, and the idea that anyone can create art. They then get a second generation who want to do more sophisticated, interesting, things.

And then you get a couple of things happening at once – you get a group of people who move even further on from the "sophisticated" work, and who create art that's even more intellectually complex and which only appeals to people who have a lot of time to study the work intensely (this is not necessarily a bad thing, but it is a thing) and another group whose reaction is to say "let's go back to the simple original style".

We'll see this playing out in rock music over the course of the seventies, in particular, but in the fifties it was happening in jazz. As artists like John Coltrane, Eric Dolphy, Thelonius Monk and Charles Mingus were busy pushing the form to its harmonic limits, going for ever-more-complex music, there was a countermovement to create simpler, more blues-based music.

In the US, this mostly took the form of rhythm and blues, but there was also a whole movement of youngish men who went looking for the obscure heroes of previous generations of jazz and blues music, and brought them out of obscurity. That movement didn't get much traction in the jazz scene in America – though it did play into the burgeoning folk scene, which we'll talk about in the next volume. But it made a huge difference in the UK.

In the UK, there were a lot of musicians – mostly rich, young, white men, though they came from all social classes and backgrounds, and mostly based in London – who idolised the music made in New Orleans in the 1920s. These people – people like Humphrey Lyttleton, Chris Barber, George Melly, Ken Colyer, and Acker Bilk – thought not only that bebop and modern jazz were too intellectual, but many of them thought that even the Kansas City jazz of the 1930s which had led to swing – the music of people like Count Basie or Jesse Stone – was too far from the true great music, which was the 1920s hot Dixieland jazz of people like King Oliver, Sidney Bechet, and Louis Armstrong. Any jazz since then was suspect, and they set out to recreate that 1920s music as accurately as they could. They were playing traditional jazz – or trad[13], as it was known.

These rather earnest young men were very much the same kind of people as those who would, ten years later, form bands like the Rolling Stones, the Yardbirds, and the Animals, and they saw themselves as scholars as much as those later musicians did. They were looking at the history, and trying to figure out how to recapture the work of other people. They were working for cultural preservation, not to create new music themselves as such – although many of them became important musicians in their own right.

Skiffle started out as a way for trad musicians who played brass instruments to save their lips. When the band that at various times was led by Ken Colyer or Chris Barber used to play their sets, they'd

---

[13]Some, like Melly, would make a distinction between "trad jazz" and "revivalist jazz". This distinction was very important to some of these musicians, but is irrelevant to us, and has been largely ignored by everyone since.

take a break in the middle so their lips wouldn't wear out, and originally this break would be taken up with Colyer's brother Bill playing his old seventy-eight records and explaining the history of the music to the audience – that was the kind of audience that this kind of music had, the kind that wanted a lecture about the history of the songs.

But eventually, the band figured out that you could do something similar while still playing live music. If the horn players either switched to string instruments for a bit, played percussion on things like washboards, or just sat out, they could take a break from their main set of playing Dixieland music and instead play old folk and blues songs. They could explain the stories behind those songs in the same way that Bill Colyer had explained the stories behind his old jazz records, but they could incorporate it into the performance much more naturally.

And so in the middle of the Dixieland jazz, you'd get a breakout set, featuring a lineup that varied from week to week but would usually be Chris Barber on double bass instead of his usual trombone, Colyer and Tony Donegan on guitar, Alexis Korner on mandolin, and Bill Colyer on washboard percussion.

And when, for an early radio broadcast, Bill Colyer was asked what kind of music this small group were playing, he called it "skiffle". And so Ken Colyer's Skiffle Group was born.

In its original meaning "skiffle" was one of many slang terms that had been used in the 1920s in the US for a rent party. It was never in hugely wide use, but it was referenced in, for example, the song "Chicago Skiffle" by Jimmy O'Bryant's Famous Original Washboard Band.

We haven't talked about rent parties before, but they were a common thing in the early part of the twentieth century, especially in black communities, and especially in Harlem in New York. If the rent was due and you didn't have enough money to pay for it, you'd clear some space in your flat, get in some food and alcohol, find someone you knew who could play the piano, or even a small band, and let everyone know there was a party on. They'd pay at the door, and hopefully you'd get enough money to cover the cost of your food, some money for the piano player, and the rent for the next month.

Many musicians could make a decent living playing a different rent party every day, and musicians like Fats Waller and James P. Johnson spent much of their early careers playing rent parties.

If a band, rather than a single piano player, played at a rent party, it would not be a big professional band, but it would be more likely to be a jug band or a coffee pot band – people using improvised household equipment for percussion along with string instruments like guitars and banjos, harmonicas, and similar cheap and portable instruments.

This kind of music would have gone unremembered, were it not for Dan Burley. Dan Burley was a pioneering black journalist who worked as an editor for *Ebony* and *Jet* magazines, and also edited most of Elijah Mohammed's writings, as well as writing a bestselling dictionary of Jive slang. He was also, though, a musician – he'd been a classmate of Lionel Hampton, in fact, and co-wrote several songs with him – and in the late 1940s he put together a band which also included Brownie and Sticks McGhee (although Sticks was then performing under the name of "Globe Trotter McGhee"). They called themselves Dan Burley and His Skiffle Boys, and it was them that Bill Colyer was remembering when he gave the style its name.

The trad jazz scene in Britain, like the overlapping traditional folk scene, had a great number of left-wing activists, and so at least some of the bands were organised on left-wing, co-operative, lines. That was certainly the case for Ken Colyer's band. But then Colyer wanted to sack the bass player and the drummer, because he didn't think they could play well, and the guitarist, now calling himself Lonnie Donegan after his favourite blues singer, because he hated him as a person. As Chris Barber later said, "Anyone who's ever dealt with Lonnie hates his guts, but that's no reason to fire him."

The band weren't too keen on this "firing half of what was meant to be a workers' co-operative" idea, took a vote, and kicked Colyer and his brother out instead. Colyer then made several statements about how he'd been going to leave them anyway, because they kept doing things like wanting to play ragtime or Duke Ellington songs or other things that weren't completely pure New Orleans jazz.

The result was two rival bands, one headed by Colyer, and one headed by Chris Barber, which became known unsurprisingly as the Chris Barber band.

Barber is one of the most important figures in British jazz, although he entered the world of music almost accidentally. He was in the audience watching a band play when the trombonist leaned over in the middle of the show and asked him if he wanted to buy a trombone. Barber asked how much it was, and the trombonist said "five pounds ten". As Barber happened to have exactly five pounds and ten shillings in his pocket at the time, and he couldn't see any good reason not to own a trombone, he ended up with it, and then he had to learn how to play it. But he learned it well enough that by the time the group kicked the Colyers out, he was the obvious choice to lead the band.

Both bands were still wanted by the record label, and so at short order the Chris Barber band had to go into the studio to record an album that would compete with the second album by Colyer. But they didn't have enough material to make an album, or at least not enough material that wasn't being done by every other trad band in London.

So then the idea struck them to record some of the skiffle music they'd been playing in between sets, as a bit of album filler.

They weren't the first band to do this – in fact Colyer's own band had done the same some months previously. Colyer's new band featured clarinettist Acker Bilk, who would later become the very first British person ever to have a number one record in the US, and it also featured Alexis Korner in its skiffle group. That skiffle group, made up of Ken Colyer, Bill Colyer, Alexis Korner, and Mickey Ashman, recorded several songs on the second Colyer band album, including "Midnight Special" by Lead Belly.

But what the members of the Barber band came up with, more or less accidentally, was something that was a lot closer to the rock and roll that was just starting to be a force in the US than it was to anything else that was being recorded in the UK. In fact there's a very strong argument to be made that rock music – the music from the sixties onwards, made by guitar bands – as opposed to rock and roll – a music created in the 1950s, originally mostly by black people, and often featuring piano and saxophone – had its origins in these tracks as much as it did in anything created in the USA.

The important thing about this – something that is very easy to miss with hindsight, but is absolutely crucial – is that these skiffle groups were the first bands in Britain where the guitar was front and centre. Normally, the guitar would be an instrument at the back, in the rhythm section – Britain didn't have the same tradition of country and blues singers as the US did, and it was still more or less unknown to have a singer accompanying themselves on a guitar, as opposed to the piano.

That changed with skiffle. And in particular, a record that changed the world almost as much as "Rock Around the Clock" had was this band's version of "Rock Island Line", featuring Lonnie Donegan on vocals.

"Rock Island Line" is a song that's usually credited to Huddie Ledbetter, who is better known as Lead Belly – but, as with many things, the story is a little more complicated than that.

Ledbetter was one of the pioneers of what we now think of as folk music. He had spent multiple terms in prison – for carrying a pistol, for murder, for attempted murder, and for assault – and the legend has it that at least twice he managed to get himself pardoned by singing for the State Governor. The legend here is slightly inaccurate – but not as inaccurate as it may sound.

Ledbetter was primarily a blues musician, but he was taken under the wing of John and Alan Lomax, two left-wing collectors of folk songs, who brought him to an audience primarily made up of white urban leftists – a very different audience from that of most black performers of the time. As well as being a performer, Ledbetter would assist the Lomaxes in their work recording folk songs, by going into prisons and talking to the prisoners there, explaining what it was the Lomaxes were doing – a black man who had spent much of his life in prison was far more likely to be able to explain things in a way that prisoners understood than two white academics were going to be able to.

Ledbetter was, undoubtedly, a songwriter of real talent, but "Rock Island Line" itself isn't an original song. It dates back to 1930, only a few years before Lead Belly's recording, and it was written by Clarence Wilson, an engine-wiper for the Rock Island railway company. Wilson was also part of the Rock Island Colored Quartet, one of several vocal groups who were supported by the railway as a PR move to boost its brand.

In that iteration of the song, it was essentially an advertising jingle. But within four years it had been taken up by singers in prisons, and had transmuted into the kind of train song that talks about the train to heaven and redemption from sin. In this iteration, it's closer to another song popularised by Lead Belly, "Midnight Special", or to Rosetta Tharpe's "This Train", than it is to an advertisement for a particularly good train line.

Lead Belly took the song for his own, and added verses. He also added spoken introductions, which varied every time, but eventually coalesced into a story about a train driver who pretends his train is carrying livestock rather than pig iron in order to avoid waiting while another train passed him.

And it's that song, an advertising jingle that had become a gospel song that had become a song about a trickster figure of a train driver, that Lonnie Donegan performed, with members of Chris Barber's Jazz Band.

The song had become popular among trad jazzers, and one version of "Rock Island Line" that Donegan would definitely have heard is George Melly's version from 1951. Unlike Donegan's version, this was never a hit, and Melly later admitted that this lack of success was one of the reasons he wasn't a particular fan of Donegan – but Donegan definitely attended a concert where Melly performed the song, several years before recording his own version.

Melly's version was so unsuccessful, in fact, that it seems never to have been reissued in any format that will play on modern equipment – it's not only never been released as a download or on CD, it's never even been released on *vinyl* to the best of my knowledge – and it's never been digitised by any of the many resources I consult for archival 78s, so I've been unable to listen to the song in order to see how close it is to Donegan's version.

The only digital copy of it I've ever been able to find out about was when an Internet radio show devoted to old 78s played it on one episode nearly six years ago, but the MP3 of that episode is no longer in the station's archives, and the DJ hasn't responded to my emails.

So I've no idea to what extent George Melly's version was responsible for Donegan choosing that song to record, but it's safe to say that Melly's version didn't have whatever magic Donegan's had that made him into arguably the most influential British musician of his generation.

Donegan's version starts similarly to Lead Belly's, but he tells the story differently. In his version, the line runs down to New Orleans, which is not where the real-life Rock Island Line runs — Billy Bragg suggests in his excellent book on skiffle that this was a mishearing by Donegan of "Mule-ine", from one of Lead Belly's recordings — and instead of having to wait "in the hole" — wait at the side while another train goes past, the driver lies in order to avoid paying a toll (which wasn't a feature on American railways).

Amazingly, Donegan's version of the song's intro became the standard, even for American musicians who presumably had some idea of American geography or the workings of American railways. Johnny Cash's 1957 version, for example, starts with an almost word-for-word copy of Donegan's introduction.

But it wasn't the story that made Donegan's version successful — rather, it was the way it became a wailing, caterwauling, whirlwind of energy, unlike anything else ever previously recorded by a British musician, and far more visceral even than most American rock and roll records of the period.

"Rock Island Line" was originally put out as an album track on the Chris Barber album, but was released as a single under Donegan's name a year later, and shot to number one in the UK charts. But while it seemed like it was just a novelty hit at first, it soon became apparent that it was much more than that — and it could be argued that, other than "Rock Around the Clock", it was the most important single record we've covered here. Because "Rock Island Line" created the skiffle craze, and without the skiffle craze everything would be totally different. Soon there were dozens of bands, up and down the UK, playing whitebread versions of 1920s and 30s black American folk songs.

The thing about the skiffle craze was that, unlike every popular music format before – and most since – skiffle could be emulated by anyone. It helped if you had a guitar or a banjo, of course, or maybe a harmonica, but the other instruments that were typically used were made out of household items – a washboard, played with a thimble; a tea-chest bass, made with a tea-chest and a broom handle; possibly a jug, or comb and paper.

(Of course, ironically, many of these things later became obsolete, and now the only place you're likely to find a washboard is in a music shop, being sold at an outrageously high price for people who want to play skiffle music).

This was in stark contrast to other musical genres. An electric guitar, or a piano, or a saxophone or trumpet or what have you, required a significant investment, money that most people simply didn't have.

Because one thing we've not mentioned yet, but which is hugely important here, is just how poor Britain was in 1954.

The USA was going through a post-war boom, because it was the only major industrialised nation in the world that hadn't had much of its industrial capacity destroyed in the war, and so it had become the world's salesman. If you wanted to buy consumer goods of any type, you bought American, because America still had factories, and it had people who could work in them rather than having to rebuild bombed-out cities. Much of the story of rock and roll ties in with this – this is the time when America was in the ascendant as a world power.

The UK, on the other hand, had gone through two devastating wars in a forty-year period, and basically had to rebuild all its major cities from scratch. And it wasn't helped by the US suddenly, in August 1945. withdrawing all its help for Britain in what had been the Lend-Lease programme. Fifty-five percent of the UK's GDP in the second world war had been devoted to the war, and it ended up having to take out a massive loan from the US to replace the previous aid it had been given. That loan was agreed in 1946, and the final instalment of it was paid in 2006.

The result of this economic hardship was that the post-war years were a time of terrible deprivation in the UK, to the extent that rationing only ended in July 1954 – nine years after World War II ended, and a week before "Rock Island Line" was recorded.

In fact, rationing in the UK ended the day before Elvis Presley recorded "That's All Right, Mama", so if we want to draw a line in the sand and say "this is where the 1950s of the popular imagination, as opposed to the 1950s of the calendar, started", that would be as good a date as any to set.

Bear all this in mind as the story goes forward, and it'll explain a lot about British attitudes to America, in particular – Britain looked to America with a combination of awe and envy, resentment and star-struck admiration, and a lot of that comes from the way that the two countries were developing economically during this time.

So, around the country, teenagers were looking for an outlet for their music, and they could easily see themselves as Lonnie Donegan, the lad from Scotland brought up in London. Half the teenagers in the country bought themselves guitars, or made basses out of tea-chests.

And Lonnie Donegan was even a big star in the US! All the music papers were saying so! Maybe, just maybe, it was possible for you to go and become famous in the US as well!

Because, surprisingly, Donegan's record did make the top ten in the pop charts in the USA, in what became the first example of a long line of white British men with guitars gaining commercial success in the US by selling the music of the US' own black people back to white teenagers. Donegan wasn't really a big star over there, but he was close enough that the British music papers, buoyed by patriotism, could pretend he was.

In fact, Donegan wasn't quite a one-hit wonder in the USA – he was a two-hit wonder, first with "Rock Island Line", and a few years later with the novelty song "Does Your Chewing Gum Lose its Flavour on the Bedpost Overnight?" – but he still made more of an impact there than any other British musician of his generation.

Any version of "Rock Island Line" recorded by an American after 1955 would be based around Donegan's version. Bobby Darin's first single, for example, was a cover version of Donegan's record, in a reversal of the usual process which would involve British people copying the latest American hit for the domestic market. It was the first time since Ray Noble in the 1930s that a British musician had achieved any kind of level of popular success in the USA at all, and the British music public were proud of Donegan.

Except, that is, for the trad jazz fans who were Donegan's original audience. For a lot of them, Donegan was polluting the purity of the music. The trad jazz *musicians* usually didn't mind this. But the purists in the music papers really, really, disliked Donegan.

Not that credibility mattered – after all, as the session guitarist Bert Weedon said to Donegan, "You're the first man to have made any money out of the guitar. Bloody well done!" And while Donegan didn't make any more than his initial sixteen pound session fee – his fee for the entire Chris Barber album from which "Rock Island Line" was taken – from the initial recording, he did indeed become financially very successful from his follow-up hits like "Puttin' on the Style".

"Puttin' on the Style" was famously parodied by Peter Sellers, but there's another recording of that song which probably shows its cultural impact better. There is a very, very, low-fidelity recording in existence, and easily findable online, of a teenage skiffle group performing the song in 1957 at Woolton Village Fete. Later, on the same day that recording was made, the sixteen-year-old boy singing lead on the song would be introduced properly for the first time to another teenager, who he would invite to join the group. But it'll be a while yet before we talk about John Lennon and Paul McCartney properly.

"The Wallflower"

We've talked a little about answer songs before, when we were talking about "Hound Dog" and "Bear Cat", but we didn't really go into detail there. But answer songs were a regular thing in the 1950s, and responsible for some of the most well-known songs of the period. In the blues, for example, Muddy Waters' "Mannish Boy" is an answer song to Bo Diddley's "I'm a Man", partly mocking Diddley for being younger than Waters. But "I'm a Man" was, in itself, a response to Waters' "Hoochie Coochie Man".

And, the "Bear Cat" debacle aside, this was an understood thing. It was no different to the old blues tradition of the floating lyric – you'd do an answer song to a big hit, and hopefully get a little bit of money off its coattails, but because everyone did it, nobody complained about it being done to them. Especially since the answer songs never did better than the original. "Bear Cat" might have gone to number three, but "Hound Dog" went to number one, so where was the harm?

But there was one case where an answer song became so big that it started the career of a blues legend, had a film named after it, and was parodied across the Atlantic.

The story starts, just like so many of these stories do, with Johnny Otis. In 1953, Otis discovered a Detroit band called the Royals, who had recently changed their name from the Four Falcons to avoid confusion with another Detroit band, the Falcons – this kind of confusion of names was common at the time, given the way every vocal group in the country seemed to be naming themselves after birds. Shortly after Otis discovered them, their lead singer was drafted, and Sonny Woods, one of the band's members, suggested that as a replacement they should consider Hank Ballard, a friend of his who worked on the same Ford

245

assembly line as him. Ballard didn't become the lead singer straight away – Charles Sutton moved to the lead vocal role at first, while Ballard took over Sutton's old backing vocal parts – but he slowly became more important to the band's sound.

Ballard was an interesting singer in many ways – particularly in his influences. While most R&B singers of this time wanted to be Clyde McPhatter or Wynonie Harris, Ballard was a massive fan of Gene Autry, the country and western singer who was hugely influential on Bill Haley and Les Paul. Despite this, though, his vocals didn't sound like anyone else's before him. You can find singers later on who sounded like Ballard – most notably both Jackie Wilson and Chubby Checker started out as Hank Ballard soundalikes – but nobody before him who sounded like that.

Once Ballard was in the group, they had that thing that every band needed to stand out – a truly distinctive sound of their own.

Otis became the band's manager, and got them signed to King Records. Their first few singles were all doo wop ballads, many of them written by Otis, and they featured Sutton on lead. They were pleasant enough, but nothing special, though one song Otis wrote for them, "Every Beat of My Heart", later became a million seller for Gladys Knight and the Pips. But there's nothing about that track that really stands out – it could be any of a dozen or so vocal groups of the time. But that started to change when Hank Ballard became the new lead singer on the majority of their records. Around that time, the band also changed its name to The Midnighters, as once again they discovered that another band had a similar-sounding name. And it was as the Midnighters that they went on to have their greatest success, starting with "Get It".

"Get It" was the first of a string of hits for the band, but it's the band's second hit that we're most interested in here. Hank Ballard had been a fan of Billy Ward and his Dominoes, and their hit "Sixty Minute Man", which had been considered a relatively filthy song for the time period.

"Get It" had itself been mildly risqué for the period, but Ballard wanted to write something closer to "Sixty Minute Man", and so he came up with a song that he initially titled "Sock It To Me, Mary".

Ralph Bass, the producer, thought the song was a little too strong for radio play, and so the group reworked it in the studio, with the new title being taken partially from the name of the engineer's wife, Annie. The song they eventually recorded was called "Work With Me Annie".

The song's lyrics, things like "Annie please don't cheat/Give me all my meat," are certainly suggestive, but it wouldn't set too many people on the warpath in 2019. In 1954, though, that kind of thing was considered borderline pornographic. "Give me all my meat?" That's... well, no-one seemed sure quite what it was, but it was obviously filthy and should be banned.

So of course it went to number one in the R&B chart. Getting banned on the radio has always been a guaranteed way to have a hit. And it helped that the song was ridiculously catchy, the kind of thing that you keep humming for weeks

The Midnighters followed up with a song that was even more direct – "Sexy Ways". That, too, went right up the charts. But "Work With Me Annie" had been such a success that the band recorded two direct followups – "Annie Had a Baby" and "Annie's Aunt Fanny".

And they weren't the only ones to record answer songs to their record. There were dozens of them – even a few years later, in 1958, Buddy Holly would be singing about how "Annie's been working on the midnight shift". But we want to talk about one in particular, here. One sung from the perspective of "Annie" herself.

Jamesetta Hawkins did not have the easiest of lives, growing up. She went through a variety of foster homes, and was abused by too many of them. But she started singing from a very early age, and had formal musical training. Sadly, that training was by another abuser, who used to punch her in the chest if she wasn't singing from the diaphragm. But she still credited that training with the powerful voice she developed later.

Jamesetta was another discovery of Johnny Otis. When she was introduced to Otis, at first he didn't want a new girl singer, but she impressed him so much that he agreed to sign her – so long as she got her parents' permission, because she was only sixteen. There was one problem with that. She didn't know her father, and her mother was in jail. So she faked a phone call – "calling her mother" while keeping a finger on the phone's button to ensure there was no actual call. She later provided him with a forged letter.

Meanwhile, Jerry Leiber and Mike Stoller, Otis' former colleagues, were working on their own records with the Robins. The Robins had been through a few lineup changes, recorded for half a dozen small labels, and several of them had, on multiple occasions, had run-ins with the law. But they'd ended up recording for Spark Records, the label Leiber and Stoller had formed with their friend Lester Sill.

Their first record to become really, really big, was "Riot in Cell Block #9". Like many Leiber and Stoller songs, this combined a comedy narrative – this time about a riot in a jail, a storyline not all that different from their later song "Jailhouse Rock" – with a standard blues melody.

"Riot" is probably the first record to incorporate the influence of the famous stop-time riff which Willie Dixon had come up with for Muddy Waters. This is the "da da da-da da" riff one can hear in everything from Waters' "Mannish Boy" to Peggy Lee's "I'm a Woman" (another Leiber and Stoller song). But it had first been used (as far as I can tell – remembering that there is never a true "first") in Waters' "Hoochie Coochie Man", which first hit the R&B charts in March 1954.

The Robins' record came out in May 1954. So it's likely that Leiber and Stoller heard "Hoochie Coochie Man" and immediately wrote "Riot".

However, they had a problem – Bobby Nunn, the Robins' bass singer, simply couldn't get the kind of menacing tones that the song needed – he was great for joking with Little Esther and things of that nature, but he just couldn't do that scary growl.

Or at least, that's the story as Leiber and Stoller always told it. Other members of the Robins later claimed that Nunn had refused to sing the lead, finding the lyrics offensive. Terrell Leonard said "We didn't understand our heritage. These two white songwriters knew our culture better than we did. Bobby wouldn't do it."

But they knew someone who would. Richard Berry was a singer with a doo wop group called The Flairs, who recorded for Modern and RPM records. In particular, they'd recorded a single called "She Wants to Rock", which had been produced by Leiber and Stoller.

That song was written by Berry, but you can hear a very clear stylistic connection with Leiber and Stoller's work. They were obviously sympathetic, musically, and Leiber and Stoller remembered him and liked his voice. They got him to sing the part that Nunn would otherwise have sung, and "Riot in Cell Block #9" became a massive hit, though Berry never saw much money from it. This would end up being something of a pattern for Richard Berry's life, sadly. Berry was one of the most important people in early rock and roll, but his work either went uncredited or unpaid, or sometimes both.

But one thing that "Riot in Cell Block #9" did was cement Berry's reputation within the industry as someone who would be able to turn in a good vocal, at short notice, on someone else's record.

And so, when it came time for Jamesetta Hawkins to record the new answer song for "Work With Me Annie", and they needed someone to be Henry, who Annie was engaging in dialogue, Johnny Otis called in Berry as well. Otis always liked to have a bit of saucy, sassy, back-and-forth between a male and female singer, and that seemed particularly appropriate for this song.

The record Otis, Hawkins, and Berry came up with was a fairly direct copy of "Work With Me Annie", but even more blatant about its sexuality. The record was called "The Wallflower", but everyone knew it as "Roll With Me Henry". The song was credited to Jamesetta, under the new name Johnny Otis had given her, a simple reversal of her forename. Etta James was on her way to becoming a star.

The song as recorded is credited to Hank Ballard, Etta James, and Johnny Otis as writers, but Richard Berry always claimed he should have had a credit as well, claiming that his vocal responses were largely improvised. This is entirely plausible – Berry was a great songwriter himself, who wrote several classic songs, and they sound like the kind of thing that one could come up with off the cuff.

It's also certainly the case that there were more than a few records released around this time that didn't go to great lengths to credit the songwriters accurately, especially for contributions made in the studio during the recording session.

"The Wallflower" went to number one on the R&B charts, but it didn't become the biggest hit version of that song, because once again we're looking at a white person copying a black person's record and making all the money off it. And Georgia Gibbs' version is one of those ones which we can't possibly justify as being a creative response. It's closer to the Crew Cuts than to Elvis Presley – it's a note-for-note soundalike cover, but one which manages to staggeringly miss the point, not least because Gibbs changes the lyrics from "Roll with me, Henry" to the much less interesting "Dance with me, Henry".

On the other hand, it did have two advantages for the radio stations – the first was that Gibbs was white, and the second was that it was less sexually explicit than Etta James' version. "The Wallflower" may not sound particularly explicit to our ears, but anything that even vaguely hinted at sexuality, especially women's sexuality, and most especially black women's sexuality, was completely out of the question for early-fifties radio.

This wasn't the only time that Georgia Gibbs ripped off a black woman's record – her cover version of LaVern Baker's "Tweedle Dee" also outsold Baker's original, and was similarly insipid compared to its inspiration. But at least in this case Etta James got some of the songwriting royalties, unlike LaVern Baker, who didn't write her record.

And again, this is something we've talked about a bit and we will no doubt talk about more – it's people like Georgia Gibbs who created the impression that all white rock and roll stars of the fifties merely ripped off black musicians, because there were so many who did, and who did it so badly.

Some of the records we'll be talking about as important in this series are by white people covering black musicians, but the ones that are actually worth discussing were artists who put their own spin on the music and made it their own. You might argue about whether Elvis Presley or Arthur Crudup recorded the better version of "That's All Right, Mama", or whether Jerry Lee Lewis improved on Big Maybelle's original "Whole Lotta Shakin'" but it's an argument you can have, with points that can be made on both sides. Those records aren't just white people cashing in on black musicians' talent, they're part of an ongoing conversation between different musicians – a conversation which, yes, has a racial power dynamic which should not be overlooked and needs to be addressed, but not an example of an individual white person deliberately using racism to gain success which should rightfully be a black person's.

You can't say that for this Georgia Gibbs record. It was an identical arrangement, the vocal isn't an interpretation as much as just existing, and the lyrics have been watered down to remove anything that might cause offence. No-one – at least no-one who isn't so prudish as to actually take offence at the phrase "roll with me" – listening to the two records could have any doubt as to which was by an important artist and which was by someone whose only claim to success was that she was white and the people she was imitating weren't.

Etta James later rerecorded the track with those lyrics herself. If you can't beat 'em, join 'em, I suppose. After all, "Dance With Me Henry" was an absolutely massive, huge hit. It was so popular that it spawned answer songs of its own. Indeed, even the Midnighters themselves recorded an answer to the answer – Gibbs' version, not Etta James' – when they recorded "Henry's Got Flat Feet, Can't Dance No More".

And "Dance With Me Henry" got into the popular culture in a big way. The song was so popular that Abbot and Costello's last film was named after it, in a hope of catching some of its popularity. And it inspired other comedy as well.

And here, again, we're going to move briefly over to the UK. Rock and roll hadn't properly hit Britain yet, though as it turns out it was just about to. But American hit records did get heard over here, and "Dance With Me Henry" was popular enough to come to the notice of the Goons.

The Goon Show was the most influential radio show of the 1950s, and probably of all time. The comedy trio of Spike Milligan, Peter Sellers, and Harry Secombe are namechecked as an influence by every great British creative artist of the 1960s and 70s, pretty much without exception. Not just comedians – though there wouldn't be a Monty Python, for example, without the Goons – but musicians, poets, painters. To understand British culture in the fifties and sixties, you need to understand the Goons. And they made records at times – and one of the people who worked with them on their records was a young producer named George Martin.

George Martin had a taste for sonic experimentation that went well with the Goons' love of sound effects and silly voices, and in 1955 they went into the studio to record what became a legendary single – Spike Milligan and Peter Sellers performing "Unchained Melody", which had been one of the biggest hits of the year in a less comedic version.

That track became legendary because it didn't see a legal release for more than thirty years. The publishers of "Unchained Melody" wouldn't allow them to release such a desecration of such a serious, important, work of art, and it and its B-side weren't released until the late 1980s, although the record was widely discussed. It became something of a holy grail for fans of British comedy, and was only finally released at all because George Martin's old friend, and Goon fan, Paul McCartney ended up buying the publishing rights to "Unchained Melody". And because that single was left unreleased for more than thirty years, so was its B-side.

That B-side was a reworking of "Dance With Me Henry" as a duet between the Goon characters Henry Crun and Minnie Bannister, two extremely elderly and forgetful characters. Whether that's a more or less respectful cover version than Georgia Gibbs', I'll let you decide, though of course, in the context of a British music scene that was currently going through the skiffle craze, that version of "Dance With Me Henry" would have seemed almost normal.

Back in the US, Richard Berry was back at work as a jobbing musician. He wrote one song, between sets at a gig, which he scribbled down on a napkin and didn't record for two years, but "Louie Louie" didn't seem like the kind of thing that would have any commercial success, so he stuck to recording more commercial material, like "Yama Yama Pretty Mama". We'll pick back up with Richard Berry in a couple of years' time, when people remember that song he wrote on the napkin.

Meanwhile, Etta James continued with her own career. She recorded a follow-up to "The Wallflower", "Hey Henry", but that wasn't a hit, and was a definite case of diminishing returns. But her third single, "Good Rockin' Daddy", was a top ten R&B hit, and showed she could have a successful career.

But after this, it would be five years before she had another hit, which didn't happen until 1960, when after signing with Chess Records she released a couple of hit duets with Harvey Fuqua, formerly of the Moonglows.

Those duets saw the start of an incredible run of hits on the R&B charts, including some of the greatest records ever made. While we're unlikely to be covering her more as the story goes on – her work was increasingly on the borderline between blues and jazz, rather than being in the rock and roll style of her early recordings with Johnny Otis – she had an incredible career as one of the greatest blues singers of her generation, and continued recording until shortly before her death in 2011. She died three days after Johnny Otis, the man who had discovered her all those decades earlier.

"Pledging My Love"

A content warning: this chapter contains a description of a death by gunshot. I am not using any of the more explicit descriptions of this death, though I do describe some aspects of it, but talking about that subject at all can be upsetting, so if you're likely to be disturbed by that, please skip to the next chapter.

Johnny Ace was born John Alexander Jr – he used a stage name because his mother didn't approve of secular music – and he was part of a group of musicians called the Beale Streeters.

To understand the importance of this group of people, you have to understand Memphis and why it was important.

American regional musical culture could be incredibly specific, and different cities had different specialities. That's changed somewhat now, as transport and communications have got so much better, but certainly in the first half of the twentieth century you'd find that cities a hundred or so miles apart had taken a lot of the same musical influences but put them together in radically different ways.

And Memphis, in particular, was an unusual city for the southern US. It was still an intensely racist city by any normal standards, and it was segregated, and thus still home to countless horrors and crimes against humanity. But *for the Southern US* black people led comparatively comfortable lives, simply because Memphis was very close to fifty percent black in the early decades of the twentieth century – and was actually majority-black in the late nineteenth.

In 1878, there was a plague – yellow fever swept the city – and it took an immense toll. Before the 1878 plague, there were fifty-five thousand people living in Memphis. Afterward there were fourteen thousand, and twelve thousand of those were black. The plague killed seventy-five percent of the white people living in Memphis, but only seven percent of the black people. Even though white people moved back into the city and eventually became the majority again, and even though they had all the institutional power of a racist state on their side, there was less of a power imbalance in Memphis, and the white ruling classes simply couldn't keep black people down as thoroughly as in other Southern cities.

Memphis' regional speciality is the blues, and its first great musical hero was W.C. Handy. Even though Handy only lived in Memphis for a few years, having been born in Alabama and later moving to New York, he is indelibly associated with Memphis, and with Beale Street in particular.

Handy claimed to have invented the blues, though his blues wasn't much like what we'd call "the blues" these days, and often had an element of the tango about it. He was certainly the first person to have any kind of hit with blues songwriting, back in a time when hits in music were measured by sheet music sales, before recorded music had become more than an interesting novelty.

So Memphis was, as far as the wider world was concerned, and certainly as far as anyone in Memphis itself was concerned, the birthplace of the blues. And Beale Street, more than any other part of Memphis, was *the* blues area. Everyone knew it.

Beale Street was *the* centre of black culture, not just for Memphis, but for the whole of Tennessee, in the late forties and early fifties. It wasn't actually called Beale Street on the maps until 1955, but everyone referred to it as "Beale Street" anyway. By 1950 people were already complaining about the fact that the "old" Beale Street had gone.

Beale Street was where Lansky's was – the place where the coolest people bought their clothes. There was Schwab's Dry Good Store, where you could buy everything you wanted. And there was the Beale Street Blues Boys, or the Beale Streeters – accounts vary as to what they actually called themselves. They weren't a band in a traditional sense, but there were a few of them who got together a lot, and when they would make records, they would often play on each others tracks. There was the harmonica player Junior Parker, who would go on to record for every Memphis-based label, often recording in the Sun studios, and who would write songs like "Mystery Train". There was the piano player Roscoe Gordon, who had a unique off-beat way of playing that would later go on to be a massive influence on ska and reggae music. There was the singer Bobby "Blue" Bland, one of the most important blues singers of all time, and there was guitarist Riley King, who would later be known as "the blues boy", before shortening that and becoming just "B.B." King. And there was Johnny Ace, another piano player and singer.

But the Beale Street Blues Boys slowly drifted apart. Riley King went off and started cutting his own records for RPM, one of the myriad tiny labels that had sprung up to promote R&B music. And Bobby Bland got drafted, but before he had to go off to be in the armed forces, he went into Sam Phillips' studio and cut a few sides, which were released on Duke Records, backed by the Beale Streeters, with B.B. King on guitar and Johnny Ace on the piano.

Shortly after this, Ace's first single came out almost by accident. He was playing piano at one of the Bobby Bland sessions, this time not at Sam Phillips' studio, and Bland couldn't get the lyrics to his song right. In the session downtime, Ace started singing Ruth Brown's hit "So Long".

Dave Mattis, Duke Records' owner, thought that what Ace was doing sounded rather better than the song they were meant to be recording, and so they changed it up just enough for it to count as "an original", with Ace coming up with a new melody and Mattis writing new lyrics, and "My Song" by Johnny Ace was created.

This would be how all Ace's records would be created from that point on. They would take a pop standard or another song that Ace knew, someone would write new lyrics, and then Ace would come up with a new melody while keeping the chord progression and general feel the same. It was a formula that would lead to a string of hits for Ace.

"My Song" might not sound very rock and roll, but the B-side was a jump boogie straight out of the Big Joe Turner style – "Follow the Rules".

The A-side went to number one on the R&B charts, and was the first of eight hits in a row. Ace's singles would typically have a ballad on the A-side and a boogie number on the B-side. This was a typical formula for the time – you might remember that Cecil Gant had a similar pattern of putting a ballad on one side and a boogie on the other. The idea was to maximise the number of buyers for each single by appealing to two different audiences. And it seemed to work. Ace became very, very popular.

In fact, he became too popular. Duke Records couldn't keep up with the demand for his records, and Don Robey, the owner of Peacock Records, stepped in, buying them out.

Don Robey had a reputation for violence. He was also, though, one of the few black businessmen in a white-dominated industry, and it might be argued that you can only get to that kind of status with a certain amount of unethical practices.

His business manager and unacknowledged partner, Evelyn Johnson, was by all accounts a far nicer person than Robey. She did the day-to-day running of the businesses, drew up the business plans, and basically did everything that an owner would normally be expected to, while Robey took the money.

Johnson did everything for Robey. When he'd decided to put out records, mostly to promote the blues singer Clarence "Gatemouth" Brown, who he managed, Johnson asked him how they were going to go about this, and Robey said "Hell, I don't know! That's for you to find out!"

So Johnson figured out what to do – you call the Library of Congress. They had all the forms necessary for copyright registration, and whenever they didn't have something, they would give her the details of the organisation that did. She got every copyright and record-related form from the Library of Congress, BMI, and other organisations, and looked over them all. Everything that looked relevant, she filled out. Everything that didn't, she kept in case it was useful later, in a file labelled, "It could be in here".

Johnson ran the record label, she ran the publishing company, and she ran *and owned* the booking agency. The booking agency started the model that companies like Motown would later use – cleaning the acts up, giving them lessons in performance, buying them clothes and cars, giving them spending money. She lost money on all the artists that were recording for Robey's labels, where the performances turned into a loss-leader for the record labels, but she made the money back on artists like B.B. King or Ike and Tina Turner, who just turned up and did their job and didn't have to be groomed by the Johnson/Robey operation.

She never got the credit, because she was a black woman, while Don Robey was a man, but Evelyn Johnson pretty much single-handedly built up the careers of every black artist in Texas, Tennessee, Mississippi or California during the early part of the 1950s.

From this point on, Duke became part of the Don Robey empire, run by Evelyn Johnson. For a while, Dave Mattis was a silent partner, but when he noticed he was getting neither money nor a say, he went to see Robey to complain. Robey pulled a gun on Mattis, and bought out Mattis for a tiny fraction of what his share of the record company was actually worth.

Once Robey had bought Duke, Ace started working with Johnny Otis as many of the other Duke and Peacock artists did, and his records from then on were recorded in Houston, usually with the Johnny Otis band, and with Otis producing, though sometimes Ace's own touring band would play on the records instead.

Ace's formula owed a lot to Charles Brown's sophisticated West Coast blues. Brown was the missing link between the styles of Nat "King" Cole and Ray Charles, and his smooth lounge blues was an important precursor to a lot of the more laid back kinds of soul music.

Now, there is a very important point to be made here, and that is that Johnny Ace's music was *extremely* popular with a black audience. He didn't get a white audience until after his death, and that audience was largely only interested in one record – "Pledging My Love". It's important to point this out because for much of the time after his death his music was dismissed by white music critics precisely because it didn't fit their ideas of what black music was, and they assumed he was trying to appeal to a white audience. In fact there's a derogatory term for the smooth-sounding blues singers, which I won't repeat here, but which implies that they were "white on the inside".

Nothing could be further from the truth. As Johnny Otis said, Ace was "too smooth for the white critics and white writers for a long time." He pointed out that this was "white arrogance", and that it implied that "black people are not the best judge of what was the best art to come out of the community, but the white writers are." Otis' point, which I agree with, was that, in his words, "you have to take your cue from the people of the community. They know better than you what they like and what is black artistry."

Ace's music – yearning ballads about unrequited love, sung in a smooth, mellow, voice – didn't fit with white preconceptions about the proper music that black men should be making, and so for decades his work was more or less airbrushed out of history. It was inconvenient for the white myth makers to have a black man playing sophisticated music.

But that music was hugely popular among black audiences. "The Clock", for example, went to number one on the R&B charts, and stayed on the charts from June through October 1953. His follow-ups to "The Clock" weren't as big, and there was a sign he was entering diminishing returns, but his records stayed on the charts for longer than most, and as a result his releases were also less frequent. Don Robey stockpiled his recordings, putting out just one single every six months, waiting for the previous single to fall off the charts before releasing the next one. This stockpiling would prove very lucrative for him.

Because while Ace was a sophisticated performer, he lived a less sophisticated life. One of his hobbies was to drive at top speed, while drunk, and shoot the zeroes out of road signs. With a lifestyle like that, it is probably not all that surprising that Ace didn't live to a ripe old age, but the story of his death is still one that might be shocking or upsetting, and one that is still sad even though it was probably inevitable.

The last song Johnny Ace played live was "Yes, Baby" – a duet with Big Mama Thornton, who had been his regular touring partner for quite a while. The two would tour together and Thornton would be backed by Ace's band, with another pianist. Ace would take over from the pianist for his own set, and then the two of them would duet together.

Ace's live shows were a big draw. Evelyn Johnson said on several occasions that Ace was so popular that she used his popularity to make deals on less popular acts – if you wanted to book Johnny Ace you had to book B.B. King or Bobby "Blue" Bland as well, and those acts built their own followings through playing those gigs, often on the same bill as Ace and Big Mama Thornton.

By all accounts the show in Houston on Christmas Day was a massively enjoyable one – right up until the point that it very suddenly wasn't.

The rumour that went round in the days after his death was that he was killed playing Russian roulette. That's still what most people who talk about him think happened. This would have been a tragic way to go, but at least he would have known the possible consequences, and you have to think that no-one is going to play Russian roulette unless they have some sort of death wish.

And there were other rumours that went around – one that persists to this day is that Little Esther was present. She wasn't, as far as I can tell.

And the darkest rumours, repeated by people who like to sensationalise things, claim that it was a hit from Don Robey, that Ace was planning on changing record labels.

But that's not what actually happened. What happened is much more upsetting, and even more pointlessly tragic.

Johnny Ace was backstage in Houston with a bunch of people – Big Mama Thornton and the band's bass player Curtis Tilman were there, as were Ace's girlfriend and some other people. It was Christmas day, they were killing time between sets, and they'd been drinking. Ace was waving a gun around and making people nervous. He was in a bad mood because he had a toothache, and he was feeling tired and annoyed.

Accounts vary slightly as to what happened next, but Big Mama Thornton's was given as a legal deposition only a couple of hours after his death, before exaggeration set in.

"Johnny was pointing this pistol at Mary Carter and Joe Hamilton. He was kind of waving it around. I asked Johnny to let me see the gun. He gave it to me and when I turned the chamber a .22 cal. Bullet fell out in my hand. Johnny told me to put it back in where it wouldn't fall out. I put it back and gave it to him. I told him not to snap it to nobody. After he got the pistol back, Johnny pointed the pistol at Mary

Carter and pulled the trigger. It snapped. Olivia was still sitting on his lap. I told Johnny again not to snap the pistol at anybody. Johnny then put the pistol to Olivia's head and pulled the trigger. It snapped. Johnny said, 'I'll show you that it won't shoot.' He held the pistol up and looked at it first and then put it to his head. I started towards the door and heard the pistol go off. I turned around and saw Johnny falling to the floor. I saw that he was shot and I run on stage and told the people in the band about it."

According to Evelyn Johnson, Ace's hair stood on end from the shock, and he died with "a smirky little grin on his face, and his expression was 'What'd I say?'"

He was only twenty-five, and he'd been the most successful rhythm and blues singer of the previous year. When Cash Box, the trade paper, polled disc jockeys in December 1954 to find out who the most played artist of 1954 had been, Ace was the clear favourite. Shortly after his death, Duke Records announced that he had had three records top one and three quarter million sales the previous year. That is, to put it bluntly, a ludicrous amount – almost nothing sold that much, and one is tempted to believe that Duke were slightly manipulating the figures – but that it's at all plausible says a lot about how popular Johnny Ace was at the time.

After Ace's death, "Pledging My Love" instantly became his biggest hit. The credited songwriters for "Pledging My Love" are Don Robey and Fats Washington, the lyricist behind many of B.B. King's songs from this period, but it's safe to say that Ace himself wrote the music, with Robey taking the credit.

Robey apparently never wrote a song in his life, but you wouldn't believe it from the songwriting credits of any record that was put out by Duke or Peacock Records. There, Don Robey, or his pseudonym Deadric Malone, would appear to be one of the most prolific songwriters of all time, writing in a whole variety of different styles – everything from "Love of Jesus" to "Baby, What's Your Pants Doing Wet?" In total, he's credited as writer for 1200 different songs.

"Pledging My Love" was released only days before Ace's death, and the initial expectation was that it would follow the diminishing returns that had set in since "The Clock", becoming a modest but not overwhelming hit. Instead, it became a massive smash hit, and his biggest record ever, and it gained him a whole new fanbase – white teenagers, who had previously not been buying his records in any large numbers.

Black people in the fifties mostly still bought 78s, because they tended to be poorer and so not buying new hi-fi equipment when they could still use their old ones. 45s, in the R&B market, were mostly for jukeboxes. But for the first time ever, the pressing plant that dealt with Duke's records couldn't keep up with the demand for 45s – so much so that the record was held back on the jukebox charts, because the label couldn't service the demand. The records were being bought by young white teenagers, instead of his previous older black audiences – although that other audience still bought the record.

Ace's death came at a crucial transition point for the acceptance of rhythm and blues among white record buyers, and "Pledging My Love" acted as a catalyst. Until a couple of years earlier, songs owned by ASCAP, the performing rights society that dealt only with "respectable" composers for the Tin Pan Alley publishing houses, made up about eight times as many hits as songs owned by BMI, who dealt with the blues and hillbilly musicians. But in early 1955, eight of the ten biggest hits were BMI songs. "Pledging My Love" came at precisely the right moment to pick up on that new wave. There were white cover versions of the record, but people wanted the original, and Johnny Ace's version made the pop top twenty.

What none of this did was give Ace's family any money. Don Robey told them, after Ace's death, that Ace owed *him* money rather than the other way round.

And Ace and his family didn't receive even the songwriting royalties Ace *was* owed for the few songs he was credited with. While Robey was registered with BMI, and registered the songs with them, he had a policy of keeping his artists as ignorant as possible of the business side of things, and so he didn't let Ace know that Ace would also have to register with BMI to receive any money. Because of this, his widow didn't even know that BMI existed until James Salem, Ace's biographer, told her in the mid-nineties, and it was only then that she started to get some of the songwriting royalties she and her children had been entitled to for forty-plus years worth of sales and radio play.

Robey wasn't the only one making money from Ace. Cash-in tribute records were released, including records by Johnny Moore's Blazers (featuring Linda Hayes on vocals), Johnny Fuller, Vanetta Dillard, the Five Wings and the Rovers.

All of these records were incredibly tasteless – usually combining a bunch of quotes from Ace's lyrics to provide his "last letter" or a letter from heaven or similar, and backing them with backing tracks that were as close as possible to the ones Ace used.

And after Don Robey had completely scraped the barrel of unreleased Ace recordings, he tried to sign Johnny Ace's brother, St. Clair Alexander, to a record deal, but eventually decided that Alexander wasn't quite good enough (though Alexander would spend the next few decades performing a tribute show to his brother, which many people thought was quite decent). Instead, Robey persuaded a blues singer named Jimmie Lee Land to perform as "Buddy Ace" in the hope of milking it some more, and put out press releases claiming that "Buddy" was Johnny Ace's brother. Buddy Ace's first record was released simultaneously with the last tracks from Johnny that were in the vault, putting out adverts talking about "the last record on the immortal Johnny Ace to complete your collection" and "the first record on the versatile Buddy Ace to start your collection".

Buddy Ace actually made some very strong records, but he didn't really sound much like Johnny, and nor did he duplicate Johnny's success, though he continued as a moderately successful performer until the day he died – which was, rather eerily, while performing in Texas, forty years to the day after Johnny Ace died.

But Robey wanted to milk the catalogue, and tried in 1957 to resuscitate the career of his dead star by getting the Jordanaires, famous for backing Elvis Presley, to overdub new backing vocals on Ace's hits. This musical graverobbing was not successful, and all it did was sour Johnny Otis on Robey, as Robey had agreed that Otis' productions would remain untouched. Even forty years afterwards – and twenty years after Robey's death – it would still infuriate Otis.

But probably the most well-known of all the posthumous releases to do with Johnny Ace came in 1983, when Paul Simon wrote and recorded "The Late Great Johnny Ace", a song which linked Ace with two other Johns who died of gunshot wounds – Lennon and Kennedy. It was released on Simon's *Hearts and Bones*, an album that was steeped in nostalgia for the music of the period when rhythm and blues was just starting to turn into rock and roll. The period defined by the late, great, Johnny Ace.

"Ko Ko Mo"

"Aruba, Jamaica..."

No, sorry, this is not that "Kokomo", which much as I love the Beach Boys is *not* going to make this history. Instead it's a song that is now almost completely forgotten but which was one of the most important records in early rock and roll.

And I do mean both that it has been almost completely forgotten and that it was hugely important. This song seems just to have fallen out of the collective memory altogether, to the extent that I only found out about it by reading old books and asking "what is this 'Ko Ko Mo' they're talking about?"

Because it was important enough that all of the best books on R&B history – most of which were written in the sixties or seventies, when the events I've been talking about were far fresher in the memory – mentioned it, and said it was one of the most important records of 1954.

And the fact is, there is an interesting story buried in there, the story of how "Ko Ko Mo" by Gene and Eunice was two of the most important records in early rock and roll.

But there's another story there too – the story of how a record can completely disappear from the cultural memory. Because even in those books which mention it... that's all they do. They just mention this record's existence, giving it no more than a few sentences. In most of these chapters, I end up cutting a lot of material, because there's far more to say than will fit into ten pages or so. Here...there's nothing to cut. The sum total of all the information out there, in the whole world, as far as I can tell, is in a single eleven-page CD booklet.

To talk about "Ko Ko Mo", first we're going to have to talk about Shirley and Lee. Shirley and Lee were "the sweethearts of the blues", a New Orleans R&B duo who recorded in Cosimo Matassa's studio. They weren't a real-life couple, but their publicity suggested that they were, and their songs made up a continuing story of an on-again off-again romance. Their first single, "I'm Gone", reached number two on the R&B charts, and had back-and-forth vocals, singing to each other as if they were in a relationship. You can trace a line from them through Sonny and Cher or Johnny Cash and June Carter — duet partners whose appeal was partly due to their offstage relationships. Of course in Shirley and Lee's case this was faked, but the audiences didn't know that, at least at the time.

Shirley and Lee were popular enough that they inspired a whole host of imitators. We've mentioned Ike and Tina Turner before, and we're likely to talk about them again, but there was also Mickey and Sylvia, whose "Love is Strange" we'll be looking at later.

Those three duo acts all knew each other — for example, Mickey and Sylvia sang and played on, and co-produced, Ike and Tina Turner's "I Think It's Going to Work Out Fine". But there was one other duo act who tried to make a success out of the Shirley and Lee formula, and who didn't know those other groups, and it's them we're going to be looking at here.

Unlike Shirley and Lee, Gene and Eunice were a real-life couple, and so they didn't have to fake things the way Shirley and Lee did. Gene Forrest had been a jobbing singer for several years. He started out recording solo records for John Dolphin's label Recorded In Hollywood.

"Recorded in Hollywood" was a bit of a misnomer, but that label name itself tells you something about the rampant racism of American society in the 1950s. You see, John Dolphin wasn't actually based in Hollywood because when he'd tried to open his first business there — a record shop — he'd been unable to, because Dolphin was black, and black people weren't allowed to own businesses in Hollywood. So he named his record shop "Dolphin's of Hollywood" anyway, and opened it in a different part of Los Angeles.

But even though Dolphin was a victim of racism, he was also a beneficiary of it, and this just goes to show how revoltingly endemic racism was in the US in this time period. Because the original location for Dolphin's of Hollywood was on Central Ave, which at the time was the centre for black businesses in LA, in the same way that Beale Street was in Memphis or Rampart Street in New Orleans.

But Central Ave only became a centre for black business because of one of the worst acts of racism in America's history. Most of the businesses there were originally owned by Japanese people. When, during World War II, Japanese people in America, and Japanese-Americans, were interred in concentration camps for the duration of the war, those businesses became vacant, and the white owners of the properties were desperate for someone to rent them to, so they "allowed" black people to rent them. There was a big campaign in the black local press at the time to encourage black entrepreneurs to take over these vacant properties, and part of the campaign was to tell people that if they didn't start businesses there then Jews would instead.

Yes.

Sadly society in the US at that time was just *that* fractally racist.

But John Dolphin managed to build himself a very successful business, and he essentially dominated rhythm and blues in Los Angeles in the 1950s. As well as having a record shop, which stayed open twenty-four hours a day, he also owned a radio station, which broadcast from the front window of the record shop, with DJs such as Hunter Hancock and Johnny Otis. Those DJs would tell everyone they were broadcasting from Dolphin's, so the listeners would come along to the shop.

And Dolphin innovated something that may have changed the whole of music history – he deliberately targeted both his radio station and his record shop at white teenagers, realising that they would buy music by black musicians if they knew about it, and that they had more money than the black community. As a result, his record shop often had queues out the door of white teenagers eager to buy the latest R&B records, and through the influence of his DJs the whole of the West Coast music scene became strongly influenced by the music people like Otis and Hancock would play.

And then on top of that, in what, depending on how you look at it, was a great act of corporate synergy or something that should have brought action by antitrust agencies. Dolphin owned record labels. And his promise to artists was "We'll record you today and you'll have a hit tonight" – because anything recorded on his labels would instantly go into heavy rotation on his radio station and be pushed in his record shop. Gene Forrest's records were an example.

What that didn't mean for the musicians, though, was any money. Dolphin paid a flat fee for his recordings, took all the publishing rights, and wouldn't pay royalties. But for many musicians this was reasonable enough at the time – the idea for them was that they'd make records for Dolphin to build themselves a name, then move on to a label which paid them reasonable amounts of money. As Dolphin never signed anyone to a multi-record contract, they could easily move on after making a record or two for him.

Sadly for Gene the promise of "a hit tonight" didn't pay off, and after three singles for Recorded in Hollywood, he moved first to RPM Records, one of the many blues and R&B labels that was operating at the time, and then to Aladdin Records for a one-off single backed by a band called the Four Feathers. That would be the only record they would make together, but the connection with Aladdin Records would prove to be important.

Shortly after that record came out, Forrest met a young singer named Eunice Levy, after she'd done well at Hunter Hancock's talent show. Initially they started working together because the Four Feathers were looking for a female harmony vocalist, but soon they became romantically involved, and started working as a duo rather than as part of a larger group, and recording for Combo Records.

Combo was a tiny label owned by the trumpet player Jake Porter, and most of the records it released were recorded in Porter's basement. Gene and Eunice's only record for Combo, "Ko Ko Mo", is a fairly typical rhythm and blues record for 1954. It varies simply between a verse in tresillo rhythm, trying for something of the sound of Fats Domino's records, and a more straightforward shuffle on the choruses, going between them rather awkwardly.

The reason for the awkward transition is simple enough – it's a song made up from ideas from two different songwriters bolted together. Gene came up with the verse, while Eunice came up with the chorus – she was inspired by the town of Kokomo, Indiana. Jake Porter is the third credited songwriter, and it's not entirely certain what, if anything, he contributed – Porter was the owner of the record label, and label owners often took credit they didn't deserve. But on the other hand, Porter was himself a musician, and he'd performed with Lionel Hampton and Benny Goodman, among others, so it's not unreasonable that he might have actually contributed to the songwriting.

The duo were backed on the record by "Jonesy's Combo", who are credited on the record along with Gene and Eunice.

But there's another version of "Ko Ko Mo, credited to Gene and Eunice with *Johnny's* Combo. The Johnny in this case is Johnny Otis, whose band backs the singers on that version. It sounds very close to identical to the original – even though I'm sure Johnny Otis could easily have got the record sounding smoother and with more of a groove if he had been allowed.

You see, Gene was still under contract with Aladdin Records as a solo artist following his one single with them, and when they found that he had put out a record that might have some success with a competing label, they decided that they had to have their own version, and pulled rank, getting him to rerecord the track as closely as he could to the original recording. Eunice wasn't contracted to Aladdin, but given that the alternative was presumably a lawsuit, she went along with it. Gene and Eunice were now an Aladdin Records act, and their next few records would all be released on that label. The recording replicated the original as closely as possible, and both records even had B-sides which were identical-sounding recordings of the same song.

Once Combo Records found out, they started an advertising war with Aladdin. It was bad enough that other people were recording the song and having hits with it, but the same act putting out the record on two different labels, that was obviously unacceptable, and the two labels started to put out competing adverts in the trade journals, Aladdin's adverts saying "Don't Be Fooled, *THIS* is the Gene and Eunice Ko Ko Mo!", while Combo's said "This is it! The *original* Ko Ko Mo!"

Billboard counted the two records as the same for chart purposes – no-one could be bothered keeping track of which version of "Ko Ko Mo" it was that was played on the radio or on a jukebox. As far as the public were concerned, it was all one record, and that one record ended up going to number six on the R&B charts.

But Gene and Eunice weren't the only ones to have a hit with "Ko Ko Mo". The song became the subject of almost a feeding frenzy of cover versions. The first, by Marvin and Johnny, came out only a month after the original recording, but there were dozens upon dozens of them. The Crew Cuts, Louis Armstrong, the Flamingos, Rosemary Clooney's sister Betty... everyone was recording a version of "Ko Ko Mo", within a month or two of the single coming out.

The best explanation anyone can come up with for the massive, improbable, success of the song in cover versions is that it was one of the few R&B singles of the time to be completely free of sexual innuendo. While R&B records of the time mostly sound completely clean to modern ears, to radio programmers at the time records like "The Wallflower" and "Hound Dog" were utterly scandalous, and required substantial rewriting if they were going to play to white audiences.

But "Ko Ko Mo" had such a simplistic lyric that there was no problem with it, and the result was that everyone could record it and have a hit with the white audience, leading to it even being recorded by Perry Como.

And that was the biggest hit of all. Como was the person with whom the song became associated, although thankfully for all concerned he made no further rock and roll records. And even Como's version is probably more rocking than that by Andy Griffith – yes, that Andy Griffith, the 50s sitcom actor.

It's notable that the trade magazines advertised Como's version of "Ko Ko Mo" as a rock and roll record – this was in very early 1955, after "Rock Around the Clock" had been released, but well before it became a hit. But rock and roll was already a phrase that was in use for the style of music, at least among the trade magazines.

Normally this kind of cover version would have brought at least a reasonable amount of money to the songwriters – and as Gene and Eunice were the writers, that should have given them a large amount of money. However, after they sold the song to one publishing company, Aladdin claimed that they owned the publishing, again due to their existing contract with Gene Forrest. So everybody got a share of the money from the hit record, except for the people who wrote and sang it.

Gene and Eunice's next single was "This is My Story". There was a problem, though. "Ko Ko Mo" was going up the charts, and "This is My Story" was about to be released. They needed to go out on tour to capitalise on the first, promote the second, and generally get themselves into a position where they could have a career with some sort of possibility of lasting.

And Eunice was pregnant, with Gene's child.

Obviously, she couldn't go out on the road and tour, especially in the kind of conditions in which black artists had to tour in the 1950s, often sleeping on fans' floors because there were no hotels that would take black people.

There was only one thing for it. They would have to get in a replacement Eunice. They auditioned several singers, before eventually settling on Linda Hayes, the sister of Tony Williams of the Platters. Hayes didn't sound much like Eunice, but she looked enough like her that she could do the job. Hayes had a relatively decent minor career herself, singing lead on several records with her brother's group before putting out a few records of her own.

So Gene toured with Linda as a substitute Eunice while Eunice was on what amounted to maternity leave, and that worked well enough. "This is My Story" went to number eight on the R&B charts, and it looked like Gene and Eunice were on their way to permanent stardom.

Unfortunately, that wasn't the case, and by the time Eunice got back from maternity leave, the duo's career stalled. They recorded several more records for Aladdin, and tried various different tactics to repeat their early success, including having their records produced by the great Earl Palmer. None of that did any good as far as charting goes. "This is My Story" was their last chart hit for Aladdin, and after the recordings with Earl Palmer in 1958, the label dropped them.

They recorded for several more labels, with mixed results. For a while, Eunice returned to Combo records – unsurprisingly, after what had happened with Gene's contract, Jake Porter didn't want to have anything to do with Gene, but Eunice released a couple of unsuccessful tracks with them.

So, why did Gene and Eunice become completely forgotten? Why, outside the liner notes for a single out-of-print CD booklet and a Wikipedia article based substantially on that booklet, have I been able to find a grand total of four paragraphs or so of text about them in any reliable source? And why does even that set of liner notes start with the sentence "Gene & Eunice's story is muddled, confusing, and largely unknown"?

I think this comes back to something that has been an underlying theme of this book from the start – the fact that great art comes from scenes as much as it does from individuals.

This is not the same as saying that great *artists* aren't individuals, but that the music we remember tends to come out of reinforcing groups of artists, not just collaborating but providing networks for each other, acting as each other's support acts, promoting each other's material. I mentioned when I was talking about Mickey and Sylvia, Shirley and Lee, and Ike and Tina Turner that all three of these acts knew and worked with each other. None of them worked with Gene and Eunice, and Gene and Eunice just don't seem to have had any particular network of musicians with whom they collaborated. The collaboration with Johnny Otis just seems to have been a one-off job for him, and bringing in Linda Hayes doesn't seem to have led to any further connections with the people she worked with.

With almost every act we've talked about, you find them turning up in unexpected places in biographies of other acts, and even the one-hit wonders who had hits that people remembered continued being parts of other musicians' lives. Gene and Eunice just didn't. But without those connections, without making themselves part of a bigger story, they didn't become part of the cultural memory. Most of the acts that covered "Ko Ko Mo" were people like Perry Como or Louis Armstrong who aren't part of the rock and roll canon, and so the record seems to have turned into a footnote. But that wasn't quite the end of their influence.

Jamaica always had a soft spot for US R&B of the Fats Domino type, and Gene and Eunice, with their adaptations of Dave Bartholomew's New Orleans style, became mildly successful in Jamaica. In particular, their record "The Vow", which had been one of their last

Aladdin releases, got covered on Coxsone Dodd's Studio One records, the label that basically pioneered ska, rocksteady, and reggae music in Jamaica. In 1965, Studio One released a cover version of "The Vow", performed by Bunny and Rita – as in Bunny Wailer, of the Wailers, and Rita Anderson, who would later also join the Wailers and become better known by her married name after she married Bunny's bandmate Bob Marley.

Gene and Eunice attempted a reunion in the eighties. They didn't get on well enough to make it work, but Eunice did get to record one last single as a solo artist, under her new married name Eunice Russ Frost. On "Real Reel Switcher" she was backed by the classic fifties rhythm section of Red Callender and Earl Palmer.

Gene remained out of the spotlight until his death in 2003, but Eunice would occasionally perform at conventions for fans of doo wop and R&B until she died in 2002. She never got to recapture her early success, but she did, at least, know there were still people out there who remembered "Ko Ko Mo".

"Earth Angel"

When you're dealing with music whose power lies in its simplicity, as early rock and roll's does, you end up with music that relies on a variety of formulae, and whose novelty relies on using those formulae in ever-so-slightly different ways.

This is not to say that such music can't be original, but that its originality relies on using the formulae in original ways, rather than in doing something completely unexpected.

And one of the ways in which early rock and roll was formulaic was in the choice of chord sequence. When writing a fifties rock and roll song, you basically had four choices for chord sequence, and those four choices would cover more than ninety percent of all records in the genre. There was the twelve-bar blues, the basis for songs like "Hound Dog", or "Roll Over Beethoven", or "Shake, Rattle, and Roll". There's the variant eight-bar blues, which most of the R&B we've talked about uses. Eight-bar blues is actually a few different related chord sequences rather than a single one, but they all have similar effects, and they're pretty much interchangeable

Then there's the three-chord trick, which is similar to the twelve bar blues but just cycles through the chords I IV V IV I IV V IV – this is the chord sequence for "La Bamba", "Louie Louie", "Twist and Shout", and "Hang On Sloopy". If a sixties garage band could play it, and it sounded vaguely Latin, it was probably a three-chord trick.

And finally, there's the doo wop chord sequence. This is actually two very slightly different chord sequences – I , vi, ii, V and I, vi, IV, V. But those two sequences are so similar that we'll just lump them both in under the single heading of "the doo wop chord sequence" from now on. If you don't know anything about music theory, the ii chord (the minor second) and the IV chord (the major fourth) in a key share two of their three notes – the two sequences are so interchangeable that any song written with one sequence can be played with the other. So for our purposes, it's all one sequence.

And that may be the most important chord sequence ever, just in terms of the number of songs which use it. It's the progression that lies behind thirties songs like "Blue Moon", and the version of "Heart and Soul" most people can play on the piano (the original song is slightly different), but it's also in "Oliver's Army" by Elvis Costello, "Enola Gay" by Orchestral Manoeuvres in the Dark, "Million Reasons" by Lady Gaga, "I'm the One" by DJ Khaled. . . whatever genre of music you like, you almost certainly know and love dozens of songs based on that progression. (And you almost certainly hate dozens more. It's also been used in a *lot* of big ballads that get overplayed to death, and if you're not the kind of person who likes those records, you might end up massively sick of them.)

But while it has been used in almost every genre of music, the reason why we call this progression the doo wop progression is that it's behind almost every doo wop song of the fifties and early sixties. "Duke of Earl", "Why Do Fools Fall in Love", "In the Still of the Night", "Sh-Boom" – it forms the basis of more hit records in that genre than I could name. It would be easier to name the doo wop songs that *don't* use that progression.

And in this chapter we're going to look at a song that cemented that sequence as the doo wop standard, imitated by everyone, and which managed to become a massive hit despite containing almost nothing at all original.

The Penguins were a vocal group, that formed out of the maelstrom of vocal groups in LA in the fifties, in the scene around Central Ave.

One thing you'll notice when we talk about vocal groups, especially in LA, is that it gets very confusing very fast with all the different bands swapping members and taking each others' names. So for clarity, the Hollywood Flames, featuring Bobby Byrd, were different from the Famous Flames, who also featured Bobby Byrd, who wasn't the same Bobby Byrd as the Bobby Byrd who was a Hollywood Flame. And when we talk about bird groups, we're talking about groups named after birds, not groups featuring Bobby Byrd. And the two members of the Hollywood Flames who were previously in a bird group called the Flamingos weren't in the bird group called the Flamingos that people normally mean when they talk about the Flamingos, they were in a different band called the Flamingos that went on to become the Platters. Got that?

I'm sorry. I know that makes no sense, but that should hopefully give you some idea of what the experience of tracing these groups' histories feels like. Even the sources I'm consulting for this, written by experts who've spent decades trying to figure out who was in what band, often admit to being very unsure of their facts. Vocal groups on the West Coast in the US were far more fluid than on the East Coast, and membership could change from day to day and hour to hour.

But now, I'll try to give you as accurate and straightforward a picture of the actual development of the Penguins as I can. It's a convoluted story, but I'll try to make it easy to follow.

We'll start with the Hollywood Flames. The Hollywood Flames initially formed in 1948, at one of the talent shows that were such important incubators of black musical talent in the 1950s. In this case, they all separately attended a talent show at the Largo Theatre in Los Angeles, where so many different singers turned up that instead of putting them all on separately, the theatre owner told them to split into a few vocal groups.

Shortly after forming, the Hollywood Flames started performing at the Barrelhouse Club, owned by Johnny Otis, and started recording under a variety of different names. Their first release was as "The Flames", and came out in January 1950.

Another track they recorded early on was "Tabarin", by an aspiring songwriter named Murry Wilson. Murry Wilson would never have much success as a songwriter, but we'll be hearing about him a lot in volumes two and three of this series, as he went on to manage his sons' group, the Beach Boys.

At some point in late 1954, Curtis Williams, one of the Hollywood Flames, left the group. It seems likely, in fact, that the Hollywood Flames split up in late 1954 or early 55, and reformed later – throughout 1955 there were a ton of records released featuring various vocalists from the Hollywood Flames in various combinations, under other band names, but in the crucial years of 1955 and 1956, when rock and roll broke out, the Hollywood Flames were not active, even though later on they would go on to have quite a few minor hits.

But while the band wasn't active, the individuals were, and Curtis Williams took with him a song he had been working on with another member, Gaynel Hodge. That song was called "Earth Angel", and when he bumped into his old friend Cleve Duncan, Williams asked Duncan if he'd help him with it. Duncan agreed, and they worked out an arrangement for the song, and decided to form a new vocal group, each bringing in one old friend from their respective high schools. Duncan brought in Dexter Tisby, while Williams brought in Bruce Tate. They decided to call themselves The Penguins, after the mascot on Kool cigarettes.

Williams and Tate had both attended Jefferson High School, and now is as good a time as any to talk about that school. Because Jefferson High School produced more great jazz and R&B musicians than you'd expect from a school ten times its size, or even a hundred. Etta James, Dexter Gordon, Art Farmer, Johnny "Guitar" Watson, Barry White, Richard Berry... The great jazz trumpeter Don Cherry actually got in trouble with his own school because he would play truant – in order to go and play with the music students at Jefferson High.

And this abundance of talent was down to one good teacher – the music teacher Samuel Browne, who along with Hazel Whittaker and Marjorie Bright was one of the first three black teachers to be employed to teach secondary school classes in LA.

Several of the white faculty at Jefferson asked to be transferred when he started working at Jefferson High, but Browne put together an astonishing programme of music lessons at the school, teaching the children about the music that they cared about – jazz and blues – while also teaching them to play classical music. He would have masterclasses taught by popular musicians like Lionel Hampton or Nat "King" Cole, and art musicians like William Grant Still, the most important black composer and conductor in the classical world in the mid-twentieth century. It was, quite simply, the greatest musical education it was possible to have at that time, and certainly an education far beyond anything that most poor black kids of the time could dream of. Half the great black musicians in California in the forties and fifties learned in Browne's lessons.

And that meant that there was a whole culture at Jefferson High of taking music seriously, which meant that even those who weren't Browne's star pupils knew it was possible for them to become successful singers and songwriters.

Jesse Belvin, who had been a classmate of Curtis Williams and Gaynel Hodge when they were in the Hollywood Flames, was himself a minor R&B star already, and he would soon become a major one. He helped Williams and Hodge with their song "Earth Angel", and it has a great deal of melodic resemblance to his first hit; a song called "Dream Girl".

But that's not the only part of "Earth Angel" that was borrowed. There's the line "Will you be mine?", which had been the title of a hit record by the Swallows. The arrangement comes straight from "I Know" by the Hollywood Flames, recorded when Williams was still in the band with Hodge.

And most importantly, the Hollywood Flames had, a while earlier, been asked to record a demo for a local songwriter, Jessie Mae Robinson. That song, "I Went to Your Wedding", later became a hit for the country singer Patti Page.

The middle eight of "I Went to Your Wedding" was melodically identical to the middle eight of "Earth Angel", and the two had very similar sets of lyrics, too. Compare "I Went to Your Wedding":

> She came down the aisle, wearing a smile
>
> A vision of loveliness
>
> I uttered a sigh, whispered goodbye
>
> Goodbye to my happiness

With "Earth Angel"

> I fell for you and I knew
>
> The vision of your loveliness
>
> I hoped and I pray that someday

I'll be the vision of your happiness

The song was a Frankenstein's monster, bolted together out of bits of spare parts from other songs, But like the monster, it took on a life of its own. And the spark that gave it life came from Dootsie Williams.

Dootsie Williams was the owner of Doo-Tone Records, and was a former musician, who had played trumpet in jazz and R&B bands for several years before realising that he could make more money by putting out records by other people.

His first commercial successes came not from music at all, but from comedy. Williams was a fan of the comedian Red Foxx, and wanted to put out albums of Foxx's live set. Foxx initially refused, because he thought that if he recorded anything then people wouldn't pay to come and see his live shows. However, he became short of cash and agreed to make a record of his then-current live set. *Laff of the Party* became a massive hit, and more or less started the trend for comedy albums.

Williams wasn't, primarily, a record-company owner, though. He was like Sam Phillips – someone who provided recording services – but his recordings were songwriters' demos, and so meant to be for professionals, unlike the amateurs Phillips recorded.

The Penguins would record some of those demos for him, performing the songs for the songwriters who couldn't sing themselves, and as he put it "I had the Penguins doing some vocals and they begged me 'Please record us so we can get a release and go on the road and get famous' and all that. They kept buggin' me 'til I said, 'Okay, what have you got?'"

Their first single, credited to "The Dootsie Williams Orchestra, with Vocal by The Penguins" didn't even feature the Penguins on the other side. The song itself, "There Ain't No News Today", wasn't an original to the band, and it bore more than a slight resemblance to records like Wynonie Harris' "Who Threw the Whiskey in the Well?"

But the "what have you got?" question had also been about songs. Williams was also a music publisher, and he was interested in finding songs he could exploit, not just recordings. As he put it, talking to Johnny Otis:

"They said, 'We got a song called "Earth Angel" and a song called "Hey Señorita".' Of course, 'Earth Angel' was all messed up, you know how they come to you. So I straightened it out here and straightened it out there, and doggone, it sounded pretty good."

"Earth Angel" was not even intended to be an A-side, originally. It was tossed off as a demo, and a demo for what was expected to be a B-side. The intended A-side was "Hey Señorita". Both tracks were only meant to be demos, not the finished recordings, and several takes had to be scrapped because of a neighbour's dog barking.

But almost straight away, it became obvious that there was something special about "Earth Angel". Dootsie Williams took the demo recording to Dolphin's of Hollywood, the most important R&B record shop on the West Coast.

As we discussed last chapter,as well as being a record shop and the headquarters of a record label, Dolphin's also broadcast R&B radio shows from the shop. And Dolphin's radio station and record shop were aimed, not at the black adult buyers of R&B generally, but at teenagers.

And this is something that needs to be noted about "Earth Angel" – it's a song where the emphasis is definitely on the "Angel" rather than on the "Earth". Most R&B songs at the time were rooted in the real world – they were aimed at adults and had adult concerns like sex, or paying the rent, or your partner cheating on you, or your partner cheating on you because you couldn't pay the rent and so now you had no-one to have sex with. There were, of course, other topics covered, and we've talked about many of them, but the presumed audience was someone who had real problems in their life – and who therefore also needed escapist music to give them some relief from their problems.

On the other hand, the romance being dealt with in "Earth Angel" is one that is absolutely based in teenage romantic idealisations rather than in anything like real world relationships.

(This is, incidentally, one of the ways in which the song resembles "Dream Girl", which again is about a fantasy of a woman rather than about a real woman).

The girl in the song only exists in her effects on the male singer – she's not described physically, or in terms of her personality, only in the emotional effect she has on the vocalist.

But this non-specificity works well for this kind of song, as it allows the listener to project the song onto their own crush without having to deal with inconvenient differences in detail – and as the song is about longing for someone, rather than being in a relationship with someone, it's likely that many of the adolescents who found themselves moved by the song knew almost as little about their crush as they did about the character in the song.

The DJ who was on the air when Dootsie Williams showed up was Dick "Huggy Boy" Hugg, possibly the most popular DJ on the station. Huggy Boy played "Earth Angel" and "Hey Señorita", and requests started to come in for the songs almost straight away. Williams didn't want to waste time rerecording the songs when they'd gone down so well, and released it as the final record.

Of course, as with all black records at this point in time, the big question was which white people would have the bigger hit with it? Would Georgia Gibbs get in with a bland white cover, or would it be Pat Boone? As it turns out, it was the Crew Cuts, who went to number one (or number three, I've seen different reports in different sources) on the pop charts with their version.

After "Sh-Boom", the Crew Cuts had briefly tried to go back to barbershop harmony with a version of "The Whiffenpoof Song", but when that did nothing, in quick succession they knocked out hit, bland, covers first of "Earth Angel" and then of "Ko Ko Mo", which restored them to the top of the charts at the expense of the black originals.

But it shows how times were slowly changing that the Penguins' version also made the top ten on the pop charts, as Johnny Ace had before them. The practice of white artists covering black artists' songs would continue for a while, but within a couple of years it would have more-or-less disappeared, only to come back in a new form in the sixties.

The Penguins recorded a follow-up single, "Ookey Ook". That, however, wasn't a hit. Dootsie Williams had been refusing to pay the band any advances on royalties, even as "Earth Angel" rose to number one on the R&B charts, and the Penguins were annoyed enough that they signed with Buck Ram, the songwriter and manager who also looked after the Platters, and got a new contract with Mercury.

Williams warned them that they wouldn't see a penny from him if they broke their contract, but they reasoned that they weren't seeing any money from him anyway, and so decided it didn't matter. They'd be big stars on Mercury, after all. They went into the studio to do the same thing that Gene and Eunice had done, rerecording their two singles and the B-sides, although these recordings didn't end up getting released at the time.

Unfortunately for the Penguins, they weren't really the band that Ram was interested in. Ram had used the Penguins' current success as a way to get a deal both for them and for the Platters, the group he really cared about. And once the Platters had a hit of their own – a hit written by Buck Ram – he stopped bothering with the Penguins. They made several records for Mercury, but with no lasting commercial success. And since they'd broken their contract with Doo-Tone, they made no money at all from having sung "Earth Angel".

At the same time, the band started to fracture. Bruce Tate became mentally ill from the stress of fame, quit the band, and then killed someone in a hit-and-run accident while driving a stolen car. He was replaced by Randy Jones. Within a year Jones had left the band, as had Dexter Tisby. They returned a few months after that, and their replacements were sacked, but then Curtis Williams left to rejoin the Hollywood Flames, and Teddy Harper, who had been Dexter Tisby's replacement, replaced Williams. The Penguins had basically become Cleve Duncan, who had sung lead on "Earth Angel", and any selection of three other singers, and at one point there seem to have been two rival sets of Penguins recording.

By 1963, Dexter Tisby, Randy Jones, and Teddy Harper were touring together as a fake version of the Coasters, along with Cornell Gunter who was actually a member of the Coasters who'd split from the other three members of *his* group. You perhaps see now why I said that stuff at the beginning about the vocal group lineups being confusing.

At the same time, Cleve Duncan was singing with a whole other group of Penguins, recording a song that would never be a huge hit but would appear on many doo wop compilations – so many that it's as well known as many of the big hits, "Memories of El Monte". That song was written in 1963 by Frank Zappa and Ray Collins, both later of the Mothers of Invention, and its lyrics hark back to the innocent days of the mid-fifties.

It's fascinating to listen to that song, and to realise that by the very early sixties, pre-British Invasion, the doo wop and rock-and-roll eras were already the subject of nostalgia records. Pop not only will eat itself, but it has been doing almost since its inception.

Meanwhile, there were lawsuits to contend with. "Earth Angel" had originally been credited to Curtis Williams and Gaynel Hodge, but they'd been helped out in the early stages of writing it by Jesse Belvin, and then Cleve Duncan had adjusted the melody, and Dootsie Williams claimed to have helped them fix up the song.

Belvin had been drafted into the army when "Earth Angel" had hit, and when he got out he was broke, and he was persuaded by Dootsie Williams, who still seems to have held a grudge about the Penguins breaking their contract, to sue over the songwriting royalties. Belvin won sole credit in the lawsuit, and then signed over that sole credit to Dootsie Williams, so (according to Marv Goldberg) for a while Dootsie Williams was credited as the only writer.

Luckily, for once, that injustice was eventually rectified. These days, thankfully, the writing credits are split between Curtis Williams, Jesse Belvin, and Gaynel Hodge, and in 2013 Hodge, the last surviving co-writer of the song, was given an award by BMI for the song having been played on the radio a million times. Hodge and the estates of his co-writers receive royalties for its continued popularity.

Curtis Williams and Bruce Tate both died in the 1970s. Jesse Belvin died earlier than that, but we'll look at his life and death in a later chapter. Dexter Tisby seems to be still alive, as is Gaynel Hodge. And Cleve Duncan continued performing with various lineups of Penguins until his death in 2012, making a living as a performer from a song that sold twenty million copies but never paid its performers a penny. He always said that he was always happy to sing his hit, so long as the audiences were happy to hear it, and they always were.

"Ain't That a Shame"

As you'll remember from the chapter on "Lawdy Miss Clawdy", after his brief split from Imperial Records, and thus from working with Fats Domino, Dave Bartholomew had returned to Imperial after Domino helped him on "Lawdy Miss Clawdy", and the two of them resumed their collaboration.

The first new track they recorded together was an instrumental called "Dreaming", featuring members of both Domino's touring band and of Bartholomew's studio band. It's credited on the label to Bartholomew as a writer, but other sources have the instrumental being written by Domino.

Whoever wrote it, the most popular hypothesis seems to be that the song was written as a tribute to Domino's manager, Melvin Cade, who had died only five days before the session. Domino had been sleeping in the back of Cade's car, as Cade had been speeding to get them to a show that they were late for. Cade had lost control of the car, which had been thrown ten feet into the air in a collision. Domino and the other passengers were uninjured, but Cade died of his injuries.

While this was obviously tragic, it turned out to be to Domino's benefit – Domino's contract with Cade had given Domino only a hundred and fifty dollars a day from his shows, with Cade keeping the rest – which might often be several times as much money. With Cade's death, Domino was free from that contract, and so the beginning of September 1952, with the death of Cade and the renewal of Domino and Bartholomew's partnership, marks the start of the second phase of Fats Domino's career.

It also marked the resumption of Domino and Bartholomew's strained songwriting partnership – although this is using "strained" in a fairly loose sense, given that they continued working with each other for decades. But like with so many musical partnerships where the whole is greater than the sum of the parts, both men did consider their own contribution to be the more important. Bartholomew considered himself to be the more important writer because he came up with literate stories with narrative arcs and punchlines, coupled with sophisticated musical ideas, while Domino considered himself more important because he came up with relatable, simple, ideas and catchy hooks.

And, of course, Domino's piano style and distinctive voice were crucial in the popularity of the records, just as Dave Bartholomew's arrangement and production ideas were.

And the difference in their attitudes shows up in, for example, "Going to the River", one of the first fruits of their renewed collaboration. Dave Bartholomew called that "a nothing song" – and it's easy to see what he means. Other than the tresillo bassline, there's not much of musical interest there. You've got Domino playing his usual triplets in the right hand on the piano, but rather than the drums emphasising the backbeat, they're mostly playing the same triplets as the piano. The chord sequence is nothing special. and the lyrics were simplistic.

But at the same time, the track did go to number two on the R&B charts, and probably would have gone to number one if it hadn't been for a cover version by Chuck Willis which went to number four. For once it wasn't a white man having a hit with a black man's song, but another black man, who'd heard Domino perform it live before the record was released and got in quickly with his own version.

On the other hand, it wasn't like Domino was the perfect judge of what made a hit, either. Bartholomew wrote the song "I Hear You Knocking" for Domino, but when Domino decided not to record it, Bartholomew recorded it for another artist on Imperial Records, Smiley Lewis, getting the great New Orleans piano player Huey "Piano" Smith to play in an imitation of Domino's style. That went to number two on the R&B charts, and a cover version by the white singer Gale Storm went to number two on the pop charts.

So both Domino and Bartholomew were capable of coming up with big hits in the style they perfected together, and both were capable of dismissing a potential hit when it wasn't their own idea. But their partnership was so successful that Dave Bartholomew actually regarded Smiley Lewis as a "bad luck singer", because when Bartholomew wrote and produced for him, the records would only sell a hundred thousand copies or so, compared to the much larger numbers of records that Domino sold.

Domino was becoming huge in the R&B world – in early 1954 Billboard listed him as the biggest selling R&B star in the country – and he was managing to cope with it better than most. While he would miss the occasional gig from drinking a little too much, and he'd sleep around on the road more than a married man should, he was essentially a well-adjusted, private, man, who had five kids, phoned home to his wife every night, and never touched anything stronger than alcohol.

That wasn't true of the rest of his band, however. In the 1950s, heroin was the chic drug to be taking if you were a touring musician, and many of Domino's touring band members were users. He would often have to pay to get his guitarist's instrument out of the pawn shop, so they could go on tour, and once even had to pay off the guitarist's back child support, to get him out of jail, as he would keep spending all his money on heroin.

The one who came out worst, sadly, was Jimmy Gilchrist, who would sing with Domino's backing band as the support act. Gilchrist died of an overdose during one of Domino's tours in early 1954. Domino replaced him with a new support act, Jalacey Hawkins, but he only lasted a couple of weeks. According to Domino, he fired Jalacey for being too vulgar on stage, and screaming, but Screamin' Jay Hawkins, as he would soon become known, claimed instead that it was because Domino was jealous of Hawkins' cool leopard-skin suit.

But through this turmoil, Domino and Bartholomew, with Cosimo Matassa in the control room, continued recording a whole string of hits – "Please Don't Leave Me", "Rose Mary", "Something's Wrong", "You Done Me Wrong", and "Don't You Know" all went top ten on the R&B charts. For two and a half years, from September 1952 through March 1955, they would dominate the rhythm and blues charts, even though most white audiences had little idea who Fats Domino was.

But slowly Domino was noticing that more and more white teenagers were starting to come to his shows – and he also started incorporating a few country songs and old standards into his otherwise R&B-dominated act, catering slightly more to a pop audience.

Their first crossover hit definitely has more of Domino's fingerprints on it than Bartholomew's. Bartholomew was unimpressed at the session, saying that the song didn't tell a complete story. Once it became a hit, though, Bartholomew would soften on the song, saying "'Ain't That a Shame' will never die, it will be here when the world comes to an end."

He may not have been a particular fan of the song, but you'd never know it from his arrangement. Take, for example, the way the horn section in the intro punctuates the words. It doesn't just go "You made me cry", but "You made – BAM BAM – me cry – BAM BAM". That's the kind of arrangement decision that can only be made by someone with a real feel for the material. And this is where Dave Bartholomew's real importance to the records he was making with Fats Domino comes in. It's all well and good Bartholomew doing great arrangements and productions for his own songs, or songs mostly written by him, but he put the same thought and attention into the arrangements even where the song was not to his taste and wasn't his idea.

Domino's biographer Rick Coleman – to whose biography of Domino I'm extremely indebted for the chapters on Domino – suggests that Dave Bartholomew's arrangement owes a little to the old Dixieland jazz standard "Tin Roof Blues". I can sort of hear it, but I'm not entirely convinced.

Another possible influence on "Ain't That a Shame" is a record by Lloyd Price, who of course had worked with both Domino and Bartholomew earlier. His "Ain't it a Shame" doesn't sound much like "Ain't That a Shame", but it does have a very Fats Domino feel, and it would be very surprising if neither Bartholomew nor Domino had heard it given their previous collaborations. Indeed, early pressings of "Ain't That a Shame" mistakenly called it "Ain't It a Shame", presumably because of confusion with the Lloyd Price song.

Bartholomew and Matassa also put more thought into the production than was normal at this time. When mastering Domino's records, now that Matassa's studio had finally switched to tape from cutting directly on to wax, they would speed up the tape slightly – a trick which made Domino's voice sound younger, and which emphasised the beat more. This sort of thing is absolutely basic now, but at the time it was extraordinarily unusual for any rhythm and blues records to have any kind of production trickery at all. It also had another advantage, because as Cosimo Matassa would point out, it would change the key slightly so it wouldn't be in a normal key at all. So when other people tried to cover Domino's records "they couldn't find the damn notes on the piano!"

Of course, with success came problems of its own. When Domino was sent on a promotional tour of local radio stations, DJs would complain to Lew Chudd of Imperial Records that Domino didn't speak English. He did speak English – though it was his second language, after Creole French – but he spoke English with such a thick accent that many people from outside Louisiana didn't recognise it as English at all.

Domino's relative lack of fluency in English is possibly also why he wrote such simple lyrics – a fact that was mocked on national TV when Steve Allen, the talk show host, read out the lyrics to "Ain't That a Shame" in a mock "poetry recital", to laughter from the studio audience, causing Bartholomew and Domino to feel extremely upset.

Of course, this is an easy trick to play, as almost all song lyrics sound puerile when recited pompously enough, and without the musical accompaniment. For example, try reading the following out loud:

Lets go to church, next Sunday morning

We'll see our friends on the way

We'll stand and sing, on Sunday morning

And I'll hold your hand as we pray

Sounds ridiculous, doesn't it? That, of course, is a lyric written by Steve Allen, who despite having written 8500 songs by his own count, never wrote one as good as "Ain't That a Shame".

As with all black hits at this time, there was a terrible white cover, in this case by Pat Boone. Boone's cover version came out almost before Domino's did, thanks to Bill Randle. Bill Randle was a DJ in Cleveland, a colleague of Alan Freed, who is now a much better-known

DJ, but in the early fifties Randle was possibly the best-known DJ in America. While Freed only played black rhythm and blues records, Randle, whose first radio show was called "the Inter-Racial Goodtime Hour", played records by both black and white people. As the country's biggest DJ, he was sent an advance copy of "Ain't That a Shame", and he liked it immensely. According to Lew Chudd, "He liked it because it was ignorant, because he was an English professor". That's sort of true – Randle wasn't a professor at the time, but in the 1960s he ended up getting degrees in law, journalism, sociology, and education, and a doctorate in American Studies, all while continuing to work as a DJ.

Randle would regularly send copies of new R&B records to white record executives he knew, and it was because of Randle that the Crew Cuts and the Diamonds, among others, first heard the black recordings whose style they stole. In this case, he sent his acetate copy of "Ain't That a Shame" to Randy Wood, the owner of Dot Records, a label set up specifically to record white cover versions of black records.

Randle was an odd case, in this respect, because he *was* someone who truly loved rhythm and blues, and black music, and would play it regularly on his show – early on, he had actually been fired from one of his first radio jobs for playing a Sister Rosetta Tharpe record, though he was soon rehired. But he seems to have truly bought into the idea that the white cover versions of black records did help the black performers.

There are very few examples of how little that was the case more blatant than that of Boone, a man whose attitude is best summed up by the fact that when he recorded his version, he tried to change the lyrics to "Isn't That a Shame" because he thought "Ain't" ungrammatical.

In a 1977 interview, Domino said of Boone's cover 'When I first heard it I didn't like it. It took two months to write and he put it out almost the same time I did. It kind of hurt. The publishing companies don't care if a thousand people make it." Talking to Domino's biographer Rick Coleman, Dave Bartholomew was characteristically more forthright. "Pat Boone was a lucky white boy. He wasn't singing shit. Randy Wood was doing un-Constitutional type stuff. He was successful with it, but that don't make it right!"

Bill Randle would play both versions of the record on his show, and both went to number one in Cleveland as a result. But in the rest of the country, the clean-cut white man was miles ahead of the fat black man with a flat top from New Orleans.

Boone's misunderstanding typifies the cultural ignorance that characterised white cover versions of R&B hits in this period. A few months later, a similar thing would happen again with Domino's hit "Bo Weevil", and here the racial dynamics were more apparent.

The song was covered by Teresa Brewer, and obviously her version did better on the charts. But the thing is, that song celebrates boll weevils – pests which destroy cotton, and which have become regarded in African-American folklore as humorous trickster figures, because they bankrupted plantation owners – and while boll weevils didn't reach the USA until after slavery had ended, you can understand how a pest that destroys the livelihood of cotton plantation owners might have a rather different reputation among black people than white.

But despite these white covers, Domino continued to make inroads into the white market himself. And for all that Domino's music seems easygoing, it was enough that even before his proper crossover into the pop market, Domino had shows cancelled because the promoters or local government couldn't handle the potential of riots breaking out at his shows. That only increased when "Ain't That a Shame" hit, and white teenagers wanted to come to the shows. Police would try to shut them down, because white and black kids dancing together was illegal, and often shows would be cancelled because of the police's heavy-handed tactics – for example, at one show in Houston, the police tried in vain to stop the dancing, and eventually said that only whites would be allowed to dance, so Domino stopped the show, and the kids in the audience defiantly sang "Let the Good Times Roll" at the police. At another show in San Jose, someone threw a lit string of firecrackers into the audience, leading to a dozen people requiring medical treatment and another dozen being arrested.

"Ain't That a Shame" was one of two hit songs recorded on the same day. The other, "All By Myself", would also become a number one hit on the R&B charts.

While "All By Myself" was credited to Domino and Bartholomew, it was based very closely on an old Big Bill Broonzy record. While the verses are quite different, the choruses are identical. Domino here for the first time plays in his two-beat piano style, yet another of the New Orleans rhythms that Domino and Bartholomew would incorporate into Domino's hits.

A standard two-beat rhythm is the rhythm one finds in polkas, or in, say, Johnny Cash records – that boom-chick, boom-chick, walking or marching rhythm. But the New Orleans variant of it, which as far as I can tell was first recorded when Domino recorded "All By Myself", isn't boom-chick boom-chick, but is rather boom-boom-chick, boom-boom-chick, with quavers on the first beat, and slightly swinging the quavers. Indeed by doing it two-handed (with the bass booms in the left hand and the treble chicks in the right), Domino also sneaks in a bass quaver at the end of the "chick", syncopating it, so it comes out as "a-boom-boom-chick, a-boom-boom-chick".

The two-beat rhythm would become as important a factor in Domino's future records as his rolling piano triplets and Dave Bartholomew's tresillo rhythms already had been. Domino's music was about rhythm and groove, and whereas most of his contemporaries were content to stick with one or two simple rhythms, Domino and Bartholomew would stack all of these different rhythmic patterns on top of each other.

A lot of this is the basic musical vocabulary of anyone working in any of the musics influenced by New Orleans R&B these days, which includes all of reggae and ska as well as most African-American musical idioms, but that vocabulary was being built in these sessions. Domino and Bartholomew weren't the only ones doing it – Professor Longhair and Huey "Piano" Smith and Mac Rebennack were all contributing, and all of these performers would take each other's material and put their own unique spin on it – but they were vital parts of creating these building blocks that would be used by musicians to this day.

"Ain't That a Shame" was just the start of Domino's rock and roll stardom. He would go on to have another seven R&B number ones after this, and his records would consistently chart on the R&B charts for the next seven years – he would have, in total, forty top ten hits on the R&B chart in his career. But what was more remarkable was the number of pop chart hits he would have. He had fourteen pop top twenty hits between 1955 and 1961, eleven of them going top ten, including classics like "I'm in Love Again", "I'm Walkin'", "Blue

Monday", "Valley of Tears", "I Want to Walk You Home" and "Walking to New Orleans". Almost all of his hit singles were written by the Bartholomew and Domino songwriting team, and almost all of them were extraordinarily good records – there were almost no fifties rockers who had anything like Domino's consistent quality. So we'll be seeing Fats Domino again in a future chapter, when he finds his thrill on Blueberry Hill. . .

"Tweedle Dee"

We talked back in the chapter on "Ko Ko Mo" about how the copyright law in the 1950s didn't protect arrangements, and how that disproportionately affected black artists. But that doesn't mean that the black artists didn't fight back. Today we're going to talk about LaVern Baker, who led the fight for black artists' rights in the 1950s, But she was also one of the most successful female R&B artists of the fifties, and would deserve recognition even had she never been a campaigner.

LaVern Baker was born Delores Evans, but she took her father's surname, Baker, as a stage name – although she took on many different names in the early stages of her career.

Music ran in her family. Her aunt, for example, was Merline Johnson, the "Yas Yas Girl", who had been a mildly successful blues singer in the thirties and forties, and had performed with musicians such as Big Bill Broonzy and Blind John Davis.

Young Delores idolised her aunt, as well as her more distant relative, the blues singer Memphis Minnie, and by the time she was twelve she was recording with Lester Melrose, the producer at RCA who also worked with Baker's relatives. However, those early recordings only produced one single, under another name, which sold so poorly that when she was interviewed in the 1990s Baker would say that she only knew of one person who owned a copy, and that person wouldn't even make a cassette copy for Baker.

When Baker became a full time singer in her late teens, she wasn't performing as LaVern Baker, but as "Little Miss Sharecropper". She was, in fact, basically a tribute act to "Little Miss Cornshucks", a novelty blues singer whose act had her dressed as an innocent, unsophisticated, farm-girl.

Little Miss Cornshucks seems to have had personal problems that limited her success – she was an alcoholic and married to a drug dealer – but she was hugely influential on a lot of the rhythm and blues artists who recorded for Atlantic in the early 1950s, as she was a favourite of the label's owner, Ahmet Ertegun. In particular, Ruth Brown's first hit single on Atlantic, "So Long", was a cover version of Cornshucks' local hit version of the song from the forties.

Little Miss Cornshucks never did particularly well on the national scene, but she was popular enough in Chicago that the club owners wanted to put on an act who could capitalise on that popularity. And so, like Little Miss Cornshucks, Little Miss Sharecropper would go on stage carrying a straw basket, barefoot, in ragged clothes and a straw hat. She was not exactly happy about this act, but she still gave her all in her performances, and quickly established a reputation as an excellent blues singer around the Midwest – first in Chicago and later in Detroit. She also recorded at least a few singles as Little Miss Sharecropper, including an early attempt at jumping on the rock bandwagon, "I Want to Rock".

While in Detroit, she also played a big part in teaching a young singer named Johnnie Ray how to sing the blues. Ray went on to be the biggest teen idol of the early 1950s, and most of the gimmicks the young singer used to make his audience of teenage girls swoon for him were things that LaVern Baker had taught him how to do, mostly things she'd picked up from Al Jolson.

Ray was a singer who many listeners thought at first was himself a black woman, and so there are a *lot* of racial dynamics at play there, in a black woman who had to perform as a caricature of ignorant black femininity teaching a white man who sang like a black woman how to perform by getting him to copy the stage presence of a blackface minstrel act.

Both Ray and Baker were hugely influenced by another singer, Dinah Washington, as almost all R&B singers, especially women, were at this time. Washington worked on the borders of jazz and R&B, but slightly over to the jazz side rather than to the R&B one, and so while she didn't make rock and roll music herself, or even proto-rock and roll, without her we would have no Ray Charles or Aretha Franklin, no Etta James or LaVern Baker.

Washington was the consummate blues stylist, but the music she sang was a combination of traditional pop, jazz, blues, R&B, and torch songs. Like so many of the early stars of R&B, she started out as a member of Lionel Hampton's band, singing with him for a couple of years in the late 1940s, before she went solo and started performing her own music.

Washington didn't hit the pop charts with any regularity until 1959, but she was a regular at the top of the R&B charts right from the beginning of her career, and one thing you'll notice if you read the biographies of any singer at all from this time period is them saying how much they wanted to sound like Washington specifically. Washington's commercial peak came rather later than her peak in influence, and she only played a very indirect part in the history of rock and roll, but it was a very large indirect part.

While Baker was performing as Little Miss Sharecropper, she also recorded for a lot of different labels, under a variety of different names. But none of these records sold outside the cities Baker was playing in, and she remained unknown elsewhere until 1953, when she signed with Atlantic Records.

Her first single for Atlantic, "Soul on Fire" was credited to Baker plus one of Ahmet Ertegun's pseudonyms and was, for the time, a remarkably intense record. Before it was released, she got the chance to go overseas for the first time. She joined a touring show called The Harlem Melody in late 1953, and travelled to Europe with that tour. The rest of the acts eventually moved on, and moved back to the USA, but Baker decided to stay on performing in Milan, and occasionally also performing in France. She didn't learn to speak the language, but was successful there until she got a telegram from her agent telling her to get back home because she had a hit record.

"Soul on Fire" wasn't actually a hit, but it was a successful enough single that Atlantic were convinced that Baker was someone worth investing in, and so they had called her back for another session. This time it was for a bit of pop fluff called "Tweedle Dee".

"Tweedle Dee" was a clear attempt at another "Ko Ko Mo" – an R&B record with a vaguely Latin beat, and with lyrics consisting of platitudes about love and gibberish nonsense syllables. And early 1955 was the very best possible time to release something like that. Baker turned in a great vocal on a song that didn't really deserve it, but her conviction alone gave the record enough power that it rose to number fourteen on the pop charts.

But Baker's hit was another one to fall foul of Georgia Gibbs.

Gibbs was a popular singer from the big band era, who'd had hit records with things like "If I Knew You Were Coming I'd Have Baked a Cake". But when musical fashions changed, Gibbs took to recording hits by black artists in soundalike versions, as we've already seen in the chapter on "The Wallflower".

In the case of "Tweedle Dee", Gibbs and her producers hired the same arranger and musicians who'd played on Baker's record, and even tried to hire the same engineer, (Tom Dowd, of Atlantic Records, who turned them down) just in case they had a single scrap of originality left in their sound somewhere. They were attempting, as far as possible, to make the exact same record, just with a white woman as the credited artist.

It's a distinction I've made before, but it's one that continues to need to be made – there is a continuum of cover versions, and not all are created equal. In the case of white artists in the fifties covering black artists, there is always a power imbalance there – there are always opportunities the white artist can take that the black artist can't – but there is a huge, clear, distinction between on the one hand a transformative cover like Elvis Presley doing "That's All Right, Mama", where the artist totally recasts it into his own style, and on the other hand... well, on the other hand hiring the same arranger and musicians to rerecord a track note-for-note.

And Baker certainly thought there was a difference. She had nothing against white singers performing in black idioms or singing other people's songs – again, she had helped make Johnnie Ray into the star that he became – but someone just straight out copying every single element of one of her records and having a bigger hit with it was a step too far. And unlike many of the other artists of the time, Baker decided she was going to do something about it.

The thing you need to understand here is that while Baker later estimated that she had lost as much as fifteen thousand dollars – in 1955 dollars – on lost sales because of Gibbs, she was not particularly interested in the money. What she was interested in was the exposure that radio play, in particular, would bring her. And it was the radio play, more than anything else, that was the big problem for her, and for other black artists.

Audiences weren't finding out about Baker's record as much as they should have, because the radio was playing Gibbs' record and not Baker's. Without that radio exposure, Baker lost out on sales, and lost out on new fans who might like her other records.

Baker decided that she had to fight back against this.

One thing she did was a simple publicity stunt – Baker had to travel on a long-distance flight, and before she did so, she took out a life insurance policy, putting Gibbs down as the beneficiary, because if Baker died then Gibbs would no longer have a career without having anyone to copy. But she did more than that.

She also lobbied Congressman Charles Diggs Jr, for help. Diggs was the first black Congressman from Michigan, and he was a pioneer in civil rights in US electoral politics. He had only just been elected when Baker contacted him, but he would soon rise to national attention with his publicising of the case of Emmett Till, a fourteen-year-old black child who had been brutally murdered because he had been accused of whistling at a white woman.

In her open letter to Diggs, Baker said "After an investigation of the facts, you might see some wisdom in introducing a law to make it illegal to duplicate another's work. It's not that I mind someone singing a song that I wrote or have written for me by someone, but I bitterly resent their arrogance in thefting my music note-for-note".

Now, I have to admit that here I've hit a bit of a wall in my researches, because I have found three different, contradictory, stories about what resulted from this, and I can't find any evidence to distinguish between them in any of the books I've consulted or on the Internet.

One version is that nothing followed from this as far as legislation goes, and that Diggs did nothing.

Another, which I've only found in the book "Blue Rhythms", was that Congress passed a bill which stated that on any record released, sixteen to twenty-four bars of the arrangement had to be different from any other version. Now, frankly, I find this rather difficult to believe — it doesn't fit with anything else I know about the history of the record industry and copyright law, and I can't find any evidence of it anywhere else, but the article in that book quotes Baker as saying this, and as also saying that she kept a copy of the bill in her house for a long time after it passed.

And the third story, which seems the most plausible, but which again I've been unable to confirm, is that Diggs set up a Congressional committee to look into changes to the copyright law, that it investigated what changes could be made, but that it ultimately didn't lead to any laws being passed.

But what definitely happened, largely as a result of the publicity campaign by Baker and the unwelcome attention it drew to the racism of the music industry, is that the practice of making white note-for-note cover versions began to fall out of favour.

Georgia Gibbs' record label announced that after "Dance With Me Henry" she wasn't going to cover any more R&B songs (they claimed that this was because R&B was falling out of favour with the public and nobody liked it anyway, and anyway those grapes were sour), while WINS radio in New York decided it was going to ban copy records altogether. They said that they were going to continue to play cover versions — where an artist recorded someone else's song in their own style, changing the arrangement — but that they weren't going to play straight copies any more. Other stations followed suit.

While Georgia Gibbs' label had said after the "Tweedle-Dee" controversy that Gibbs would not be cutting any more material from this R&B fad, two years on things had changed, and they tried the same trick again, taking Baker's new single "Tra La La" and having Gibbs record a cover version of that.

"Tra La La" was a success, but Gibbs' producers had rather missed the point. "Tra La La" wasn't the side of Baker's record that people were listening to. Instead, everyone was listening to "Jim Dandy" on the other side. While "Tra La La" was another song in the style of "Tweedle Dee", "Jim Dandy" was something altogether rawer, and more... rock and roll.

And this is, I think, the ultimate reason that the white copycats of black music stopped, at least in this form. They could see that people were buying the black musicians' records, but they couldn't see *why* they were buying them. None of the people who were making what amounted to photocopies of the black musicians' records could actually understand the music that they were parasites on. They had no creativity themselves, and relied merely on being able to duplicate someone else's work without understanding it. That's no basis on which to build a career.

"Tra La La" went to number twenty-four on the pop charts for Gibbs, but "Jim Dandy" went to number seventeen for Baker. Gibbs would never have another top thirty hit again.

And so, as this story goes on, we will occasionally have reason to note a white cover version of a black record, but they will become less and less relevant. The dominance of acts like the Crew Cuts and Georgia Gibbs was a brief one, and while they were able to hold back the careers of people like LaVern Baker, they weren't able to be anything themselves other than dead ends, both artistically and commercially.

Gibbs' version wasn't the only cover version of "Tweedle-Dee" by a white person. Elvis Presley was regularly performing the song live as he started his touring career. He never cut the song in the studio, but he would perform it on the radio on occasion.

Indeed, Baker's influence on Presley seems to be rather underrated – as well as performing "Tweedle Dee" live in 1955, he also recorded two other songs that year which Baker also recorded – "Tomorrow Night" and "Harbor Lights". While neither of those songs were original to Baker, it's probably more than just coincidence that he would record so many songs that she sang.

LaVern Baker had a whole run of hits in the late fifties, but she became dissatisfied with the material she was given by Atlantic. While she gave great performances on "Tweedle Dee", "Tra La La", "Ting a Ling", "Humpty Dumpty Heart" and the rest of the songs she was ordered to sing, they were not really the kind of songs that she'd always wanted to perform. She'd wanted to be a torch song singer, and while some of the material she was given, like "Whipper Snapper" by Leiber and Stoller, was superior early rock and roll, a lot of it was novelty gibberish.

You can hear what she could do with something a bit more substantial on "I Cried a Tear", which went to number two on the R&B charts and number twenty-one on the pop charts. "I Cried a Tear" is still ultra-simplistic in its conception, but it's structured more like the songs that Baker had grown up on, and she gives a performance that is more suited to a torch song than to fifties rock and roll.

Having a hit with a track like that – a waltz ballad – gave Baker and her producers the confidence to branch out with her material. In 1958 she would record an entire album of old Bessie Smith tracks, which doesn't quite match up perhaps to the quality of Smith's recordings of the songs, but isn't an embarrassment in comparison with them, which says something.

Baker would have ten years of moderate chart success, making the hot one hundred with everything from the Leiber and Stoller gospel song "Saved" (another song which Elvis later covered) to "Fly Me to the Moon" to "Think Twice", a great soul duet with Jackie Wilson, her last R&B top forty hit, in 1965.

The hits dried up after 1965, and even a novelty song about Batman in 1966 couldn't get her back into the charts, and even before that she had moved more into performing jazz and blues rather than her old rock and roll hits. After her second marriage, to the comedian Slappy White, broke up, she went on a USO tour to perform for troops in Vietnam, where she fell ill. A doctor advised her to stay in a warm climate for her health, and so she got a permanent position as a troop entertainer in the Philippines, where she stayed for twenty-two years.

After the revolution which brought democracy to the Philippines and the subsequent closure of the base where she was working, Baker returned to the US.

Much as she'd taken over from Ruth Brown as Atlantic Records' biggest female star of the 1950s, now she took over from Brown in her role in the Broadway revue "Black and Blue", singing blues songs from the twenties and thirties, and had something of a career renaissance.

Her health problems got worse, and by the mid nineties she was performing from a wheelchair – both her legs had been amputated due to complications from diabetes. She never made as much money as she should have, but she was one of the first recipients of a lifetime achievement award from the Rhythm and Blues Foundation (which she had helped Ruth Brown set up, though Baker was never as antagonistic towards the record companies as Brown), and she was the second female solo artist to be inducted into the Rock and Roll Hall of Fame, after Aretha Franklin. For someone who prized recognition over money, maybe that was enough. She died in 1997, aged 67.

"Sincerely"

Chess Records is one of those labels, like Sun or Stax or PWL, which defined a whole genre. And in the case of Chess, the genre it defined was the electric Chicago blues. People like Muddy Waters, Elmore James, Howlin' Wolf, Little Walter, and Willie Dixon all cut some of their most important recordings for the Chess label. I remember when I was just starting to buy records as a child, decades after the events we're talking about, I knew before I left primary school that Chess, like Sun, was one of the two record labels that consistently put out music that I liked.

And yet when it started out, Chess Records was just one of dozens of tiny little indie blues labels, like Modern, or RPM, or King Records, or Duke or Peacock, many of which were even putting out records by the same people who were recording for Chess. So over the next three chapters, we're going to talk about how Chess ended up being the one label that defined that music in the eyes of many listeners, and how that music fed into early rock and roll.

And to start with, we're going to talk about Harvey Fuqua. Harvey was the nephew of Charlie Fuqua of the Ink Spots, and as you might imagine, having an uncle in the most important black vocal group in history gave young Harvey Fuqua quite an impetus, even though the two of them weren't close.

Fuqua started a duo with his friend Bobby Lester after they both got out of the military. Fuqua would play piano, and they would both sing. The two of them had a small amount of success, touring the South, but then shortly after their first tour Fuqua had about the worst thing possible happen to him – there was a fire, and both his children died in it. Understandably, he didn't want to stay in Louisville Kentucky, where he'd been raising his family, so he and his wife moved to Cleveland.

When he got to Cleveland, he met up again with an old friend from his military days, Danny Coggins. The two of them started performing together with a bass singer, Prentiss Barnes, under the name The Crazy Sounds.

The style they were performing in was called "vocalese", and it's a really odd style of jazz singing. The easiest way to explain it is the opposite of scat singing. In scat, you improvise a new melody with nonsense lyrics – that's the standard form of jazz singing.

In vocalese, on the other hand, you do the opposite. You come up with proper lyrics, not just nonsense syllables, and you put them to a pre-recorded melody. The twist is that the pre-recorded melody you choose is a melody that's already been improvised by an instrumentalist. So for example, you could, as Eddie Jefferson, who is credited as the inventor of vocalese, did, take Coleman Hawkins' great sax solo on "Body and Soul" and add lyrics singing Hawkins' praises, singing them to the melody he had improvised.

The Crazy Sounds performed this kind of music as a vocal trio for a while, but their sound was missing something, and eventually Fuqua travelled down to Kentucky and persuaded Bobby Lester to move to Cleveland and join the Crazy Sounds. They became a four-piece, and slowly started writing their own new material in a more R&B style.

They performed together a little, and eventually auditioned at a club called the Loop, where they were heard by a blues singer called Al "Fats" Thomas. Thomas was very impressed by the Crazy Sounds, and immediately phoned his friend, the DJ Alan Freed.

Alan Freed is a difficult character to explain, and his position in rock and roll history is a murky one. He was the first superstar DJ, and he was the person who more than anyone else made the phrase "rock and roll" into a term for a style of music, rather than, as it had been, just a phrase that was used in some of that music.

Freed had not started out as a rhythm and blues or rock and roll DJ, and in fact had no great love for the music when he started playing it on his show. He was a lover of classical music – particularly Wagner, whose music he loved so much that he named one of his daughters

Sieglinde. But he named his first daughter Alana, which shows his other great love, which was for himself.

Freed had been a DJ for several years when he was first introduced to rhythm and blues music, and he'd played a mixture of big band music and light classical, depending on what the audience wanted. But then, in 1951, something changed. Freed met Leo Mintz, the owner of a record shop named Record Rendezvous, in a bar. Mintz discovered that Freed was a DJ and took him to the shop. Freed later mythologised this moment, as he did a lot of his life, by talking about how he was shocked to see white teenagers dancing to music made by black people, and he had a sort of Damascene conversion and immediately decided to devote his show to rhythm and blues.

The reality is far more prosaic. Mintz, whose business actually mostly sold to black people at this point, decided that if there was a rhythm and blues radio show then it would boost business to his shop, especially if Mintz paid for the radio show and so bought all the advertising on it. He took Freed to the shop to show him that there was indeed an audience for that kind of music, and Freed was impressed, but said that he didn't know anything about rhythm and blues music. Mintz said that that didn't matter. Mintz would pick the records – they'd be the ones that he wanted his customers to buy – and tell Freed what to play. All Freed had to do was to play the ones he was told and everything would work out fine.

The music Mintz had played for Freed was, according to Freed later, people like LaVern Baker – who had not yet become at all well known outside Detroit and Chicago at the time – but Mintz set about putting together selections of records that Freed should play. Those records were mostly things with gospel-sounding vocals, a dance beat, or honking saxophones, and Freed found that his audiences responded astonishingly well to it.

Freed would often interject during records, and would bang his fists on the table or other objects in time to the beat, including a cowbell that he had on his desk – apparently some of his listeners would be annoyed when they bought the records he played to find out half the sounds they'd heard weren't on the record at all.

Freed took the stage name "Moondog", after a blind New York street musician and outsider artist of that name. Freed's theme song for his radio show was "Moondog Symphony", by Moondog, a one-man-band performance credited to "Moondog (by himself) playing drums, maracas, claves, gourds, hollow legs, Chinese block and cymbals."

When Fats Thomas got the Crazy Sounds an audition with Freed, Freed was impressed enough that he offered them a management contract. Being managed by the biggest DJ in the city was obviously a good idea, so they took him up on that, and took his advice about how to make themselves more commercial, including changing their name to emphasise the connection to Freed. They became first the Moonpuppies and then the Moonglows.

Freed set up his own record label, Champagne Records, and released the Moonglows' first single, "I Just Can't Tell No Lie". According to Freed's biographer John A. Jackson, Freed provided additional percussion on that song, hitting a telephone book in time with the rhythm as he would on his show. I don't hear any percussion on there other than the drum kit, but maybe you can, if you have better ears than me.

This was a song that had been written by the Moonglows themselves, but when the record came out, both sides were credited to Al Lance – which was a pseudonym for Alan Freed. And so the DJ who was pushing their record on the radio was also their manager, and the owner of the record company, and the credited songwriter. Unsurprisingly, then, Freed promoted "I Just Can't Tell No Lie" heavily on his radio show, but it did nothing anywhere outside of Cleveland and the immediately surrounding area. Danny Coggins quit the group, fed up with their lack of success, and he was replaced by a singer who variously went under the names Alex Graves, Alex Walton, Pete Graves, and Pete Walton. Freed closed down Champagne Records.

For a time it looked like the Moonglows' career was going to have peaked with their one single, as Freed signed another vocal group, the Coronets, and got them signed to Chess Records in Chicago.

Chess was a blues label, which had started in 1947 as Aristocrat Records, but in 1948 it was bought out by two brothers, Leonard and Phil Chess, who had emigrated from Poland as children and Anglicised their names. Their father was in the liquor business during the Prohibition era, which in Chicago meant he was involved with Al Capone, and in their twenties the Chess brothers had started running nightclubs in the black area of Chicago.

Chess, at its start, had the artists who had originally recorded for Aristocrat – people like Muddy Waters and Sunnyland Slim, and they also licensed records made by Sam Phillips in Memphis, and because of that put out Jackie Brenston's "Rocket "88"" and early recordings by Howlin' Wolf, before just poaching Wolf for their own label.

By 1954, thanks largely to their in-house bass player and songwriter Willie Dixon, Chess had become known as the home of electric Chicago blues, and were putting out classic after classic in that genre. But they were still interested in putting out other styles of black music too, and were happy to sign up doo wop groups.

The Coronets put out a single, "Nadine", on Chess, which did very well. The credited writer was Alan Freed. Their follow-up single did less well, though, and Chess dropped them.

But Freed had been trying for some time to make a parallel career as a concert promoter, and indeed a few months before he signed the Moonglows to a management contract he had put on what is now considered the first major rock and roll concert – the Moondog Coronation Ball, at the Cleveland Arena. That show had been Freed's first inkling of just how popular he and the music he was playing were becoming – twenty thousand people tried to get into the show, even though the arena only had a capacity of ten thousand, and the show had to be cancelled after the first song by the first performer, because it was becoming unsafe to continue.

But Freed put on further shows at the arena, with better organisation, and in August 1953 he put on "the Big Rhythm and Blues Show". This featured Fats Domino and Big Joe Turner, and the Moonglows were also put on the bill. As a result of their appearance on the show, they got signed to Chance Records, a small label whose biggest act was the doo wop group The Flamingos. Freed didn't own this label of course, but by this time he'd got into the record distribution business, and the distribution company he co-owned was Chance's distributor in the Cleveland area. The other co-owner of the distributor was the owner of Chance Records, and Freed's brother was the distributor's vice-president and in charge of running it.

The Moonglows' first single on Chance, a Christmas single, did nothing in the charts, but they followed it with a rather unusual choice.

"Secret Love" was a hit for Doris Day, from the soundtrack of her film *Calamity Jane*. In the context of the film, which has a certain amount of what we would now call queerbaiting, that song can be read as a song about lesbianism or bisexuality. But that didn't stop a lot of male artists covering it for other markets.

We've talked before about how popular songs would be recorded in different genres, and so Day's pop version was accompanied by Slim Whitman's country version and one by the Moonglows. Unfortunately, a fortnight after the Moonglows released their version, the Orioles, who were a much more successful doo wop group, released their own record of the song, and the two competed for the same market. However, "Secret Love" did well enough, given a promotional push by Freed, that it became apparent that the Moonglows could have a proper career.

It sold over a hundred thousand copies, but then the next few records on Chance failed to sell, and Chance closed down when their biggest act, the Flamingos, moved first to Parrot Records, and then quickly on to Chess.

It seemed like everything was against the Moonglows, but they were about to get a big boost, thanks in part to a strike.

WINS radio in New York had been taken over at a rock-bottom price by an investment consortium who wanted to turn the money-losing station into a money-maker. It had a powerful transmitter, and if they could boost listenership they would almost certainly be able to sell it on at a massive profit.

One of the first things the new owners did was to sack their house band – they weren't going to pay musicians any more, as live music was too expensive. This caused the American Federation of Musicians to picket the station, which was expected and understandable.

But WINS also had the broadcast rights to the New York Yankees games – indeed, the ball games were the only really popular thing that the station had. And so the AFM started to picket Yankee Stadium too.

On the week of the starting game for what looked to be the Yankees' sixth World Series win in a row.

That game would normally have had the opening ball thrown by the Mayor of New York, but the Mayor, Robert Wagner, rather admirably refused to cross a picket line. The Bronx borough president substituted for him – and threw the opening ball right into the stomach of a newspaper photographer.

WINS now desperately needed something to go right for them, and they realised Freed's immense drawing power. They signed him for the unprecedented sum of seventy-five thousand dollars a year, and Freed moved from the mid-market town of Cleveland to a huge, powerful, transmitter in New York. He instantly became the most popular DJ in New York, and probably the best-known DJ in the world.

And with his great power came record labels wanting to do Freed favours. He was already friends with the Chess brothers, and with the sure knowledge that any record the Moonglows put out would get airplay from Freed, they eagerly signed the Moonglows and put out "Sincerely".

"Sincerely" featured Bobby Lester on lead vocals, but the song was written by Harvey Fuqua. Or, as the label credited it, Harvey Fuqua and Alan Freed. But while those were the two credited writers, the song owes more than a little to another one. The bridge for "Sincerely" is almost identical to that from "That's What You're Doing to Me" by Billy Ward and the Dominoes, written by Billy Ward.

So while I'm critical of Freed for taking credit where it's not deserved, it should be remembered that Fuqua wasn't completely clean when it came to this song either.

"Sincerely" rose to number one on the R&B charts, thanks in large part to Freed's promotion. It knocked "Earth Angel" off the top, and was in turn knocked off by "Pledging My Love", and it did relatively well in the pop charts, although once again it was kept off the top of the pop charts by an insipid white cover version, this time by the McGuire Sisters.

Chess wanted to make as much out of the Moonglows as they could, and so they decided to release records by the group under multiple names and on multiple labels. So while the Moonglows were slowly rising up the charts on Chess, The Moonlighters put out another single, "My Loving Baby", on Checker.

There were two Moonlighters singles in total, though neither did well enough for them to continue under that name, and on top of that they also provided backing vocals on records by other Chess artists. Most notably, they sang the backing vocals on "Diddley Daddy" by Bo Diddley.

The Moonglows or Moonlighters weren't the only ones performing under new names though. The real Moondog had, once Freed came to New York, realised that Freed had taken his name, and sued him. Freed had to pay Moondog five thousand seven hundred dollars, and stop calling himself Moondog. He had to switch to using his real name. And along with this, he changed the name of his show to "The Rock and Roll Party".

The term "rock and roll" had been used in various contexts before, of course, but it had not been applied to a form of music on a regular basis. Freed didn't want to get into the same trouble with the phrase "rock and roll" as he had with the name "Moondog", and so he formed a company, Seig Music, which was owned by himself, the promoter Lew Platt, WINS radio, and the gangs–. I'm sorry, the legitimate businessman and music publisher Morris Levy. We'll be hearing more about Levy later. This company attempted to trademark the phrase "rock and roll", and started using it for Freed's now-branded "Rock and Roll Shows", both on radio and on stage.

The only problem was that the phrase caught on too much, thanks to Freed's incessant use of the phrase on his show – there was no possible way they were going to be able to collect royalties from everyone who was using it, and so that particular money-making scheme faltered.

The Moonglows, on the other hand, had a run of minor hits. None were as big as "Sincerely", but they had five R&B top ten hits and a bunch more in the top twenty. The most notable, and the one people remember, is "Ten Commandments of Love", from 1958. But that song wasn't released as by "the Moonglows", but by "Harvey and the Moonglows".

There was increasing tension between the different members of the band, and songs started to be released as by Harvey and the Moonglows or by Bobby Lester and the Moonglows, as Chess faced the fact that the group's two lead singers would go their separate ways.

Chess had been contacted by some Detroit-based songwriters, who were setting up a new label, Anna, and wanted Chess to take over the distribution for it.

By this point, Harvey Fuqua had divorced his first wife, and was working for Chess in the backroom as well as as an artist, and he was asked by Leonard Chess to go over and work with this new label. He did – and he married one of the people involved, Gwen Gordy. Gwen and her brother ended up setting up a lot of different labels, and Harvey got to run a few of them himself – there was Try-Phi, and Harvey Records. There was a whole family of different record labels owned by the same family, and they soon became quite successful.

But at the same time, Fuqua was still performing and recording for Chess, including successful duets with Etta James. Both he and Bobby Lester were performing with rival groups of Moonglows, who both continued recording for Chess. Harvey's Moonglows was an entire other vocal group, a group from Washington DC called the Marquees, who'd had one single out, "Wyatt Earp". That single had been co-written by Bo Diddley, a Chess artist who had tried to get the group signed to Chess. When they'd been turned down, Diddley took them to Okeh instead.

Fuqua hired the Marquees and renamed them, and they recorded several tracks as Harvey and the Moonglows, and while none of them were very successful commercially, some of them were musically interesting. One in particular, "Mama Loocie", featured a lead from a great young vocalist who would in 1963 become Harvey Fuqua's brother-in-law, when he married Gwen's sister Anna.

That record didn't do much, but that singer was to go on to bigger and better things, as was Harvey Fuqua, when one of the Gordy family's labels became a little bit better known than the rest, with Fuqua working for it as a record producer and head of artist development.

But the story of Motown Records, and of that singer, Marvin Gaye, is for another time...

"Maybellene"

In this chapter, we're going to talk about the most important single record Chess ever put out, and arguably the most important artist in the whole history of rock music.

But first, we're going to talk about something a lot more recent. We're going to talk about "Old Town Road" by Lil Nas X. This is a song put out late in 2018 by a rapper, but it reached number nineteen in the country charts. Because it's a country song. It's a song with banjo and mandolin, with someone singing in a low Johnny Cash style voice about riding a horse while wearing a cowboy hat. It's clearly country music if anything at all is country music. But it was taken off the country music charts the week it would otherwise have made number one, in a decision that Billboard was at pains to say was nothing at all to do with Lil Nas X's race.

A hint – if you have to go to great lengths to say that the thing you're doing isn't racist, it's probably racist.

Because genre labels have always been about race, and about policing racial boundaries in the US, since the very beginning. Remember that when Billboard started the R&B charts they were called the "race music" charts. You had the race music charts for black people, the country charts for lower-class whites, and the pop charts for the respectable white people. That was the demarcation, and that still is the demarcation.

But people will always want to push against those constraints. And in the 1950s, just like today, there were black people who wanted to make country music. But in the 1950s, unlike today, there was a term for the music those people were making. It was called rock and roll. For about a decade, from roughly 1955 through 1965, "rock and roll"

317

became a term for the music which disregarded those racial boundaries. And since then there has been a slow but sure historical revisionism.

The lines of rock and roll expand to let in any white man, but they constrict to push out the women and black men who were already there. But there's one they haven't yet been able to push out, because this particular black man playing country music was more or less the embodiment of rock and roll.

Chuck Berry was, in many ways, not at all an admirable man. He was one of all too many rock and roll pioneers to be a sex offender (and again, please see the disclaimer in the introduction for my thoughts about that – nothing I say about his work should be taken to imply that I think that work mitigates some of the awful things he did) and he was also by all accounts an unpleasant person in a myriad other ways. As I talked about in that disclaimer, we will be dealing with many awful people in this series, because that's the nature of the history of rock and roll, but Chuck Berry was one of the most fundamentally unpleasant, unlikeable, people we'll be looking at.

Nobody has a good word to say about him as a human being, and he hurt a lot of people over his long life. When I talk about his work, or the real injustices that were also done to him, I don't want to forget that.

But when it comes to rock and roll, Chuck Berry may be the single most important figure who ever lived, and a model for everyone who followed.

To talk about Chuck Berry, we first of all have to talk about Johnnie Johnson. Johnnie Johnson was a blues piano player, who had got a taste of life as a professional musician in the Marines, where he'd played in a military band led by Bobby Troup, the writer of "Route 66" among many other songs. After leaving the Marines, he'd moved around the Midwest, playing blues in various bands, before forming his own trio, the Johnnie Johnson Trio, in St Louis.

That trio consisted of piano, saxophone, and drums – until New Year's Eve 1952, when the saxophone player had a stroke and couldn't play. Johnson needed another musician to play with the trio, and needed someone quick, but it was New Year's Eve – every musician he could think of would be booked up. Except for Chuck Berry. Berry was a guitarist he vaguely knew, and was different in every way from Johnson. Where Johnson was an easy-going, fat, jovial, man, who had no ambitions other than to make a living playing boogie woogie piano, Chuck Berry had already served a term in prison for armed robbery, was massively ambitious, and was skinny as a rake.

But he could play the guitar and sing well enough, and the customers had hired a trio, not a duo, and so Chuck Berry joined the Johnnie Johnson Trio.

Berry soon took over the band, as Johnson, a relatively easy-going person, saw that Berry was so ambitious that he would be able to bring the band greater success than they would otherwise have had. And also, Berry owned a car, which was useful for transporting the band to gigs. And so the Johnnie Johnson trio became the Chuck Berry Trio.

Berry would also play gigs on the side with other musicians, and in 1954 he played guitar on a session for a calypso record on a local independent label, "Oh Maria" by Joe Alexander and the Cubans. However, when Berry tried to get that label to record the Chuck Berry Trio, they weren't interested. But then Berry drove to Chicago to see one of his musical heroes, Muddy Waters.

We've talked about Waters before, but only in passing – but Waters was, by far, the biggest star in the Chicago electric blues style, whose driving, propulsive, records were more accessible than Howlin' Wolf but still had some of the Delta grit that was missing from the cleaner sounds of people like T-Bone Walker. Berry stayed after the show to talk to his idol, and asked him how he could make records like Waters did. Waters told him to go and see Leonard Chess at Chess Records. Berry went to see Chess, who asked if Berry had a demo tape. He didn't, but he went back to St Louis and came back the next week with a wire recording of four newly-recorded songs.

The first thing he played was a blues song he'd written called "The Wee Wee Hours". That was too generic for Chess – and the blues they put out tended to be more electric Chicago blues, rather than the Nat Cole or Charles Brown style Berry was going for there. But the next song he played had them interested.

Berry had always been interested in playing as many different styles of music as he could – he was someone who was trying to incorporate the sounds of Louis Jordan, Muddy Waters, Charlie Christian, and Nat "King" Cole, among others. And so as well as performing blues, jazz, and rhythm and blues music, he'd also incorporated a fair amount of country and western music in his shows. And in particular, he was an admirer of Bob Wills and his Texas Playboys, and he would perform their song "Ida Red" in shows, where it always went down well.

Berry would perform that song live, but messed around and changed the lyrics a lot – he eventually changed the title to "Ida May", for a start – and when he performed the song for Leonard Chess, Chess thought it sounded great. There was only one problem – he thought the name made it too obvious where Berry had got the idea, and he wanted it to sound more original. They tried several names and eventually hit on "Maybellene", after the popular cosmetics brand, though they changed the spelling.

"Ida Red" wasn't the only influence on "Maybellene" though. There was another song called "Oh Red", a hokum song by the Harlem Hamfats, which Larry Birnbaum, in *Before Elvis*, suggests was the only influence on "Maybellene". Birnbaum contends that Berry was misremembering the song, as both songs have "Red" in the titles.

I disagree – I think it's fairly clear that "Maybellene" is inspired both by "Ida Red"'s structure and patter-lyric verse and by "Oh Red"'s chorus melody. And it wasn't just Bob Wills' version of "Ida Red" that inspired Berry. There's a blues version, by Bumble Bee Slim, which has a guitar break that isn't a million miles away from what Berry was doing.

And there's another influence as well. Berry's lyrics were about a car chase – to try to catch up with a cheating girlfriend – and are the thing that makes the song so unique. They – and the car-horn sound of the guitar – seem to have been inspired by a hillbilly boogie song called "Hot Rod Racer" by Arkie Shibley and his Mountain Dew Boys, which had been a successful enough country song that it spawned at least three hit cover versions, including one by Red Foley.

Berry took all these Western Swing, blues, and hillbilly boogie influences and turned them into something new. Even this early, you can already see the Chuck Berry style fully formed. Clean blues guitar, as clean as someone like T-Bone Walker, but playing almost rockabilly phrases – this is closer to the style of Elvis' Sun records than it is to anything else that Chess were putting out – and punning, verbose, witty lyrics talking about something that would have a clear appeal to people half his age. All of future rock is right there.

The lineup on the record was the Chuck Berry trio – Berry on guitar, Johnson on piano, and Ebby Hardy on drums – augmented by two other musicians. Jerome Green, the maraca player, is someone we'll be talking about in the next chapter, but it's worth here talking about Willie Dixon, the bass player, because he is probably the single most important figure in the whole Chess Records story.

Dixon had started out as a boxer – he'd been Joe Louis' sparring partner – before starting to play a bass made out of a tin can and a single string for him by the blues pianist Leonard Caston. Dixon and Caston formed an Ink Spots-style group, The Five Breezes. But when America joined in World War II, Dixon's music career went on hold, as he was a conscientious objector, unwilling to fight in defence of a racist state, and so he spent ten months in prison. He joined Chess in 1951, shortly after Leonard Chess took over full control of the company by buying out its original owner – right after the club Chess had been running had mysteriously burned down, on a day it was closed, giving him enough insurance money to buy the whole record company.

And Dixon was necessary because among Leonard Chess' flaws was one fatal one – he had no idea what real musical talent was or how to find it. But he did have the second-order ability to find people who could recognise real musical talent when they heard it, and the willingness to trust those people's judgment. And Dixon was not only a real talent himself, but he could bring out the best in others, too.

Dixon was, effectively, the auteur behind almost everything that Chess Records put out. As well as a session bass player who played on almost every Chess release that wasn't licensed from someone else, he was also their staff producer, talent scout, and staff songwriter, as well as a solo artist under his own name. To all intents and purposes, Willie Dixon *was* the Chicago blues, and when the second generation of rock and rollers started up in the 1960s – white boys with guitars from England – it was Willie Dixon's songs that formed the backbone of their repertoire.

Just a few of the songs he wrote that became classics include "Little Red Rooster" for Howlin' Wolf, "Bring it on Home" for Sonny Boy Williamson II, "You Need Love" for Muddy Waters . . . You get the idea. In any other session he played on – in any other room he ever entered – Dixon would be the most important songwriter in the room. But as it turned out, on this occasion, he was only the second-most important and influential songwriter there, as "Maybellene" would be the start of a run of singles that is unparalleled for its influence on rock and roll music. It was the debut of the single most important songwriter in rock and roll history.

Of course, Chuck Berry isn't the only credited songwriter – and, separately, he may not have been the song's only writer. But these two things aren't linked.

Leonard Chess was someone who had a reputation for not being particularly fair with his artists when it came to contracts. A favourite technique for him was to call an artist and tell him that he had some new papers to sign. He would then leave a bottle of whisky in the office, and not be in when the musician turned up. His secretary would say "Mr. Chess has been delayed. Help yourself to a drink while you wait in the office". Chess would only return when the musician was totally drunk, and then get him to sign the contract. That wouldn't work on Berry, who didn't drink, but Chess did manage to get Berry to sign two thirds of the rights to "Maybellene" over to people who had nothing to do with writing it – Russ Fratto and Alan Freed.

Freed had already taken the songwriting credit for several songs by bands that he managed, none of which he wrote, but now he was going to take the credit for a song by someone he had never met – Chess added his name to the credits as a bribe, in order to persuade him to play the song on his radio show. Russ Fratto, meanwhile, was the landlord of Chess Records' offices and owned the stationery company that printed the labels Chess used on their records. It's been said in a few places that Fratto was given the credit because the Chess brothers owed him money, so they gave him a cut of Berry's royalties to pay off their own debt.

But while Freed and Fratto took unearned credit for the song, it's at least arguable that so did Chuck Berry.

Who wrote what on the songs credited to Berry has always been a matter of some dispute. After they stopped working together, Johnnie Johnson started to claim that he deserved co-writing credit for everything that was credited to Berry on his own. Johnson claimed that while Berry wrote the lyrics by himself, the band as a whole worked out the music, and that Berry's melody lines would be based on Johnson's piano parts.

It's impossible to say with certainty who did what – Johnson sued Berry in 2000, but the case was dismissed because of the length of time between the songs being written and the case being brought. And Johnson worked with Berry on almost all his albums before that so we don't have any clear guides as to what Berry's music sounded like without Johnson.

Given Berry's money-grubbing, grasping, nature, and his willingness to see every single interaction as about how many dollars and cents were in it for Chuck Berry, I have no trouble believing that Berry would take the credit for other people's work and not think twice about it, so I can fully believe that Johnson worked with him on the music for the songs. On the other hand, most of the songs in question were based around very basic blues chord changes, and the musical interest in them comes almost solely from Berry's guitar licks – Johnnie Johnson was a very good blues piano player just like a thousand other very good blues piano players, but Chuck Berry's guitar style is absolutely distinctive, and unlike anything ever recorded before.

But the crucial evidence as to how much input or lack of it Johnson had on the writing process comes with the keys Berry chose. Maybellene is in B♭. A lot of his other songs are in E♭. These are not keys that any guitarist would normally choose to write in. If you're a guitarist, writing for the guitar, you'd probably choose to write in E or A if you're playing the blues, D if you're doing folkier stuff, maybe G or C if you're doing something poppier and more melodic. These are easy keys for the guitar, the keys that every guitarist's fingers will automatically fall into unless they have a good reason not to.

E♭ and B♭, though, are fairly straightforward keys on the piano if you're playing the blues. And they're keys that are absolutely standard for a saxophone player – alto saxes are tuned to an E♭, tenor saxes to B♭, so if you're a band where the sax player is the most important instrumentalist, those are the keys you're most likely to choose, all else being equal.

Now, remember that Chuck Berry replaced the saxophone player in Johnnie Johnson's band. Once you know that it seems obvious what's happened – Berry has fit himself in around arrangements and repertoire that Johnson had originally worked up with a sax player, playing in the keys that Johnson was already used to. When they worked out the music for Berry's songs, that was the pattern they fell into.

So, I tend to believe Johnson that the backings were worked out between them after Berry wrote the lyrics. Johnson's contribution seems to have come somewhere between that of an arranger and of a songwriter, and he deserves some credit at least morally, if not under the ridiculous legal situation that made arrangements uncopyrightable.

"Maybellene"'s success was in part because of a very deliberate decision Berry had made years earlier, having noted the success of white performers singing black musicians' material, and deciding that he was going to try to get the white people to buy his recordings rather than the cover versions, by singing in a voice that was closer to white singers than the typical blues vocalist. While it caused him problems in early days, notably with him turning up to gigs only to be told, often with accompanying racial slurs, that they'd expected the performer of "Maybellene" to be a white man and he wasn't allowed to play, his playing-down of his own blackness also caused a major benefit – he became one of the only black musicians to chart higher than the white cover version.

It would normally be expected that "Maybellene" would be overshadowed on the charts by Marty Robbins' version, especially since Marty Robbins was a hugely popular star, and Berry was an unknown on a small blues label. Instead, as well as going to number one on the R&B charts, Berry's recording went to number five on the pop charts. And other recordings by him would follow over the next few years.

He was never a consistent chart success – in fact he did significantly less well than his reputation in rock and roll history would suggest – but he notched several top ten hits on the pop charts.

"Maybellene" did so well that even "The Wee Wee Hours", released as the B-side, went to number ten on the R&B charts. Berry's next single was a "Maybellene" soundalike – "Thirty Days". It's a great track, but it didn't do quite so well on the charts – it went to number two on the R&B charts, and didn't hit the pop charts at all. The single after that, "No Money Down", did less well again. But Berry was about to turn things around again with his next single.

"Roll Over Beethoven" is, as far as I can tell, the first time that rock and roll started the pattern of self-mythologising that would continue throughout the genre's history. Of course, there had been plenty of records before this that had talked about the power of music or how much the singer wanted to make you dance, or whatever, but this one is different in a couple of ways. Firstly, it's talking about recorded music specifically – Berry isn't wanting to go out and listen to a band play live, but he wants to listen to the DJ play his favourite record instead. And secondly, he's explicitly making a link between his music – "these rhythm and blues" – and the music of the rockabilly artists from Memphis – "don't step on my blue suede shoes".

And Berry's music did resemble the Memphis rockabilly more than it resembled anything else. Both had electric lead guitars, double bass, drums, and reverb, and no saxophone and little piano. Both sang sped-up hillbilly boogies with a hard backbeat. Rock and roll was, as we have seen, a disparate genre at first, and people would continue to pull from a whole variety of different sources. But working independently and with no knowledge of each other, a white country hick from Tennessee and a sophisticated black urbanite from the Midwest had hit upon almost exactly the same formula, and Berry was going to make sure that he made the connection as clear as possible.

If there's a moment that rock and roll culture coalesced into a single thing, it was with "Roll Over Beethoven". And Berry now had his formula worked out. The next thing to do was to get rid of the band. "Roll Over Beethoven" was the penultimate single credited to Chuck Berry & His Combo, rather than to just Chuck Berry. We'll look at the last one, recorded at the same session, in a few chapters.

"Bo Diddley"

One of the many injustices in copyright law – and something that we'll have a lot of cause to mention during the course of this series – is that, for the entire time period covered by this series, it was impossible to copyright a groove or a rhythm, but you could copyright a melody line and lyric. And this has led to real inter-racial injustice.

In general, black musical culture in the USA has emphasised different aspects of musical invention than white culture has. While white American musical culture – particularly rich white musical culture – has stressed inventive melodies and harmonic movement – think of, say, Burt Bacharach or George Gershwin – it has not historically stressed rhythmic invention. On the other hand, black musical culture has stressed that above everything else – you'll notice that all the rhythmic innovations we've talked about so far, like boogie woogie, and the backbeat, and the tresillo rhythm, all came from black musicians.

That's not, of course, to say that black musicians can't be melodically inventive or white musicians rhythmically – I'm not here saying "black people have a great sense of rhythm" or any of that racist nonsense. I'm just talking about the way that different cultures have prioritised different things.

But this means that when black musicians have produced innovative work, it's not been possible for them to have any intellectual property ownership in the result. You can't steal a melody by Bacharach, but anyone can play a song with a boogie beat, or a shuffle, or a tresillo. . . or with the Bo Diddley beat.

Elias McDaniel's distinctive sound came about because he started performing so young that he couldn't gain entrance to clubs, and so he and his band had to play on street corners. But you can't cart a

327

drum kit around and use it on the streets, so McDaniel and his band came up with various inventive ways to add percussion to the act. At first, they had someone who would come round with a big bag of sand and empty it onto the pavement. He'd then use a brush on the sand, and the noise of the brushing would provide percussion – at the end of the performance this man, whose name was Sam Daniel but was called Sandman by everyone, would sweep all the sand back up and put it back into his bag for the next show.

Eventually, though, Sandman left, and McDaniel hit on the idea of using his girlfriend's neighbour Jerome Green as part of the act.

For all Jerome's importance to music, there is astonishingly little information about him. He doesn't even have a Wikipedia page, and you'll find barely more than a few paragraphs about him online. No-one even knows when he was born or died – *if* he died, though he seems to have disappeared around 1972. And this is quite astonishing when you consider that Green played on all Bo Diddley's classic records, and sang duet on a few of the most successful ones, *and* he played on many of Chuck Berry's, and on various other records by Willie Dixon, Otis Spann, the Moonglows and more. Yet when you Google him, the third hit that comes up is about Robson Green and Jerome Flynn, a nineties soft-pop duo who span out of a soap opera.

At first, Jerome's job within McDaniel's group was to pass the hat around and collect the money, but McDaniel decided to build Jerome a pair of maracas, and teach him how to play. And he learned to play very well indeed, adding a Latin sound to what had previously been just a blues band.

Jerome's maracas weren't the only things that Elias McDaniel built, though. He had a knack for technology, though he was always rather modest about his own abilities. He built himself one of the very first tremolo systems for a guitar, making something out of old car bits and electronic junk that would break the electronic signal up. Before commercial tremolo systems existed, McDaniel was the only one who could make his guitar sound like that.

The choppy guitar, with its signal breaking up deliberately, and the maracas being shook frantically, gave McDaniel's music a rhythmic drive unlike anything else in rock and roll.

McDaniel and his band eventually got their music heard by Leonard Chess at Chess Records. Chess was impressed by a song called "Uncle John", which had lyrics that went "Uncle John's got corn ain't never been shucked/Uncle John's got daughters ain't never been... to school"; but he said the song needed less salacious lyrics, and he suggested retitling it "Bo Diddley", which also became the stage name of the man who up until now had been called Elias McDaniel.

The new lyrics were inspired by the black folk song "Hambone", which a few years earlier had become a novelty hit, and whose lyrics in turn were related to the old folk song "Hush Little Baby".

When talking about "Hambone", I have to be careful, because here I'm talking about something that's from a different culture from my own, and my understanding of it is that of an outsider. To me, "Hambone" seems to be a unified thing that's part song, part dance, part game. But my understanding may be very, very flawed, and I don't want to pretend to knowledge I don't have.

But as is my best understanding, "Hambone", like many folk songs, is not in itself a single song, but a collection of different songs with similar elements. The name comes from a dance which, it is said, dates back to enslaved people attempting to entertain themselves. Slaves in most of the US were banned from using drums, because it was believed they might use them to send messages to each other, so when they wanted to dance and sing music, they would slap different parts of their own bodies to provide percussive accompaniment.

Now, I tend to be a little dubious of narratives that claim that aspects of twentieth-century black culture date back to slavery or, as people often claim, to Africa. A lot of the time these turn out to be urban myths of the "ring a ring a roses is about the bubonic plague" kind. One of the real tragedies of slavery is that the African culture that the enslaved black people brought over to the US was largely lost in the ensuing centuries, and so there's a very strong incentive to try to find things that could be a continuation of that. But that's the story around "Hambone", which is also known as the "Juba beat".

Another influence Diddley would always cite for the lyrical scansion is the song "Hey Ba-Ba-Re-Bop", which he would usually misremember as having been by either Cab Calloway or Louis Jordan, but was actually by Lionel Hampton, based on Helen Humes' earlier "Be Baba Leba".

But the important thing to note is that the rhythm of all these records is totally different from the rhythm of the song "Bo Diddley". There's a bit of misinformation that goes around in almost every article about Diddley, saying "the Bo Diddley beat is just the 'Hambone' beat", and while Diddley would correct this in almost every interview he ever gave, the misinformation would persist – to the point that when I first heard "Hambone" I was shocked, because I'd assumed that there must at least have been some slight similarity. There's no similarity at all.

And that's not the only song where I've seen claims that there's a Bo Diddley beat where none exists. The PhD thesis[14] on the development of the backbeat which I mentioned in the chapter on "Roll 'Em Pete" claims that the beat appears on about thirteen records before Diddley's, mostly by people we've discussed before, like Louis Jordan, Johnny Otis, Fats Domino, and Roy Brown.

But having listened to the tracks mentioned there, they mostly have something that's *sort of* the Bo Diddley beat, but not really, among their other rhythms. It's most notable among the cited songs at the very start of "That's Your Last Boogie" by Joe Swift, accompanied by Johnny Otis.

But the beat there is a standard clave beat – it's sort of like the tresillo, with an extra bom-bom on the end. Bom bom-bom, bom-bom. That's not the Bo Diddley beat. The Bo Diddley beat actually varies subtly from bar to bar, and while it stresses the five beats of the clave, it doubles many of them – "chunka chunka chunk" instead of "bom bom-bom". It's not the clave, and nor is it the "shave and a haircut, two bits" rhythm other people seem to claim for it.

Most ridiculously, Wikipedia even claims that the Andrews Sisters' version of Lord Invader's great calypso song, "Rum and Coca Cola", has the Bo Diddley beat, when to my ears the only similarity to "Bo Diddley" is that both records feature maracas. Incidentally, that song was, in the Andrews Sisters version, credited to a white American thief rather

---

[14]https://www.tagg.org/xpdfs/TamlynPhD1.pdf

than to the black Trinidadian men who wrote it. Sadly appropriate for a song about the exploitation of Trinidadians for "the Yankee dollar".

None of these records have the Bo Diddley beat, despite what anyone might say. None of them even sound very much like Diddley's beat at all.

The origins of the Bo Diddley beat were, believe it or not, with Gene Autry. We've talked before about Autry, who was the biggest Western music star of the late thirties and early forties, and who inspired all sorts of people you wouldn't expect, from Les Paul to Hank Ballard. But Diddley hit upon his rhythm when trying to play Autry's "I've Got Spurs That Jingle Jangle Jingle". I don't see any resemblance there, but Diddley consistently claimed that as his inspiration.

And if you become familiar with his later work, it becomes clear that Diddley truly loved the whole iconography of the Western, and country music. He did albums called *Have Guitar Will Travel* (named after the Western TV show *Have Gun Will Travel*) and *Bo Diddley is a Gunslinger*. Diddley's work is rooted in black folklore – things like hambone, but also the figure of Stagger Lee and other characters like the Signifying Monkey – but it should be understood that black American folklore has always included the image of the black cowboy.

The combination of these influences – the "Hambone" lyrical ideas, the cowboy rhythm, and the swaggering character Diddley created for himself – became "Bo Diddley", the song.

The B-side to the record, meanwhile, was maybe even more important. It's also an early example of Diddley not just reusing his signature rhythm. The popular image of Diddley has him as a one-idea artist remaking the same song over and over again – and certainly he did often return to the Bo Diddley beat – but he was a far more interesting artist than that, and recorded in a far wider variety of styles than you might imagine. And in "I'm a Man" he took on another artist's style, beating Muddy Waters at his own game.

"I'm a Man" was a response to Waters' earlier "Hoochie Coochie Man", which we discussed back in the chapter on "The Wallflower".

"Hoochie Coochie Man" had been written by Willie Dixon for Waters, and managed to sum up everything about Waters' persona in a way that Waters himself had never managed with his own songs. It combined sexual braggadocio with hoodoo lore – the character Waters was singing in was possessed of supernatural powers, from the day he was born, and he used those powers to "make pretty women jump and shout". He had a black cat bone, and a mojo, and a John the Conqueror root.

It was a great riff, and a great persona, and a great record. But it was still a conventionally structured sixteen-bar blues, with the normal three chords that almost all blues records have.

But Bo Diddley heard that and decided that was two chords too many. When you've got a great riff, you don't *need* chord changes, not if you can just hammer on that riff. So he came up with a variant of Dixon's song, and called it "I'm a Man". In his version, there was only the one chord.

Willie Dixon guested on bass for that song, as it wasn't felt that Diddley's own bass player was getting the feeling right. There were also some changes made to the song in the studio. As Diddley put it later, "They wanted me to spell 'man', but they weren't explaining it right. They couldn't get me to spell 'man'. I didn't understand what they were talking about!"

But eventually he did sing that man is spelled m-a-n, and the song went on to be covered by pretty much every British band of the sixties, and become a blues standard. The most important cover version of it though was when Muddy Waters decided to make his own answer record to Diddley, "Mannish Boy", in which he stated that he was a man, not a boy like Diddley. Diddley got a co-writing credit on that, though Willie Dixon, whose riff had been the basis of "I'm a Man", didn't.

And then there was Etta James' answer record, "W.O.M.A.N.", which once again has wild west references in it. And that... "inspired" Jerry Leiber and Mike Stoller to write "I'm a Woman" for Peggy Lee, a song which like James' spells out the word "woman" and uses the "Hoochie Coochie Man" riff.

Of course, none of those records, except Muddy Waters', gave Bo Diddley a writing credit, just as Diddley didn't credit Dixon for his riff.

At the same session as the single was recorded, Diddley's harmonica player, Billy Boy Arnold, recorded a single of his own, backed by Diddley and his band. "I'm Sweet on you Baby" wasn't released at the time, but it's a much more straightforward blues song, and more like Chess' normal releases.

Despite putting out a truly phenomenal single, Diddley hit upon a real problem with his career, and one that would be one of the reasons he was never as popular as contemporaries like Chuck Berry. The problem, at first, looked like anything but. He was booked on the Ed Sullivan Show to promote his first single.

The Ed Sullivan Show was the biggest TV show of the fifties and sixties. A variety show presented by the eponymous Sullivan, who somehow even after twenty years of presenting never managed to look or sound remotely comfortable in front of a camera, it was the programme that boosted Elvis Presley from stardom to superstardom, and which turned the Beatles from a local phenomenon in the UK and Europe into the biggest act the world had ever seen.

Getting on it was the biggest possible break Diddley could have got, and it should have made his career. Instead, it was a disaster, all because of a misunderstanding.

At the time, the country song "Sixteen Tons" by Tennessee Ernie Ford was a big hit, and Diddley liked the song enough that he would later record his own version of it. And so he was singing it to himself in his dressing room. One of the production staff happened to walk past and hear him, and asked if he could perform that song on the show. Diddley assumed he was being asked if he would do it as well as the song he was there to promote, and was flattered to be asked to do a second song.

When he got out on to the stage he saw the cue card saying "Bo Diddley Sixteen Tons", assumed it meant the song "Bo Diddley" followed by the song "Sixteen Tons", and so he launched into "Bo Diddley".

After all, why would he go on the show to promote someone else's record? He was there to promote his own debut single. So of course he was going to play it.

This was not what the production person had intended, and was not what Ed Sullivan wanted. Backstage, there was a confrontation that got so heated that Diddley had to be physically restrained from beating Sullivan with his guitar after Sullivan called Diddley a "black boy" (according to Diddley, "black" at that time and in that place, was a racial slur, though it's the polite term to use today). Sullivan yelled and screamed at Diddley and told him he would be blacklisted from network TV, and would certainly never appear on Sullivan's show again under any circumstances. After that first TV appearance, it would be seven years until Diddley's second.

And unlike all his contemporaries he didn't even get to appear in films. Even Alan Freed, who greatly respected Diddley and booked him on his live shows, and who Diddley also respected, didn't have him appear in any of the five rock and roll films he made. As far as I can tell, the two minutes he was on the Ed Sullivan show is the only record of Bo Diddley on film or video from 1955 through 1962.

And this meant, as well, that Chess put all their promotional efforts behind Chuck Berry, who for all his faults was more welcome in the TV studios. If Diddley wanted success, he had to let his records and live performances do the work for him, because he wasn't getting any help from the media.

Luckily, his records were great. Not only was Diddley's first hit one of the great two-sided singles of all time, but his next single was also impressive. The story of "Diddley Daddy" dates back to one of the white cover versions of "Bo Diddley". Essex Records put out a cover version by Jean Dinning, produced by Dave Miller, who had earlier produced Bill Haley and the Comets' first records.

As with Georgia Gibbs' version of "Tweedle Dee", the record label wanted to make the record sound as much like the original as possible, and so tried to get the original musicians to play on it, and made an agreement with Chess. They couldn't get Bo Diddley himself, and without his tremolo guitar it sounded nothing like the original, but they did get Willie Dixon on bass, Diddley's drummer Clifton James (who sadly isn't the same Clifton James who played the bumbling sheriff in *Live and Let Die* and *Superman II*, though it would be great if he was), and Billy Boy Arnold on harmonica.

But Billy Boy Arnold made the mistake of going to Chess and asking for the money he was owed for the session. Leonard Chess didn't like when musicians wanted paying, and complained to Bo Diddley about Arnold. Diddley told Arnold that Chess wasn't happy with him, and so

Arnold decided to take a song he'd written, "Diddy Diddy Dum Dum", to another label rather than give it to Chess. He changed the lyrics around a bit, and called it "I Wish You Would".

Arnold actually recorded it for Vee-Jay Records on the very day that Bo Diddley's second single was due to be recorded, and the Diddley session was held up because nobody knew where Arnold was. They eventually found him and got him to Diddley's session – where Diddley started playing "Diddy Diddy Dum Dum". Leonard Chess suggested letting Arnold sing the song, but Arnold said "I can't – I just recorded that for Vee-Jay", and showed Chess the contract.

Diddley and Harvey Fuqua, who was there to sing backing vocals with the rest of the Moonglows, quickly reworked the song. Arnold didn't want to play harmonica on something so close to a record he'd just made, though he played on the B-side, and so Muddy Waters' harmonica player Little Walter filled in instead. The new song, entitled "Diddley Daddy", became another of Diddley's signature songs.

But the B-side, "She's Fine, She's Mine", was the one that would truly become influential. That song was later slightly reworked, by Willie Cobbs, into "You Don't Love Me", a song which was covered by pretty much every white guitar band of the late sixties – the Grateful Dead, Quicksilver Messenger Service, the Allman Brothers, Steve Stills and Al Kooper... the list goes on.

Cobbs' song itself was also slightly reworked, by Dawn Penn, in 1967, and became a minor reggae classic. Twenty-seven years later, in 1994, Penn rerecorded her song, "You Don't Love Me (No, No, No)" based on Cobbs' song, based on Bo Diddley's song, and it became a worldwide smash hit, with Diddley getting co-writing credit.

And *that* has later been covered by Beyoncé and Rihanna, and sampled by Ghostface Killah and Usher. And that's how important Bo Diddley was at this point in time. The B-side to his less-good follow-up to his debut provided enough material for sixty years' worth of hits in styles from R&B to jam band to reggae to hip-hop.

And the song "Bo Diddley" itself, of course, would provide a rhythm for generations of musicians to take, everyone from Buddy Holly with "Not Fade Away", to George Michael with "Faith", to U2 with "Desire".

Because that rhythm was so successful – even though most of the success went to white people who didn't credit or pay Diddley – people tend to think of Diddley as a one-idea musician, which is far from the truth. Like many of his contemporaries he only had a short period where he was truly inventive – his last truly classic track was recorded in 1962. But that period was an astoundingly inventive one.

In his first four tracks, Diddley had managed to record three of the most influential tracks in rock history. But the next time we look at him, it will be with a song he wrote for other people – a song that would indirectly have massive effects on the whole of popular music.

"Only You"

The story of the Platters is intimately tied up with another story we've already talked about – that of the Penguins and "Earth Angel". As a result, this chapter tells a lot of the same story as that one, from an alternative perspective. But in both cases Buck Ram ends up being the villain.

As I mentioned back then, there was a lot of movement between different vocal groups, and the Platters were very far from an exception. It's hard to talk about how they formed in the way I normally would, where you talk about these three people meeting up and then getting a friend to join them, and their personalities, and so on, because none of the five people who sang on their biggest hits were among the six people who formed the original group they came from.

The Platters started out as The Flamingos – this isn't the same group as the more well-known Flamingos, but a different group, whose lineup was Cornell Gunter, Gaynel Hodge (who was also in the Hollywood Flames at the same time), Gaynel's brother Alex Hodge, Joe Jefferson, Richard Berry, and Curtis Williams.

But very quickly, the Flamingos started to lose members to other, more popular, groups. The first to leave was Curtis Williams, who went on to join the Hollywood Flames, and from there joined the Penguins.

Richard Berry, meanwhile formed a band called the Hollywood Blue-jays and got Cornell Gunter into the group. They recorded one single for John Dolphin's record label, before renaming themselves the Flairs and moving over to Flare records, where they would record singles such as "She Wants to Rock", which we talked about in the episode on "The Wallflower". Both Berry and Gunter would later go on to work with Leiber and Stoller, with Gunter joining the Coasters.

So the Flamingos had produced some great talents, but those talents' departure left some gaping holes in the lineup. Eventually, the Flamingos settled into a new lineup, consisting of Gaynel Hodge, Alex Hodge, David Lynch (not the same one as the film director), and Herb Reed.

That lineup was not very good, though, and they didn't have a single singer who was strong enough to sing lead. Even so, the demand for vocal groups at the time was so great that they got signed by Ralph Bass, who was currently working for Federal Records, producing among other artists a singer called Linda Hayes.

We've mentioned Linda Hayes a few times previously, though you might not recognise the name. She was one of the people who had tried to cash in on Johnny Ace's death with a tribute record, "Why Johnny Why", and she was also the one who had replaced Eunice in Gene and Eunice when she went on maternity leave. We find her popping up all over the place when there was a bandwagon to jump on, and at the time we're talking about she'd just had an actual hit because of doing this.

Willie Mabon had just had a hit with "I Don't Know", which had reached number one on the R&B chart and had spawned a country cover version by Tennessee Ernie Ford. And so Hayes had put out an answer record, "Yes, I Know (What You're Putting Down)"

Hayes' answer went to number two on the R&B charts, and she was suddenly someone it was worth paying attention to. As it turned out, she would only have one other hit, in 1954. But she introduced Ralph Bass to her brother, Tony Williams, who wanted to be a singer himself.

Williams joined the Flamingos as their lead singer, and their first recording was as the vocal chorus on "Nervous Man Nervous" by Big Jay McNeely, one of the all-time great saxophone honkers, who had previously played with Johnny Otis' band.

Shortly after that, the Flamingos were due to have their own first recording session, when a problem hit. There were only so many names of birds that groups could use, and so it wasn't surprising that someone else was using the name "the Flamingos", and that group got a hit record out. So they decided that since records were often called "platters" by disc jockeys, they might as well call themselves that.

The Platters' first single, "Hey Now", did absolutely nothing. They put out a few more recordings, but nothing clicked, and nobody, Ralph Bass included, thought they were any good. Gaynel Hodge finally got sick of splitting his time between groups, and left the group, to continue with the Hollywood Flames.

The group seemed like they might be on the way out, and so Tony Williams went to his sister's manager, Buck Ram, and asked him if he'd be Williams' manager as a solo singer. Ram listened to him, and said he was interested, but Williams should get himself a group to sing with. Williams said that, well, he did already have a group. Ram talked to Ralph Bass and took the Platters on as a project for himself.

Ram is unusual among the managers of this time, in that he was actually a musician and songwriter of some ability himself. He had obtained a law degree, mostly to please his parents, but Ram was primarily a songwriter.

Long before he went into music management Ram was writing songs, and was getting them performed by musicians that you have heard of. And he seems to have been part of the music scene in New York in the late thirties and early forties in a big way, having met Duke Ellington in a music arranging class both were taking, and having been introduced by Ellington to people like Chick Webb, Cab Calloway, and Ellington's publishers, Mills Music.

Ram's first big success as a songwriter was "I'll Be Home For Christmas", which had been a hit for Bing Crosby and would later become a standard.

The story of "I'll Be Home For Christmas" was a rather controversial one – Ram had written, on his own, a song called "I'll Be Home For Christmas (Tho Just In Memory)", and had registered the copyright in December 1942, but hadn't had it recorded by anyone. A few months later, he talked to his acquaintances Walter Kent and Kim Gannon about it, and was shocked when Crosby released a single written by them which bore a strong resemblance to Ram's song. His publishers, Mills Music, sued and got Ram credited on future releases. Buck Ram would end up fighting a lot of lawsuits, with a lot of people.

But while that biggest credit was the result of a lawsuit, Ram was also, as far as I can tell, an actual songwriter of great ability. Where other managers got themselves credited on songs that they didn't write and in some cases had never heard, to the best of my knowledge there has never been any suggestion that Buck Ram wasn't the sole author of the Platters songs he's credited for.

I'm so used to this working the other way, with managers taking credit for work they didn't do, that I still find it difficult to state for certain that there wasn't some sort of scam going on, but Ram had songwriting credits long before getting into the business side of things – songs like "Chew, Chew, Chew Your Bubblegum", which he wrote with Chick Webb for Ella Fitzgerald to sing.

He spent several years working as a songwriter and arranger in New York, but made the mistake of moving West in order to get into the film music business, only to find that he couldn't break into the market and had to move into management instead. But making music, rather than managing it, was his first love, and he saw the Platters as a means to that end – raw material he could mould in his own image.

Ram signed the Platters, now a four-piece consisting of Tony Williams, Alex Hodge, David Lynch, and Herb Reed, to a seven-year contract, and started trying to mould them into a hit act.

The first single they released after signing with Ram was one which, rather oddly, featured Herb Reed on lead vocals on both sides, rather than their normal lead Tony Williams, "Roses of Picardy".

They still had the problem, though, that they simply weren't very good at singing. At the time, they didn't know how to sing in harmony – they'd just take turns singing lead, and often not be able to sing in the same key as each other.

This didn't have much success, but Ram had an idea. In the forties, he'd managed and written for a group called the Quin-Tones. There were several groups of that name over the years, but this one had been a white vocal group with four men and one woman. They weren't very successful, but working with them had given Ram a taste for the particular vocal blend that comes from having four men and one woman.

This had been a popular group style in the 1940s, thanks to the influence of the Modernaires – the vocal group who sang with the

Glenn Miller Orchestra – but had largely fallen out of favour in the 50s. Ram decided to reform the Platters along these lines.

The woman he chose to bring into the group was a singer Gaynel Hodge knew called Zola Taylor. Taylor had been recording as a solo artist, with little success, but she had a good sound on her recordings for RPM Records. With Zola in the group, Ram's ideal vocal sound was almost complete. But they hadn't quite got themselves together – after all, there was still an original member left!

But Alex Hodge wouldn't last long, as he was arrested for marijuana possession, and he was replaced by Paul Robi. Gaynel Hodge now claims that this wasn't the real reason that Alex Hodge was sacked – he says that Ram and Herb Reed conspired to get rid of Alex, who in Gaynel's telling had been the original founder of the group, because he knew too much about the music business and was getting suspicious that Ram was ripping him off. Either way, the last original member was now gone, and the Platters were Tony Williams, Zola Taylor, Herb Reed, Paul Robi, and David Lynch.

This would now be the lineup that would stay together for the rest of the 1950s and beyond.

Before that change though, the Platters had recorded a song that had sounded so bad that Ram had persuaded the label not to release it.

"Only You" was a song that Ram had written with the intention of passing it on to the Ink Spots, but for whatever reason he had never got round to it, though he'd written for the Ink Spots before – they'd released his "I'll Lose a Friend Tomorrow" in 1946.

He later said that he'd decided against giving "Only You" to the Ink Spots because they'd split up before he had a chance. That's not accurate – the Ink Spots were still around when the earliest recordings of the song by the Platters were made. More likely, he just didn't like the song. After he wrote it, he stuck the sheet music in a box, where it languished until Jean Bennett, his assistant, was moving things around and the box fell apart. Bennett looked at the song, and said she thought it looked interesting. Ram said it was rubbish, but Bennett put the sheet music on top of Ram's piano. When Tony Williams saw it, he insisted on recording it. But that initial recording seemed to confirm

Ram's assessment that the song was terrible − it didn't help that the group were completely off-key when they recorded it.

During this period the band were also recording tracks backing Linda Hayes, and indeed there was also a brother-sister duet credited to Linda Hayes and Tony Williams (of the Platters), "Oochie Pachie", which was very much in the "Ko Ko Mo" style.

And again, Hayes was trying to jump on the bandwagons, recording "My Name Ain't Annie" with the Platters on backing vocals, in the hope of getting some of the money that was going to Hank Ballard and Etta James.

But none of those records sold at all, and despite Ram's best efforts it looked like the Platters were simply not going to be having any recording success any time soon. Federal dropped them, as it looked likely they were going to do nothing.

But then, the group got very lucky. Buck Ram became the manager of the Penguins, another group that had formed out of the primal soup of singers around LA. The Penguins had just had what turned out to be their only big hit, with "Earth Angel", and Mercury Records were eager to sign them. Ram agreed to the deal, but only on the condition that Mercury signed the Platters as well.

Once they were signed, Ram largely gave up on the Penguins, who never had any further success. They'd served his purpose, and got the group he really cared about signed to a major label.

There was a six-month break between the last session the Platters did for Federal and the first they did for Mercury. During that time, there was only one session − as backing vocalists for Joe Houston, on a forgettable record called "Shtiggy Boom". But they spent that six months practising, and when they got into the studio to record "Only You" for Mercury, they suddenly sounded good.

Everything had fallen into place. They were now a slick, professional group. They'd even got good enough that they could incorporate mistakes when they worked − on an early take, Williams' voice cracked on the word "only", and he apologised to Ram, who said, "no, it sounded good, use it".

And "Only You" became one of those songs that defines an era. More than any of the doo wop songs we've covered previously, it's the epitome of 1950s smooth balladry. It was a massive hit – it spent thirty weeks on the R&B charts, seven of them at number one, and twenty-two weeks on the pop charts, peaking at number five.

Federal rush-released the awful original recording to cash in, and Ram and Mercury took them to court, which eventually ruled in favour of Federal being allowed to put out their version, but the judge also said that that decision might well turn out to be more harmful to Federal than to Mercury. The Federal version didn't chart.

The follow-up to "Only You", a song called "The Great Pretender", also by Ram, was even bigger. And this started a whole string of hits – "The Magic Touch", "Twilight Time", "Smoke Gets in Your Eyes"... most of these weren't quite as long-lasting as their first two massive hits, but they were regulars at the top of the pop charts. The Platters were, in many ways, the 1950s equivalent to the Ink Spots, and while they started off marketed as a rock and roll group, they soon transitioned into the more lucrative adult market, recording albums of standards.

But having emulated the Ink Spots in their biggest hits, the Platters also, sadly, emulated the Ink Spots in the way they fell apart. Unfortunately, the only book I've been able to find that talks about the Platters in any depth is written by someone working for Buck Ram's organisation, and so it has a very particular biased take on the legal disputes that followed for the next sixty years.

I've tried to counter this by at least skimming some of the court documents that are available online, but it's not really possible to get an accurate sense, either from court filings from 2011 or the mid-eighties, or from a self-published and self-defensive book from 2015, what actually happened between the five Platters, Ram, and Ram's assistant Jean Bennett back in the late 1950s.

What everyone seems to agree on, though, is that soon after the Platters were signed to Mercury, a corporation was set up, "Five Platters Inc.", which was controlled by Buck Ram and had all the members of the Platters as shareholders. The Platters, at the time, assigned any rights they had to the band's name to this corporation.

But then, in 1959, Tony Williams, who had always wanted a solo career, decided he wanted to pursue one more vigorously. He was going to leave the group, and he put out a solo album. Indeed, it seems to have been Buck Ram's plan from the very start to get Williams to be a solo artist, while keeping the Platters as a hit group – he tried to find a replacement for Williams as early as 1956, although that didn't work out.

For a while, Williams continued in the Platters, while they looked for a replacement, but his solo career didn't go wonderfully at first. He wasn't helped by all four of the male Platters being arrested, allegedly as customers of sex workers, but in fact because they were sharing their hotel room with white women. All charges against everyone involved were later dropped, but this meant that it probably wasn't the best time for Williams to be starting a solo career.

But by 1961, Williams had managed to extricate himself from the Platters, and had been replaced by a young singer called Sonny Turner, who could sound a little like Williams. The record company were so convinced that Williams was the important one in the Platters, though, that on many of their recordings for the next year or two Mercury would take completed recordings by the new Platters lineup and overdub new lead vocals from Williams.

But one at a time the band members left, following Williams. And as each member left, they sold their shares in Five Platters Inc. to Buck Ram or to one of Ram's companies. By 1969 Herb Reed was the only member of the classic lineup still in the group, and then he left the group too, and Buck Ram and his companies continued putting out groups with no original members as the Platters.

Now, this doesn't mean that the real members stopped touring as the Platters. After David Lynch left in 1967, for example, he formed a group called "The Original Platters", and got both Zola Taylor and Paul Robi into the group. Tony Williams, Herb Reed, and Sonny Turner all also formed their own groups which toured under the Platters name, competing with the "official" Buck Ram Platters.

There followed forty years of litigation between Ram's companies and various Platters members. And the judgements went both ways, to the point that I can't make accurate judgements from the case documents I've been able to find online.

As best as I can understand it, there was a court ruling back in 1974 that the whole purpose of Five Platters Inc. had been to illegally deprive the band members of their ownership in the band name, that it was a sham corporation, and that Buck Ram had illegally benefited from an unfair bargaining position. Shortly after that, it was ruled that FPI's trademark in the Platters name was void. But then there were other cases which went the other way, and Five Platters Inc. insisted that the band members had mostly left because they were alcoholics who didn't want to tour any more, and that they'd given up their rights to the band name of their own free will.

Meanwhile, over a hundred fake Platters groups with no original members went out on the road at various points. There have been almost as many fake Platters as there have fake Ink Spots.

The band name issues were finally resolved in 2011. By that point Buck Ram was long dead, as were all the members of the classic Platters lineup except Herb Reed. A judge finally ruled that Herb Reed had the rights to the name, and that Five Platters Inc. had never owned the name. Just before that ruling, Five Platters Inc., which was now run by Jean Bennett, announced that they were going to retire the name. Herb Reed died in 2012, shortly afterwards, though the company he licensed the name to still licenses a band to tour as the Platters.

Gaynel Hodge, however, is still alive, the last surviving member of the original Platters, and he still performs with his own Platters group, performing songs the Platters recorded after he left.

Gaynel Hodge was a major figure in the California music industry. He'll be turning up in all sorts of odd places in this series, as he was involved in a lot of very important records. And we'll definitely be seeing more of both Richard Berry and Cornell Gunter later as well. And meanwhile, somewhere out there are multiple groups of people who've never met anyone who sang on "Only You", singing that song right now and calling themselves the Platters.

"I Got A Woman"

Let's talk about melisma.

One of the major things that you'll notice about the singers we've covered so far is that most of them sound very different from anyone who's been successful as a pure vocalist in the last few decades. There's a reason for that.

Among the pop songwriters of the thirties, forties, and fifties – not the writers of blues and country music so much, but the people writing Broadway musicals and the repertoire the crooners were singing – melisma was absolutely anathema.

Melisma is a technical musical term, but it has a simple meaning – it's when you sing multiple notes to the same syllable of lyric. This is something that has always existed since people started singing – for example, at the start of "The Star-Spangled Banner", "Oh say. . . ", there are two notes on the syllable "oh". That's melisma.

But among the songwriters who were registered with ASCAP in the middle of the last century, there was a strongly-held view that this was pure laziness. You wrote one syllable of lyric for one note of melody, and if you didn't, you were doing something wrong. The lyricist Sammy Cahn used to talk about how he wrote the lyric to "Pocketful of Miracles" – "Practicality doesn't interest me" – but then the composer wrote a melody with one more note per line than he'd written syllables for the lyric. Rather than let the song contain melisma, he changed it to "pee-racticality dee-oesn't interest me".

That was the kind of thing songwriters would do to avoid even the hint of melisma. And singers were the same. If you listen to any of the great voices of the first part of the twentieth century – Sinatra, Bing Crosby, Tony Bennett – they will almost without exception hit the note

347

dead on, one note per syllable. No ornamentation, no frills. There were a few outliers – Billie Holiday and Ella Fitzgerald, for example, would both use a little melisma (Holiday more than Ella) to ornament their sound – but generally that was what good singing was. You sang the notes, one note per syllable.

And this was largely the case in the blues, as well as in the more upmarket styles. The rules weren't stuck to quite as firmly there, but still, you'd mostly sing the song as it was written, and it would largely be written without melisma.

There was one area where that was not the case – gospel, specifically black gospel.

We looked at gospel already, of course, but we didn't talk about this particular characteristic of the music. You see, in black gospel – and pretty much only in black gospel music, at the time we're talking about – the use of melisma was how you conveyed emotion. You ornamented the notes, you'd sing more notes per syllable, and that was how you showed how moved you were by the spirit.

And these days, that style is what people now think of as good or impressive singing. There are a lot of class and race issues around taste in this that I'm not going to unpick here – we've got a whole nine more volumes in which to discuss these things, after all – but when you hear someone on *The Voice* or *American Idol* or *The X Factor* trying to impress with their vocals, it's their command of melisma they're trying to impress with. The more they can ornament the notes, the more they fit today's standards of good singing.

And that changed because, in the 1950s, there was a stream of black singers who came out of the gospel tradition and introduced its techniques into pop music.

Before talking about that, it's worth talking about the musical boundaries we're going to be using in this series. While it's called "A History of Rock Music in 500 Songs", I am not planning on using a narrow definition of "rock music", because what counts as rock tends to be retroactively redefined to exclude branches of music where black people predominate. So for example, there's footage of Mohammed Ali calling Sam Cooke "the greatest rock and roll singer in the world", and at the time absolutely nobody would have questioned Cooke being called "rock and roll", but these days he would only be talked about as a soul singer.

And much of the music that we would now call soul was so influential on the music that we now call rock music that it's completely ridiculous to even consider them separately until the late seventies at the earliest. So while we're going to mostly look at music that has been labelled rock or rock and roll, don't be surprised to find soul, funk, hip-hop, country, or any other genre that has influenced rock turning up. And especially don't be surprised to see that happening if it was music that was thought of as rock and roll at the time, but has been retroactively relabelled.

So in this chapter, we're going to talk about a record that's been widely credited as the first soul record, but which was released as rock and roll. And we're going to talk about a musician who cut across all the boundaries that anyone tries to put on music, a man who was equally at home in soul, jazz, R&B, country, and rock and roll. We're going to talk about the great Ray Charles.

Ray Charles had an unusual upbringing – though perhaps one that's not as unusual as people would like to think. As far as I can tell from his autobiography, he was the product of what we would now call a polyamorous relationship. His father was largely absent, but he was brought up by his mother, who he called "Mama", and by his father's wife, who he called "Mother". Both women knew of, approved of, and liked each other, as far as young Ray was concerned.

His given name was Ray Charles Robinson, but he changed it when he became a professional musician, due to the popularity of the boxer Sugar Ray Robinson, whose peak years were around the same time as Charles' – he didn't want to be confused with another, more famous, Ray Robinson. From a very young age, he was fascinated by the piano, and that fascination intensified when, before he reached adolescence, he became totally blind.

That blindness would shape his life, even though – and perhaps because – he had a strong sense of independence. He wasn't going to let his disability define him, and he often said that the three things that he didn't want were a dog, a cane, and a guitar, because they were the things all blind men had.

Now, I want to make it very clear that I'm not talking here about the rights and wrongs of Charles' own attitude to his disability. I'm disabled myself, but his disability is not mine, and he is from another generation. I'm just stating what that attitude was, and how it affected his life and career. And the main thing it did was make him even more fiercely independent. He not only got about on his own without a cane or a dog, he also at one point even used to go riding a motorbike by himself.

Other than his independence, the main thing everyone noted about the young Ray Charles Robinson was his proficiency on the piano, and by his late teens he was playing great jazz piano, inspired by Art Tatum, who like Ray was blind. Tatum was such a proficient pianist that there is a term in computational musicology, the tatum, meaning "the smallest time interval between successive notes in a rhythmic phrase".

Charles never got quite that good, but he was inspired by Tatum's musicality, and he became a serious student of the instrument, becoming a very respectable jazz pianist.

When his mother died, when he was fifteen, Charles decided to leave school and set up on his own as a musician. Initially, he toured only round Georgia and Florida, and early on he made a handful of records. His very earliest recordings, oddly, sound a lot like his mature style – his first record, "Wondering and Wondering", was almost fully-formed mature Ray Charles.

He moved to the West Coast, and unsuccessfully auditioned to play piano with Lucky Millinder's band, and would occasionally play jazz with Bumps Blackwell and Dizzy Gillespie. But while his association with Bumps Blackwell would continue long into the future, playing jazz wasn't how Ray Charles was going to make his name.

On the West Coast in the late forties and early fifties, the most popular style for black musicians was a particular kind of smooth blues, incorporating aspects of crooning alongside blues and jazz. Two of the biggest groups in the R&B field were the Nat "King" Cole Trio and Johnny Moore's Three Blazers featuring Charles Brown. Both of these had very similar styles, featuring a piano player who sang smooth blues, with an electric guitarist and a bass player, and sometimes a drummer.

We've mentioned Nat "King" Cole before, but it's still hard for modern listeners to remember that before his massive pop success with ballads like "Unforgettable", Cole was making music which may not have been quite as successful commercially, but which was incredibly influential on the burgeoning rock music field.

A typical example of the style is Cole's version of "Route Sixty-Six", which bears a remarkable similarity to Chuck Berry's early recordings. Berry would often say that while Louis Jordan's was the music he would play to try to make a living, Nat "King" Cole was the musician he most liked to listen to, and the Chuck Berry Trio was clearly an attempt to emulate this style. Ray Charles' early recordings, for Swing Time Records, were likewise in Cole's style.

The other group I mentioned, The Three Blazers, were very much in the same style as the Nat Cole Trio, but were a couple of rungs down the entertainment ladder, and Charles Brown, their singer, would be another huge influence on Ray Charles early on.

Charles formed his own trio, the McSon Trio (the "Son" came from the Robinson in his own name, the "Mc" from the guitarist's name), but they quickly changed their name to the Ray Charles Trio, as their pianist and singer became the obvious star of the show.

Charles soon tired of running his own trio, though, and went fully solo, travelling to gigs on his own and working with local pickup bands rather than having his own steady musicians. This also gave him the opportunity to collaborate with a wider variety of other musicians than having a fixed band would.

Around this time Charles was introduced by Bumps Blackwell to Quincy Jones, with whom he would go on to collaborate in various ways for much of the rest of his career. But his most important collaboration early on was with the blues musician Lowell Fulson. Fulson was one of the pioneers of the smooth West Coast blues sound, and Charles became his pianist and musical director for a short time.

So Charles was splitting his time between making his own Nat Cole or Charles Brown style records, touring on his own, and touring with Fulson. He also worked on other records for other musicians. The most notable of these was a blues classic, by another of the greats of West Coast blues, "The Things That I Used to Do" by Guitar Slim.

Slim was one of the great blues guitarists of the 1950s, and he was also one of the great showmen, whose performance style included things like a guitar cord that was allegedly three hundred and fifty feet long, so he could keep his guitar plugged into the amplifier but walk through the crowd and even out into the street, while still playing his guitar. Slim would later be a huge influence on musicians like Jimi Hendrix, but "The Things That I Used to Do", his most famous record, is as much Charles' record as it is Guitar Slim's – Charles produced, arranged, and played piano, and the result sounds far more like the work that Charles was doing at the time than it does Guitar Slim's other work, though it still has Slim's recognisable guitar sound.

Charles finally got the opportunity to stand out when he moved from Swing Time to Atlantic Records. While several of the Swing Time recordings were minor successes, people kept telling him how much he sounded like Nat Cole or Charles Brown. But he realised that it was unlikely that anyone was telling Nat Cole or Charles Brown how much they sounded like Ray Charles, and that he would never be in the first rank of musicians unless he got a style that was uniquely his.

Everything changed with "Mess Around", which was his first major venture into the Atlantic house style. The credits for "Mess Around" claim it's written by Ahmet Ertegun, but it should really be credited as a traditional song arranged by Ray Charles, Jesse Stone, and Ertegun.

Rather surprisingly, given the habit of record executives of just taking credit for something that they had nothing to do with, Ertegun did contribute to the songwriting. He told Charles to play some piano in the style of Pete Johnson, and Charles responded by playing "Cow Cow Blues", a 1928 song by Cow Cow Davenport. Ertegun came up with some new words for that, mostly based around traditional floating lyrics. Jesse Stone came up with an arrangement, and the result was titled "Mess Around".

For his next few records, Charles was one of many artists making records with the standard Atlantic musicians and arrangers – the same people who were making records with Ruth Brown or LaVern Baker. By this point, he had gained enough confidence in the studio that he was able to sing like himself, not like Charles Brown or Nat Cole or anyone else. The music he was making was generic R&B, but records like "It Should Have Been Me", his third Atlantic single, didn't sound like anyone else at all.

"Mess Around" and "It Should Have Been Me" were Charles' two biggest hits to date, both making the top five on the R&B charts. His breakout, though, came with a song that he based around a gospel song. At this time, gospel music was not much of an influence on most of the rhythm and blues records that were charting, but as Charles would later say, "the church was something which couldn't be taken out of my voice even if I had wanted to take it out. Once I decided to be natural, I was gone. It's like Aretha: She could do "Stardust," but if she did her thing on it, you'd hear the church all over the place."

Charles had now formed his own band, which was strongly influenced by Count Basie. The Count Basie band was one of the bands that had most influenced early R&B, and its music was exactly the kind of combination of jump band and classy jazz that Charles liked. Charles' modelled his band on them, though in a slimmed down lineup because of the practicalities of touring with a big band in the fifties. He had three sax players, piano, bass, drums, two trumpets, and a trombone, and he added a girl group, called the Raelettes, who were mostly former members of a girl group called the Cookies (who would go on to have a few hits themselves over the years).

Charles was now able to record his own band, rather than the Atlantic session musicians, and have them playing his own arrangements rather than Jesse Stone's. And the first recording session he did with his own band produced his first number one. Charles' trumpet player, Renald Richard, brought Charles a set of blues lyrics, and Charles set them to a gospel tune he'd been listening to.

The Southern Tones were a gospel act recording for Duke Records, and they never had much success. They'd be almost forgotten now were it not for one record, their version of "It Must Be Jesus". Charles took that melody, and the lyrics that Renald Richard had given him, and created a record which was utterly unlike anything else that had ever been recorded. This was a new fusion of gospel, the blues, big band jazz, and early rock and roll. Nobody had ever done anything like it before. In the context of 1954, when every fusion of ideas from different musics, and every new musical experiment, was labelled "rock and roll", this was definitely a rock and roll record, but in later decades they would say that this music had soul.

That song, "I Got a Woman", was close enough to gospel to cause Charles some very real problems. Gospel singers who went over to making secular music were considered by their original fans to be going over to the side of the Devil. It wasn't just that they were performing secular music – it was very specifically that they were using musical styles that were created in order to worship God, and turning them to secular purposes.

And this criticism was applied, loudly, to Charles, even though he had never been a gospel singer. But while the gospel community was up in arms, people were listening. "I Got a Woman" went to number one on the R&B charts, and quickly entered the stage repertoire of another musician who had church music in his veins, as it became part of Elvis' regular set.

And so even as it kicked off a whole new genre, "I Got a Woman" became a rock and roll standard. It would be covered by the Everly Brothers, the Beatles, the Monkees... it would be easier to list the musicians of the fifties and sixties who didn't cover it. Even the Western Swing group The Maddox Brothers and Rose covered it, though their version, titled "The Death of Rock and Roll", credited the song as a traditional one arranged by Fred Maddox, rather than to Charles and Richard.

Ray Charles was, in the minds of his detractors, debasing something holy, but those complaints didn't stop Charles from continuing to re-work gospel songs and turn them into rock and roll classics. For his next single, he took the old gospel song "This Little Light of Mine", and reworked it into "This Little Girl of Mine".

He had hit on a formula that any other musician would have happily milked for decades. But Ray Charles wasn't a musician who would stick to just one style of music. This wandering musical mind would ensure that for the next few years Ray Charles would be probably the most vital creative force in American music, but it also meant that he would swing wildly between commercial success and failure.

After a run of huge hits in 1954, 55, and 56 – classic songs like "Hallelujah, I Love Her So", "Drown in My Own Tears", and "Lonely

Avenue" – he hit a dry patch, with such less-than-stellar efforts as "My Bonnie" and "Swanee River Rock". But you can't keep a good man down for long, and when we next look at Ray Charles, in 1959, we'll see him once again revolutionise both rock and roll and the music he invented, the music that we now call soul.

"Mystery Train"

By the end of 1955, Elvis Presley was poised to become one of the biggest artists in the world, but to do that, he would have to leave the record label that had got him to that point, and the man who had mentored him. To tell that story – how Elvis came to leave Sun Records and become a major label artist, and how he got a new, much less benevolent, mentor, we're going to tell a tale of two Parkers.

The first Parker we're going to talk about is Junior Parker, the blues musician who had been one of the Beale Streeters with Johnny Ace, Bobby "Blue" Bland, and B.B. King.

Junior Parker had been working with Howlin' Wolf for a while, before in 1952 he formed his own band, the Blue Flames (which should not be confused with all the other Flames bands we've talked about – for some reason there is a profusion of Flames that we'll be dealing with well into the seventies). Ike Turner discovered them, and initially got them signed to Modern Records, though as with many Modern Records acts they were recording mostly in Sam Phillips' studio. After one single, featuring Turner on piano, Parker and his band started recording directly for Sun Records.

The first single they recorded for Sun was a minor hit, but wasn't particularly interesting – "Feelin' Good" was basically a John Lee Hooker knock-off. But it's their second single for Sun we want to talk about here, and both sides of it. The A-side of Junior Parker and the Blue Flames' second Sun single is one of the best blues records Sun ever put out, "Love My Baby".

That record was one that Sam Phillips – a man who made a lot of great records – considered among the greatest he'd ever made. Talking to his biographer Peter Guralnick about it decades later, he said "I

357

mean you tell me a better record that you've ever heard," and Guralnick couldn't.

But it was the B-side that made an impression. The B-side was a song called "Mystery Train".

That song actually dates back to the old folk song, "Worried Man Blues", which was recorded in 1930 by the Carter Family. The Carter Family were, along with Jimmie Rodgers, the people who defined what country music is. Everyone in country music followed from either the Carters or Rodgers, and we'll be seeing some members of the extended Carter family much later. But the important thing here is that A.P. Carter, the family patriarch, was one of the most important songwriters of his generation, but he would also go out and find old folk songs that he would repurpose and credit himself with having written.

"Worried Man Blues" was one of those, and contained a line, "the train arrived, sixteen coaches long," which became part of the floating lyrics that all blues singers could call upon, and wa used as the opening line for "Mystery Train" more than twenty years later.

That song's composition was credited to Parker and to Sam Phillips. Phillips would later claim that he made three major changes to the song, and that these were why he got the co-writing credit. The first was to give the song the title "Mystery Train", which has been a big part of the song's appeal ever since. The second was to insist that the number of coaches for the train should be sixteen – Parker had been singing "fifty coaches long". And the final one was to suggest that the band start the song slowly and build up the tempo like a train gathering steam.

Parker and his Blue Flames also backed Rufus Thomas on "Tiger Man", a song that Elvis would later go on to perform in the sixties, and would play as a medley with "Mystery Train" in the seventies.

The Rufus Thomas connection proved a signifier of what was to come. Don Robey was still annoyed with Sam Phillips over "Bear Cat", the track that Phillips had produced for Thomas as an answer to "Hound Dog", and Robey would take pleasure in poaching Phillips' artists for his own label. Phillips was soon reading in Cash Box magazine that Robey was grooming Little Junior Parker for big things. Robey signed Parker to an exclusive contract, and even an unsuccessful hundred-thousand-dollar lawsuit from Sam Phillips couldn't stop Robey from having Parker on his label.

Junior Parker would go on to have a distinguished career in R&B, having occasional hit singles until shortly before his death from a brain tumour in 1971.

Luckily for Phillips, he had other artists he could work with, not least of them Elvis Presley. But before we talk more about Elvis, let's talk about that other Parker.

Tom Parker was to become the most well-known manager in the music industry, even though for most of his career he only managed one act, so we're going to look at him in some detail, as he became the template for all the worst, most grasping, managers in the music business. When we deal with Allen Klein or Peter Grant or Don Arden in future volumes, we'll be dealing with people who are following in the Colonel's footsteps.

It's difficult to separate fact from fiction in the case of Colonel Parker, though there are biographies devoted entirely to doing so, with some success. What we know for sure was that Parker was an undocumented immigrant to the United States, originally from the Netherlands, who had taken the name Parker upon his arrival.

We also know that the same day that he disappeared from his home in the Netherlands to travel to the US for the final time, a woman was found bludgeoned to death in his home town. And we know that he was dishonourably discharged from the US Army as a psychopath. And that there were rumours around his home town decades later that Parker was responsible for the murder.

We also know that he desperately hid his undocumented status long past the time when he would have been eligible for citizenship, and that he completely cut off all contact with his family, even though he had been close to them before emigrating.

Whether he was a killer or not, Parker was certainly an unsavoury character – as, to be fair, were most people involved in the business side of the music industry in the 1950s. He had his start in the entertainment industry as a con-man, and throughout his life he loved to manipulate people, playing humiliating practical jokes on them that weren't so much jokes as demonstrations of his power over them. He was, by all accounts, a cruel man who loved to hurt people – except when he loved to be outlandishly sentimental towards them instead, of course.

Parker had started out as a carny – working in travelling shows, doing everything from running a dancing chicken show (in which he'd put a hot-plate under a chicken's feet so it would keep lifting its legs up and look like it was dancing) to telling fortunes, to being the person whose job it was to tempt the geek to come back to the show with a bottle of whisky when he became too sickened by his job.

(The geek, for those who don't know, was a person in a carnival who would perform acts that would disgust most people, such as biting the head off live chickens, to the amused disgust of the audience. Usually a geek would be someone who had severe mental health and substance abuse problems, degrading himself as the only way to make enough money to feed his habit.)

All this had taught Parker a lot – it had led him to the conclusion that audiences were there to be ripped off, and that absolutely nothing mattered to them other than the promise of sexuality. As far as Parker was concerned, in showbusiness it didn't matter what the show was – what mattered was how you sold it to the audience, and how much merchandise you could sell during the show.

In his time with the carnivals, Parker had become extremely good at creating publicity stunts. One that he did many times was to fake a public wedding. He and a female staff member would pretend to be just two customers in love, and they would "get married" at the top of the Ferris wheel, drawing huge crowds.

It was during World War II that Parker had moved into country music promotion. He first became involved in music when he got to know Gene Austin, one of the biggest stars of the 1920s. Austin had been a huge star, but by the time Parker got to know him in the late thirties, he was much less popular.

Parker helped him organise some shows (according to some claims, Parker was his manager, though other sources disagree), but at this time Austin had fallen on such hard times that he would fill his car at a petrol station, pay by cheque, and then tell them that his autograph was probably worth more than the money, so why not just leave that cheque uncashed and frame it?

Parker learned a valuable lesson from Austin, with whom he would remain friends for years. That lesson was that the stars come and go, and rise and fall in popularity, but managers can keep making money no matter how old they are. Parker determined to get into music management. And given that he didn't actually like music himself, he decided to go for the music of the common people, the music that was selling to the same people who'd been coming to the carnivals. Country music.

And so to start with he put on a show by the up-and-coming star Roy Acuff.

In later years Roy Acuff would become, for a time, the single biggest star in country music, and Hank Williams would say of him, "For drawing power in the South, it was Roy Acuff, then God." But in 1941 he was merely very popular, rather than a superstar.

And Parker had used his promotional knowledge to make the show he promoted one of the biggest in Acuff's career thus far. In particular, he'd tried a new trick that no-one else had ever done before. He'd cut a deal with a local grocery chain that they would sell cut-price tickets to anyone who brought in a clipping from a newspaper. This meant that the show had, in effect, multiple box offices, while the grocery chain paid for the advertising to increase their own footfall.

Having seen what kind of money he could make from country music, Parker approached Acuff about becoming Acuff's manager. Acuff was initially interested, but after a couple of dates he was put off from working further with Parker, because Parker had what Acuff thought an un-Christian attitude to money. Acuff was playing dates for fixed fees, and Parker started insisting that as well as the fixed fee, Acuff should get a percentage of the gross. Acuff didn't want to be that grasping, and so he gave up on working with Parker – though as a consolation, Acuff did give Parker a stake in his merchandising – Parker got the rights to market Roy Acuff Flour in Florida.

But Acuff did more than that. He pointed Parker in the direction of Eddy Arnold, a young singer who was then working with Pee Wee King's Golden West Cowboys. He told Parker that Arnold would almost certainly be going solo soon, and that he would need a manager.

Arnold was a fan of Gene Austin, and so eagerly linked up with Parker. Parker quickly got Arnold signed to RCA records as a solo artist, and Arnold's second single, in 1945, "Each Minute Seems Like a Million Years", reached number five in the country charts.

Eddy Arnold was to go on to become one of the biggest stars in country music, and that was in large part because of the team that Tom Parker built around him. Parker would handle the management, Steve Sholes, the head of country and R&B at RCA, would handle the record production. Parker cut a deal with Hill and Range music publishers so that Arnold would perform songs they published in return for kickbacks, and any songs that Arnold wrote himself would go through them. And the William Morris Agency would handle the bookings.

Both Sholes and Arnold were given money by Hill and Range for Arnold recording the publishers' songs, Parker had Sholes in his pocket because he knew that Sholes was taking kickbacks and could inform Sholes' bosses at RCA, and Parker in turn took twenty-five percent of the twenty thousand dollar bribe that Hill and Range paid Arnold, as Arnold's manager.

This whole team, put together by a mutual love of ripping each other and their artists off, would go on to work with Parker on every other artist he managed, and would be the backbone of his success in the industry.

Parker soon used his music industry connections to get an honorary Colonel's commission from Louisiana Governor Jimmie Davis, himself a former country musician, and from that point until the end of his life insisted on being addressed as "Colonel", even though in reality he was a draft-dodger who had deliberately piled on weight during the Second World War so he could become too fat to draft.

But Parker and Arnold eventually split up – Parker was originally meant to be Arnold's exclusive manager, but in 1953 Arnold found out that Parker was putting together a tour of other RCA acts, headed by Hank Snow. Arnold fired the Colonel, and the Colonel quickly instead became the "exclusive" manager of Hank Snow.

Of course, Parker didn't leave his association with Eddy Arnold empty handed – he insisted on Arnold giving him a severance package of fifty thousand dollars, because of how much money Arnold was making from the contracts that Parker had negotiated for him.

His association with Hank Snow would only last two years, and would break up very acrimoniously – with Snow later saying "I have worked with several managers over the years and have had respect for them all except one. Tom Parker was the most egotistical, obnoxious human being I've ever had dealings with."

The reason Snow said this was because the Colonel tricked Snow out of the greatest business opportunity in the history of the music business. The two of them had formed a management company to manage other artists, and when Parker found another artist he wanted to manage, Snow naturally assumed that they were partners – right up until he discovered they weren't.

Since his first single, Elvis Presley had been putting out singles on Sun that largely stuck to the same formula – a blues number on one side, a country number on the other, and a sparse backing by Elvis, Scotty, and Bill.

In general, the blues sides were rather better than the country sides, not least because the country sides, after the first couple of singles, started to be songs that were especially written for Elvis by outside songwriters, and tended to be based on rather obvious wordplay – songs like "I'm Left, You're Right, She's Gone". The blues songs, on the other hand, were chosen from among Elvis' own favourites and songs that got kicked around in the studio.

This would set the template for his work in the future – whenever Elvis got to choose his own material, and follow his own instincts, the results would be good music. Whenever he was working on music that was chosen for him by someone else – even someone as sympathetic to his musical instincts as Sam Phillips – the music would suffer, though at this stage even the songs Elvis wasn't as keen on sounded great.

By the time of Elvis' last Sun single, he had finally made one more change that would define the band he would work with for the rest of the fifties. He had introduced a drummer, DJ Fontana, and while Fontana didn't play on the single – session drummer Johnny Bernero played on it instead – he would be a part of the core band from now on. The trio of Elvis, Scotty, and Bill had now become a singer and his backup band – Elvis Presley and the Blue Moon Boys.

The A-side of Elvis' fifth single for Sun Records was one of those country songs that had been written especially for Elvis, "I Forgot to Remember to Forget". It's a perfectly adequate country pop song, but the B-side, his version of "Mystery Train", was astonishing.

It was actually a merger of elements from the A-side and the B-side of Junior Parker's single, as "Love My Baby" provided the riff that Scotty Moore used on Elvis' version of "Mystery Train". Elvis, Scotty, and Bill melded the two different songs together, and they came up with something that would become an absolute classic of the rockabilly genre.

The song was probably chosen because Sam Phillips was one of the credited songwriters – as he was currently battling Don Robey in court over Junior Parker, he naturally wanted to make as much money off his former artist as he could. But at the same time, it was a song Elvis clearly liked, and one he would still be performing live in the 1970s. This wasn't a song that was being forced on to Elvis.

Indeed, Elvis almost certainly saw Junior Parker live when he was playing with the Beale Streeters – B.B. King would talk in later years about the teenage Elvis having been one of the very few white people who went to see them, and even allowing for later exaggerations, it's likely that he did see them at least a few times.

So this was one of those rare cases where the financial and artistic incentives perfectly overlapped.

But while he was recording for Sun, Elvis was also touring, and he was drawing bigger and bigger crowds, and they were going wilder and wilder. And when Tom Parker saw one of those crowds, he knew he had to have Elvis. He didn't understand at all why those girls were screaming at him – he would never, in all his life, ever understand the appeal of Elvis' music – but he knew that a crowd like that would spend money, and he definitely understood that.

Parker worked on Elvis, and more importantly he worked on Elvis' family – and even more importantly than that, he got Hank Snow to work on Elvis' family. Elvis' parents were big Hank Snow fans, and after being told by their idol how much the Colonel had helped him they were practically salivating to get Elvis signed with him.

Elvis himself was young, and naive, and would go along with whatever his parents suggested. Carl Perkins would later describe him as the most introverted person ever to enter a recording studio, and he just wanted to make some money to look after his parents. His daddy had a bad back and couldn't work, and his mama was so tired and sick all the time. If they said the Colonel would help him earn more money, well, he'd do what his parents said. Maybe he could earn them enough money to buy them a nice big house, so his mama could give up her job. They could maybe raise chickens in the yard.

It was only after the documents were signed that Snow realised that the contracts didn't mention himself at all. His partner had cut him out, and the two parted company.

Meanwhile, Sam Phillips was finding some more country singers he could work with, and starting to transition into country and rockabilly rather than the blues. A couple of months before "Mystery Train", he put out another single by a two-guitar and bass rockabilly act – "Hey Porter" by Johnny Cash and the Tennessee Two, although right now Cash didn't seem to be star material.

Colonel Parker knew that if Elvis was to become the star he could become, he would have to move to one of the major labels. Sun Records was a little nothing R&B label in Memphis; it barely registered on the national consciousness. If Elvis was going to do what Tom Parker wanted him to do, he was going to have to move to a big label – a big label like RCA Records. Colonel Parker was in the country music business after all, and if you were going to be anything at all in the country music business, you were going to work in Nashville. Not Memphis. Parker started hinting to people that Sam Phillips wanted to sell Elvis' contract, without bothering to check with Phillips.

The problem was that Sam Phillips didn't want to give up on Elvis so easily. Phillips was, after all, a great judge of talent, and not only had he discovered Elvis, he had nurtured his ability. It was entirely likely that without Sam Phillips, Elvis would never have been anything more than a truck driver with a passable voice. Elvis the artist was as much the creation of Sam Phillips as he was of Elvis Presley himself.

But there was a downside to Elvis' success, and it was one that every independent label dreads. Sun Records was having hits. And the last thing you want as an indie is to have a hit.

The problem is cashflow. Suppose the distributors want a hundred thousand copies of your latest single. That's great! Except they will not pay you for several months – if they pay you at all. And meanwhile, you need to pay the pressing plant for the singles before you get them to the distributors. If you've been selling in small but steady numbers and you suddenly start selling a lot, that can destroy your company. Nothing is more deadly to the indie label than a hit.

And then on top of that there was the lawsuit with Don Robey over Junior Parker. That was eating Phillips' money, and he didn't have much of it.

But at that point, Sam Phillips didn't have any artists who could take Elvis' place. He'd found the musician he'd been looking for – the one who could unite black and white people in Phillips' dream of ending racism. So he came up with a plan. He decided to tell Tom Parker that Elvis' contract would be for sale, like Parker wanted – but only for $35,000.

Now, that doesn't sound like a huge amount for Elvis' contract today, but in 1955 that would be the highest sum of money ever paid for a recording artist's contract. It was certainly an absurd amount for someone who had so far failed to trouble the pop charts at all. Phillips' view was that it was a ridiculous amount to ask for, but if he got it he could cover his spiralling costs, and if he didn't – as seemed likely – he would still have Elvis.

As Phillips later said, "I thought, hey, I'll make 'em an offer that I know they will refuse, and then I'll tell 'em they'd better not spread this poison any more. I absolutely did not think Tom Parker could raise the $35,000, and that would have been fine. But he raised the money, and damn, I couldn't back out then."

He gave the Colonel an unreasonably tight deadline to get him a five thousand dollar non-refundable deposit, and another unreasonably tight deadline to get the other thirty thousand. Amazingly, the Colonel called his bluff. He got him the five thousand almost straight away out of his own pocket, and by the deadline had managed to persuade

Steve Sholes at RCA to pay it back to him, to pay Sam Phillips the outstanding thirty thousand, and to pay Elvis a five thousand dollar signing bonus – of which, of course, a big chunk went directly into Tom Parker's pocket.

RCA quickly reissued "I Forgot to Remember to Forget" and "Mystery Train", while they were waiting for Elvis' first recording session for his new label. With Elvis was now on a major label, and Sam Phillips had to find a new rockabilly star to promote. Luckily, there was a new young country boy who had come to audition for him. Carl Perkins had definite possibilities.

"Tutti Frutti"

There are a handful of musicians in the history of rock music who seem like true originals. You can always trace their influences, of course, but when you come across one of them, no matter how clearly you can see who they were copying and who they were inspired by, you still just respond to them as something new under the sun.

And of all the classic musicians of rock and roll, probably nobody epitomises that more than Little Richard. Nobody before him sounded like he did, and while many later tried – everyone from Captain Beefheart to Paul McCartney – nobody ever quite sounded like him later.

And there are good reasons for that, because Little Richard was – and still is – someone who is quite unlike anyone else.

This chapter is the point where we see queer culture becoming a major part of the rock and roll story – we've dealt with possibly-LGBT people before, of course, with Big Mama Thornton, Sister Rosetta Tharpe, and Johnnie Ray, but this is the first time that an expression of sexuality has become part and parcel of the music itself.

And here, again, I have to point out that I am going to get things very wrong when I'm talking about Little Richard. I am a cis straight white man in Britain in the twenty-first century. Little Richard is a queer black man from the USA, and we're talking about the middle of the twentieth century. I'm fairly familiar with current British LGBT+ culture, but even that is as an outsider. I am trying, always, to be completely fair and to never say anything that harms a marginalised group, but if I do so inadvertently, I apologise.

When I say he's queer, I'm using the word not in its sense as a slur, but in the sense of an umbrella term for someone whose sexuality and gender identity are too complex to reduce to a single label, because he has at various times defined himself as gay, but he has also had relationships with women, and because from reading his autobiography there are so many passages where he talks about wishing he had been born a woman that it may well be that had he been born fifty years later he would have defined himself as a bisexual trans woman rather than a gay man. I will still, though, use "he" and "him" pronouns for him, because those are the pronouns he uses himself.

Here we're again going to see something we saw with Rosetta Tharpe, but on a much grander scale – the pull between the secular and the divine.

You see, as well as being some variety of queer, Little Richard is also a very, very, religious man, and a believer in a specific variety of fundamentalist Christianity that believes that any kind of sexuality or gender identity other than monogamous cis heterosexual is evil and sinful and the work of the Devil. He believes this very deeply and has at many times tried to live his life by this, and does so now. I, to put it as mildly as possible, disagree. But to understand the man and his music at all, you have to at least understand that this is the case. He has swung wildly between being almost the literal embodiment of the phrase "sex and drugs and rock and roll" and being a preacher who claims that homosexuality, bisexuality, and being trans are all works of the literal Devil – several times he's gone from one to the other. As of 2017, and the last public interview I've seen with him, he has once again renounced rock and roll and same-sex relationships. I hope that he's happy in his current situation.

But at the time we're talking about, he was a young person, and very much engaged in those things.

Richard Penniman was the third of twelve children, born to parents who had met at a Pentecostal holiness meeting when they were thirteen and married when they were fourteen. Of all the children, Richard was the one who was most likely to cause trouble. He had a habit of playing practical jokes involving his own faeces – wrapping them up and giving them as presents to old ladies, or putting them in jars in the pantry for his mother to find.

But he was also bullied terribly as a child, because he was disabled. One of his legs was significantly shorter than the other, his head was disproportionately large, and his eyes were different sizes. He was also subjected to homophobic abuse from a very early age, because the gait with which he walked because of his legs was vaguely mincing.

At the age of fourteen, he decided to leave school and become a performer. He started out by touring with a snake-oil salesman.

Snake oil is a traditional Chinese medicine, about which there have been claims made for centuries, and those claims might well be true. But snake oil in the US was usually a mixture of turpentine, tallow, camphor, and capsaicin. It wasn't much different to Vicks' VaporRub and similar substances, but it was sold as a cure-all for serious illnesses.

Snake-oil salesmen would travel from town to town selling their placebo, and they would have entertainers performing with them in order to draw crowds. The young Richard Penniman travelled with "Doc Hudson", and would sing the one non-religious song he knew, "Caldonia" by Louis Jordan. The yelps and hiccups in Jordan's vocals on that song would become a massive part of Richard's own vocal style.

Richard soon left the medicine show, and started touring with a band, B. Brown and His Orchestra, and it was while he was touring with that band that he grew his hair into the huge pompadour that would later become a trademark, and he also got the name "Little Richard". However, all the musicians in the band were older than him, so he moved on again to another touring show, and another, and another.

In many of these shows, he would perform as a female impersonator, which started when one of the women in one of the shows took sick and Richard had to quickly cover for her by putting on her costume, but soon he was performing in shows that were mostly drag acts, performing to a largely gay crowd.

It was while he was performing in these shows that he met the first of his two biggest influences. Billy Wright, like Richard, had been a female impersonator for a while too. Like Richard, he had a pompadour haircut, and he was a fairly major blues star in the period from 1949 through 1951, being one of the first blues singers to sing with gospel-inspired mannerisms.

Richard became something of a Billy Wright wannabe, and started incorporating parts of Wright's style into his performances. He also learned that Wright was using makeup on stage – Pancake 31 – and started applying that same makeup to his own skin, something he would continue to do throughout his performing career.

Wright introduced Richard to Zenas Sears, who was one of the many white DJs all across America who were starting to become successful by playing black music and speaking in approximations of African-American Vernacular English – people like Alan Freed and Dewey Phillips.

Sears had connections with RCA Records, and impressed by Richard's talent, he got them to sign him. Richard's first single was called "Every Hour", and was very much a Billy Wright imitation. It was so close to Wright's style, in fact, that Wright soon recorded his own knock-off of Richard's song, "Every Evening".

At this point Richard was solely a singer – he hadn't yet started to play an instrument to accompany himself. That changed when he met Esquerita.

Esquerita was apparently born Stephen Quincey Reeder, but he was known to everyone as "Eskew" Reeder, after his initials, and that then became Esquerita, partly as a pun on the word "excreta".

Esquerita was another gay black R&B singer with a massive pompadour and a moustache. If Little Richard at this stage looked like a caricature of Billy Wright, Esquerita looked like a caricature of Little Richard. His hair was even bigger, he was even more flamboyant, and when he sang, he screamed even louder. And Esquerita also played the piano.

Richard – who has never been unwilling to acknowledge the immense debt he owed to his inspirations – has said for years that Esquerita was the person who taught him how to play the piano, and that not only was his piano-playing style a copy of Esquerita's, Esquerita was better. It's hard to tell for sure exactly how much influence Esquerita actually had on Richard's piano playing, because Esquerita himself didn't make any records until after Richard did, at which point he was signed to his own record deal to be basically a Little Richard clone, but the records he did make certainly show a remarkable resemblance to Richard's later style.

Richard soon learned to play piano, and he was seen by Johnny Otis, who was impressed. Otis said, "I see this outrageous person, good-looking and very effeminate, with a big pompadour. He started singing and he was so good. I loved it. He reminded me of Dinah Washington. He did a few things, then he got on the floor. I think he even did a split, though I could be wrong about that. I remember it as being just beautiful, bizarre, and exotic, and when he got through he remarked, "This is Little Richard, King of the Blues," and then he added, "And the Queen, too!" I knew I liked him then."

Otis recommended Richard to Don Robey, of Peacock Records, and Robey signed Richard and his band the Tempo Toppers. In early 1953, with none of his recordings for RCA having done anything, Little Richard and the Tempo Toppers went into the studio with another group, the Deuces of Rhythm, to record four tracks, issued as two singles.

Neither had any success, and Richard did not get on very well at all with Don Robey. Robey was not the most respectful of people, and Richard let everyone know how badly he thought Robey treated his artists. Robey responded by beating Richard up so badly that he got a hernia which hurt for years and necessitated an operation.

Richard would record one more session for Peacock, at the end of the year, when Don Robey gave him to Johnny Otis to handle. Otis took his own band into the studio with Richard, and the four songs they recorded at that session went unreleased at the time, but included a version of "Directly From My Heart to You", a song Richard would soon rerecord, and another song called "Little Richard's Boogie".

Nobody was very happy with the recordings, and Richard was dropped by Peacock. He was also, around the same time, made to move away from Macon, Georgia, where he lived, after being arrested for "lewd conduct" – what amounted to consensual voyeurism.

The Tempo Toppers had split up, Richard had been dumped by two record labels, his father had died recently, he had no band, and he wasn't allowed to live in his home town any more. Things seemed pretty low.

But before he'd moved away, Richard had met Lloyd Price, and Price had suggested that Richard send a demo tape in to Specialty Records, Price's label. The tape lay unlistened at Specialty for months, and it was only because of Richard's constant pestering for them to listen to it that Bumps Blackwell, who was then in charge of A&R at Specialty, eventually got round to listening to it.

This was an enormous piece of good fortune, in a way that neither of them fully realised at the time. Blackwell had been a long-time friend and colleague of Ray Charles. When Charles' gospel-influenced new sound had started making waves on the charts, Art Rupe, Specialty's owner, had asked Blackwell to find him a gospel-sounding R&B singer of his own to compete with Ray Charles.

Blackwell listened to the tape, which contained two songs, and he could tell this was someone with as much gospel in his voice as Ray Charles had. Blackwell and Rupe made an agreement with Don Robey to buy out his contract for six hundred dollars, and one gets the impression that Robey would have paid them six hundred dollars to get rid of Richard had they asked him.

They knew that Richard liked the music of Fats Domino, and so they decided to hold their first session at Cosimo Matassa's studio, where Domino recorded, and with the same session musicians that Domino used. Blackwell also brought in two great New Orleans piano players, Huey "Piano" Smith and James Booker, both of whom were players in the same style as Domino.

All of these people were veterans of sessions either for Domino or for artists who had worked in Domino's style, like Lloyd Price or Smiley Lewis. The only difference here was that it would be Bumps Blackwell who did the arrangement and production, rather than Dave Bartholomew like on Domino's records.

However, the session didn't go well at all. Blackwell had heard that Richard was an astounding live act, but he was just doing nothing in the studio. As Blackwell later put it "If you look like Tarzan and sound like Mickey Mouse it just doesn't work out."

They did record some usable material – one of Richard's originals, "Wonderin'" came out fine, and they recorded "I'm Just a Lonely, Lonely, Guy" by a young songwriter called Dorothy LaBostrie, which seemed to go OK. They also cut a decent version of "Directly From My Heart to You".

So they had a couple of usable songs, but usable was about all you could say for them. They didn't have anything that would make an impact, nothing that would live up to Richard's potential.

So Blackwell called a break, and they headed off to get themselves something to eat, at the Dew Drop Inn. And something happened there that would change Little RIchard's career forever.

The Dew Drop Inn had a piano, and it had an audience that Little Richard could show off in front of. He went over to the piano, started hammering the keys, and screamed out "A wop bop a loo mop, a good goddamn!"

On hearing Richard sing the song he performed then, Bumps Blackwell knew two things pretty much instantly. The first was that that song would definitely be a hit if he could get it released. And the second was that there was no way on Earth that he could possibly put it out.

"Tutti Frutti" started as a song that Richard sang more or less as a joke. There is a whole undercurrent of R&B in the fifties which has very, very, sexually explicit lyrics. "Tutti Frutti" in its original form was part of this undercurrent, and had lyrics that were clearly not broadcastable – "A wop bop a loo mop, a good goddamn/Tutti Frutti, good booty/If it don't fit, don't force it, you can grease it, make it easy". But Bumps Blackwell thought that there was something that could be made into a hit there.

Handily, they had a songwriter on hand. Dorothy LaBostrie was a young woman he knew who had been trying to write songs, but who didn't understand that songs had to have different melodies – all her lyrics were written to the melody of the same song, Dinah Washington's "Blowtop Blues".

But her lyrics had showed promise, and so Blackwell had agreed to record one of her songs, "I'm Just a Lonely, Lonely, Guy", with Richard. LaBostrie had been hanging round the studio to see how her song sounded when it was recorded, so Blackwell asked her to do a last-minute rewrite on "Tutti Frutti", in the hope of getting something salvageable out of what had been a depressing session. But there was still a problem – Richard, not normally a man overly known for his modesty, became embarrassed at singing his song to the young woman.

Blackwell explained to him that he really didn't have much choice, and Richard eventually agreed to sing it to her – but only if he was turned to face the wall, so he couldn't see this innocent-looking young woman's face.

(I should note here that both Richard and LaBostrie have told different stories about this over the years – both have claimed on several occasions that they were the sole author of the song and that the other didn't deserve any credit at all. But this is the story as it was told by others who were there.)

LaBostrie's new lyrics were rudimentary at best. "I got a girl named Sue, she knows just what to do". But they fit the metre, they weren't about anal sex, and so they were going to be the new lyrics.

The session was running late at this point, and when LaBostrie had the lyrics finished there was only fifteen minutes to go. It didn't matter that the lyrics were trite. What mattered was that they got a track cut to salvage the session. Blackwell didn't have time to teach the piano players the song, so he got Richard to play the piano himself. They cut the finished track in three takes, and Blackwell went back to California happy he at last had a hit.

"Tutti Frutti" was, indeed, a massive hit. It went to number twenty-one on the pop charts. But... you know what comes next. There was an inept white cover version, this time by Pat Boone.

Boone's version changes the lyrics. In Richard's version, after all, he seems interested in both Sue and Daisy. A good Christian boy like Pat Boone couldn't be heard singing about such immorality, so rather than sing about how Daisy "knows how to love me, yes indeed", Boone sings "She's a real gone cookie/Yes, sirree/But pretty little Susie is the gal for me"

That one-line change (and a couple of other spot changes to individual words to make things into full sentences) seems to be why a songwriter called Joe Lubin is also credited for the song on Boone's version. Getting a third of a song like "Tutti Frutti" for that little work sounds like a pretty good deal, at least for Lubin, if not for Richard.

Another way in which Richard got less than he deserved was that the publishing was owned by a company owned by Art Rupe. That company licensed the song to Specialty Records for half the normal mechanical licensing rate – normally a publishing company would charge two cents per record pressed for their songs, but instead Specialty only had to pay one cent. This sort of cross-collateralisation was common with independent labels at the time, but it still rankled to Richard when he figured it out.

Not that he was thinking about contracts at all at this point. He was becoming a huge star, and that meant he had to *break* a lot of contracts. He'd got concert bookings for several months ahead, but those bookings were in second-rate clubs, and he had to be in Hollywood to promote his new record and build a new career. But he also didn't want to get a reputation for missing gigs. There was only one thing to do – hire an impostor to be Little Richard at these low-class gigs.

So while Richard went off to promote his record, another young singer from Georgia with a pompadour and a gospel feel was being introduced with the phrase "Ladies and gentlemen—the hardest-working man in showbusiness today—Little Richard!"

When James Brown went back to performing under his own name, he kept that introduction...

Meanwhile, Richard was working on his second hit record. He and Blackwell decided that this record should be louder, faster, and more raucous than "Tutti Frutti" had been. If Pat Boone wanted to cover this one, he'd have to work a lot harder than he had previously.

The basis for "Long Tall Sally" came from a scrap of lyric written by a teenage girl. Enotris Johnson had written a single verse of lyric on a scrap of paper, and had walked many miles to New Orleans to show the lyric to a DJ named Honey Chile. (Bumps Blackwell describes her as having walked from Opelousas, Mississippi, but there's no such place – Johnson appears to have lived in Bogalusa, Louisiana). Johnson wanted to make enough money to pay for hospital for her sick aunt – the "Aunt Mary" in the song, and thought that Little Richard might sing the song and get her the money.

What she had was only a few lines, but Honey Chile had taken Johnson on as a charity project, and Blackwell didn't want to disappoint such an influential figure, so he and Richard hammered something together, which became "Long Tall Sally".

The song, about a "John" who "jumps back in the alley" when he sees his wife coming while he's engaged in activities of an unspecified nature with Sally, who is long, tall, and bald, once again stays just on the broadcastable side of the line, while implying sex of a non-heteronormative variety, possibly with a sex worker. Despite this, and despite the attempts to make the song uncoverably raucous, Pat Boone still sold a million copies with his cover version.

So Little Richard had managed to get that good clean-cut whole-some Christian white boy Pat Boone singing songs which gave him a lot more to worry about than whether he was singing "Ain't" rather than "Isn't". But Richard was also becoming a big star himself – and he was getting an ego to go along with it. And he was starting to worry whether he should be making this devil music at all. When we next look at Little Richard, we'll see just how the combination of self-doubt and ego led to his greatest successes and to the collapse of his career.

"Why Do Fools Fall In Love?"

The story of Frankie Lymon and the Teenagers is a story of heartbreak and early death, a story of young people of colour having their work become massively successful and making no money off it because of wealthy businessmen stealing their work. But it's also a story of what happens when you get involved with the Mafia before you hit puberty, and your career peaks at thirteen.

The Teenagers started when two black teenagers from New York, Jimmy Merchant and Sherman Garnes, left the vocal group they'd formed, which was named "The Earth Angels" after the Penguins song, and hooked up with two Latino neighbours, Joe Negroni and Herman Santiago. They named themselves the Ermines. Soon after, they were the support act for local vocal group the Cadillacs, who had had a minor hit with "Speedoo".

They were impressed enough by the Cadillacs that in honour of them they changed their name, becoming the Coup de Villes, and after that the Premiers.

They used to practice in the hallway of the apartment block where Sherman Garnes lived, and eventually one of the neighbours got sick of hearing them sing the same songs over and over. The neighbour decided to bring out some love letters his girlfriend had written, some of which were in the form of poems, and say to the kids "Why don't you turn some of these into songs?"

And so they did just that – they took one of the letters, containing the phrase "why do birds sing so gay?" and Santiago and Merchant worked out a ballad for Santiago to sing containing that phrase.

Soon after this, the Premiers met up with a very young kid, Frankie Lymon, who sang and played percussion in a mambo group.

I suppose I should pause here to talk briefly about the mambo craze. Rock and roll wasn't the only musical style that was making inroads in the pop markets in the fifties – and an impartial observer, looking in 1953 or 1954, might easily have expected that the big musical trend that would shape the next few decades would be calypso music, which had become huge in the US for a brief period. But that wasn't the only music that was challenging rock and roll. There were a whole host of other musics, usually those from Pacific, Latin-American and/or Caribbean cultures, which tend to get lumped together as "exotica" now, and mambo was one of those.

This was a craze named after a song by the Cuban bandleader Perez Prado, "Mambo Jambo". That song was popular enough that soon everyone was jumping on the bandwagon, and so for example, Bill Haley and the Comets recorded "Mambo Rock".

Lymon was easily persuaded instead to join the Premiers. He was the young kid who hung around with them when they practiced, not the leader, and not even a major part of the group. Not yet, anyway.

Everything changed for the group when Richie Barrett heard them singing on a street corner near him.

These days, Barrett is best-known for his 1962 single "Some Other Guy", which was later covered by the Beatles, among others, but at the time he was the lead singer of a group called the Valentines.

He was also working for George Goldner at Rama Records as a talent scout and producer, doing the same kind of things that Ike Turner had been doing for Chess and Modern, or that Jesse Stone did for Atlantic – finding the acts, doing the arrangements, doing all the work involved in turning some teenage kid into someone who could become a star.

Goldner was someone for whom most people in the music industry seemed to have a certain amount of contempt – he was, by most accounts, a fairly weak-willed figure who got himself into great amounts of debt with dodgy people. But one thing they're all agreed on is that he had a great ear for a hit, because as Jerry Leiber put it he had the taste of a fourteen-year-old girl.

George Goldner had actually got into R&B through the mambo craze. When Goldner had started in the music industry, it had been as the owner of a chain of nightclubs which featured Latin music. The clubs became popular enough that he also started Tico Records, a label that put out Latin records, most notably early recordings by Tito Puente.

When the mambo boom hit, a lot of black teenagers started attending Goldner's clubs, and he became interested in the other music they were listening to. He started first Rama Records, as a label for R&B singles, and then Gee Records, named after the most successful record that had been put out on Rama, "Gee", by the Crows.

Goldner had a business partner, Morris Levy, and Levy was not someone you wanted involved in your business in any way.

In this series we're going to talk about a lot of horrible people – and in fact we've already covered more than a few of them – yet Morris Levy was one of the worst people we're going to look at. While most of the people we've discussed are either terrible people in their personal life (if they were a musician) or a minor con artist who ripped off musicians and kept the money for themselves, Morris Levy was a terrible human being *and* a con artist, someone who used his Mafia connections to ensure that the artists he ripped off would never even think of suing him, because they valued their lives too much.

Levy had been the founder of Birdland, the world-famous jazz club, in the 1940s, but when ASCAP came to him asking for the money they were meant to get for their songwriters from live performances, Levy had immediately seen the possibilities in music publishing.

Levy then formed a publishing company, Patricia Music, and a record label, Roulette, and started into the business of properly exploiting young black people, not just having them work in his clubs for a night, but having them create intellectual property he could continue exploiting for the rest of his life.

Indeed, Levy was so keen to make money off dubious intellectual property that he actually formed a company with his friend Alan Freed which attempted to trademark the phrase "rock and roll", on the basis that this way any records that came out labelled as such would have to pay them for the privilege. Thankfully, the term caught on so rapidly that there was no way for them to enforce the trademark, and it became genericised.

But this is who Levy was, and how he made his money – at least his more legitimate money. Where he got the rest from is a matter for true crime books.

There are several people who report death threats, or having to give up their careers, or suddenly move thousands of miles away from home, to avoid Levy's revenge on artists who didn't do exactly what he said. So when we're looking at a group of literal teenage kids – and black teenagers at that, with the smallest amount of institutional privilege possible – you can be sure that he was not going to treat them with the respect that they were due.

But at the start of their career, the group didn't yet have to worry about Levy. That would come later. For now, they were dealing with George Goldner, and Goldner was someone who was actually concerned with the music, and who had been producing hits consistently for the last few years.

When Richie Barrett brought the Premiers to Goldner, he was intrigued because two of the members were Latino, and he was such a lover of Latin music. But he quickly latched on to the potential of Frankie Lymon as a star. Lymon was a captivating performer, and when you watch video footage of him now you can't help but think of Michael Jackson, who followed almost exactly the same early career trajectory a decade later.

While the other band members were the normal kind of teenage kids who joined doo wop groups, and were clearly a little reserved, Lymon just went for it, working the crowd like a young James Brown with absolutely no self-consciousness at all.

He also had a gorgeous falsetto voice, and knew how to use it. As we've seen, many of the doo wop groups of the fifties weren't particularly proficient singers, but Lymon did have a real vocal talent. He was clearly a potential star.

Frankie Lymon wasn't even originally meant to be the lead singer on "Why Do Fools Fall in Love?" – that distinctive falsetto that makes the record so memorable was a late addition. The song was originally meant to be sung by Herman Santiago, and it was only in the studio that the song was rearranged to instead focus on the band's youngest – and youngest-sounding – member.

When the record came out, it wasn't credited to the Premiers, but to "The Teenagers, featuring Frankie Lymon". Goldner hadn't liked the group's name, and decided to focus on their big selling point – their youth, and in particular the youth of their new lead singer.

Much of the work to make the record a hit was done not by the Teenagers or by Goldner, but by the session saxophone player Jimmy Wright, who ended up doing the arrangements on all of the Teenagers' records, and whose idea it was to start them with Sherman Garnes' bass intros.

As with so many of these records, there was a white cover version that came out almost immediately – this time by the Diamonds, a group of Canadians who copied the formula of their fellow countrymen the Crew Cuts and more or less cornered the market in white remakes of doo wop hits.

But in a sign of how the times were changing, the Diamonds' version of the song only went to number twelve, while the Teenagers' version went to number six, helped by a massive push from Morris Levy's good friend Alan Freed.

Partly this may have been down to the fact that all the Diamonds were adults, and they simply couldn't compete with the novelty sound of a boy who sounded prepubescent, singing in falsetto.

Falsetto had, of course, always been a part of the doo wop vocal blend, but it had been a minor part up to this point. Lead vocals would generally be sung in a smooth high tenor, but would very rarely reach to the truly high notes. Lymon, by virtue of his voice not yet having broken, introduced a new timbre into rock and roll lead vocals, and he influenced almost every vocal group that followed. There might have been a Four Seasons or a Jan and Dean or a Beach Boys without Lymon, but I doubt it.

There was also a British cover version, by Alma Cogan, a middle-of-the-road singer known as "the girl with the giggle in her voice". This sort of thing was common in Britain well into the sixties, as most US labels didn't have distribution in the UK, and so if British people wanted to hear American rock and roll songs, they would often get them in native cover versions. Cogan was a particular source of these, often recording songs that had been R&B hits.

The Teenagers followed the success of "Why Do Fools Fall in Love?" with "I Want You to Be My Girl", which did almost as well, reaching a peak of number thirteen in the pop charts. But the singles after that did less well, although "I'm Not a Juvenile Delinquent" became a big hit in the UK.

The record label soon decided that Lymon needed to become a solo star, rather than being just the lead singer of the Teenagers. Quite why they made this decision was difficult to say, as one would not normally deliberately break up a hit act. But presumably the calculation was that they would then have two hit acts – solo Frankie Lymon, and the Teenagers still recording together. It didn't work out like that.

Lymon inadvertently caused another crisis in the ongoing battle of rock and roll versus racism. Alan Freed had a new TV series, *The Big Beat*, which was a toned-down version of Freed's radio show. By this point, real rock and roll was already in a temporary decline as the major labels fought back, and so Freed's show was generally filled with the kind of pre-packaged major label act, usually named Bobby, that we'll be talking about when we get to the later fifties. For all that Freed had a reputation as a supporter of black music, what he really was was someone with the skill to see a bandwagon and jump on it.

But still, some of the black performers were still popular, and so Freed had Lymon on his show. But his show was aimed at a white audience, and so the studio audience was white, and dancing. And Frankie Lymon started to dance as well. A black boy, dancing with a white girl.

This did not go down well at all with the Southern network affiliates, and within a couple of weeks Freed's show had been taken off the TV.

And that appearance, the one that destroyed Freed's show, was almost certainly Lymon's very first ever solo performance. One might think that this did not augur well for his future career, and that assessment would be largely correct.

Neither Lymon nor the Teenagers would ever have another hit after they split. The last few records credited to Frankie Lymon and the Teenagers were in fact Lymon solo recordings, performed with other backing singers. "Goody Goody" did manage to reach number twenty on the pop charts, but everything after that did worse.

Lymon's first credited solo single, "My Girl", failed to chart. He continued making records for another couple of years, but nothing came of any of them, and when his voice broke he stopped sounding much like himself. The last recording he made that came even close to being a hit was a remake of Bobby Day's "Little Bitty Pretty One" from 1960.

And the Teenagers didn't fare much better. They went through several new lead singers – there was Billy Lobrano, a white kid who according to Jimmy Merchant sounded more like Eddie Fisher than like Lymon, and there was Freddie Houston, who would go on to be the lead singer in one of the many Ink Spots lineups touring in the sixties.

After these false starts, the Teenagers started trying to focus on the other original group members, for example calling themselves "Sherman and the Teenagers" when performing the Leiber and Stoller song "The Draw". But nothing they tried had the same sound as they'd had with Lymon, and they eventually hit on the idea of getting a woman into the group instead. They got in Sandra Doyle, who would later be Zola Taylor's replacement in the Platters, and struggled on until 1961, when they finally split up.

Lymon's life after leaving the Teenagers was one of nothing but tragedy. He married three times, the last two bigamously, and his only child died two days after the birth. Lymon would apparently regularly steal from Zola Taylor, who became his second wife, to feed his heroin addiction.

He briefly reunited with the Teenagers in 1965, but they had little success. He spent a couple of years in the army, and appeared to have got himself clean, and even got a new record deal. But the night before he was meant to go back into the studio, he fell off the wagon, for what would be the last time.

Frankie Lymon died, aged just twenty-five, and a has-been for almost half of his life, of a heroin overdose, in 1968.

The other Teenagers would reunite, with Lymon's brother joining them briefly, in the 70s. Sherman Garnes died in 1977, and Joe Negroni in 1978, but Santiago and Merchant continued, off and on, with a lineup of the Teenagers – a version of the band continues to this day, still featuring Herman Santiago, and Merchant remained with the band until his retirement a few years ago.

But their first hit caused legal problems.

"Why Do Fools Fall In Love?" was written by Herman Santiago, with the help of Jimmy Merchant. But neither Santiago or Merchant were credited on the song when it came out. The credited songwriters for the song are Frankie Lymon – who did have some input into rewriting it in the studio – and Morris Levy, who had never even heard the song until after it was a massive hit.

George Goldner was originally credited as Lymon's co-writer, and of course Goldner never wrote it either, but at least he was in the studio when it was recorded. But when Levy bought out Goldner's holdings in his companies, he also bought out his rights to songs he was credited for, so Levy became the legal co-writer of "Why Do Fools Fall in Love?"

In 1992 Santiago and Merchant finally won the credit for having written "Why Do Fools Fall in Love?", but in 1996 the ruling was over-turned. They'd apparently waited too long to take legal action over having their song stolen, and so the rights reverted to Lymon and Morris Levy – who had never even met the band when they wrote the song.

But, of course, Lymon wasn't alive to get the money. But his widow was. Or rather, his widows, plural, were. In the 1980s, three separate women claimed to be Lymon's widow and thus his legitimate heir. One was his first wife, who he had married in 1964 while she was still married to her first husband. One was Zola Taylor, who Lymon supposedly married bigamously a year after his first marriage, but who couldn't produce any evidence of this, and the third was either his second or third wife, who he married bigamously in 1967 while still married to his first, and possibly his second, wife. That third wife eventually won the various legal battles and is now in charge of the Frankie Lymon legacy.

"Why Do Fools Fall in Love?" has gone on to be a standard, recorded by everyone from Joni Mitchell to the Beach Boys to Diana Ross. But Frankie Lymon and the Teenagers stand as a cautionary tale, an example that all too many people were still all too eager to follow.

"Blue Suede Shoes"

While Elvis Presley had moved from Sun to RCA, that didn't mean that Sam Phillips had given up on recording rock and roll music. Far from it. With the amount of money that RCA had paid for Elvis' contract, Sun Records was for the first time on a completely secure footing, and now Phillips could really begin work on making the music that would come to define his legacy.

Because now, Sun Records shifted almost entirely from being a blues label to being a rockabilly label. We've not talked much about rockabilly as a genre, and that's because until now we've only heard one person performing it. But while Elvis was arguably the first rockabilly artist, it wasn't until Elvis had left Sun that the floodgates opened, and Sam Phillips started producing the records that defined the genre as a genre, rather than as the work of a single individual.

The rockabilly sound was, in essence, created in Sun studios. And rockabilly is one of those sounds that purists, at least, insist had a very, very specific meaning. It had to have slapback echo on the vocals, it had to have an electric lead guitar and slapback bass. It basically had to have all the elements of Elvis' very earliest records. You could add a few other elements, like piano or drums – mostly because anything else would exclude Jerry Lee Lewis – but no horns or strings, no backing vocals, nothing that would take away from the very primitive sound. And no steel guitar or fiddle, either – that would tip it over into country.

There were, of course, other people who produced rockabilly records, and we'll look at some of them in this volume and the next. But when they did, they were all copying the sound that Sam Phillips created.

Because after Elvis stopped recording for Sun, Sam Phillips and his small staff discovered enough young, exciting, musicians that Sun

Records was assured a place in music history, even though its biggest artist was gone.

The first of the new artists Phillips discovered was someone who came to Sun when Elvis was still on the label – a young man named Carl Perkins.

Perkins, like many of the pioneers of rock and roll music, had grown up dirt-poor. His parents were sharecroppers, who were illiterate enough that they misspelled their own surname on his birth certificate – they spelled it Perkings, though he always used Perkins in later life. His family had been so poor that when young Carl, inspired by listening to the Grand Ole Opry on the radio, asked if he could have a guitar, his parents couldn't afford one, and so his father made him one from a cigar box and a broom handle. However, young Carl got good enough that soon his dad bought him a real guitar. He was so poor that when he broke strings, he had to tie them together because he couldn't afford new ones, and he ended up developing a unique guitar style – bending strings to get different notes rather than fretting them normally – to avoid the knots in the strings, which hurt his fingers.

When he was fourteen, Perkins wrote his first song, and it again shows just how poor he was. That first song, "Movie Magg" invites the song's subject to go to the cinema with him – and to ride on a mule to get there. Because in the time and place where Perkins grew up, it was actually considered slightly classier to ride a mule to the cinema than to take a car, because if anyone did have a car, it was one that was so broken down and rusted that it was actually less impressive than a mule.

All of Perkins' early work is like that, rooted in a poverty far deeper than almost anyone reading this will be able to understand. It's music based in the country music he heard growing up, and it's music that could only be made by someone who spent his childhood picking cotton for pennies an hour in order to help his family survive.

When Perkins had learned to play the guitar well enough to play lead, he taught his brother Jay to play rudimentary rhythm parts. Jay loved music as much as Carl did, but the two brothers had slightly different tastes in country music. Carl was a massive fan of the inventor of bluegrass, Bill Monroe, who sang high, driving, harmony-filled songs of longing. Jay, on the other hand, preferred Ernest Tubb's low, honky tonk, music.

They taught their younger brother Clayton to play a little bass, even though he wasn't a music lover especially – Clayton loved drinking and fighting and not much else. But he had a reasonable sense of rhythm, so they could teach him the three places to put his fingers on most country songs, and let him figure out the rest with practice. Their friend Fluke Holland joined on drums, and the Perkins Brothers Band was born.

The Perkins brothers spent the next several years honing their craft playing some of the roughest bars in Tennessee. They had to develop an ability to play dance music for venues where it was customary to buy two bottles of beer at a time, one to drink, and one to smash over someone else's head. You didn't want to use an empty bottle for your smashing, as there was no weight to them, but a full bottle of beer would put someone out of commission very quickly.

So they very quickly developed a style that was rooted in honky-tonk music, but which was totally oriented around getting people dancing. It had elements of bluegrass, Western Swing, the blues, and anything else that could possibly be used to get a crowd of drunks dancing, if you only had two guitars, a double bass, and a drum kit. Both Carl and Jay would take turns singing lead, and when they ran out of songs to perform, Carl would improvise new ones around standard chord changes. He had the ability to improvise words and music off the top of his head – and he'd remember a good chorus or a good line and reuse it, so these improvised songs slowly became standard, structured, parts of their set.

They were soon able to make a full-time living playing music for bars full of angry drunk men, and for several years they did just that, starting from before it was even legal for them to enter the bars they were playing. They had no ambition to do anything else – they were just glad to be earning a living doing something that was fun.

Slowly but surely, Carl Perkins started to carve out a unique sound for the band, at least on the songs that he wrote and sang. He didn't know what it was that he was doing, but he knew it was different, and that no-one else was doing anything like it. Until one day he heard someone who was.

When Carl Perkins heard Elvis singing "Blue Moon of Kentucky" on the radio, he knew that there was someone else who was out there doing the same kind of thing as him. He was even singing a song by Carl's favourite, Bill Monroe.

If this Elvis Presley kid could become a star making that kind of music, maybe so could Carl himself. He and his brothers went to see Elvis live, and while Jay and Clayton took a dislike to Elvis – deciding that because he paid any attention to his appearance he must be gay, and therefore in their opinion worthy of nothing but contempt – Carl saw something else.

He determined right then that he was going to go to Sun Records and demand an audition. If they would put that Elvis boy's records out, then surely they would put his out too?

The Perkins Brothers Band all piled into a single car, and drove down to Memphis, to 706 Union Ave. They went in to see the people at Sun Records – and were turned away. Marion Keisker told them that they weren't auditioning right then, and that they didn't need any new singers. When Carl Perkins told her that they sounded a bit like Elvis, she was even more dismissive – they didn't need another Elvis. They'd already got one.

They trudged back despondently to the car, deciding that their dream of stardom was at an end. But as they were doing so, a Cadillac pulled up and a man got out of it. They decided that the only person who would be driving a Cadillac to that studio must be the owner of the record label, so they went over to him and told him what had happened.

And Sam Phillips agreed with Keisker. He wasn't after anyone else right now. He had enough acts. And Carl was devastated. According to Perkins, Phillips later told him "I couldn't say no. Never have I [seen] a pitifuller-looking fellow as you looked when I said, 'I'm too busy to listen to you.' You overpowered me." He relented, and told them that he'd give them a quick listen, but it had to be quick as he was busy that day.

They went into the studio and started running through their set. They got through a verse of the first song, and Phillips stopped them.

He wasn't interested in anything like that. They started another song. Again, Phillips stopped them and said he wasn't interested. They were about to go home, but then Carl asked if he could try just one more song. He started up that song he had written when he was fourteen, "Movie Magg".

The band joined in, and as they played through the song, Carl noticed something. Sam Phillips hadn't stopped them from playing. He sat through the whole thing, listening intently.

When they got to the end, he said that if they came back with a few more songs that sounded like that, they might just be worth recording. The band were pleased, but Phillips also said something else, to Carl alone, that was more worrying. He told Carl that there was no place for any lead vocals by his brother Jay. "There's already one Ernest Tubb in the world. No-one needs another one."

Without them having fully realised it at the time, the Perkins Brothers Band had now become Carl Perkins and his band.

When they came back a few weeks later, they had worked out a few more songs. Phillips put out "Movie Magg", backed with a ballad Carl had written, "Turn Around", but he didn't put these out on Sun. Rather, he put them out on a new label, Flip, that didn't pay union scale. Flip only put out records around Tennessee, and the idea was that these would be audition records – Phillips would see how the records would do locally, without paying full royalties and without paying expensive shipping costs or for a large print run. Phillips was in financial trouble at the time, and he was trying to find ways to cut costs.

"Movie Magg" did well enough on Flip that for the next Carl Perkins single, Phillips moved him on to Sun Records proper. This followed the same formula as the first single, pairing an uptempo A-side with a B-side ballad in the Hank Williams vein. The A-side, "Gone Gone Gone", was one of Carl's improvised songs – every take of it was different, although they were all based around the same basic idea, which was riffing on the old phrase, "It must be jelly, 'cause jam don't shake like that".

"Gone Gone Gone" wasn't a hit, but it sold well enough, and Phillips arranged for Perkins to go out on tour, on a bill with Elvis and another new Sun signing, Johnny Cash. It was on this tour that Cash made a suggestion to Perkins that would change Perkins' life.

Cash remembered a fellow serviceman, a black man named C.V. Wright, had referred to his service issue shoes as "blue suede shoes", and he told Perkins that he should write a song about that. Perkins dismissed the idea. What the hell did he know about shoes, anyway? And what kind of song could you write about them? The idea was ridiculous.

The tour went well, apart from one incident – Perkins and Presley had been talking about their mutual love for the song "Only You", and that inspired Perkins to add the song to his own setlist. That irritated Presley, who had been planning to perform the song himself the same night, and Presley felt that Perkins' performance had upstaged him. The two remained friends, but would never perform on the same bill again. Elvis did, however, take Carl out clothes shopping, and show him how to dress in a more sophisticated manner on stage.

Shortly after that tour, Perkins was performing another show, when he noticed someone in the audience berating his date, "Don't step on my suedes!" He started thinking about what kind of person would find his shoes so important, and started thinking about pride, and about people who don't have anything. The idea merged with Cash's mention of blue suede shoes, and Perkins found himself one night getting out of bed, playing his electric guitar unplugged, so as not to disturb his wife, and writing a song he called "Blue Swade Shoes" – he didn't know how "suede" was spelled. Two days later, on December 19, 1955, he was in the studio recording it.

Perkins was certain that this was going to be it. This was his breakthrough record. But at the same time he was getting depressed about his prospects. He had a wife and kids to support, and he was earning so little money from his music that he was having to do farm work as a side job in order to make enough money to buy his kids Christmas presents. The people at this side job were often astonished that "that singer fella" was there. Everyone around knew him from his stage shows, and they all knew he'd put out records. Surely he was rich now, and didn't need to be doing such menial work?

He was at a low, and that didn't get better when he finally got his complimentary copies of his new single. They arrived through the post and, as often happened with records at that time, they'd got smashed into bits. He wanted to have his own copies of the record, of course, so he went into town to the shop that sold records, and asked for a copy. He was horrified at what he saw. Instead of a proper record – a big ten inch thing with a tiny little hole in the middle, made out of shellac – he was confronted with something only seven inches across, made of some kind of plastic, and with a big hole in the middle.

He explained that no, he wanted his record, and the store owner replied that this was his record. He came home with this little floppy thing and cried, explaining to his wife that they'd messed up his record in some way, and that he was ruined. Eventually they figured out that this was OK, and that what the store owner had told Carl had been correct – these new vinyl records were apparently what all the kids wanted instead of what Carl thought of as real records.

"Blue Suede Shoes" was an obvious hit, but the B-side, "Honey Don't", got more than a little airplay as well. "Blue Suede Shoes" was such a smash hit that Steve Sholes of RCA called Sam Phillips, worried. When he'd signed Elvis, had he backed the wrong horse? Phillips assured Sholes that he hadn't.

As it turned out, "Blue Suede Shoes" and Elvis' first single for RCA, "Heartbreak Hotel", were racing up the charts at the same time as each other. "Heartbreak Hotel" ended up at number one, and "Blue Suede Shoes" at number two, and both were crossover hits, making the top two in both pop and country and the top five in R&B.

"Blue Suede Shoes" was so popular, in fact, that at one point it was being performed simultaneously on two different TV shows – at the same time as Carl Perkins was appearing on *The Ozark Jubilee*, his very first TV appearance, Presley was on *Stage Show* on another network, performing his cover version of it.

Presley's version wasn't released as a single until a few months later – they'd come to a gentleman's agreement that he wouldn't affect Perkins' sales – but it was put out as the opening track on Presley's first album, and as a track on an EP. When Presley's version finally came out as a single, towards the end of the year, it made the top twenty and brought in further royalties for Perkins.

Perkins' version of "Blue Suede Shoes" and Elvis' had a few crucial differences other than just their performer. Perkins' version is more interesting rhythmically at the start – it has a stop-time introduction which essentially puts it into $\frac{6}{4}$ time before settling into $\frac{4}{4}$. Elvis, on the other hand, stayed with a $\frac{4}{4}$ beat all the way through. Elvis' performance is all about keeping up a sense of urgency, while Perkins is about building up tension and release.

Elvis' introduction is "Well, it's one for the money," BAM, "two for the show", BAM... it's a record that's all about that initial urgency. By contrast Perkins' seems to stall after every line, as if it's hesitant, as if he doesn't really want to get started. But at the same time that gives it a rhythmic interest that isn't there in Presley's version. Perkins' original is the more sophisticated, musicianly, record. Most cover versions since have followed Presley's version, with the notable exception of John Lennon's live cover version from 1969, which follows the pattern of Perkins'.

Unfortunately, Perkins' career was then derailed in a tragic accident. On his way to perform on *The Perry Como Show* on TV, Perkins' car hit a truck. The truck driver was killed, and Perkins and his brother Jay were both hospitalised. They got better, but their career had lost momentum – and by the time they were completely well, Sam Phillips was rather more interested in his next big thing.

Phillips did, however, get Perkins a Cadillac of his own, like the one Perkins had been impressed by when he first met Phillips. He told Perkins that he'd planned to do this for the first Sun Records artist to have a million-seller, which "Blue Suede Shoes" was. Perkins was less impressed when he found out that the Cadillac wasn't a gift, but had been paid for out of Perkins' royalties, and that eventually started a lifelong series of royalty disputes between the two men, with Perkins never believing he had received all the money that was rightfully his.

Perkins would never have another hit as a performer, and his career would be defined by that one song, but he continued making great records, including some that would inspire some of the most important musicians in the world, and would rightfully become classics.

But it's "Blue Suede Shoes" which ensured his place in music history, and which sixty-three years later, more than any other record, sums up that point in 1956 when two country boys from Tennessee were chasing each other up the charts and defining the future of rock and roll.

"I Walk the Line"

This series is about the history of rock music, but one of the things we're going to learn as the story goes on is that the history of any genre in popular music eventually encompasses them all. And at the end of 1955, in particular, there was no hard and fast distinction between the genres of rock and roll, rhythm and blues, and country music.

So in this chapter we're going to talk about someone who, to many, epitomises country music more than any other artist, but who started out recording for Sam Phillips at Sun, making music that was stylistically indistinguishable from any of the other rockabilly artists there, and whose career would intertwine with all of them for decades to come.

Johnny Cash's birth name was actually J.R. Cash – initials rather than a full name – and that was how he was known until he joined the Air Force. His parents apparently had a disagreement over what their son's name should be, and so rather than give him full names, they just gave him initials.

The Air Force wouldn't allow him to just use initials as his name, so he changed his name to John R. Cash. It was only once he became a professional musician that he took on the name Johnny Cash. He still never had a middle name, just a middle initial.

While he was in the military, he'd been the very first American to learn that Stalin had died, as he'd been the radio operator who'd intercepted and decoded the Russian transmissions about it. But the military had never been the career he wanted. He wanted to be a singer. He just didn't know how.

After returning to the US from his stint in the Air Force in Germany, aged twenty-two, Cash got married and moved to Memphis, to be near his brother. Cash's brother introduced him to two of his colleagues,

Luther Perkins and Marshall Grant. Both Perkins and Grant could play
a little guitar, and they started getting together to play a little music,
sometimes with a steel player called Red Kernodle.

They were very, very, unskilled musicians, but that didn't matter.
They had a couple of things that mattered far more than skill. They
had a willingness to try anything if it might sound good, and they had
Cash's voice, which even as a callow young man sounded like he had
been carved out of rock and imbued with the spirit of an Old Testament
prophet. Cash never had a huge range, but his voice had a sonority to
it that was quite astonishing, a resonant bass-baritone that demanded
you pay attention to what it had to say.

And Cash had a determination that he was going to become a
famous singer. He had no idea how one was to go about this, but he
knew it was what he wanted to do.

To start with, they mostly performed the gospel songs that Cash
loved. This was the music that is euphemistically called Southern
Gospel, but which is really white gospel. Cash had had a religious
experience as a kid, when his elder brother, who had wanted to become a priest, had died and had had a deathbed vision of heaven and
hell, and Cash wanted to become a gospel singer to pay tribute to his
brother while also indulging his own love of music.

But then at one of their jam sessions, Cash brought in a song he
had written himself, called "Belshazzar", based on a story from the
Bible. The other two were amazed. Not so much by the song itself,
but by the fact that you could write a song at all. The idea that songs
were something you write was not something that had really occurred
to them.

Cash, Perkins, and Grant all played acoustic guitar at first, and
none of them were particularly good. They were mostly just hanging
out together, having fun. They were just singing stuff they'd heard
on the radio, and they particularly wanted to sound like the Louvin
Brothers.

They were having fun together, but that was all. But Cash was
ambitious to do something more. And that "something more" took
shape when he heard a record, one that was recorded the day after the

plane that took Cash back into the US touched down – Elvis Presley singing "That's All Right, Mama".

He liked the sound of that record a lot. And what he liked even more was hearing the DJ, after the song was played, say that the record was out on Sun Records, a label based in Memphis itself.

Johnny, Luther, and Marshall went to see Elvis, Scotty, and Bill perform, playing on the back of a flatbed truck and just playing the two songs on their single. Cash was immediately worried – Elvis was clearly a teenager, and Cash himself was a grown man of twenty-two. Had he missed his chance at stardom? Was he too old?

Cash had a chat with Elvis, and went along again the next night to see the trio performing a proper set at a nightclub, and this time he talked with Scotty Moore and asked him how to get signed to Sun.

Moore told him to speak to Sam Phillips, and so Cash got hold of Sun's phone number and started calling, asking to speak to Phillips, who was never in – he was out on the road a lot of the time, pushing the label's records to distributors and radio stations.

But Cash also knew that he was going to have to do something more to get recorded. He was going to have to turn his little guitar jam sessions into a proper group like Elvis, Scotty, and Bill, not just three people bashing away together at acoustic guitars. They sometimes had Red on steel guitar, but they still needed some variety. Cash was obviously going to be the lead singer, so it made sense for him to stick with the acoustic rhythm guitar. Luther Perkins got himself an electric guitar and started playing lead lines which amounted to little more than boogie-woogie basslines transposed up an octave.

Marshall Grant, meanwhile, got himself a double bass, and taped markers on it to show him where the notes were. He'd never played one before, so all he could do was play single notes every other beat, with big gaps between the notes – he couldn't get his fingers between the notes any faster.

This group was clearly not anything like as professional as Presley and his group, but they had something. Their limitations as musicians meant that they had to find ways to make the songs work without relying on complicated parts or virtuoso playing. As Luther Perkins would later put it, "You know how all those hot-shot guitarists race their fingers all over the strings? Well, they're looking for the right sound. I found it."

But Cash was still, frankly, a little worried that his group weren't all that great, and when he finally went to see Sam Phillips in person, having failed to get hold of him on the phone, he went alone.

Phillips was immediately impressed by Cash's bearing and presence. He was taller, and more dignified, than most of the people who came in to audition for Phillips. He was someone with presence, and gravitas, and Phillips thought he had the makings of a star.

The day after meeting Phillips for the first time, Cash brought his musician friends around as well, and Johnny, Luther, Marshall, and Red all had a chat with Phillips. Phillips explained to them that they didn't need to be technically great musicians, just have the right kind of sound.

The four of them rehearsed, and then came back to Phillips with some of the material they'd been practising. But when it came time to audition, their steel player got so scared that he couldn't tune his guitar, his hands were shaking so much. Eventually he decided that he was holding the other three back, and left the studio, and the audition continued with just the group who had now become the Tennessee Three – a name they chose because while they all now lived in Tennessee, none of them had originally come from there.

Phillips liked their sound, but explained that he wasn't particularly interested in putting out gospel music. There's an urban legend that Phillips said "go home and sin, then come back with a song I can sell", though this was denied by Cash. But it is true that he'd had no sales success with gospel music, and that he wanted something more commercial.

Whatever Phillips said, though, Cash took the hint, and went home and started writing secular songs. The one he came back to Phillips with, "Hey Porter", was inspired by the sound of the railway, and had a boom-chick-a-boom rhythm that would soon become Cash's trademark. Phillips liked it, and the Tennessee Three set to recording it.

Or at least that was what they were called when they recorded it, but by the time it was released Sam Phillips had suggested a slight name change, and the single came out under the name Johnny Cash and the Tennessee Two.

As the Tennessee Two didn't have a drummer, Cash put paper between the strings and the fretboard of his acoustic guitar to deaden the sound and turn it into something that approximated the sound of a snare drum. The resulting boom-chick sound was one that would become a signature of Cash's recordings for the next few decades, a uniquely country music take on the two-beat rhythm. That sound was almost entirely forced on the group by their instrumental limitations, but it was a sound that worked.

The song Cash brought in to Phillips as a possible B-side was called "Folsom Prison Blues", and it was only an original in the loosest possible sense. Before going off to Germany with the air force, Cash had seen a film called *Inside the Walls of Folsom Prison*, and it had given Cash the idea that someone should write a song about that. But he'd put the idea to the back of his mind until two other inspirations arrived.

The first was a song called "Crescent City Blues", which he heard on a Gordon Jenkins album that a fellow airman in Germany owned. Jenkins' song in turn is also strongly inspired by another song, also titled "Crescent City Blues", by the boogie-woogie pianist Little Brother Montgomery. But Jenkins' song provided more than a close model for Cash's song.

The first two verses for Jenkins' song go:

> I hear the train a-comin, it's rolling 'round the bend
>
> And I ain't been kissed lord since I don't know when
>
> The boys in Crescent City don't seem to know I'm here
>
> That lonesome whistle seems to tell me, Sue, disappear
>
> When I was just a baby my mama told me, Sue
>
> When you're grown up I want that you should go and see and do
>
> But I'm stuck in Crescent City just watching life mosey by
>
> When I hear that whistle blowin', I hang my head and cry

The second musical inspiration for Cash's prison song was a song by Cash's idol, Jimmie Rodgers, "Blue Yodel #1", also known as "T For Texas". Rodgers' line "I'm gonna shoot poor Thelma, just to see her jump and fall" hit Cash hard, and he realised that the most morally bankrupt person he could imagine was someone who would kill someone else just to watch them die.

He put this bleak amorality together with the idea of a song about Folsom, and changed just enough of the words to "Crescent City Blues" that it worked with this new concept of the character, and he titled the result "Folsom Prison Blues".

Cash's new song started:

> I hear the train a-comin, it's rolling 'round the bend
>
> And I ain't seen the sunshine since I don't know when
>
> I'm stuck in Folsom Prison and time keeps dragging on
>
> But that train keeps a-rollin' on down to San Antone
>
> When I was just a baby my mama told me, Son
>
> Always be a good boy, don't ever play with guns
>
> But I shot a man in Reno, just to watch him die
>
> When I hear that whistle blowin', I hang my head and cry

And it followed the pattern of Jenkins' original all the way through, keeping Jenkins' melody and the majority of his lyrics.

Sam Phillips didn't think that was suitable as the B-side to "Hey Porter", and they eventually went for a sad song that Cash had written titled "Cry Cry Cry", but "Folsom Prison Blues" was put aside as a future possibility.

When the contract was drawn up, the only person who was actually signed to Sun was Cash – Phillips didn't want to be tied to the other two musicians. But while only Cash was signed to the label, they split the money more or less equitably, in a forty-thirty-thirty split (other sources say that the split was completely equal).

"Hey Porter" and "Cry Cry Cry" both charted, and "Folsom Prison Blues" became Cash's second single, and one of the songs that would define him for the rest of his career. It went to number four on the country and western chart, and established him as a genuine star of country music.

It's around this time that Sun signed Carl Perkins, which caused problems. Cash resented the way that he was being treated by Phillips as being less important than Perkins. He thought that Phillips was now only interested in his new star, and wasn't going to bother promoting Cash's records any more. This would be a recurring pattern with Phillips over the next few years – he would discover some new star and whoever his previous favourite was would be convinced that Phillips no longer cared about them any more. This is ultimately what led to Sun's downfall, as one by one his discoveries moved on to other labels that they believed valued them more than Phillips did.

Phillips, on the other hand, always argued that he had to put in more time when dealing with a new discovery, because he had to build their career up, and that established artists would always forget what he'd done for them when they saw him doing the same things for the next person.

That's not to say, though, that Cash disliked Perkins. Quite the contrary. The two became close friends – though Cash became even closer with Clayton Perkins, Carl's wayward brother, who had a juvenile sense of humour that appealed to Cash. Cash and Carl Perkins even co-wrote a song, "All Mama's Children", which became the B-side to Perkins' "Boppin' the Blues".

It's not the greatest song either man ever wrote, by any means, but it was the start of a working relationship that would continue off and on for decades, and which both men would benefit from significantly.

By this point, Cash had started to build a following, and as you might expect given his inspiration, he was following the exact same career path as Elvis Presley. He was managed by Elvis' first proper manager, Bob Neal, and he was given a regular slot on the Louisiana Hayride, the country music radio show that Elvis had built his reputation on. But this meant that Cash was being promoted alongside Carl Perkins, as a rock and roll star.

This would actually do wonders for Cash's career in the long term. A lot of people who wouldn't listen to anything labelled country were fans of Cash in the mid fifties, and remained with him, and this meant that his image was always a little more appealing to rock audiences than many other similar singers. You can trace a direct line between Cash being promoted as a rock and roller in 1955 and 56, and his comeback with the American Recordings series more than forty years later.

But when Cash brought in a new song he'd written, about his struggle while on the road to be true to his wife (and, implicitly, also to his God), it caused a clash between him and Sam Phillips.

That song was quite possibly inspired by a line in "Sixteen Tons", the big hit from Tennessee Ernie Ford that year, which Cash fell in love with when it came out, and which made Cash a lifelong fan of its writer Merle Travis.

He never made the connection publicly himself, but one line in "Sixteen Tons", "Can't no high-toned woman make me walk the line", almost definitely stuck in Cash's mind, and it became the central image of a song he wrote while on the road, thinking about fidelity in every sense.

"I Walk the Line" was the subject of a lot of debate between Cash and Phillips, neither of whom were entirely convinced by the other's argument. Cash was sure that the song was a good one, maybe the best song he ever wrote, but he wanted to play it as a slow, plaintive, lovelorn ballad. Phillips, on the other hand, wasn't so impressed by the song itself, but he thought that it had some potential if it was sped up to the kind of tempo that "Hey Porter", "Cry Cry Cry" and "Folsom Prison Blues" had all been performed in – a rock and roll tempo, for Cash's rock and roll audience. Give it some rhythm, and some of the boom-chika-boom, and there might be something there.

Cash argued that he didn't need to. After all, the other song he had brought in, one that he cared about much less and had originally written to give to Elvis, was a rock and roll song. The lyrics even went "Get rhythm if you get the blues".

That song itself would go on to become a hit for Cash, and a staple of his live shows, but Phillips didn't see a reason why, just because one side of the record was uptempo, the other shouldn't be as well. He wanted the music to be universal, rather than personal, and to his mind a strong rhythm was necessary for universality.

They eventually compromised and recorded two versions, a faster one recorded the way Phillips wanted it, and a slower one, the way Cash liked it. Cash walked out convinced that Phillips would see reason and release the slower version. He was devastated to find that Phillips had released the faster version.

Cash later said, "The first time I heard it on the radio, I called him and said, 'I hate that sound. Please don't release any more records. I hate that sound.' "

But then the record became a massive hit, and Cash decided that maybe the sound wasn't so bad after all. It went to number one on the country jukebox chart, made the top twenty in the pop charts, and sold more than two million copies as a single. Phillips had unquestionably had the right instincts, commercially at least.

"I Walk the Line" has a very, very, unusual structure. There's a key change after every single verse. This is just not something that you do, normally. Most pop songs will either stay in one key throughout, have a different key for different sections (so they might be in a minor key for the verse and a major key for the chorus, for example) or have one key change near the end, to give the song a bit of a kick. Here, the first verse is in F, then it goes up a fourth for the second verse, in B♭. It goes up another fourth, to E♭, for the third verse, then for the fourth verse it's back down to B♭, and the fifth verse it's back down to F, though an octave lower.

(For those wondering about those keys, either they're playing with capoes or, more likely, Sam Phillips sped the track up a semitone to make it sound faster.)

And this is really very, very, clever in the way it sets the mood of the song. The song starts and ends in the same place both musically and lyrically – the last verse is a duplicate of the first, though sung an octave lower than it started – and the rising and falling overall arc of the song suggests a natural cycle that goes along with the metaphors in the lyrics – the tides, heartbeats, day and night, dark and light. The protagonist of the song is walking a thin line, wobbling, liable at any moment to fall over to one side or another, just like the oscillation and return to the original tonal centre in this song. What sounds like a relatively crude piece of work is, when listened to closely, a much more inventive record.

And this is true of the chord sequences in the individual verses too. The verses only have three chords each – the standard three chords that most country or blues songs have, the tonic, subdominant and dominant of the key. But they're not arranged in the standard order that you'd have them in, in a three-chord trick or a twelve-bar blues. Instead the verses all start with the dominant, an unusual, unstable, choice that came about from Cash having once threaded a tape backwards and having been fascinated by the sound. The dominant is normally the last chord. Here it's the first.

The backwards tape is also one story as to where he got the idea of the humming that starts every verse – though Cash also used to claim that the humming was so he could find the right note because there were so many key changes.

This is not a song that's structured like a normal country and western song, and it's quite an extraordinarily personal piece of work. It's an expression of one man's very personal aesthetic, no matter how much Sam Phillips altered it to fit his own ideas of what Cash should be recording. It's an utterly idiosyncratic, utterly strange record, and a very strong contender for the best thing Sun Records ever put out, which is a high bar to meet. The fact that this sold two million copies in a country market that is usually characterised as conservative shows just how wrong such stereotypes can be.

It was a masterpiece, and Johnny Cash was set for a very, very, long and artistically successful career.

But that career wouldn't be with Sun. His life was in turmoil, the marriage that he had written so movingly about trying to keep together was falling apart, and he was beginning to think that he would do better doing as Elvis had and moving to a major label. Soon he would be signed to Columbia, the label where he would spend almost all his career, but we'll have one last glimpse of him at Sun. before he went off to Columbia and superstardom, at the start of the next volume.

"Heartbreak Hotel"

When we left Elvis last, his manager, Colonel Tom Parker, had managed to get him signed to RCA Records for a sum of money far greater than anything anyone had paid for a singer before, after Sam Phillips made what seemed like a ludicrous demand just to get Parker out of his hair.

And this was a big deal. Sun Records, as we've seen, was a tiny regional operation. It was able to generate massive hits for Carl Perkins and Johnny Cash after Elvis left, but that's only because of the cash the label was able to make from the Elvis deal. It's safe to say that the whole genre of rockabilly was funded by that one deal. RCA, on the other hand, was one of the biggest labels in the world.

The first thing RCA did was to reissue his last Sun single, "I Forgot to Remember to Forget", backed with "Mystery Train". With RCA's backing, the single did far better than it had on Sun, hitting number one on the country charts at the beginning of 1956.

But was that enough to make the money RCA had paid for Elvis worth it? When Elvis went into the studio on January 10 1956, two days after his twenty-first birthday, the pressure was on him to record something very special indeed.

Before going into the studio, Elvis had been sent ten demos of songs to consider for this first session. The song he ended up choosing as the main one for the session, though, was a song by someone he already knew – and for which he had a third of the songwriting credit.

Mae Axton was an odd figure. She was an English teacher who had a sideline as a freelance journalist. One day she was asked by a magazine she was freelancing for to write a story about hillbilly music, a subject about which she knew nothing. She went to Nashville to interview the singer Minnie Pearl, and while she was working on her story, Pearl introduced her to Fred Rose, the co-owner of Acuff-Rose Publishing, the biggest publishing company in country music. And Pearl, for some reason, told Rose that Mae, who had never written a song in her life, was a songwriter.

Rose said that he needed a new novelty song for a recording session for the singer Dub Dickerson that afternoon, and asked Mae to write him one. And so, all of a sudden, Mae Axton was a songwriter, and she eventually wrote over two hundred songs, starting with her early collaborations with Dickerson.

She was still also a freelance journalist, though, and it was easy for her to make a sidestep into publicity for hillbilly acts. For a time she was Hank Snow's personal publicist, and she would often work with Colonel Parker on promoting shows when they came through Florida, where she lived.

She'd interviewed Elvis when he came to Florida, and had immediately been struck by him. He'd talked to her about how amazed he was by how big the ocean was, and how he'd give anything to have enough money to bring his parents down to Florida to live there. She said later, "That just went through my heart. 'Cause I looked down there, and there were all these other kids, different show members for that night, all the guys looking for cute little girls. But his priority was doing something for his mother and daddy."

She promised she'd write him a song, and by the end of the year, she had one for him.

"Heartbreak Hotel" was, initially, the work of Tommy Durden, a country singer and songwriter.

As Durden used to tell it, he was inspired by a newspaper story of a man who'd died by suicide, who had been found with no identification on him and a note that simply read "I walk a lonely street".

Later research has suggested that rather than a suicide, the story Durden had read was probably about an armed robber, Alvin Krolik, who had been shot dead in the course of committing a robbery. Krolik had, a few years earlier, after confessing to a string of other robberies, made the news with a partial autobiography he'd written containing the lines "If you stand on a corner with a pack of cigarettes or a bottle and have nothing to do in life, I suggest you sit down and think. This is the story of a person who walked a lonely street. I hope this will help someone in the future."

Whatever the actual story, it inspired Durden, who had a few lines of the song, and he played what he had to Mae Axton. She thought a lot about the phrase, and eventually came to the conclusion that what you'd find at the end of a lonely street was a heartbreak hotel. The two of them finished the song off, with the help of Glenn Reeves, a rockabilly singer who refused to take credit for his work on the song, because he thought it was ridiculous.

Reeves did, though, record the demo for them. They'd already decided that the song should be pitched to Elvis, and so Reeves impersonated Presley. A lot of people have claimed that Elvis copied that recording exactly, phrasing and all. Comparing the two recordings, though, shows that that's not the case. Elvis definitely found it easier to record a song when he'd heard someone else doing it in an approximation of his style, and in the sixties he often would just copy the phrasing on demos.

But in the case of "Heartbreak Hotel", Elvis is not copying Reeves' phrasing at all. The two are similar, but that's just because Reeves is imitating Elvis in the first place. There are dozens of tiny choices Elvis makes throughout the song which differ from those made by Reeves, and it's clear that Elvis was thinking hard about the choices he was making.

When Mae played him the song, insisting to him that it would be his first million seller, his reaction on hearing it was "Hot dog, Mae! Play it again!" He instantly fell in love with the song, which reminded the young blues-lover of Roy Brown's "Hard Luck Blues".

Elvis got a third of the songwriting credit for the song, which most people have said was insisted on by the Colonel – and certainly other songs Elvis recorded around that time gave him a credit for that reason. But to her dying day Mae Axton always said that she'd cut him in on the song so he might be able to get that money to buy his parents a house in Florida.

The session to record "Heartbreak Hotel" started with the engineers trying – and failing – to get a replica of Sam Phillips' slapback echo sound, which was a sound whose secret nobody but Phillips knew. Instead they set up a speaker at one end of the room and fed in the sound from the mics at the other end, creating a makeshift echo chamber which satisfied Chet Atkins but threw the musicians, who weren't used to hearing the echo live rather than added after the fact.

Atkins isn't the credited producer for "Heartbreak Hotel" – that's Steve Sholes, the A&R man at RCA Records who had signed Presley – but by all accounts Atkins was nominally in charge of actually running the session. And certainly there would be no other reason for having Atkins there – he played guitar on the record, but only adding another acoustic rhythm guitar to the sound, which was frankly a waste of the talents of probably the greatest country guitarist of his generation.

That said, Atkins didn't do that much production either – according to Scotty Moore, his only suggestion was that they just keep doing what they'd been doing.

To start the session off, they recorded a quick version of "I Got a Woman", the Ray Charles song, which had been a staple of Elvis' live act since it had been released. After that, the remainder of the first session was devoted to "Heartbreak Hotel", a record that has a sense of thought that's been put into the arrangement that's entirely absent from the Sun Records arrangements, which mostly consist of "start the song, play the song through with a single solo, and end the song". The whole point of those records was to capture a kind of spontaneity, and you can't do much to play with the dynamics of an arrangement when there are only three instruments there. But now there were six – Scotty Moore and Bill Black were there as always, as was D.J. Fontana, who had joined the band on drums in 1955 and was recording for the first time, along with Atkins and piano player Floyd Cramer, who played on many of the biggest hits to come out of Nashville in the fifties and sixties.

Atkins and Cramer are two of the principal architects of what became known as "the Nashville Sound" or "Countrypolitan" – there are distinctions between these two styles for those who are interested in the fine details of country music, but for our purposes they're the same, a style of country music that pulled the music away from its roots and towards a sound that was almost a continuation of the pre-rock pop sound, all vocal groups and strings, with little in the way of traditional

country instrumentation like fiddles, mandolins, banjos, and steel guitars. And there's an element of that with their work with Presley, too
– the rough edges being smoothed off, everything getting a little bit
more mannered. But at this point it seems still to be working in the
record's favour.

After recording "Heartbreak Hotel", they took a break before spending another three-hour session recording another R&B cover that was
a staple of Elvis' stage show, "Money Honey".

Along with the addition of Atkins and Cramer, there were also
backing vocalists for the very first time. Now this is something that
often gets treated as a problem by people coming to Elvis' music fresh
today. Backing vocals in general have been deprecated in rock and
roll music for much of the last fifty years, and people think of them
as spoiling Elvis' artistry. There have even been releases of some of
Elvis' recordings remixed to get rid of the backing vocals altogether
(though that's thankfully not possible with these 1956 records, which
were recorded directly to mono).

But the backing vocals weren't an irritating addition to Elvis' artistry.
Rather, they were the essence of it, and if you're going to listen to Elvis
at all, and have any understanding of what he was trying to do, you
need to understand that before anything else.

Elvis' first ambition – the aspiration he had right at the beginning
of his career – was to be a member of a gospel quartet. Elvis wanted to
have his voice be part of a group, and he loved to sing harmony more
than anything else. He wanted to sing in a gospel quartet before he
ever met Sam Phillips, and as his career went on he only increased the
number of backing vocalists he worked with – by the end of his career he
would have J.D. Sumner and the Stamps (a Southern Gospel group),
and the Sweet Inspirations (the girl group who had backed Aretha
Franklin), *and* Kathy Westmoreland, a classically-trained soprano, all
providing backing vocals.

However, the backing vocalists on this initial session weren't yet
the Jordanaires, the group who would back Elvis throughout the fifties
and sixties. One of the Jordanaires was there – Gordon Stoker – but
the rest of them weren't hired for the January sessions, as Steve Sholes
wanted to use members of a group who were signed with RCA in their

own right – the Speer Family. So Ben and Brock Speer joined Elvis and Stoker to make an unbalanced gospel quartet, with too many tenors and no baritone.

When Elvis found out at a later session that this had happened as a cost-cutting measure, he insisted that all the Jordanaires be employed at his future sessions.

The next day, to end the sessions, they regrouped and cut a couple of ballads. "I'm Counting On You" was rather mediocre, but "I Was the One" ended up being Elvis' personal favourite track from the sessions. At the end of the sessions, Steve Sholes was very unsure if he'd made the right choice signing Elvis. He only had five tracks to show for three sessions in two days, when the normal thing was to record four songs per session – Elvis and his group were so slow partly because they were used to the laid-back feel of the Sun studios, with Sam Phillips never clock-watching, and partly because Elvis was a perfectionist. Several times they'd recorded a take that Sholes had felt would be good enough to release, but Elvis had insisted he could do it better. He'd been right – the later versions were an improvement – but they had remarkably few tracks that they could use.

Many of those who'd loved Elvis' earlier work were astonished at how bad "Heartbreak Hotel" sounded to them. The reverb, sounding so different from the restrained use of slapback on the Sun records, sounded to many ears, not least Sam Phillips', like a bad joke – Phillips called the result "a morbid mess". Yet it became a smash hit. It went to number one on the pop charts, number one in country, and made the top five in R&B. This was the moment when Elvis went from being a minor country singer on a minor label to being Elvis, Elvis the Pelvis, the King of Rock & Roll.

After the sessions that produced "Heartbreak Hotel", Elvis went back into the studio twice more and recorded a set of songs – mostly R&B and rockabilly covers – for his first album. Almost all of these were Elvis' own choice of material, and so while his versions of "Blue Suede Shoes" or "Tutti Frutti" didn't match the quality of the originals, they were fine performances and perfect for album tracks. While the "Heartbreak Hotel" session had been in Nashville – a natural choice, since it was both relatively close to Elvis' home town of Memphis, and the capital of country music, and Elvis was still supposedly a country artist – the next couple of sessions were in New York, timed to coincide with Elvis' appearances on TV.

Starting with the low-rated *Stage Show*, a programme that was presented by the swing bandleaders Tommy and Jimmy Dorsey, Elvis quickly moved up the ladder of TV shows, appearing first with Milton Berle, then with Steve Allen, and then finally on the Ed Sullivan show. On his first appearances, you can see the Elvis that people who knew him talked about – even as he's working the audience with what looks like the utmost confidence, you can see his fingers twitching wildly in a way he's not properly conscious of, and you can tell that under the mask of the sex symbol is the quiet country boy who would never meet anyone's eye.

Each show caused more controversy than the last, as first Elvis' hip gyrations got him branded a moral menace, then he was forced to sing while standing still, and then only filmed from the waist up. Those shows helped propel "Heartbreak Hotel" to the top of the charts, but the Colonel decided that Elvis probably shouldn't do too much more TV – if people could see him without paying, why would they pay to see him? No, Elvis was going to be in films instead.

But all that work meant that Elvis' fourth set of sessions for RCA was fairly disastrous, and ended up with nothing that was usable. Elvis had been so busy promoting "Heartbreak Hotel" that he hadn't had any chance to prepare material, and so he just went with Steve Sholes' suggestion of "I Want You, I Need You, I Love You". But the session went terribly, because Elvis had no feel for the song at all. Normally, Elvis would learn a song straight away, after a single listen, but he just couldn't get the song in his head. They spent the whole session working on that single track, and didn't manage to get a usable take recorded at all. Steve Sholes eventually had to cobble together a take using bits of two different performances, and no-one was happy with it, but it reached number one on the country chart and number three on the pop charts. It was hardly "Heartbreak Hotel" levels of success, but it was OK.

It was the B-side of that single that was really worth listening to. A leftover from the album sessions, it was, like Elvis' first single, a cover version of an Arthur Crudup song. And "My Baby Left Me" also gave D.J. Fontana his first chance to shine, on the brief drum solo intro.

By this point, it was very clear that if Elvis was given control of the studio and singing material he connected with, he would produce great things. And if he was doing what someone else thought he should be doing, he would be much less successful.

A couple of months later Elvis and the group were back in the studio cutting what would become their biggest double-sided hit, both songs definitely chosen by Elvis. These days their cover version of Big Mama Thornton's "Hound Dog" is the better-known of the two sides they cut that day, but while that's an excellent track – and one that bears almost no relation to Thornton's original – the A-side, and the song that finally convinced several detractors, including Sam Phillips, that Elvis might be able to make decent records away from Sun, was "Don't Be Cruel", a song written by Otis Blackwell, but credited to Blackwell and Presley, as the Colonel insisted that his boy get a cut for making it a hit.

Otis Blackwell is another person who we'll be hearing from a lot, as he wrote a string of hits, including several for Elvis, who he never met – the one time he did have a chance to meet him, he declined, as he'd developed a superstition about meeting the man who'd given him his biggest hits. At this time, Blackwell had just written the song "Fever" for Little Willie John, which was about to become a big hit for Peggy Lee, in a version with different lyrics, and Blackwell was at the start of an impressive career.

Elvis' performance on "Don't Be Cruel" showed a lightness of touch that had been absent on his earlier RCA records. He was finally in control of the sound he wanted in the studio. "Don't Be Cruel" took twenty-eight takes, and "Hound Dog" thirty-one, but you'd never believe it from the light, frothy, sound that "Don't Be Cruel" has in its finished version, where Elvis sounds as playful as if he was improvising the song on the spot.

Both sides of the record went to number one – first "Don't Be Cruel" went to number one and "Hound Dog" to number two, and then they swapped over. Between them they spent eleven weeks at the top of the charts.

But even as Elvis was starting to take complete control in the studio, that control was starting to be taken away from him by events. His next session after the one that produced "Hound Dog" and "Don't Be Cruel" was one he had not been expecting. When he'd signed to make his first film, a Western called *The Reno Brothers*, he'd expected it to be a straight acting role with no songs – he wanted to follow the path of people like Frank Sinatra, who had parallel careers in the cinema and in music, and he also hoped that he could emulate his acting idols, Marlon Brando and James Dean.

But by the time he came to make the film, several songs had been added – and he found out, to his annoyance, that he wasn't allowed to use Scotty, Bill, and D.J. on the soundtrack, because the film company didn't think they could sound hillbilly enough. They were replaced with Hollywood session musicians, who could do a better job of sounding hillbilly than those country musicians could. Elvis didn't have any say over the material either, although he did like the main ballad that was going to be used in the film – the other three songs were among the most mediocre he'd do in the fifties.

By the time *The Reno Brothers* was finished, it had been renamed *Love Me Tender*, and we'll be picking up on Elvis' film career in the next volume...

"Please Please Please"

There is a type of musician we will come across a lot as our story progresses. He is almost always a man, and he is usually regarded as a musical genius. He will be focused only on two things – his music and his money – and will have basically no friends, except maybe one from his childhood. He has employees, not friends. And he only hires the best – his employees do staggering work while being treated appallingly by him, and he takes all the credit while they do most of the work. Yet at the same time, the work those employees do ends up sounding like that genius, and when they go on to do their own stuff without him, it never sounds quite as good. That one percent he's adding does make the difference. He's never really liked as a person by his employees, but he's grudgingly respected, and he's loved by his audience.

There are people like that in every creative field – one thinks of Stan Lee in comics, or Walt Disney in film – but there are a lot of them in music, and they are responsible for an outsized portion of the most influential music ever made. And James Brown is almost the archetypal example of this kind of musician.

James Brown had a hard, hard childhood. His mother left his father when James was four – stories say that Brown's father pulled a gun on her, so her wanting to get away seems entirely reasonable, but she left her son with him, and James felt abandoned and betrayed for much of his life. A few years later his father realised that he didn't have the ability to look after a child by himself, and dumped James on a relative he always called an aunt, though she was some form of cousin, to raise. His aunt ran a brothel, and it's safe to say that that was not the best possible environment in which to raise a young child. He later said that he was in his teens before he had any underwear that was bought from a shop rather than made out of old sacks. In later life, when other people would talk about having come from broken homes and having been abandoned by their fathers, he would say "How do you think I feel? My father *and my mother* left me!"

But he had ambition. Young James had entered – and won – talent shows from a very young age – his first one was in 1944, when he was eleven, and he performed "So Long", the song that would a few years later become Ruth Brown's first big hit, but was then best known in a version by the Charioteers.

He loved music, especially jazz and gospel, and he was eager to learn anything he could about it. The one form of music he could never get into was the blues – his father played a little blues, but it wasn't young James' musical interest at all – but even there, when Tampa Red started dating one of the sex workers who worked at his aunt's house, young James Brown learned what he could from the blues legend.

He learned to sing from the holiness churches, and his music would always have a gospel flavour to it. But the music he liked more than anything was that style of jazz and swing music that was blending into what was becoming R&B. He loved Count Basie, and used to try to teach himself to play "One O'Clock Jump", Count Basie's biggest hit, on the piano.

That style of music wouldn't show up in his earlier records, which were mostly fairly standard vocal group R&B, but if you listen to his much later funk recordings, they owe a lot to Basie and Lionel Hampton. The music that Brown became most famous for is the logical conclusion to the style that those musicians developed – though we'll talk more about the invention of funk, and how funk is a form of jazz, in a future volume.

But his real favourite, the one he tried to emulate more than any other, was Louis Jordan. Brown didn't get to see Jordan live as a child, but he would listen to his records on the radio and see him in film shorts, and he decided that more than anything else he wanted to be like Jordan. As soon as he started performing with small groups around town, he started singing Jordan's songs, especially "Caldonia", which years later he would record as a tribute to his idol.

But as you might imagine, life for young James Brown wasn't the easiest, and he eventually fell into robbery. This started when he was disciplined at school for not being dressed appropriately – so he went out and stole himself some better clothes. He started to do the same for his friends, and then moved on to more serious types of theft, including cars, and he ended up getting caught breaking into one.

At the age of sixteen, Brown was sent to a juvenile detention centre, on a sentence of eight to sixteen years, and this inadvertently led to the biggest piece of luck in his life, when he met the man who would be his mentor and principal creative partner for the next twenty years. There was a baseball game between inmates of the detention centre and a team of outsiders, one of whom was named Bobby Byrd, and Byrd got talking to Brown and discovered that he could sing. In fact Brown had put together a little band in the detention centre, using improvised instruments, and would often play the piano in the gym. He'd got enough of a reputation for being able to play that he'd acquired the nickname "Music Box" – and Byrd had heard about him even outside the prison.

At the time, Byrd was leading a gospel vocal group, and needed a new singer, and he was impressed enough with Brown that he put in a word for him at a parole hearing and helped him get released early. James Brown was going to devote his life to singing for the Lord, and he wasn't going to sin any more.

He got out of the detention centre after serving only three years of his sentence, though you can imagine that to a teen there was not much "only" about spending three years of your life locked up, especially in Georgia in the 1940s, a time and place when the white guards were free to be racially abusive to an even greater extent than they are today. And for the next ten years, throughout his early musical career, Brown would be on parole and in danger of being recalled to prison at any time.

Brown ended up joining Byrd's sister's gospel group, at least for a while, before moving over to Byrd's own group, which had originally been a gospel group called the Gospel Starlighters, but by now was an R&B group called the Avons. They soon renamed themselves again, to the Flames, and later to the Famous Flames, the name they would stick with from then on (and a name which would cause a lot of confusion, as we've already talked about the Hollywood Flames, who featured a different Bobby Byrd).

Brown's friend Johnny Terry, who he had performed with in the detention centre, also joined the group. There would be many lineups of the Famous Flames, but Brown, Byrd, and Terry would be the nucleus of most of them.

Brown was massively influenced by Little Richard, to the extent that he was essentially a Little Richard tribute act early on. Brown felt an immediate kinship with Richard's music because both of them were from Georgia, both were massively influenced by Louis Jordan, and both were inspired by church music. Brown would later go off in his own direction, of course, but in those early years he sounded more like Little Richard than like anyone else.

In fact, around this time, Little Richard's career was doing so well that he could suddenly be booked into much bigger halls than he had been playing. He still had a few months' worth of contracts in those old halls, though, and so his agent had a brainwave. No-one knew what Richard looked like, so the agent got Brown and the Flames to pretend to be Little Richard and the Upsetters and tour playing the gigs that Richard had been booked into. Every night Brown would go out on stage to the introduction, "Please welcome the hardest working man in showbusiness today, Little Richard!", and when he finished ghosting for Little Richard, he liked the introduction enough that he would keep it for himself, changing it only to his own name rather than Richard's.

Brown would perform a mixture of Richard's material, his own originals, and the R&B songs that the Flames had been performing around Georgia. They'd already been cutting some records for tiny labels, at least according to Brown's autobiography, mostly cover versions of R&B hits, but Brown's imitation of Richard went down well enough that Richard's agent, Clint Brantley, decided to get the group to record a demo of themselves doing their own material.

They chose to do a song called "Please, Please, Please", written by Brown and Johnny Terry. The song was based on something that Little Richard had scribbled on a napkin, which Brown decided would make a good title for a song. The song fits neatly into a particular genre of R&B ballad, typified by for example, Richard's "Directly From My Heart to You", though both that song and "Please Please Please" owe more than a little to "Shake a Hand" by Faye Adams, the song that inspired almost all slow-burn blues ballads in this period. Another key to the song came when Brown heard the Orioles' version of Big Joe Williams' "Baby Please Don't Go", and used their backing vocal arrangement.

The Famous Flames were patterning themselves more and more on two groups – Billy Ward and the Dominoes, whose records with Clyde McPhatter as lead singer had paved the way for vocal group R&B as a genre, and Hank Ballard and the Midnighters, whose "Work With Me Annie" had had, for the time, a blatant sexuality that was unusual in successful records. They were going for energy, and for pure expression of visceral emotion, rather than the smooth sophisticated sounds of the Platters or Penguins.

They were signed to Federal Records by Ralph Bass. Bass was absolutely convinced that "Please Please Please" would be a hit, and championed the Flames in the face of opposition from his boss, Syd Nathan. Nathan thought that the song just consisted of Brown screaming one word over and over again, and that there was no way on earth that it could be a hit. In Brown's autobiography (not the most reliable of sources) he even claims that Bass was sacked for putting out the record against Nathan's will, but then rehired when the record became a hit. I'm not sure if that's literally true, but it's a story that shows the emotional truth of the period – Bass was the only person at the record company with any faith in the Famous Flames.

But the song became hugely popular. The emotion in Brown's singing was particularly effective on a particular type of woman, who would feel intensely sorry for Brown, and who would want to make that poor man feel better. Some woman had obviously hurt him terribly, and he needed the right woman to fix his hurt. It was a powerful, heartbreaking, song, and an even more powerful performance.

The song would eventually become one of the staples in the group's live repertoire, and they would develop an elaborate routine about it. Brown would drop to his knees, sobbing, and the other band members would drape him in a cape – something that was inspired by a caped wrestler, Gorgeous George – and try to lead him off stage, concerned for him. Brown would pull away from them, feigning distress, and try to continue singing the song while his bandmates tried to get him off the stage.

Sometimes it would go even further – Brown talks in his autobiography about one show, supporting Little Richard, where he climbed into the rafters of the ceiling, hung from the ceiling while singing, and dropped into the waiting arms of the band members at the climax of the show.

But there was trouble in store. The record reached number six on the R&B chart and supposedly sold between one and three million copies, though record companies routinely inflated sales by orders of magnitude at this point. But it was credited to James Brown and the Famous Flames, not just to the Famous Flames as a group. When they started to be billed that way on stage shows, too, the rest of the band decided that enough was enough, and quit en masse.

Bobby Byrd and Johnny Terry would rejoin fairly shortly afterwards, and both would stay with Brown for many more years, but the rest of the group never came back, and Brown had to put together a new set of Famous Flames, starting out almost from scratch. He had that one hit, which was enough to get his new group gigs, but everything after that flopped, for three long years.

Records like "Chonnie On Chon" tried to jump on various bandwagons – from listening to that one, you can hear that there was still a belief among R&B singers that if they namechecked Annie from "Work With Me Annie" by the Midnighters, they would have a hit – but despite him singing about having a rock and roll party, the record tanked:

Brown and his new group of Flames had to build up an audience more or less from nothing. And it's at this point – when Brown was the undisputed leader of the band – that he started his tactic of insisting on absolute discipline in his bands. Brown took on the title "the hardest working man in showbusiness", but his band members had to work equally hard, if not harder. Any band member whose shoes weren't shined, or who missed a dance step, or hit a wrong note on stage, would be fined. Brown took to issuing these fines on stage – he'd point at a band member and then flash five fingers in time to the music. Each time he made his hand flash, that was another five dollar fine for that musician. Audiences would assume it was part of the dance routine, but the musician would know that he was losing that money.

But while Brown's perfectionism verged on the tyrannical (and indeed sometimes surpassed the tyrannical), it had results.

Brown knew, from a very early age, that he would have to make his success on pure hard work and determination. He didn't have an especially good voice (though he would always defend himself as a singer – when someone said to him "all you do is grunt", he'd respond, "Yes, but I grunt *in tune*"). And he wasn't the physical type that was in fashion with black audiences at the time. While I am absolutely not the person to talk about colourism in the black community, there is a general consensus that in that time and place, black people were more likely to admire a black man if he was light-skinned, had features that didn't fit the stereotype of black people, and was tall and thin. Brown was very dark, had extremely African features, and was short and stocky.

So he and his group just had to work harder than everyone else. They spent three years putting out unsuccessful singles and touring the chitlin circuit. We've mentioned the chitlin circuit in passing before, but now is probably the time to explain this in more detail.

The chitlin circuit was an informal network of clubs and theatres that stretched across the USA, catering almost exclusively to black audiences. Any black act – with the exception of a handful of acts who were aiming at white audiences, like Harry Belafonte or Nat "King" Cole – would play the chitlin circuit, and those audiences would be hard to impress. As with poor audiences everywhere, the audiences wanted value for their entertainment dollar, and were not prepared to tolerate anything less than the best.

The worst of these audiences was at the amateur nights at the Apollo Theater in Harlem. The audiences there would come prepared with baskets full of rotten fruit and eggs to throw at the stage. But all of the audiences would be quick to show their disapproval.

But at the same time, that kind of audience will also, if you give them anything more than their money's worth, be loyal to you forever. And Brown made sure that the Famous Flames would inspire that kind of loyalty, by making sure they worked harder than any other group on the circuit. And after three years of work, he finally had a second hit.

The new song was inspired by "For Your Precious Love" by Jerry Butler, another slow-burn ballad, though this time more obviously in the soul genre.

As Brown told the story, he wrote his new song and took it to Syd Nathan at Federal, who said that he wasn't going to waste his money putting out anything like that, and that in fact he was dropping Brown from the label. Brown was so convinced it was a hit that he recorded a demo with his own money, and took it directly to the radio stations, where it quickly became the most requested song on the stations that played it.

According to Brown, Nathan wouldn't budge on putting the song out until he discovered that Federal had received orders for twenty-five thousand copies of the single.

Nathan then asked Brown for the tape, saying he was going to give Brown one more chance. But Brown told Nathan that if he was going to put out the new song, it was going to be done properly, in a studio paid for by Nathan. Nathan reluctantly agreed, and Brown went into the studio and cut "Try Me".

"Try Me" became an even bigger hit than "Please Please Please" had, and went to number one on the R&B charts and number forty-eight on the pop charts.

But once again, Brown lost his group, and this time just before a big residency at the Apollo – the most prestigious, and also the most demanding, venue on the chitlin circuit. He still had Johnny Terry, and this was the point when Bobby Byrd rejoined the group after a couple of years away, but he was still worried about his new group and how they would fare on this residency, which also featured Little Richard's old group the Upsetters, and was headlined by the blues star Little Willie John.

Brown needn't have worried. The new lineup of Famous Flames went down well enough that the audiences were more impressed by them than by any of the other acts on the bill, and they were soon promoted to co-headline status, much to Little Willie John's annoyance.

That was the first time James Brown ever played at the Apollo, a venue which in later years would become synonymous with him, and we'll pick up in later volumes on the ways in which Brown and the Apollo were crucial in building each other's reputation.

But for Brown himself, probably the most important thing about that residency at the Apollo came at the end of the run. And I'll finish this chapter with Brown's own words, from his autobiography, talking about that last night:

> The day after we finished at the Apollo I was in my room at the Theresa, fixing to leave for Washington, when somebody knocked on the door. "Come in," I said. I was gathering up my belongings, not really watching the door. I heard it open, real slow, but that was all. After a minute, when I realized how quiet it was, I turned around. There was a small woman standing there, not young, not old. I hadn't seen her since I was four years old, but when I looked at her I knew right away it was my mother.
>
> I had no idea she was coming to see me that day or any day.
>
> "I've been looking for you for a long time," I said. "I'm glad to see you."
>
> She started to smile, and when she did I could see she'd lost all her teeth.
>
> All I could think to say was, "I'm going to get your mouth fixed for you."
>
> She didn't say anything. She just walked toward me. We hugged, and then I kissed my mother for the first time in more than twenty years.

"Drugstore Rock 'n' Roll"

Sometimes a novelty act will have real talent, and sometimes the things that can bring you the most success initially can be the very things that stop you from building a career. In the case of Janis Martin, "the female Elvis Presley", those four words were the reason she became successful, and some say they are also the reason she very quickly dropped into obscurity. There are no books about Janis Martin, who as far as I can tell was the first successful female rockabilly artist. There are no films about her. There are just a handful of articles in obscure fanzines, and pages on unvisited websites, to mark the story of a true pioneer of rockabilly music.

But I don't think that the way Janis Martin's career stalled was down to that label at all. I think it stalled because of misogyny, plain and simple, and I'm going to explain why in this episode. So a warning right now – this will deal in passing with abortion and underage marriage. If you are likely to find anything dealing with those things traumatising, please skip this chapter. I won't be going into those things in any great detail, but sometimes better safe than sorry.

Janis Martin was born in 1940, and spent her early years as a child country and western act. She started playing the guitar when she was only four, holding it upright because she wasn't big enough yet to play it normally, and by the age of eleven she was a regular on The Old Dominion Barn Dance. This was at a time when the dominant force in country and western music was a series of live variety shows that would be broadcast by different radio stations, and there was a definite hierarchy there. At the very top of the chain was the Grand Ole Opry, whose performers like Roy Acuff would absolutely dominate the whole

429

medium of country music. If you were on the Opry, you were going to be a big star, and you would be heard by everyone. You'd made it.

Slightly lower than the Opry were shows like the Louisiana Hayride. The Hayride was for those who were on their way up or on their way down. Elvis Presley got a residency on the show when he went down too badly on the Opry for them to book him again, and Hank Williams started performing on it when he was dropped by the Opry for drunkenness, but it also booked acts who weren't quite well known enough to secure a spot on the Opry, people who were still building their names up.

And then, a rung below the Hayride, were shows like the Old Dominion Barn Dance. The Barn Dance had some big name acts – the Carter Family, Flatt and Scruggs, Joe Maphis – these weren't small-time no-namers by any means. But it wasn't as big as the Hayride.

Young Janis Martin was a country singer, pushed into the role by her domineering mother. But she wasn't massively interested in country music. She liked the honky-tonk stuff – she liked Hank Williams, "Because he had a little rock to his music". But she didn't like bluegrass, and she was starting to get bored with the slow country ballads that dominated the pop part of the country field.

But luckily, the further down the rungs you got, the more experimental the hillbilly shows could be, and the more they could deviate from the straight formula insisted on by the shows at the top. Shows like the Opry, while wildly popular, were also extraordinarily conservative. The Barn Dance allowed people to try things that were a little different.

Janis Martin was a little different. She changed her whole style with one twist of a radio dial, when she was thirteen. She was going through the radio stations trying to find something she liked, when she hit on a station that was playing "Mama, He Treats Your Daughter Mean" by Ruth Brown.

She immediately decided that that was what she wanted to be singing – "black R&B", as she would always put it, not country music. She immediately incorporated "Mama, He Treats Your Daughter Mean" into her set, and started adding a lot of similar songs – not just Ruth

Brown songs, though Brown would always remain her very favourite, but songs by LaVern Baker and Dinah Washington as well.

This was not normal, even for the small number of country musicians who were playing R&B songs. Generally, the few who did that were performing music originally recorded by male jump band artists like Louis Jordan or Big Joe Turner. The songs Brown, Baker, and Washington recorded were all closer to jazz than to country music, and it's actually quite hard for me to imagine how one could perform "Mama He Treats Your Daughter Mean" with country instrumentation.

But this was what Janis Martin was doing, and it went down well with the Old Dominion Barn Dance audience. What worried some of them was another change that went along with this – she started performing in a manner that they interpreted as overtly sexual. At thirteen and fourteen years old, she was dancing on the stage in a way that was often compared to Elvis Presley – someone she'd never heard of at the time, and wasn't that impressed by when she did. She preferred Carl Perkins. She wasn't intending to be vulgar or sexual – it just made no sense to her *not* to dance while she was singing uptempo R&B-style songs.

As she later said, "When I was a little girl doing all those rock 'n' roll moves on the barndances, people thought it was cute. But then, when I was fifteen or sixteen, and wearing a ponytail, and out there moving like Elvis, a lot of people thought it was vulgar."

But, at the time, the crowds at the Barndance shows were still happy to hear this music, however different it was from the country music they were used to.

Martin's big break came when two staff announcers on WRVA, the station that hosted the Barndance, Carl Stutz and Carl Barefoot, brought her a song they'd written, "Will You, Willyum?".

The song itself was not hugely impressive – it's a standard boogie rhythm country song, and like many second-rate songs of the time it tries to get itself a little second-hand excitement by namechecking another song – in this case, it references dancing with Henry, a reference to "The Wallflower". But Martin's demo of the song was enough to catch the ear of Steve Sholes, the A&R man who had signed Elvis a few months earlier, and so in March 1956, aged just fifteen, Janis

Martin was signed to RCA Records, one of the biggest labels in the country.

Sholes wanted to record "Will You, Willyum?" as her first single, but had also suggested that she try writing songs herself. Her very first attempt at writing a song took her, by her own accounts, ten or fifteen minutes to write, and ended up as the B-side. It was "Drugstore Rock 'n' Roll".

Now, this actually marks something of a turning point in our story, though it may not seem it. Up to this point, the music we've looked at broadly falls into three categories – R&B and jump band music made by and for black adults, white country musicians imitating that jump band music and generally aiming it at a younger audience, and doo wop music made by and for black teenagers.

"Drugstore Rock 'n' Roll" is the first record we've looked at – and one of the first records ever made – to deal specifically with the experience of the white teenagers who were now the music's biggest audience, and deal with it from their own perspective. This is where the 1950s of the popular imagination – letter sweaters, crewcuts, ponytails, big skirts, dancing to the jukebox, drinking a malt with two straws, the 1950s of *Happy Days* and *American Graffiti* and Archie Comics, all starts.

Now, in this, we have to consider that the micro and the macro are telling us rather different things, and that both parts of the picture are true. On the one hand, we have a teenage girl, writing her first ever song, talking about her own experiences and doing so in a musical idiom that she loves. On the other hand, we have a massive corporate conglomerate taking musical styles created by marginalised groups, removing those elements that made them distinctive to those groups, and marketing them at a more affluent, privileged, audience.

Both these things were happening at the same time, and we'll see, as we look at the next few years of rock and roll history, how an influx of well-meaning – and often great – individual white artists making music they truly believed in, and with no racist motives as individuals (indeed many of them were committed anti-racists), would still, in aggregate, turn rock and roll from a music that was dominated by black artists and created for a primarily black audience, into one that was created by and for privileged white teenagers.

Over the next few years the most popular artists in rock and roll music would go from being black men singing about gay sex and poor white sharecroppers singing about drinking liquor from an old fruit jar to being perky teenagers singing about sock hops and going steady, and Janis Martin was an early example of this. But she was still, ultimately, too individual for the system to cope with.

Given that she supposedly moved like Elvis (I say supposedly because I haven't been able to find any footage of her to confirm this) and had had a similar career path, RCA decided to market her as "the Female Elvis". They got the permission of Elvis and the Colonel to do so, though Martin only ever met Elvis twice, and barely exchanged a couple of words with him when she did.

They also got in some of the same people who performed on Elvis' records. While Elvis' own musicians weren't available, Chet Atkins, who also produced Janis' sessions, and Floyd Cramer were both on most of Janis' early recordings, and came up with a very similar sound to the Elvis records, and on at least some of her records the Jordanaires provided backing vocals, as they did for Elvis.

The first single, "Will You, Willyum?" backed with "Drugstore Rock 'n' Roll", was a hit, and went to number thirty-five in the pop charts. It sold three quarters of a million copies, and led to performances on most of the big TV shows, as well as on the Grand Ole Opry. But the follow-up, "Ooby Dooby" (a cover of a song we'll be dealing with in a couple of chapters' time) didn't do quite so well. So for her third single they tried to lean into the Elvis comparisons with. . . a song about Elvis – "My Boy Elvis".

She wasn't particularly keen on the song, but she had no control over the material she was given – back then, artists on major labels made the records they were told to make, and that was the end of it.

"My Boy Elvis" was, in fact, only one of a large number of novelty records about Elvis that hit in 1956. Novelty records were a huge part of the music industry in the 1950s and 60s, and there would not be a trend that would go by without a dozen people putting out records of one kind or another about the trend. And given that Elvis' rise to stardom was the biggest cultural phenomenon the world had ever seen, it's not surprising that a few record company owners figured that if the kids were interested in buying records by Elvis, they might be tricked into buying records about Elvis too.

A typical example of the form was "I Want Elvis For Christmas" by the Holly Twins, a song written by two aspiring songwriters – Don Kirshner, who would later become one of the most important music publishing executives in the world, and a young man named Walden Cassoto, who would soon change his name to Bobby Darin. The person impersonating Elvis on that record was a country singer called Eddie Cochran, who we'll be hearing a lot more about soon.

So these novelty records were being released left and right, but very few of them had any success. And Martin's record was no exception. Not only that, the teenage girl audience who were Elvis' biggest fanbase started to resent the marketing – which she hadn't chosen herself – comparing her to Elvis. They were in love with Elvis, and didn't like the comparison.

Janis was selling records, but not quite at the level RCA initially hoped – they were having trouble building her audience. That was because in 1956, unlike even a year or so later, record labels had no idea what to do with white rock and roll acts aimed at the teen crowd. There were Bill Haley and Elvis, who were in a league of their own, and there were the Sun Records artists who could be packaged together on tours and play to the same crowds.

But other than that, rock and roll acts played the chitlin circuit, and that was black acts for black audiences.

There was a possible solution to this problem – Elvis. Colonel Parker, Elvis' manager, was a close associate of Steve Sholes, and believed Sholes when he told Parker that Janis Martin was going places. He wanted to sign Janis to a management contract and promote Elvis and Janis as a double-bill, thinking that having a male-female act would be a good gimmick.

But her parents thought this was a bad idea. Just before she had been signed to RCA, Elvis had very publicly collapsed and been hospitalised with exhaustion through overwork. For all that Martin's mother was a pushy stage mother, she didn't want that for her daughter, and so the Colonel never got to sign Janis, and Janis never got to tour and play to Elvis' audience.

So since she had come up through the country music scene, and had been signed by RCA's country department, she was put on bills with other RCA country artists like Hank Snow.

Understandably, Martin's rock and roll style didn't really fit on the bills, and the audiences were unimpressed. No-one in RCA or her promotional team knew how to deal with a rock and roll star who wasn't the most massive thing on the charts – there was not, yet, anywhere to put a mid-range rock and roll star.

But she continued plugging away, making rockabilly records, and slowly building up a fanbase for herself. She even had a screen test with MGM, the film studio that had signed Elvis up so successfully.

But she had a problem, and one that would eventually cause the end of her career. A few months before she was signed to RCA, she had got married.

This is less odd than it might now sound. In the southern US in the 1950s, it was perfectly normal for people to get married in their early or mid teens. We will see a few more stories as the series goes on where people have married far, far, too young – in some cases, because of abuse by an older man, in other cases just because teenage hormones had convinced them that they were definitely mature enough, no matter what those old people said. In this case, she had eloped with a paratrooper, who was stationed in Germany soon after. She only told her parents about the marriage once her husband had left the country.

So everything was fine – while she might have been technically married, it wasn't like she was even on the same continent as her husband, so for all practical purposes it was exactly as if she was the single, sweet, innocent teenage girl that RCA wanted people to think she was. And she didn't see the need to tell RCA any different. What they didn't know couldn't hurt them.

And that was all fine, until her 1957 European tour. As she was going to be in Europe anyway, her husband asked for a leave of absence and spent thirty days travelling around with her. And when she got back to the US, she was pregnant.

When she informed RCA, they were furious. They couldn't have their seventeen-year-old nation's sweetheart going around being visibly pregnant – even though one of the songs they'd chosen for her to record at her first session, "Let's Elope Baby", had described her actual experiences rather better than they'd realised.

And so they came up with what they thought was the obvious solution – they tried to persuade her to get an abortion, although that was still illegal in the US at the time. She refused, and the label dropped her.

She started recording for a small label – she turned down offers from King and Decca records, and instead went with the tiny Belgian label Palette – but she never had any success, and soon split from her husband. By 1960, aged twenty, she was on to her second marriage.

Her second husband toured with her for a while, but soon told her that if she wanted to stay with him, she would have to give up on the music industry. For the next thirteen years, while she was married to him, she did just that, and her career was over.

But then, after her second marriage ended, she put together a band, Janis Martin and the Variations, and started playing gigs again. And the woman whose entire life had been controlled by other people – first her mother, then her record label, then her husband – found she liked performing again. She didn't return to full-time music, at least at first – she held down a day job as the assistant manager of a country club in Virginia – but she found that she still had fans, especially in Europe.

In the late seventies Bear Family Records, a German reissue label that specialises in doing comprehensive catalogue releases by 50s country and rock and roll artists, had put out two vinyl albums collecting everything she'd released in the fifties (and this was later put together as a single-CD set, one of their first CD releases, in the mid-eighties), and she'd become known to a new generation of rockabilly fans in Europe, as well as building up a new small fanbase in the USA. So in 1982, she travelled to Europe for the first time since that 1957 tour, and started performing for audiences who, more than anything else, wanted to hear her own song, "Drugstore Rock 'n' Roll".

For the last few decades of her life, Janis Martin would regularly tour, even though she hated flying, because she felt she owed it to the fans to let them see her perform. Her son played drums with her band, and audiences would regularly thrill to Janis, as this woman who was now a great-grandmother and looked like any other great-grandmother from Virginia, sang her songs of teenage rebellion. Her third marriage, in 1977, was to a man who had been a fan of hers during her first career, and lasted the rest of her life. She was finally happy.

And in 2006 she recorded what was intended to be a comeback album, and she was finally able to fulfil a lifetime ambition, and perform with Ruth Brown, singing the song that changed everything for her when she'd heard it more than fifty years earlier.

That was the first and only time Janis Martin and Ruth Brown would meet and perform together. Ruth Brown died in late 2006, and Janis' son died in early 2007. Janis herself died of cancer in September 2007, having outlived the man with whom she had been compared in her teens by more than thirty years, and having lived to see her work embraced by new generations. There are much worse lives for an Elvis to have had.

"Be-Bop-A-Lula"

"White face, black shirt/White socks, black shoes/Black hair, white Strat/Bled white, died black/Sweet Gene Vincent..."

So sang Ian Dury, one of the greats of the rock and roll generation that came up in the seventies, a generation that grew up on listening to Gene Vincent. In the USA, Vincent was more or less regarded as a one-hit wonder, though that one hit was one of the most memorable of the 1950s, but in the UK, he was to become one of the biggest influences on everyone who sang or played a guitar.

Gene Vincent was born Vincent Eugene Craddock, and he would have been perfectly happy in his original career as a sailor, until 1955. Then, something happened that changed his life forever. He re-enlisted in the Navy, and got a nine-hundred dollar bonus – a huge sum of money for a sailor in those days – which he used to buy himself a new Triumph racing motorbike.

The bike didn't last long, and nor did Gene's Navy career. There are two stories about the accident. The one which he told most often, and which was the official story, was that he was not at fault – a woman driving a Chrysler ran a red light and ran into him, and the only reason he didn't get compensation was that he signed some papers while he was sedated in hospital.

The other story, which he told at least one friend, was that he'd been out drinking and was late getting back to the Naval base. There was a security barrier at the base, and he tried to ride under the barrier. He'd failed, and the bike had come down hard on his left leg, crushing it.

Whatever the truth, his left leg was smashed up, and looked for a long time like it was going to be amputated, but he refused to allow this. He had it put into a cast for more than a year, after which it was put into a metal brace instead. His leg never really properly healed, and it would leave him in pain for the rest of his life. His leg developed chronic osteomyelitis, he had a permanent open sore on his shin, his leg muscles withered, and his bones would break regularly.

Then in September 1955, finally discharged from the naval hospital, Gene Vincent went to see a country music show. The headliner was Hank Snow, and the Louvin Brothers were also on the bill, but the act that changed Gene's life was lower down the bill – a young singer named Elvis Presley.

The story seems to be the same for almost every one of the early rockabilly artists, but this is the first time we've seen it happen with someone who didn't go on to sign with Sun – a young man in the Southern US has been playing his guitar for a while, making music that's a little bit country, a little bit blues, and then one day he goes to see a show featuring Elvis Presley, and he immediately decides that he wants to do that, that Elvis is doing something that's like what the young man has already started doing, but he's proved that you can do it on stage, for people.

It's as if at every single show Elvis played in 1954 and 1955 there was a future rockabilly star in the audience – and by playing those shows, Elvis permanently defined what we mean when we say "rock and roll star".

The first thing Gene did was to get himself noticed by the radio station that had promoted the show, and in particular by Sheriff Tex Davis, who was actually a DJ from Connecticut whose birth name was William Doucette, but had changed his name to sound more country. Davis was a DJ and show promoter, and he was the one who had promoted the gig that Elvis had appeared at. Gene Craddock came into his office a few days after that show, and told him that he was a singer. Davis listened to him sing a couple of songs, and thought that he would do a decent job as a regular on his Country Showtime radio show.

Soon afterwards, Carl Perkins came to town to do a show with Craddock as the opening act. It would, in fact, be his last show for a while – it was right after this show, as he travelled to get to New

York for the TV appearance he was booked on, that he got into the car crash that derailed his career. But Tex Davis asked Carl to watch the opening act and tell him what he thought. Carl watched, and he said that the boy had potential, especially one particular song, "Be-Bop-A-Lula", which sounded to Carl quite like some of his own stuff.

That was good enough for Tex Davis, who signed Craddock up to a management contract, and who almost immediately recorded some of his performances to send to Ken Nelson at Capitol Records.

Capitol at the time was the home of crooners like Frank Sinatra and Nat "King" Cole, and other than its small country music division had little connection to the new forms of music that were starting to dominate the culture. Capitol had been founded in the early 1940s by the songwriter Johnny Mercer, who wrote many standards for Sinatra, Bing Crosby, Tony Bennett and others, and also recorded his own material, like "Ac-Cent-Tchu-Ate the Positive".

Mercer was a great songwriter, but you can imagine that a record label headed up by Mercer might not have been one that was most attuned to rock and roll. However, in 1955 Capitol had been bought up by the big conglomerate EMI, and things were changing at the label.

Ken Nelson was the head of country music for Capitol Records, and is someone who has a very mixed reputation among lovers of both country music and rockabilly, as someone who had impeccable taste in artists – he also signed Buck Owens and the Louvin Brothers among many other classic country artists – but also as someone who would impose a style on those artists that didn't necessarily suit them.

Nelson didn't really understand rockabilly at all, but he knew that Capitol needed its own equivalent of Elvis Presley. So he put a call out for people to recommend him country singers who could sound a bit like Elvis. On hearing the tape that Tex Davis sent him of Gene Craddock, he decided to call in this kid for a session in Nashville.

By this point, Craddock had formed his own backing band, who became known as the Blue Caps. This consisted of guitarist Cliff Gallup, the oldest of the group and a plumber by trade, drummer Dickie Harrell, a teenager who was enthusiastic but a good decade younger than Gallup, rhythm guitarist Willie Williams, and bass player Jack Neal. They took the name "Blue Caps" from the hats they all wore on stage, which were allegedly inspired by the golf caps that President Eisenhower used to wear while playing golf. Not the most rebellious of inspirations for the group that would, more than any other rock and roll group of the fifties, inspire juvenile delinquency and youthful rebelliousness.

The session was at a studio run by Owen Bradley, who had just recently recorded some early tracks by a singer from Texas named Buddy Holly. The song chosen for the first single was a track called "Woman Love", which everyone was convinced could be a hit. They were convinced, that is, until they heard Gene singing it in the studio, at which point they wondered if perhaps some of what he was singing was not quite as wholesome as they had initially been led to believe.

Ken Nelson asked to look at the lyric sheet, and satisfied that Gene *could* have been singing "hugging" rather than what Nelson had worried he had been singing, agreed that the song should go out on the A-side of Gene's first single, which was to be released under the name Gene Vincent – a name Nelson created from Gene's forenames.

It turned out that the lyric sheet didn't completely convince everyone. Most radio stations refused to play "Woman Love" at all, saying that even if the lyrics weren't obscene – and plenty of people were convinced that they were – the record itself still was.

Or, at least, the A-side was.

The B-side, a song called "Be-Bop-A-Lula", was a different matter.

There are three stories about how the song came to have the title "Be-Bop-A-Lula". Donald Graves, a fellow patient in the naval hospital who was widely considered to have co-written the song with Gene, always claimed the song was inspired by the 1920s vaudeville song "Don't Bring Lulu".

As Tex Davis told the story, it was inspired by a *Little Lulu* comic book Davis showed Vincent, to which Vincent said, "Hey, it's be-bop a lulu!"

Davis is credited as co-writer of the song along with Gene, but it's fairly widely acknowledged that he had no part in the song's writing. Almost every source now says that Davis paid Donald Graves twenty-five dollars for his half of the songwriting rights.

Far more likely is that it was inspired by the Helen Humes song "Be Baba Leba".

That song had been rerecorded by Lionel Hampton as "Hey Ba-Ba-Re-Bop!", which had been a massive R&B hit, and the song is also generally considered one of the inspirations behind the term "bebop" being applied to the style of music.

And that's something we should probably at least talk about briefly here, because it shows how much culture changes, and how fast we lose context for things that seemed obvious at the time. The term "bebop", as it was originally used, was used in the same way we use it now — for a type of jazz music that originated in New York in the mid-1940s, which prized harmonic complexity, instrumental virtuosity, and individual self-expression. The music made by people like Charlie Parker, Oscar Peterson, Dexter Gordon, Dizzy Gillespie, and so on, and which pretty much defined what was thought of as jazz in the postwar era.

But while that was what the term originally meant, and is what the term means now, it wasn't what the term meant in 1956, at least to most of the people who used the term. Colloquially, bebop meant "that noisy music I don't understand that the young people like, and most of the people making it are black". So it covered bebop itself, but it was also used for rhythm and blues, rock and roll, even rockabilly — you would often find interviewers talking with Elvis in his early years referring to his music as "Hillbilly Bop" or "a mixture of country music and bebop".

So even though "Be-Bop-A-Lula" had about as much to do with bebop as it did with Stravinsky, the name still fit.

At that initial session, Ken Nelson brought in a few of the top session players in Nashville, but when he heard the Blue Caps play, he was satisfied that they were good enough to play on the records, and sent the session musicians home. In truth, the Blue Caps were probably best described as a mixed-ability group. Some of them were rudimentary musicians at best — though as we've seen, rockabilly, more than most genres, was comfortable with enthusiastic amateurs anyway.

But Cliff Gallup, the lead guitarist, was quite probably the most technically accomplished guitarist in the world of rockabilly. Gallup's guitar style, which involved fast-picked triplets and the use of multiple steel fingerpicks, was an inspiration for almost every rock and roll guitarist of the 1960s, and any group which had him in would sound at least decent.

During the recording of "Be-Bop-A-Lula", Dickie Harrell decided to let out a giant scream right in the middle of the song – he later said that this was so that his mother would know he was on the record. Cliff Gallup was not impressed, and wanted to do a second take, but the first take was what was used.

"Be-Bop-A-Lula" is by any standards a quite astonishing record. The lyric is, of course, absolute nonsense – it's a gibberish song with no real lyrical content at all – but that doesn't matter at all. What matters is the sound. What we have here, fundamentally, is the sound of "Heartbreak Hotel" applied to a much, much, less depressive lyric. It still has that strange morbidity that the Elvis track had, but combined with carefree gibberish lyrics in the style of Little Richard. It's the precise midpoint between "Heartbreak Hotel" and "Tutti Frutti", and is probably the record which, more than any other, epitomises 1956.

A lot of people commented on the similarity between Vincent's record and the music of Elvis Presley. There are various stories that went round at the time, including that Scotty and Bill got annoyed at Elvis for recording it without them, that Elvis' mother had told him she liked that new single of his, "Be-Bop-A-Lula", and even that Elvis himself, on hearing it, had been confused and wondered if he'd forgotten recording it.

In truth, none of these stories seem likely. The record is, sonically and stylistically, like an Elvis one, but Vincent's voice has none of the same qualities as Elvis'. While Elvis is fully in control at all times, playful and exuberant, Gene Vincent is tense and twitchy. Vincent's voice is thinner than Elvis', and his performance is more mannered than Elvis' singing at that time was.

But none of this stopped Vincent from worrying the one time he did meet Elvis, who came over and asked him if he was the one who'd recorded "Be-Bop-A-Lula". Vincent was apologetic, and explained that he'd not been intending to copy Elvis, the record had just come out like that. But Elvis reassured him that he understood, and that that was just how Gene sang.

What fewer people commented on was the song's similarity to "Money Honey". The two songs have near-identical melodies. The only real difference is that in "Be-Bop-A-Lula" Vincent bookends the song with a slight variation, turning the opening and closing choruses into twelve-bar blueses, rather than the eight-bar blues used in the rest of the song and in "Money Honey".

Luckily for Vincent, at this time the culture in R&B was relaxed enough about borrowings that Jesse Stone seems not to have even considered suing.

The follow-up to "Be-Bop-A-Lula" did much less well. "Race With the Devil" – not the same song as the one later made famous by Judas Priest – was one of the all-time great rockabilly records, but the lyrics, about a hot-rod race with the actual Devil, were, like "Woman Love", considered unbroadcastable, and this time there was no massive hit record hidden away on the B-side to salvage things.

The single after that, "Blue Jean Bop", did a little better, reaching the lower reaches of the top fifty, rather than the lower reaches of the top hundred as "Race With the Devil" had, and making the top twenty in the UK.

But there were three major problems that were preventing Vincent and the Blue Caps from having the success that it seemed they deserved.

The first was Ken Nelson. He was in charge of the material that the group were recording, and he would suggest songs like "Up a Lazy River", "Ain't She Sweet", and "Those Wedding Bells are Breaking up That Old Gang of Mine". Vincent enjoyed those old standards as much as anyone, but they weren't actually suited to the rockabilly treatment – especially not to the kind of rough and ready performances that the original lineup of the Blue Caps were suited to.

And that brings us to the second problem. There was a huge age gap, as well as disparity in ability, in the band, and Cliff Gallup, in particular, felt that he was too old to be touring in a rock and roll band, and quit the group. Gallup was actually offered a regular gig as a session guitarist by Ken Nelson, which would have meant that he didn't have to travel, but he turned it down and got a job as a high school janitor and maintenance man, just playing the occasional extra gig for pin money. When he was contacted by fans, he would get embarrassed, and he didn't like to talk about his brief time as a rock and roll star. He never signed a single autograph, and when he died in 1989 his widow made sure the obituaries never mentioned his time with Gene Vincent.

But Gallup was just the first to leave. In the first two and a half years of the Blue Caps' existence, twenty different people were members of the band. Vincent could never keep a stable lineup of the band together for more than a few weeks or months at a time.

And the third major problem... that was Vincent himself. Even before his accident, he had been an impetuous, hot-headed man, who didn't think very carefully about the possible consequences of his actions. Now he was in chronic pain from the accident, he was a rock and roll star, and he was drinking heavily to deal with the pain. This is not a combination that makes people less inclined to rash behaviour.

So, for example, he'd started breaking contracts. Vincent and the Blue Caps were booked to play a residency in Las Vegas, where they were making three thousand dollars a week – for 1956 a staggering sum of money.

But Tex Davis told Vincent that the owner of the casino wanted him to tone down some aspects of his act, and he didn't like that at all. It wasn't even enough to convince him when it was pointed out that the man doing the asking was big in the Mafia. Instead, Gene went on stage, sang one song, found Tex Davis in the crowd, caught his eye, flipped him off, and walked off stage, leaving the band to do the rest of the show without him.

Unsurprisingly, the residency didn't last very long. Equally unsurprisingly, Tex Davis decided he was no longer going to manage Gene Vincent. Legal problems around the fallout from losing his management caused Vincent to be unable to work for several months.

While both "Race With the Devil" and "Blue Jean Bop" were big hits in the UK, the closest they came to having another hit in the USA was a song called "Lotta Lovin'". That was written by a songwriter named Bernice Bedwell, who is otherwise unknown – she wrote a handful of other rockabilly songs, including another song that Vincent would record, but nothing else that was particularly successful, and there seems to be no biographical information about her anywhere.

She sold the publishing rights to the song to a Texas oilman, Tom Fleeger, who does seem to have had a fairly colourful life – he wrote a memoir, *Fidel and the Fleeg*, which I sadly haven't read, but in which he claims that Fidel Castro tried to frame him for murder in the 1940s after a dispute over a beautiful woman.

Fleeger was soon to start his own record label, Jan Records, but for now he thought that the song would be suitable for Gene Vincent, and got in touch with him. "Lotta Lovin'" was quickly recorded at Gene's first session at Capitol's new studio at the Capitol Tower in Hollywood. The B-side was a ballad called "Wear My Ring" by Warren Cassoto, the future Bobby Darin, and Don Kirshner.

"Lotta Lovin'" went to number thirteen on the pop charts, and number seven on the R&B charts, and it looked like it would revitalise Gene's career. But it was not to be. Vincent's increasingly erratic behaviour – including pulling a gun on band members on multiple occasions – and Capitol and Ken Nelson's lack of understanding of rock and roll music, meant that he quickly became a forgotten figure in the US.

But he had a huge impact on the UK, thanks to a TV producer named Jack Good.

Jack Good was the person who, more than anyone else, had brought rock and roll to British TV. He'd been the producer of *Six-Five Special*, a BBC TV show that was devoted to rock and roll and skiffle, before moving to ITV, producing its first two rock and roll shows, *Oh Boy*, and *Boy Meets Girls*. And it was Good who suggested that Vincent switch from his normal polite-looking stagewear into black leather, and that he accentuate the postural problems his disability caused him.

Vincent's appearances on *Boy Meets Girls*, dressed in black leather, hunched over, in pain because of his leg, defined for British teenagers of the 1950s what a rock and roller was meant to look like. At a time when few American rock and roll stars were visiting the UK, and even fewer were getting any exposure on the very small number of TV shows that were actually broadcast – this was when there were only two TV channels in the UK, and they broadcast for only a few hours – Gene Vincent being *here*, and on British TV, meant the world. And on a show like *Boy Meets Girls*, where the rest of the acts were people like Cliff Richard or Adam Faith, having a mean, moody, leather-clad rock and roller on screen was instantly captivating. For a generation of British rockers, Gene Vincent epitomised American rock and roll.

Until in 1960 he was on a tour of the UK that ended in tragedy. But that's a story for another time...

"Ooby Dooby"

In this chapter, we're once again going to look at a star who was discovered by Sun Records. But for once, the star we're looking at did not do his most interesting or vital work at Sun, and nor did he do the work that defined his persona there.

Indeed, this is one of the very few times that Sam Phillips and Sun Records took on someone who would become a massive, massive, star, and completely mismanaged him, misjudged his abilities totally, and did everything completely wrong, to the point where he almost destroyed his career before it began.

Roy Orbison was someone who made an unlikely rock and roll star. A quiet, unassuming, man, who rarely used an oath stronger than "Mercy", and wore dark glasses in later years to hide as much of his face as possible, he was the last person one would expect to be making music that was regarded as rebellious or exciting. And indeed, in his later years, the music he chose to make was very far from rebellious, though always rooted in rock and roll.

Orbison had grown up knowing he was going to be a singer. When he was six years old, his father had bought him a guitar and taught him the chords to "You Are My Sunshine", and by the age of ten he was already winning talent contests. But it was seeing the famous country singer Lefty Frizzell live that really convinced him.

It wasn't so much that Frizzell was a great performer – though he was pretty good, and he hugely influenced Orbison's vocal style. What really impressed young Roy Orbison, though, was seeing Frizzell, after the show, getting into a Cadillac. Orbison realised you could make real money just from singing, and started to make plans.

In his teens, he and a group of his friends formed a country and western band, the Wink Westerners (named after the small town they lived in). That band had various lineups, but it eventually settled into a two-guitar, bass, drums, and electric mandolin lineup of Orbison, Billy Pat Ellis, Jack Kenneally, Johnny Wilson, and James Morrow.

While Orbison was still in school, the band got their own radio show, one day a week, and became big enough that when the country star Slim Whitman came to town they were chosen as his backing group.

The band were primarily a country band, but like most bands of the time they would play whatever music the customers wanted to hear. In later years, Orbison would be able to pinpoint the exact moment he became a rock and roller – on New Year's Eve 1954. The band started playing "Shake, Rattle, and Roll", expecting it to finish dead on the stroke of midnight, but then Orbison looked at the clock and realised they'd started far too soon. That version of "Shake, Rattle, and Roll", which lasted for eight minutes, converted Roy Orbison. When he started playing it, rock and roll was just another form of music, but by the end he knew he wanted to play that kind of music forever. The Wink Westerners were quickly renamed the Teen Kings.

Orbison went off to university, where he heard a song called "Ooby Dooby" which was written by two classmates of his, Dick Penner and Wade Moore. They allegedly wrote it in a fifteen minute period, while on the roof of their frat house, and to be honest it sounds like fifteen minutes is about as long as it would take to write. It soon entered the set of the newly-named Teen Kings and became one of their most successful songs.

The Teen Kings soon got their own local TV series, to go with the local radio shows they already had. When the new country star Johnny Cash passed through town, he appeared on the Teen Kings' TV show, and Orbison asked him how to get signed to Sun Records. Cash gave Orbison the phone number for Sam Phillips, and told him to tell Phillips that Cash had sent him. He also advised Orbison that if he wanted to have any success as a musician, he should probably start singing in a lower register, and maybe change his name. Orbison never took that advice, and in later years he would joke with Cash about how terrible his advice was.

His advice about getting signed to Sun wasn't much better either – Orbison did indeed phone Sam Phillips and tell him Johnny Cash had said to call Phillips. Phillips responded by saying "Tell Johnny Cash he doesn't run Sun Records, I do" and slamming the phone down. So Sun Records seemed like a dead end. The Teen Kings were going to have to look elsewhere for a record contract.

So instead they went into the studio to audition for Columbia Records. They recorded two tracks at that initial session. One was "Ooby Dooby"; the other was a cover version of a song by the Clovers, "Hey, Miss Fannie".

At the time, the Teen Kings thought that they'd almost certainly get a contract with Columbia, but Columbia ended up turning them down. They did, however, like "Ooby Dooby", enough to give it to another group, Sid King and the Five Strings, who released it unsuccessfully as a single.

As they had been turned down now by both the major label Columbia and the large indie Sun, Roy and the band went into the studio with Norman Petty, a local Texas record producer, to record "Ooby Dooby" again, to be released as a single on the tiny indie label Je-Wel. It came out at almost exactly the same time as Sid King's version.

But then Sam Phillips had a change of heart. Roy still wanted to be on Sun, and pestered a local record shop owner who knew Phillips to play "Ooby Dooby" for him. Phillips eventually listened to the single and liked it, but thought that he could do a better job of it. He discovered that Orbison wasn't yet twenty-one, and so the contract he'd signed with Je-Wel was void. Phillips signed Orbison, got an injunction taken out against Je-Wel, preventing them from putting out any more copies of the single – only a few hundred ever got released – and quickly went into the studio to record a new version of the song.

And this sort of sums up the difference between Orbison's relationship with Sam Phillips and everyone else's. Every other successful musician who recorded for Sun Records recorded for them first, and owed their careers to Phillips. He'd given them the shot that no-one else would, and he'd moulded them into the artists that they would become. Even the ones who later fell out with Phillips always credited him with being the reason they'd had any success in the business.

Roy Orbison, on the other hand, had been discovered before Phillips. Phillips had turned him down, and he'd made a record somewhere else. That record was even with a producer who, in a little while, would be putting out rockabilly hits every bit as big as Phillips was. That meant that Roy Orbison would never feel, as Elvis or Johnny Cash or Carl Perkins did, that he owed his career to Sam Phillips.

The rerecorded version was, as far as Orbison's performance goes, almost identical to the original. Orbison was not a wild improviser like many of the artists with whom Phillips worked – he would work out his parts exactly, and stick to them. While Phillips would always claim in later life that his version of "Ooby Dooby" was vastly superior to the earlier one, most listeners would struggle to tell the difference.

Rather oddly, given Orbison's later career, it wasn't primarily his singing that impressed Phillips, but rather his guitar playing. Phillips would talk for the rest of his life about what a great guitarist Orbison was. Phillips would often get Orbison to play on records by other artists, and would later say that the only musician he knew who had a better sense of rhythm was Jerry Lee Lewis.

And Orbison *was* a great guitarist. He was similar to Chuck Berry in that he would play both rhythm and lead simultaneously – if you listen to the records he made where his guitar playing is prominent, you can hear him using the bass strings to keep a riff down, and then playing fills between his vocal lines.

But still, it would be several years before anyone in the record industry seemed to notice that Roy Orbison was, well, Roy Orbison.

The B-side, "Go Go Go", was recorded in a single take, and itself became a rockabilly classic – it would be one of the few rockabilly songs that Orbison would keep in his setlists in future years. It was co-written by Orbison and the band's drummer, Billy Pat Ellis, but it caused problems.

While Ellis had co-written the song, he wasn't credited on the label, which understandably caused him to get angry – it seemed like Roy was cheating him out of his royalties. And while the record had been made by Roy Orbison and the Teen Kings as a group, it seemed that all anyone was talking about was Roy Orbison, not the Teen Kings.

The group went out on tour, on a package with other Sun artists, and "Ooby Dooby" went to number fifty-nine in the pop charts and sold around two hundred thousand copies. This wasn't an amazing, ground-breaking level of success like some other Sun artists had had, but it was perfectly respectable, and was enough to see them go into the studio to record a follow-up, "Rockhouse".

"Rockhouse" was originally written by a young singer called Harold Jenkins, who was making recordings for Sun at the time, though those recordings didn't get released until after Jenkins became a country star under the name Conway Twitty. Orbison took Jenkins' demo and substantially reworked it, earning himself a co-writing credit.

The B-side was a song that Johnny Cash had written, called "Little Woolly Booger", renamed for Orbison's version to the rather more radio-friendly "You're My Baby".

"Rockhouse" didn't do very well, and the band were getting disgruntled. They felt that Sam Phillips didn't care about any of them, and they were also getting a bit sick of Roy himself, who they thought was taking too much of the spotlight. So they secretly made an agreement. At the start of a scheduled recording session, Orbison and Phillips went to the cafe next door to take a break. When they got back, they found that the Teen Kings had packed up all their gear and driven away. Roy no longer had a band.

He was absolutely devastated – the people he'd come up with as a teenager, the people he'd thought were his friends, had all deserted him. He'd been playing with these people for years, and now, just as they were starting to achieve some success, they'd decided to leave him. The session was cancelled, and Sam Phillips was so worried about Orbison that he invited the young man to stay in his house for what turned into a several-month-long stay. Phillips, who had himself suffered from severe depression, was worried about the young singer, and tried to give him life advice.

The advice that Phillips was giving Orbison had a profound effect on both Orbison and on Phillips' son Knox, who later said, "It was the first time I actually could see Sam giving someone he really cared about like Roy some hard advice — I mean, I was real young, but I thought, 'You know what? It's a different way he's saying it but it's the same advice he's been giving me. It's the same thing.' That was the first time I actually knew that Sam was just trying to make people better. I mean, he wasn't in the studio trying to inspire or record them. He could say the same thing that would teach you the same lesson if you were talking to him about charcoal or motorcycles. It was the same lesson."

For much of the next year, Orbison was essentially homeless. He spent most of his time on tour, but considered Memphis his home base, and stayed with either Sam Phillips, Johnny Cash, or Carl Perkins when he was "at home".

But he was starting to get bigger plans. He had already co-written a handful of songs, but he hadn't put serious thought into his songwriting. That changed when he went on a tour with Eddie Cochran and Gene Vincent. He realised that they – and the other people on the bill – had one hit each. Cochran would later have more, but still, Orbison wondered where those people's other hits were going to come from. Where were they going to find their material?

He didn't want to get into a position where he had to just keep playing the same hit every day for the rest of his life, and realised that the only way to ensure he would have a ready supply of new material was to write it himself, and so he started to take his songwriting seriously as his principal art. Given that the hits on Sun had dried up, in fact, he basically became a songwriter who happened to sing, rather than a singer who wrote some of his own songs.

While he continued making recordings for Sun, none of them did anything, and he later referred to some of them as among the worst records ever made. As Orbison was becoming less successful, Phillips increasingly palmed him off on his new assistant, Jack Clement, and Clement insisted on Orbison performing material for which he had no feeling. Orbison was starting to push to record ballads, but Clement knew that Roy Orbison just didn't have the voice for them.

But his songwriting was another matter. Sun artists started recording his stuff. Jerry Lee Lewis put out "Go Go Go" as the B-side to his big hit "Breathless", and the minor Sun artist Warren Smith recorded Roy's "So Long, I'm Gone".

That reached the lower reaches of the Hot 100, and so became the first thing that earned Roy some serious money since "Ooby Dooby" a year earlier. Songwriting was clearly the way forward, and he decided to write a song about his new wife, Claudette, which he pitched to the Everly Brothers when they were on a bill together, and which they decided to record.

We'll be talking about the Everly Brothers in the next volume, but the important thing to note right now is that they were a much bigger act than Roy Orbison was. Them performing one of Orbison's songs would be a massive break for him, but there was a catch. They had a deal with the publishing company Acuff-Rose that they would only perform songs that were published by that company, and Orbison had a contract with Sam Phillips that meant that Orbison's songs were all published by Phillips.

Orbison went to Phillips and explained the situation. He didn't want to record for Sun any more anyway – they weren't releasing most of what he was recording, he wasn't having any hits, and they didn't have the same ideas about what material he should be recording as he did. He wanted to assign the song to Acuff-Rose and give himself a chance at doing better than he had been.

Phillips was not happy about this. This was at almost exactly the same time that both Johnny Cash and Carl Perkins left Sun Records, and he suspected a degree of collusion between the three men – and he wasn't wrong in his suspicion. The three of them all thought that Phillips was not paying them enough royalties, was not telling them important business information, and was more interested in the latest new thing than in building the careers of people he'd already signed.

Phillips eventually made a suggestion which Orbison took up, though he later said that he didn't realise what the consequences would be. The deal was that Orbison could quit his contract, and sign with Acuff-Rose, but only by signing all the songwriting royalties for the songs he'd already recorded over to Phillips.

So Sam Phillips is now the credited songwriter for all the songs Orbison wrote and recorded during his time at Sun, and unsurprisingly Orbison resented this for the rest of his life. Most Sun artists came to believe that they had been treated badly in business dealings by Phillips, and that he hadn't properly recognised their talent. Roy Orbison, more than any of the others, actually had a case to answer here.

Sam Phillips never understood what he had in Roy Orbison until much later. With every other artist he had, he took someone raw and unsure of his own direction and moulded him into what Sam saw in him. With Orbison, he took an artist who was already a moderate success, and who had firm ideas, and kept him from doing the material that was good for him. He later said "I really have to take the blame for not bringing Roy to fruition."

As soon as the Everlys' version of "Claudette" came out, Orbison saw an immediate upswing in his fortunes. Two weeks after it came out, he called Wesley Rose at Acuff-Rose.

"How's the record doing?"

"Oh, it sold half a million already."

"Have I made any money?"

"Why, yes you have."

Roy bought a Cadillac, moved to Nashville, and quickly signed with RCA Records, who saw in him the potential to be the next Elvis. And it seemed he was following the same career path exactly, as his first recordings for RCA were with largely the same group of musicians who played on Elvis' big hits. There was no Scotty, Bill, or DJ, as they were all exclusive to Elvis, but Chet Atkins was on guitar, Floyd Cramer was on piano, and the Jordanaires were on backing vocals. But even though Roy had largely been signed on the basis of his songwriting ability, the songs they chose to record for him were once again not written by him and not his choice of material. This time they were all picked by Wesley Rose.

He was now being allowed to sing ballads, but they weren't the ballads that he wanted to be singing – they were the kind of song that anyone in the pop-country market could be singing. And still the producers didn't know how to deal with his voice. His RCA singles did even worse than his records on Sun, despite having the push of a major label behind him. Eventually the money from "Claudette" ran out, and he was dropped by RCA.

Chet Atkins, like Sam Phillips, just didn't get Roy Orbison. He would later say "We did some pretty good records, but they were typical

Nashville at that time, and we didn't reach out and try to do something different. I blame myself for that. I should have seen the greatness in him and the quality of his voice."

Orbison sold his Cadillac, and moved out of Nashville, and back to West Texas. It looked like his career was over, and he would spend his life exactly as he'd hoped he wouldn't, as a musician who'd had one minor hit and never did anything else.

But then he met a couple of people who would change the course of his life forever. But that's a story for volume two...

"I Gotta Know"

Today we're going to talk about someone whose career as a live performer spans more than seventy years. Wanda Jackson started performing in 1948, and she finally retired from live performance in March 2019, though she is, at the time of writing, working on a new album. She is only the second performer we've dealt with who is still alive and working, and she has the longest career of any of them.

Wanda Jackson is, simply, the queen of rockabilly, and she's a towering figure in the genre.

Jackson was born in Oklahoma, but as this was the tail-end of the great depression, she and her family migrated to California when she was small, as stragglers in the great migration that permanently changed California.

The migration of the Okies in the 1930s is a huge topic, and one that I don't have the space to explain in this podcast – if you're interested in it, I'd recommend as a starting point listening to the episode of the great country music podcast Cocaine & Rhinestones on "Okie From Muskogee"[15]. The very, very, shortened version is that bad advice as to best farming practices created an environmental disaster on an almost apocalyptic scale across the whole middle of America, right at the point that the country was also going through the worst economic disaster in its history. As entire states became almost uninhabitable in what became known as the Dust Bowl, three and a half million people moved from the Great Plains to elsewhere in the US, and a large number of them moved to California, where no matter what state they actually came from they became known as "Okies".

---

[15] Available at https://cocaineandrhinestones.com/

But the thing to understand about the Okies for this purpose is that they were a despised underclass – and as we've seen, members of despised underclasses often created the most exciting and innovative music.

The music made by the Okies who moved to California was far more raucous than the country music that was popular in the Eastern states, and it had a huge admixture of blues and boogie woogie in it. If you remember back in chapter three, we talked about Western Swing and the distinction in the thirties and forties between country music and western music. The "Western" in that music came from the wild west, but it also referred to the west coast and the migrants from the Dust Bowl. Of the two biggest names in Western Swing, one, Bob Wills, was from Texas but moved to Oklahoma, while the other, Spade Cooley, was from Oklahoma but moved to California.

It was the Western Swing that was being made by Dust Bowl migrants in California in the 1940s that, when it made its way eastwards to Tennessee, transmuted itself into rockabilly. And that is the music that young Wanda Jackson was listening to when she was tiny. Her father, who she absolutely adored, was a fan of Bob Wills, Spade Cooley, and Tex Williams, as well as of Jimmie Rodgers' hillbilly music and the blues. They lived in Greenfield, a town a few miles away from Bakersfield, where her father worked, and if any of you know anything at all about country music that will tell you a lot in itself. Bakersfield would become, in the 1950s, the place where musicians like Buck Owens, Merle Haggard, and Wynn Stewart, most of them from Dust Bowl migrant families themselves, developed a tough form of honky-tonk country and western that was influenced by hillbilly boogie and Western Swing.

Wanda Jackson spent the formative years of her childhood in the same musical and social environment as those musicians, and while she and her family moved back to Oklahoma a few years later, she had already been exposed to that style of music. At the time, when anyone went out to dance, it was to live music, and since her parents couldn't afford babysitters, when they went out, as they did most weekends, they took Wanda with them, so between the ages of five and ten she seems to have seen almost every great Western band of the forties.

Her first favourite as a kid was Spade Cooley, who was, along with Bob Wills, considered the greatest Western Swing bandleader of all (though his music, which to my ears is mediocre, has been rightly overshadowed by his murder of his wife – and I advise you not to look for details of that murder).

The other artist she loved though was a sibling group called The Maddox Brothers and Rose, who were a group that bridged the gap between Western Swing and the newer Bakersfield sound. The Maddox Brothers and Rose were also poor migrants who'd moved to California, though in their case they'd travelled just before the inrush of Okies rather than at the tail end of it. They're another of those groups who are often given the credit for having made the first rock and roll record, although as we've often discussed that's a largely meaningless claim. They were, however, one of the big influences both on the Bakersfield sound and on the music that became rockabilly.

Wanda loved the Maddox Brothers and Rose, and in particular she loved their stage presence – the shiny costumes they wore, and the feistiness of Rose, in particular. She decided before she was even in school that she wanted to be "a girl singer", as she put it, just like Rose Maddox.

When she was six, her father bought her a guitar from the Sears Roebuck catalogue and started teaching her chords. He played a little guitar and fiddle, and the two of them would play together every night. They'd sit together and try to work out the chords for songs they knew from the radio or records, and Wanda's mother would write down the chords in a notebook for them.

She also taught herself to yodel, since that was something that all the country and western singers at the time would do, and had done ever since the days of Jimmie Rodgers in the late twenties and early thirties. By the time she was in her early teens, she was regularly performing for her friends at parties, and her friends dared her to audition for a local radio show that played country music and had a local talent section. Her friends all went with her to the station, and she played Jimmie Rodgers' "Blue Yodel #6" for the DJ who ran the show.

To her shock, but not the shock of her friends, the DJ loved her sound, and gave her a regular spot on the local talent section of his show, which in turn led to her getting her own fifteen-minute radio show, in which she would sing popular country hits of the time period. One of the people whose songs she would perform on a regular basis was Hank Thompson.

Thompson was a honky-tonk singer who performed a pared-down version of the Bob Wills style of Western Swing. Thompson's music was using the same rhythms and instrumentation as Wills, but with much more focus on the vocals and the song than on instrumental solos. Thompson's music was one of several precursors to the music that became rockabilly, though he was most successful with mid-tempo ballads like "The Wild Side of Life".

Thompson, like Wanda, lived in Oklahoma, and he happened to be driving one day and hear her show on the radio. He phoned her up at the station and asked her if she would come and perform with his band that Saturday night. When she told him she'd have to ask her mother, he laughed at first – he hadn't realised she was only fourteen, because her voice made her sound so much older.

At this time, it was normal for bands that toured to have multiple featured singers and to perform in a revue style, rather than to have a single lead vocalist – there were basically two types of tour that happened: package tours featuring multiple different acts doing their own things, and revues, where one main act would introduce several featured guests to join them on stage. Johnny Otis and James Brown, for example, both ran revue shows at various points, and Hank Thompson's show seems also to have been in this style.

Jackson had never played with a band before, and by her own account she wasn't very good when she guested with Thompson's band for the first time. But Thompson had faith in her. He couldn't take her on the road, because she was still so young she had to go to school, but every time he played Oklahoma he'd invite her to do a few numbers with his band, mentoring her and teaching her on stage how to perform with other musicians.

Thompson also invited Jackson to appear on his local TV show, which led to her getting a TV show of her own in the Oklahoma area, and she became part of a loose group of locally-popular musicians, including the future homophobic campaigner against human rights Anita Bryant.

While she was still in high school, Thompson recorded demos of her singing and took them to his producer, Ken Nelson, at Capitol Records. Nelson liked her voice, but when he found out she was under eighteen he decided to pass on recording her, just due to the legal complications and the fact that she'd not yet finished school.

Instead, Jackson was signed to Decca Records, where she cut her first recordings with members of Thompson's band. Her first single was a duet with another featured singer from Thompson's band, Billy Gray. Thompson, who was running the session, basically forced Jackson to sing it against her objections. She didn't have a problem with the song itself, but she didn't want to make her name from a duet, rather than as a solo artist.

She might not have been happy with the recording at first, but she was feeling better about it by the time she started her senior year in High School with a top ten country single.

Her followups were less successful, and she became unhappy with the way her career was going. In particular she was horrified when she first played the Grand Ole Opry. She was told she couldn't go onstage in the dress she was wearing, because her shoulders were uncovered and that was obscene – at this time, Jackson was basically the only country singer in the business who was trying to look glamorous rather than like a farmgirl – and then, when she did get on stage, wearing a jacket, she was mocked by a couple of the comedy acts, who stood behind her making fun of her throughout her entire set. Clearly the country establishment wasn't going to get along with her at all.

But then she left school, and became a full-time musician, and she made a decision which would have an enormous effect on her. Her father was her manager, but if she was going to get more gigs and perform as a solo artist rather than just doing the occasional show with Hank Thompson, she needed a booking agent, and neither she nor her father had an idea how to get one.

So they did what seemed like the most obvious thing to them, and bought a copy of *Billboard* and started looking through the ads. They eventually found an ad from a booking agent named Bob Neal, in

Memphis, and phoned him up, explaining that Wanda was a recording artist for Decca.

Neal had heard her records, which had been locally popular in Memphis, and was particularly looking for a girl singer to fill out the bill on a tour he was promoting with a new young singer he managed, named Elvis Presley.

Backstage after her support slot on the first show of the tour, she and her father heard a terrible screaming coming from the auditorium. They thought at first that there must have been a fire, and Wanda's father went out to investigate, telling her not to come with him. He came back a minute later telling her, "You've got to come see this".

The screaming was, of course, at Elvis, and immediately Wanda knew that he was not any ordinary country singer. The two of them started dating, and Elvis even gave Wanda his ring, which is still in her possession, and while they eventually drifted apart, he had a profound influence on her.

Her father was not impressed with Elvis' performance, saying "That boy's got to get his show in order... He's all over the stage messin' around. And he's got to stop slurrin' his words, too."

Wanda, on the other hand, was incredibly impressed with him, and as the two of them toured – on a bill which also included Bob Neal's other big act of the time, Johnny Cash – he would teach her how to be more of a rock and roller like him. In particular, he taught her to strum the acoustic guitar with a single strum, rather than to hit each string individually, which was the style of country players at the time.

Meanwhile, her recording career was flagging – she hadn't had another hit with any of her solo recordings, and she was starting to wonder if Decca was the right place for her. She did, though, have a hit as a songwriter, with a song called "Without Your Love", which she'd written for Bobby Lord, a singer who appeared with her on the radio show Ozark Jubilee.

That song had gone to the top ten in the country charts, and turned out to be Lord's only hit single.

But while she could come up with a hit for him, she wasn't having hits herself, and she decided that she wanted to leave Decca. Her contract was up, and while they did have the option to extend it for another year and were initially interested in exercising the option, Decca agreed to let her go.

Meanwhile, Wanda was also thinking about what kind of music she wanted to make in the future. Elvis had convinced her that she should move into rockabilly, but she didn't know how to do it. She talked about this to Thelma Blackmon, the mother of one of her schoolfriends, who had written a couple of songs for her previously, and Blackmon came back with a song called "I Gotta Know", which Jackson decided would be perfect to restart her career.

At this point Hank Thompson went to Ken Nelson, and told him that that underage singer he'd liked was no longer underage, and would he be interested in signing her?

He definitely was interested, and he took her into the Capitol Tower to record with a group of session musicians who he employed for as many of his West Coast sessions as possible, and who were at that point just beginning to create what later became the Bakersfield sound.

The musicians on that session were some of the best in the country music field – Jelly Sanders on fiddle, Joe Maphis on guitar, and the legendary Ralph Mooney on steel guitar, and they were perfect for recording what would become a big country hit.

But "I Gotta Know" was both country and rock and roll. While the choruses are definitely country, the verses are firmly in the rock and roll genre. Now, I'm indebted to the website "Women in Rock & Roll's First Wave"[16] for this observation, but this kind of genre-mixing was very common particularly with women, and particularly with women who had previously had careers outside rock and roll and were trying to transition into it. While male performers in that situation would generally jump in head first and come up with an embarrassment like Perry Como's version of "Ko Ko Mo", female performers would do something rather different.

They would, in fact, tend to do what Jackson did here, and combine the two genres, either by having a verse in one style and a chorus in the other, as Wanda does, or in other ways, as in for example Kay Starr's "Rock and Roll Waltz".

---

[16]https://www.womeninrockproject.org/

Starr is a particularly good example here, because she's doing what a lot of female performers were doing at the time, which is trying to lace the recording with enough irony and humour that it could be taken as either a record in the young persons' style parodying the old persons' music, or a record in the older style mocking the new styles. By sitting on the fence in this way and being ambiguous enough, the established stars could back down if this rock and roll music turned out to be just another temporary fad.

Jackson isn't quite doing that, but with her Elvis-style hiccups on the line "I gotta know, I gotta know", she comes very close to parody, in a way that could easily be written off if the experiment had failed.

The experiment didn't fail, however, and "I Gotta Know" became Jackson's biggest hit of the fifties, making its way to number fifteen on the country charts – rather oddly, given that she was clearly repositioning herself for the rockabilly market, it seemed to sell almost solely to the country market, and didn't cross over the way that Carl Perkins or Gene Vincent did.

Her next single could have been the one that cemented her reputation as the greatest female rockabilly star of all, had it not been for one simple mistake. The song "Hot Dog! That Made Him Mad!" had been a favourite in her stage act for years, and she would let out a tremendous growl on the title line when she got to it, which would always get audiences worked up.

Unfortunately, she horrified Ken Nelson in the studio by taking a big drink of milk while all the session musicians were on a coffee break. She hadn't realised what milk does to a singer's throat, and when they came to record the song she couldn't get her voice to do the growl that had always worked on stage. The result was still a good record, but it wasn't the massive success it might otherwise have been.

After that failed, Ken Nelson floundered around for quite a while trying to find something else that could work for Jackson. She kept cutting rockabilly tracks, but they never quite had the power of her stage performances, and meanwhile Nelson was making mistakes in what material he brought in, just as he was doing at the same time with Gene Vincent. Just like with Vincent, whenever Wanda brought in her own material, or material she'd picked to cover by other people, it worked fine, but when Nelson brought in something it would go down like a lead balloon.

Probably the worst example was a terrible attempt to capitalise on the current calypso craze, a song called "Don'a Wanna", which was written by Boudleaux Bryant, one of the great songwriters of the fifties, but which wouldn't have been his best effort even before it was given a racist accent at Nelson's suggestion (and which Jackson cringed at doing even at the time, let alone sixty years later).

Much better was "Cool Love", which Jackson co-wrote herself, with her friend Vicki Countryman, Thelma Blackmon's daughter. That one is possibly too closely modelled after Elvis' recent hits, right down to the backing vocals, but it features a great Buck Owens guitar solo, it's fun, and Jackson is clearly engaged with the material.

But just like all the other records since "I Wanna Know", "Cool Love" did nothing on the charts — and indeed it wouldn't be until 1960 that Jackson would reach the charts again in the USA. But when she did, it would be with recordings she'd made years earlier, during the time period we're talking about now.

And before she did, she would have her biggest success of all, and become the first rock and roll star about whom the cliché really was true — even though she was having no success in her home country, she was big in Japan.

But that's a story for volume two. . .

"Train Kept A-Rollin'"

There's a tradition in rock and roll music of brothers who constantly fight, but make great music together, and we'll see plenty of them as we go through the next few decades – the Everly Brothers, Ray and Dave Davies, the Beach Boys. . . rock and roll would be very different without sibling rivalry. But few pairs of brothers have fought as violently and as often as Johnny and Dorsey Burnette. The first time Roy Orbison met them, he was standing in a Memphis radio station, chatting with Elvis Presley, and waiting for a lift. When the lift doors opened, inside the lift were the Burnette brothers, in the middle of a fist-fight.

When Dorsey was about eight years old and Johnny six, their mother bought them both guitars. By the end of the day, both guitars had been broken – over each other's heads.

And their fights were not just the minor fights one might expect from young men, but serious business. Both of them were trained boxers, and in Dorsey Burnette's case he was a professional who became Golden Gloves champion of the South in 1950, and had once fought Sonny Liston. A fight between the Burnette brothers was a real fight.

They'd grown up around Lauderdale Court, the same apartment block where Elvis Presley spent his teenage years, and they used to hang around together and sing with a gang of teenage boys that included Bill Black's brother Johnny. Elvis would, as a teenager, hang around on the outskirts of their little group, singing along with them, but not really part of the group – the Burnette brothers were as likely to bully him as they were to encourage him to be part of the gang, and while they became friendly later on, Elvis was always more of a friend-of-friends than he was an actual friend of theirs, even when he was a colleague of Dorsey's at Crown Electric. He was a little bit younger than them, and not the most sociable of people, and more importantly he didn't like their aggression – Elvis would jokingly refer to them as the Daltons, after the outlaw gang,

Another colleague at Crown Electric was a man named Paul Burlison, who also boxed, and had been introduced to Dorsey by Lee Denson, who had taught both Dorsey and Elvis their first guitar chords. Burlison also played the guitar, and had played in many small bands over the late forties and early fifties. In particular, one of the bands he was in had had its own regular fifteen-minute show on a local radio station, and their show was on next to a show presented by the blues singer Howlin' Wolf. Burlison's guitar playing would later show many signs of being influenced by Wolf's electric blues, just as much as by the country and western music his early groups were playing. Some sources even say that Burlison played on some of Wolf's early recordings at the Sun studios, though most of the sessionographies I've seen for Wolf say otherwise.

The three of them formed a group in 1952, the Rhythm Rangers, with Burlison on lead guitar, Dorsey Burnette on double bass, and Johnny Burnette on rhythm guitar and lead vocals. A year later, they changed their name to the Rock and Roll Trio.

While they were called the Rock and Roll Trio, they were still basically a country band, and their early setlists included songs like Hank Snow's "I'm Moving On". That one got dropped from their setlist after an ill-fated trip to Nashville. They wanted to get on the Grand Ole Opry, and so they drove up, found Snow, who was going to be on that night's show, and asked him if he could get them on to the show. Snow explained to them that it had taken him twenty years in the business to work his way up to being on the Grand Ole Opry, and he couldn't just get three random people he'd never met before on to the show.

Johnny Burnette replied "Fuck you", and then they turned round and drove back to Memphis. They never played a Hank Snow song live again.

It wasn't long after that, in 1953, that they recorded their first single, "You're Undecided", for a tiny label called Von Records in Boonville, Mississippi. Around this time they also wrote a song called "Rockabilly Boogie", which they didn't get to record until 1957. That has been claimed as the first use of the word "rockabilly", and Billy Burnette, Dorsey's son, says they coined the word based on his name and that of Johnny's son Rocky.

Now, it seems much more likely to me that the origin of the word is the obvious one – that it's a portmanteau of the words "rock" and "hillbilly", to describe rocking hillbilly music – but those *were* the names of their kids, so I suppose it's just about possible.

Their 1953 single was not a success, and they spent the next few years playing in honky-tonks. They also regularly played the Saturday Night Jamboree at the Goodwyn Institute Auditorium, a regular country music show that was occasionally broadcast on the same station that Burlison's old bands had performed on, KWEM. Most of the musicians in Memphis who went on to make important early rockabilly records would play at the Jamboree, but more important than the show itself was the backstage area, where musicians would jam, show each other new riffs they'd come up with, and pass ideas back and forth. Those backstage jam sessions were the making of the Rock and Roll Trio, as they were for many of the other rockabilly acts in the area.

Their big break came in early 1956, when they appeared on the *Ted Mack Amateur Hour* and won three times in a row. The *Ted Mack Amateur Hour* was a TV series that was in many ways the *X Factor* or *American Idol* of the 1950s. The show launched the careers of Pat Boone, Ann-Margret, and Gladys Knight among others, and when the Rock and Roll Trio won for the third time (at the same time their old neighbour Elvis was on the Ed Sullivan show on another channel) they got signed to Coral Records, a subsidiary of Decca Records, one of the biggest major labels in the USA at the time.

Their first attempt at recording didn't go particularly well. Their initial session for Coral was in New York, and when they got there they were surprised to find a thirty-two piece orchestra waiting for them, none of whom had any more clue about playing rock and roll music than the Rock and Roll Trio had about playing orchestral pieces.

They did record one track with the orchestra, "Shattered Dreams", although that song didn't get released until many years later. But after recording that song they sent all the musicians home except the drummer, who played on the rest of the session. They'd simply not got the rock and roll sound they wanted when working with all those musicians. They didn't need them.

They didn't have quite enough songs for the session, and needed another uptempo number, and so Dorsey went out into the hallway and quickly wrote a song called "Tear It Up", which became the A-side of their first Coral single, with the B-side being a new version of "You're Undecided".

While Dorsey wrote that song, he decided to split the credit, as they always did, four ways between the three members of the band and their manager. This kind of credit-splitting is normal in a band-as-gang, and right then that's what they were – a gang, all on the same side. That was soon going to change, and credit was going to be one of the main reasons.

But that was all to come. For now, the Rock and Roll Trio weren't happy at all about their recordings. They didn't want to make any more records in New York with a bunch of orchestral musicians who didn't know anything about their music. They wanted to make records in Nashville, and so they were booked into Owen Bradley's studio, the same one where Gene Vincent made his first records, and where Wanda Jackson recorded when she was in Nashville rather than LA. Bradley knew how to get a good rockabilly sound, and they were sure they were going to get the sound they'd been getting live when they recorded there.

In fact, they got something altogether different, and better than that sound, and it happened entirely by accident.

On their way down to Nashville from New York they played a few shows, and one of the first they played was in Philadelphia. At that show, Paul Burlison dropped his amplifier, loosening one of the vacuum tubes inside. The distorted sound it gave was like nothing he'd ever heard, and while he replaced the tube, he started loosening it every time he wanted to get that sound.

So when they got to Nashville, they went into Owen Bradley's studio and, for possibly the first time ever, deliberately recorded a distorted guitar.

I say possibly because, as so often happens with these things, a lot of people seem to have had the same idea around the same time, but the Rock and Roll Trio's recordings do seem to be the first ones where the distortion was deliberately chosen. Obviously we've already looked at "Rocket "88"'", which did have a distorted guitar, and again that was caused by an accident, but the difference there was that the accident happened on the day of the recording with no time to fix it. This was Burlison choosing to use the result of the accident at a point where he could have easily had the amplifier in perfect working order, had he wanted to.

At these sessions, the trio were augmented by a few studio musicians from the Nashville "A-Team", the musicians who made most of the country hits of the time. While Dorsey Burnette played bass live, he preferred playing guitar, so in the studio he was on an additional rhythm guitar while Bob Moore played the bass. Buddy Harmon was on drums, while session guitarist Grady Martin added another electric guitar to complement Burlison's.

The presence of these musicians has led some to assume that they played everything on the records, and that the Rock and Roll Trio only added their voices, but that seems to be very far from the case. Certainly Burlison's guitar style is absolutely distinctive, and the effect he puts on his guitar is absolutely unlike anything else that you hear from Grady Martin at this point, though Martin did, later, introduce the fuzztone to country music, with his playing on records like Marty Robbins' "Don't Worry". But that was a good five years after the Rock and Roll Trio sessions, and the most likely explanation is that Martin was inspired to add fuzz to his guitar by Paul Burlison, rather than deciding to add it on one session and then not using it again for several years.

The single they recorded at that Nashville session was one that would echo down the decades, influencing everyone from the Beatles to Aerosmith to Screaming Lord Sutch and the Savages.

The A-side, "Honey Hush", was originally written and recorded by Big Joe Turner three years earlier. It's not one of Turner's best, to be honest – leaning too heavily on the misogyny that characterised too much of his work – but over the years it has been covered by everyone from Chuck Berry to Paul McCartney, Elvis Costello to Jerry Lee Lewis. The Rock and Roll Trio's cover version is probably the best of these, and certainly the most exciting, and inspired most of those covers, but the song that really mattered to people was the B-side, a track called "Train Kept A-Rollin'".

"Train Kept A-Rollin'", like many R&B songs, has a long history, and is made up of elements that one can trace back to the 1920s, or earlier in some cases. But the biggest inspiration for the track is a song called "Cow Cow Boogie", which was originally recorded by Ella Mae Morse in 1942, but which was written for Ella Fitzgerald to sing in an Abbot and Costello film, but cut from her appearance. Fitzgerald eventually recorded her own hit version of the song in 1943, backed by the Ink Spots, with the pianist Bill Doggett accompanying them.

That song was adapted by the jump band singer Tiny Bradshaw, under the title "Train Kept A-Rollin'". Bradshaw changed the song's subject, from meeting a cowboy who sang boogie songs to a train journey, but kept the melody line and some of the rhyme scheme.

And that in turn was the basis for the Rock and Roll Trio's version of the song, which they radically rearranged to feature an octave-doubled guitar riff, apparently invented by Dorsey Burnette, but played simultaneously by Burlison and Martin, with Burlison's guitar fuzzed up and distorted. This version of the song would become a classic.

The single wasn't a success, but its B-side got picked up by the generation of British guitar players that came after, and from then it became a standard of rock music. It was covered by Screaming Lord Sutch and the Savages, the Yardbirds, Shakin' Stevens and the Sunsets, Aerosmith, Motorhead... You get the idea. By adding a distorted guitar riff, the Rock and Roll Trio had performed a kind of alchemy, which turned a simple novelty cowboy song into something that would make the repertoire of every band that ever wanted to play as loud as possible and to scream at the top of their voices the words "the train kept rolling all night long".

Sadly, the Rock and Roll Trio didn't last much longer. While they had always performed as the Rock and Roll Trio, Coral Records decided to release their recordings as by "Johnny Burnette and the Rock and Roll Trio", and the other two members were understandably furious. They were a band, not just Johnny Burnette's backing musicians.

Dorsey was the first to quit – he left the band a few days before they were due to appear in *Rock! Rock! Rock!*, a cheap exploitation film starring Alan Freed. They got Johnny Black in to replace him for the film shoot, and Dorsey rejoined shortly afterwards, but the cracks had already appeared.

They recorded one further session, but the tracks from that weren't even released as by Johnny Burnette and the Rock and Roll Trio, just by Johnny Burnette, and that was the final straw. The group split up, and went their separate ways.

Johnny remained signed to Coral Records as a solo artist, but when he and Dorsey both moved, separately, to LA, they ended up working together as songwriters.

Dorsey was contracted as a solo artist to Imperial Records, who had a new teen idol star who needed material. Ricky Nelson had had an unexpected hit after singing on his parents' TV show, and as a result he was suddenly being promoted as a rock and roll star. Dorsey and Johnny wrote a whole string of top ten hits for Nelson, songs like "Believe What You Say", "Waiting In School", "It's Late", and "Just a Little Too Much".

They also started recording for Imperial as a duo, as the Burnette Brothers, but that was soon stopped by Coral, who wanted to continue marketing Johnny as a solo artist, and they both started pursuing separate solo careers. Dorsey eventually had a minor hit of his own, "There Was a Tall Oak Tree", which made the top thirty in 1960. He made a few more solo records in the early sixties, and after becoming a born-again Christian in the early seventies he started a new, successful, career as a country singer, eventually receiving a "most promising newcomer" award from the Academy of Country Music in 1973, twenty years after his career started. He died in 1979 of a heart attack.

Johnny Burnette eventually signed to Liberty Records, and had a string of hits that, like Dorsey's, were in a very different style from the Rock and Roll Trio records. His biggest hit, and the one that most people associate with him to this day, was "You're Sixteen, You're Beautiful, And You're Mine".

That song is, of course, a perennial hit that most people still know almost sixty years later, but none of Johnny's solo records had anything like the power and passion of the Rock and Roll Trio recordings. And sadly we'll never know if he would regain that passion, as in 1964 he died in a boating accident.

Paul Burlison, the last member of the trio, gave up music once the trio split up, and became an electrician again. He briefly joined Johnny on one tour in 1963, but otherwise stayed out of the music business until the 1980s. He then got back into performing, and started a new lineup of the Rock amd Roll Trio, featuring Johnny Black, who had briefly replaced Dorsey in the group, and Tony Austin, the drummer who had joined with them on many tour dates after they got a recording contract.

He later joined "the Sun Rhythm Section", a band made up of many of the musicians who had played on classic rockabilly records, including Stan Kesler, Jimmy Van Eaton, Sonny Burgess, and DJ Fontana.

Burlison released his only solo album in 1997. That album was called *Train Kept A-Rollin'*, and featured a remake of that classic song, with Rocky and Billy Burnette – Johnny and Dorsey's sons – on vocals. He kept playing rockabilly until he died in 2003, aged seventy-four.

"Blueberry Hill"

This is the last chapter in which we're going to look at Fats Domino, although he will be mentioned in future ones. He was the one star from the pre-rock days of R&B to last and thrive, and even become bigger, in the rock and roll era, and he was, other than Elvis Presley, by far the most successful of the first wave of rock and roll stars.

And this points to something interesting – something which we haven't really pointed out as much as you might expect.

Because of that first wave of rock and rollers, by late 1956 there were only Elvis and the black R&B stars left as rock and roll stars on the US charts. The wave of white rockabilly acts that had hits throughout 1955 and 56 had all fizzled – Carl Perkins, Gene Vincent, and Bill Haley would between them never have another major hit in the US, though all of them would have success in other countries, and make important music over the next few years. Johnny Cash would have more hits, but he would increasingly be marketed as a country music star.

If we're talking about actual rock and roll hits rising to decent positions in the charts, by late 1956 you're looking at acts like Little Richard, Chuck Berry, and Fats Domino, with only Elvis left of the rockabillies.

Of course, very shortly afterwards, there would come a second wave of white rock and rollers, who would permanently change the music, and by the time we get to mid-1957 we'll be in a period where white man with guitar is the default image for rock and roll star, but in late 1956, that default image was a black man with a piano, and the black man with a piano who was selling the most records, by far, was Fats Domino.

When we left Domino, he had just had his breakout rock and roll hit, with "Ain't That a Shame". He was so successful that Imperial Records actually put out an album by him, rather than just singles, for the first time in the six years he'd been recording for them. This was a bigger deal than it sounds – rhythm and blues artists hardly ever put out albums in the fifties. The sales of their records weren't even normally directly to their audiences – they were to jukebox manufacturers.

So when Imperial put out an album, that was a sign that something had changed with Domino's audience – he was selling to white people with money. The black audience, for the most part, were still buying 78s, not even 45s – they were generally relatively poor, and not the type of people to upgrade their record players while the old ones still worked.

(This is obviously a huge generalisation, but it's true in so far as any generalisations are true.)

Meanwhile, the young white rock and roll audience that had developed all of a sudden between 1954 and 1956 was mostly buying the new 45rpm singles, but at least some of them were also buying LPs – enough of them that artists like Elvis were selling on the format.

Domino's first album, *Rock and Rollin' With Fats Domino*, was made up almost entirely of previously released material – mostly hit singles he'd had in the few years before the rock and roll boom took off, and including the songs we've looked at before. It was followed only three months later by a follow-up, imaginatively titled *Fats Domino Rock and Rollin'*. That one was largely made up of outtakes and unreleased tracks from 1953, but when it came out in April 1956 it sold twenty thousand copies in its first week on release.

That doesn't sound a lot now, but for an album aimed at a teenage audience, by a black artist, in 1956, and featuring only one hit single, that was quite an extraordinary achievement.

But Domino's commercial success in 1956 was very much overshadowed by other events, which had everything to do with the racial attitudes of the time. Because believe it or not, Fats Domino's shows were often disrupted by riots.

We've been talking about 1956 for a while, and dealing with black artists, without having really mentioned just what a crucial time this was in the history of the civil rights struggle. The murder of Emmett Till, supposedly for whistling at a white woman, had been in August 1955. Rosa Parks had refused to get to the back of the bus in December 1955, and in early 1956 a campaign of white supremacist terrorism against black people stepped up, with the firebombing of several churches and of the houses of civil rights leaders including Dr. Martin Luther King.

This, as much as anything musical, is the context you need to understand why rock and roll was seen as so revolutionary in 1956 in particular. White teenagers were listening to music by black musicians, and even imitating that music themselves, right at the point where people were having to start taking sides for or against racial justice and human decency. A large chunk of white America was more worried about the "inappropriate" behaviour of people like Rosa Parks than about the "legitimate concerns" of the firebombers.

And this attitude was also showing up in the reaction to music. In April 1956 Nat King Cole was injured on stage when a mob of white supremacists attacked him. Cole was one of the least politically vocal black entertainers, and he was appearing before an all-white audience, but he was a black man playing with a white backing band, and that was enough for him to be a target for attempted murder.

And this is the background against which you have to look at the reports of violence at Fats Domino shows. The riots which broke out at his shows throughout that year were blamed in contemporary news reports on his "pulsating jungle rhythms" – and there's not even an attempt made to hide the racism in statements like that – but there was little shocking about Domino's actual music at the time.

In fact, in 1956, Domino seemed to be trying to cross over to the country and older pop audience, by performing old standards from decades earlier. His first attempt at doing so became a top twenty pop hit. "My Blue Heaven" had originally been a hit in 1927 for the crooner Gene Austin. Domino's version gave it a mild R&B flavour, and it became a double-sided hit with "I'm in Love Again" on the other side.

And for the rest of the year, Domino would repeat this formula – one side of each of his singles would be written by Domino or his producer Dave Bartholomew, while the other side would be a song from twenty to forty years earlier. His single releases for the next eighteen months or so would include on them such standards as "I'm in the Mood for Love", "As Time Goes By", and "When My Dreamboat Comes Home".

And so, this is the music that was supposedly to blame for riots. And riots did follow Domino around everywhere he went. In Roanoake, Virginia, for example, in May, Domino was playing to a segregated crowd – whites in the balcony, black people on the floor. The way segregation worked when it came to rock and roll or R&B concerts was simple – whichever race the promoter thought would be more likely to come got the floor, the race which would have fewer audience members got the balcony.

But in this case, the promoters underestimated how many white people were now listening to this new music. The balcony filled up, and a lot of white teenagers went down and joined the black people on the ground floor. Towards the end of the show, someone in the balcony, incensed at the idea of black and white people dancing together, threw a whisky bottle at the crowd below. Soon whisky bottles were flying through the air, and the riot in the audience spread to the streets around.

The New York Times blamed the black audience members, even though it had been a white person who'd thrown the first bottle. The American Legion, which owned the concert venue, decided that the simplest solution was just to ban mixed audiences altogether – they'd either have all-white or all-black audiences.

Another riot broke out in San Jose in July, when someone threw a string of lit firecrackers into the audience. In the ensuing riot, a thousand beer bottles were broken, twelve people were arrested, and another twelve needed medical treatment.

In Houston, Domino played another show where white people were in the balcony and black people were on the dancefloor below. Some of the white people decided to join the black dancers, at which point a black policeman – trying to avoid another riot because of "race mixing" – said that everyone had to sit down and no-one could dance. But then a white cop overruled him and said that only white people could dance. Domino refused to carry on playing if black people weren't allowed to dance, too, and while that show didn't turn violent, a dozen people were arrested for threatening the police.

This is the context in which Domino was performing, and this is the context in which he had his biggest hit.

The song that was meant to be the hit was "Honey Chile", a new original which Domino got to feature in an exploitation film, *Shake, Rattle, and Rock*.

At the same session where he recorded that, he tried to record another old standard, with disappointing results.

"Blueberry Hill" was originally written in 1940 by Vincent Rose, Larry Stock, and Al Lewis. As with many songs of the time, it was recorded simultaneously by dozens of artists, but it was the Glenn Miller Orchestra who had the biggest hit with it.

After Glenn Miller, Gene Autry had also had a hit with the song. We've talked before about Autry, and how he was the biggest Western music star of the late thirties and early forties, and influenced everyone from Les Paul to Bo Diddley. Given Domino's taste for country and western music, it's possible that Autry's version was the first version of the song he came to love. But Domino was inspired to cover the song by Louis Armstrong's recording. Armstrong was, of course, another legend of New Orleans music, and his version, from 1949, had come out after Domino had already started his own career.

Domino loved Armstrong's version, and had wanted to record it for a long time, but when they got into the studio the band couldn't get through a whole take of the song. Dave Bartholomew, who hadn't been keen on recording the song anyway, said at the end of the session, "We got nuthin'".

But Bunny Robyn, the engineer at the session, thought it was salvageable. He edited together a version from bits of half-finished takes, and thanks to the absolutely metronomic time sense of Earl Palmer, he managed to do it so well that after more than thirty years of listening to the record, I'm still not certain exactly where the join is. I *think* it's just before he starts the second middle eight, just before he sings "the wind in the willow" – there's a slight change of sonic ambience there – but I wouldn't swear to it.

After Robyn edited that version together, Dave Bartholomew tried to stop it from being released, telling Lew Chudd, the owner of the record label, that releasing it would ruin Domino's career forever.

He couldn't have been more wrong. The song became Domino's biggest hit, rising to number two in the pop charts, and Bartholomew later admitted it had been a huge mistake for him to try to block it, saying that his horn arrangement for the song would be the thing he would be remembered for, and telling Domino's biographer Rick Coleman, "When I'm dead and gone a million times, they'll still be playing 'da-da-da-da-dee-dah'".

Not only was Domino's version a hit, but it was big enough that Louis Armstrong's version of the song was reissued and became a hit as well, and Elvis recorded a soundalike cover, including the piano intro that Domino had come up with, for his film *Loving You*.

The song was so big that it even revived the career of its co-lyricist, Al Lewis, whose career had been in the doldrums since a run of hits for people like Eddie Cantor in the 1930s. Lewis made a comeback as an R&B songwriter, co-writing songs like "I'm Ready", for Domino himself, and "Tears on My Pillow", for Little Anthony and the Imperials.

As always with a Fats Domino record, we're going to talk about its points of rhythmic interest. The bass-line here is not one that was used on any of the previous versions, but it was common on New Orleans R&B records – indeed it's very similar to the one Domino used on "Ain't That a Shame".

This kind of bassline has some of that Jelly Roll Morton Spanish tinge we've talked about before, when we talked about the tresillo rhythms that Dave Bartholomew brought to the arrangements. But when it's used as a piano bassline, as it is here, it comes indirectly from the boogie woogie pianist Jimmy Yancey.

Yancey made a speciality of this kind of bassline, but the man who made every New Orleans piano player start playing like that was the great boogie player Meade "Lux" Lewis, with his song "Yancey Special". Lewis named that song after Yancey, which caused a problem for him when Sonny Thompson, an R&B bandleader from Chicago, recorded an instrumental with a similar bassline, "Long Gone".

"Long Gone" went to number one on the R&B charts, and Lewis sued Thompson for copyright infringement, claiming it was too similar to "Yancey Special", because it shared the same bassline. The defendants brought out Jimmy Yancey, who said that he'd come up with that bassline long before Lewis had. Lewis didn't help himself in his testimony – he claimed, at first, that he hadn't named the song after Jimmy Yancey, but later admitted on the stand that the song called "Yancey Special" which featured a bassline in the style of Jimmy Yancey had indeed been named after Jimmy Yancey.

The plagiarism case was thrown out for that reason, but also for two others. One was that the bassline was such a simple idea that it couldn't by itself be copyrightable – which is something I would question, but I have spoken in great detail about the problems with copyright law as it comes to black American musical creation in the past, and I won't repeat myself here. The other was that by allowing the record of "Yancey Special" to come out before he'd registered the copyright, Lewis had dedicated the whole composition to the public domain, and so Thompson could do what he liked with the bassline.

That bassline became a staple of R&B music, and particularly of New Orleans R&B music. You can hear it, for example, on "I Hear You Knockin'", a 1955 hit for Smiley Lewis, arranged by Dave Bartholomew, featuring Huey "Piano" Smith playing a very Fats Domino style piano part.

Domino had used the bassline in "Ain't That a Shame", as well, and it seems to have been taken up by Bartholomew as a signature motif – he also used it in "Blue Monday", another song which he'd written for Smiley Lewis. Domino's remake of that song would become his next hit after "Blueberry Hill", and almost as big a success.

Worldwide, "Blueberry Hill" was the biggest rock and roll hit of 1956, outdoing even Elvis' "Hound Dog" and "Heartbreak Hotel" in worldwide chart positions, though none of those songs could beat "Que Sera Sera" by Doris Day – however much our popular image of the 1950s is based on ponytailed bobbysoxers, the fact remains that a sizeable proportion of the record-buying public were older and less inclined to rock than to gently sway, and for all that Domino's shows were inspiring riots wherever he went in 1956, his records were still also appealing to that older crowd.

But segregation applied here too. "Blueberry Hill" made Billboard's top thirty records of the year for country sales in its annual roundup, but it never appeared even on the top one hundred country charts during 1956 itself. We've already looked at how the recent "Old Town Road" debacle shows how musical genres are the product of rigid segregation, but nothing shows that more than this. That appearance by Domino in the top thirty sellers for the year was the only appearance by a black artist on any Billboard country charts in the fifties, and it shows that country audiences were buying Domino's records, just as his lack of appearance on all the other country charts that year shows that this wasn't being recognised by any of the musical gatekeepers, despite the evident country sensibility in his performance. Meanwhile, of course, Elvis Presley and Carl Perkins were appearing on the R&B charts as well as the country and pop ones.

1956 was the absolute peak of Domino's career in chart terms, and "Blueberry Hill" was his biggest hit of that year, but he would carry on having top twenty pop hits until 1962, by which point he had outlasted not only the first wave of rockabilly acts that came up in 1955 and 56, but almost all of the second wave that we're going to see coming up in 1957 as well. His is an immense body of work, and we've barely touched upon it in the three episodes this podcast has devoted to him. His top thirty R&B chart hits span from 1949 through to 1964, a career that covers multiple revolutions in music. When he started having hits, the biggest artists in pop music were Perry Como and the Andrews Sisters, and when he stopped, the Beatles were at the top of the charts.

The whole of New Orleans music owes a debt to Domino, and "Blueberry Hill" in particular has been cited as an influence by everyone from Mick Jagger to Leonard Cohen.

Yet Domino is curiously unacknowledged in the popular consciousness, while much lesser stars loom larger. I suspect that part of the reason for that is racism, both in ignoring a black man because he was black, and in ignoring him because he didn't fit white prejudices about black people and the music they make.

Other than drinking a bit too much, and sleeping around a little in the fifties, Domino led a remarkably non-rock-and-roll life. He was married to the same woman for sixty-one years, he rarely left his home in New Orleans, and other than a little friction between songwriting partners you'll struggle to find anyone who had a bad word to say about him. You build a legend as a rock star by shooting your bass player on stage or choking to death on your own vomit, not by not liking to travel because you don't like the food anywhere else, or by being shy but polite, and smiling a lot.

That's not how you build a reputation for rock and roll excess. But it is how you build a body of work that stands up to any artist from the mid twentieth century, and how you live a long and happy life. It's how you get the Medal of Arts awarded to you by two Presidents – George W. Bush awarded Domino with a replacement after he lost his first medal, from Bill Clinton, during Hurricane Katrina. And it's how you become so universally beloved and admired that when your home is destroyed in a hurricane, everyone from Elton John to Robert Plant will come together to record a tribute album to help raise funds to rebuild it.

Fats Domino died in 2017, sixty-eight years after the start of his career, at the age of eighty-nine. His collaborator Dave Bartholomew died in June 2019, aged one hundred. They both left behind one of the finest legacies in the histories of rock and roll, rhythm and blues, and New Orleans music.

"Brown-Eyed Handsome Man"

When we left Chuck Berry, he had just recorded and released his third single, "Roll Over Beethoven", the single which had established him as the preeminent mythologiser of rock and roll.

While these days, both sides of his next single – "Brown-Eyed Handsome Man" and "Too Much Monkey Business" – are considered rock and roll classics, neither hit the pop charts in 1956 when they were released. That's because, although they might not seem it at first glance now, both songs are tied in to a very different culture from the white teen one that was now dominating the rock and roll audience.

To see why, we have to look at the R&B tradition which Berry grew up in, and in particular we want to look once again at the work of Berry's hero Louis Jordan, and the particular type of entertainment he provided.

You see, while Louis Jordan was a huge star, and had a certain amount of crossover appeal to the white audience, he was someone whose biggest audience was black people, and in particular black adults.

The teenager as a separate audience for music didn't really become a thing in a conscious way until the mid-fifties. Before the rise of the doo wop groups, R&B music, and the jump band music before it, had been aimed at a hard-working, hard-partying, adult audience, and at a defiantly working-class audience at that – one that had a hard life, and whose reality involved cheating partners, grasping landlords, angry bosses, and a large amount of drinking when they weren't dealing with those things.

But one mistake that's always made when talking about marginalised people is to equate poverty or being a member of a racial minority with being unsophisticated. And there was a whole seam of complex, clever, ironic humour that shows up throughout the work of the jump band and early R&B musicians – one that is very different from the cornball humour that was standard in both country music and white pop.

That style of humour is often referred to as "hip" or "hep" humour, and the early master of it was probably Cab Calloway, who was also the author of a "Hepster's Dictionary" which remained for many years the most important source for understanding black slang of the twenties through forties.

This style of humour, specific to the experiences of black people, was also the basis of much of Louis Jordan's work – and Jordan was clearly influenced by Calloway. You only have to look at songs like "What's the Use of Getting Sober (When You'll Only Get Drunk Again?)".

Obviously the experience of being drunk is one that people of all races have had, but the language used in that song, the specific word choices, roots Jordan's work very firmly in the African-American cultural experience. Jordan did, of course, have a white audience, but he got that audience without compromising the blackness of his language and humour.

That humour disappears almost totally from the history of rock music when the white people start showing up, and there are only two exceptions to this. There are the Coasters, whose lyrics by Jerry Leiber manage to perfectly capture that cynical adult humour of the old-style jump bands, even when dealing with teenage frustrations rather than adult ones – and we'll look at how successfully they do that in a few weeks' time.

The other exception is, of course, Chuck Berry, who would repeatedly cite Jordan as his single biggest influence. As we continue through Berry's career we will see time and again how things that appear original to him are actually Berry's take on something Louis Jordan did.

Berry would later manage to couple Jordan's style of humour to the adolescent topics of school, dancing, cars, and unrequited love, rather than to the more adult topics of jobs, sex, drinking, and rent.

But, crucially, at the time we're looking at, he was not yet doing so. At the session in April 1956 which produced "Roll Over Beethoven", "Drifting Heart", "Too Much Monkey Business", and "Brown-Eyed Handsome Man", there were still relatively few signs that Berry was appealing to a white adolescent audience. "Very few signs" does not, of course, mean that there were *no* signs – Berry would have been able to see who it was who was turning up to his live performances – but it seems to have taken him some time to adapt his songwriting to his new audience.

Even "Roll Over Beethoven", which was, after all, a song very specifically aimed at mythologising the new music, had referred to "these rhythm and blues" rather than to rock and roll. Berry was almost thirty, and he was still in a mindset of writing songs for people his own age, for the audiences that had come to see him play small clubs in St. Louis.

Indeed, the record industry as a whole still saw the teenage audience as almost an irrelevance – other than Bill Haley and Alan Freed, very few people really realised how big that audience was. The combination of disposable income and the changes in technology that had led to the transistor radio and the 45rpm single meant that for the first time teenagers were buying their own records, and listening to them on their own portable radios and record players, rather than having to listen to whatever their parents were buying.

1956 was the year that this new factor stopped being ignorable, and Berry would become the poet laureate of teenage America, the person who more than anyone else would create the vocabulary which would be used by everyone who followed to write about the music and the interests of white teenagers.

But at this point, Berry's music was very much not that, and both "Too Much Monkey Business" and "Brown-Eyed Handsome Man" address very, very, adult concerns.

"Brown-Eyed Handsome Man", in particular, loses a lot of its context when heard today, but is an explicitly racialised song. It's worth looking at that opening verse in some detail – "arrested on charges of unemployment" is, first of all, a funny line, but it's also very much the kind of trumped-up charge that black people, especially black men, would be arrested and tried for.

And then we have the judge's wife getting the man freed because he's so attractive. This is a very, very, common motif in black folklore and blues mythology. For example, in "Back Door Man", written by Willie Dixon for Howlin' Wolf and released on Chess a few years after the time we're talking about, we have a similar situation, though in Dixon's song the judge's wife calls for the "Back door man" to be freed even though he's on trial for murder.

This is a hugely common theme in the blues – you hear it in various versions of "Stagger Lee", for example. Later this would become, thanks to these blues songs, a staple of rock and pop music too – you get the same thing in "Maxwell's Silver Hammer" by the Beatles, or Frank Zappa's "The Illinois Enema Bandit", but stripped of its original context, both those songs have a reputation, at least partly deserved, for tastelessness and misogyny.

But when this motif first came to prominence, it had a very pointed message. There is a terrible stereotype of black men as being more animal than man, and of both having insatiable sexual appetites and being irresistible to white women. This is, of course, no more true of black men than it is of any other demographic, but it was used to fuel very real moral panics about black men raping white women, which led to many men being lynched.

The trope of the women screaming out for the man to be set free, in this context, is very, very, pointed, and is owning this literally deadly negative stereotype and turning it into something to boast about.

And then there's the verse which has the brown-eyed handsome man "hit a high flyer into the stands" and go "round the third and heading for home".

Jackie Robinson, the first black man to play for a major league baseball team, had only started playing for the Dodgers in 1947, and was still playing when Berry recorded this. Robinson was a massively influential figure in black culture, and right from the start of his career, he was having records made about him, like "Did You See Jackie Robinson Hit That Ball?" by Count Basie.

It's almost impossible to state how important Jackie Robinson was to black culture in the immediate post-war period. He was a huge example of a black man breaking a colour barrier, and not only that but excelling and beating all the white people in the field. Robinson was probably the single most important figurehead for civil rights in the late forties and early fifties, even though he was – at least in his public statements – far more interested in his ability to play the game than he was in his ability to affect the course of American politics.

While obviously Robinson isn't mentioned by name in Berry's lyric, the description of the baseball player is clearly meant to evoke Robinson's image.

None of the men mentioned in the song lyric are specifically stated to be black, just "brown-eyed" – though there are often claims, which I've never seen properly substantiated, that the original lyric was "brown-skinned handsome man". That does, though, fit with Berry's repeated tendency to slightly tone down politically controversial aspects of his lyrics – "Johnny B Goode" originally featured a "coloured boy" rather than a "country boy", and in "Nadine" he was originally "campaign shouting like a Southern Democrat" rather than a "Southern diplomat".

But while the men are described in the song in deliberately ambiguous terms, the whole song is very much centred around images from black culture, and images of black men, and especially black men in contexts of white culture, usually high culture, from which they would normally be barred. Much as his idol Jordan had done earlier, Berry is repackaging black culture in a way that is relatable by a white audience, while not compromising that culture in any real way.

The flip side of "Brown-Eyed Handsome Man" is also interesting. "Too Much Monkey Business" is much more directly inspired by Jordan, but is less obviously rooted in specific black experiences. But at the same time, it is absolutely geared to adult concerns, rather than those of teenagers. At least six of the seven verses dealt with adult concerns. Over the seven verses, Berry complains about working for the US mail and getting bills, being given the hard sell by a salesman, having a woman want him to settle down with her and get married, having to go to school every day, using a broken payphone, fighting in the war, and working in a petrol station.

With the exception of the verse about going to school, these are far more the concerns of Louis Jordan, and of records like "Money Honey" or the records Johnny Otis was making, than they are of the new white teenage audience.

While both "Brown-Eyed Handsome Man" and "Too Much Monkey Business" made the top five on the R&B chart, they didn't hit the pop top forty – and "Roll Over Beethoven" had only just scraped into the top thirty. It was plain that if Berry wanted to repeat the success of "Maybellene", he would have to pivot towards a new audience. He couldn't make any more records aimed at black adults. He needed to start making records aimed at white children.

That wasn't the only change he made. The "Brown-Eyed Handsome Man" single was the last one to be released under the name "the Chuck Berry Combo". There are at least two different stories about how Berry stopped working with Ebby Hardy and Johnnie Johnson. Berry always claimed that his two band members were getting drunk all the time and not capable of playing properly. Johnson, on the other hand, always said instead that the two of them got tired of all the travelling and just wanted to stay in St. Louis.

Johnson would continue to play piano on many of Berry's recordings – though from this point on he would never be the sole pianist for Berry, as many sources wrongly claim he was. From now on, Chuck Berry was a solo artist.

The first fruit of this newfound solo stardom was Berry's first film appearance. *Rock! Rock! Rock!* is one of the more widely-available rock and roll films now, thanks to it having entered into the public domain – you can actually even watch the film through its Wikipedia page. It's not, though, a film I'd actually recommend watching at all. The plot, such as it is, consists of Tuesday Weld wanting to buy a new dress for the prom, and her dad not wanting to give her the money, and an "evil" rival for Weld's boyfriend's attentions (who you can tell is evil because she has dark hair rather than being blonde like Weld) trying to get her in trouble.

The writer, producer, and co-writer of the incidental music and title song was Milton Subotsky, who would go on to much better and more interesting things as the co-founder of Amicus Films, a British film company that made a whole host of cheap but enjoyable horror and science fiction films. Oddly enough, we'll be meeting Subotsky again.

How important the plot is can be summed up by the fact that there is a fifteen-minute sequence in this seventy-minute film, in which Weld and her friend merely watch the TV. The programme they're watching is a fictional TV show, presented by Alan Freed, in which he introduces various rock and roll acts, and this is where Berry appears.

The song he's singing in the film is his next single, "You Can't Catch Me", which had actually been recorded before "Roll Over Beethoven". But the story of the song's release is one that tells you a lot about the music business in the 1950s, and about how little the artists understood about what it was they were getting into.

At the time, it wasn't normal for R&B acts to put out albums, and so it was a sign of how much the film was aimed at the white teenage audience that a soundtrack album was considered at all. It seems to have been Alan Freed's idea. Freed was the star of the film, and the acts in it – people like LaVern Baker, the Moonglows, Johnny Burnette, and Frankie Lymon and the Teenagers – were for the most part people he regularly featured on his radio show (along with a handful of bland white novelty acts that were included in the misguided belief that the teenage audience wanted to hear a pre-teen kid singing about rock and roll).

But of course, Freed being Freed, what that meant was that the acts he included were from record labels that would bribe him, or with which he had some kind of financial relationship, and as they were on multiple different labels, this caused problems when deciding who got to put out a soundtrack album.

In particular, both the Chess brothers, whose labels had provided the Flamingos, the Moonglows, and Berry, and Morris Levy, the gangster who controlled the career of Frankie Lymon and the Teenagers, the single biggest act in the film, wanted the right to put out a soundtrack album and profit from the publicity the film would provide. All of them were "business associates" of Freed – Freed managed the Moonglows, and had been given writing credit on songs by both the Moonglows and Berry in return for playing them on his radio show, while Levy was himself Freed's manager, and had been largely responsible for getting Freed his unchallenged dominance of New York radio.

So they came to a compromise. The soundtrack album would only feature the three Chess acts who appeared in the film, and would include four songs by each of them, rather than the one song each they performed in the film. And the album would be out on Chess. But the album would include the previously-released songs that Freed was credited with co-writing, and the new songs would be published, not by the publishing companies that published those artists' songs, but by one of Levy's companies.

Chuck Berry was tricked into signing his rights to the song away by a standard Leonard Chess tactic – he was called into Chess' office to receive a large royalty cheque, and Chess asked him if while he was there he would mind signing this other document that needed signing, only could he do it in a hurry, because Chess had an urgent appointment? It was six months until Berry realised that he'd signed away the rights to "You Can't Catch Me", and twenty-eight years before he was able to reclaim the copyright for himself.

In the meantime, the rights to that one Chuck Berry song made Levy far more money than he could possibly have expected, because of the line "Here come old flat-top, he come moving up with me". In 1969, John Lennon took that line and used it, slightly altered, as the opening line for the Beatles song "Come Together".

Rather than go through the courts, Levy and Lennon came to an agreement – Lennon was going to make an album of rock and roll covers, and he would include at least three songs to which Levy owned the copyright, including "You Can't Catch Me". As a result, even after Levy finally lost the rights to the song in the early 1980s, he still continued earning money from John Lennon's cover versions of two other songs he owned, which would never have been recorded without him having owned "You Can't Catch Me".

"You Can't Catch Me" was a flop, and didn't even make the R&B charts, let alone the pop charts. This even though its B-side, "Havana Moon", would in a roundabout way end up being possibly Berry's most influential song, though that's a story for a future volume.

Berry knew he had to pivot, and fast. He wrote a new song, "Rock and Roll Music", which he thought could maybe have the same kind of success as "Roll Over Beethoven", but used the more currently-popular term rock and roll rather than talking about "rhythm and blues" as the earlier song did. But while he demoed that, it wasn't a song that he could be certain would directly get right into the head of every teenage kid in America.

For that, he turned to Johnnie Johnson again. For years, Johnson had had his own theme song at the Cosmopolitan Club. In its original form the song was based on "Honky Tonk Train Blues" by Meade "Lux" Lewis. Johnson's own take on the song had kept Lewis' intro, and had been renamed "Johnnie's Boogie".

Johnson suggested to Berry that they take that intro and have Berry play the same thing, but on the guitar. When he did, they found that when he played his guitar, it was like ringing a bell — a school bell, to be precise. And that gave Berry the idea for a lyric.

"School Day" was the pivot point, the song with which Chuck Berry turned wholly towards teenage concerns, and away from those of adults. The description of the drudgery of life in school was not that different from the descriptions of working life in "Too Much Monkey Business", but it was infinitely more relatable to the new young rock and roll audience than anything in the earlier song.

And not only that, the slow trudge of school life gets replaced, in the final verses, with an anthem to the new music, as Berry sings "Hail! Hail! Rock and roll/Deliver me from the days of old!"

"School Day" became the biggest-selling single ever to be released by Chess to that point. It hit number one on the R&B charts, knocking "All Shook Up" by Elvis off the top, and made number five on the Billboard pop charts. It charted in the UK, which given Chess' lack of distribution over here at that point was a minor miracle, and it stayed on the Billboard pop chart for an astonishing six months.

"School Day" was successful enough that Berry was given an album release of his own. *After School Session* was a compilation of tracks Berry had released as either the A- or B-sides of singles, including "School Day", "Brown-Eyed Handsome Man", "Too Much Monkey Business", and "Havana Moon", but not including "You Can't Catch Me" or the other songs on the *Rock! Rock! Rock!* compilation. It was filled out with a couple of generic blues instrumentals, but was otherwise a perfect representation of where Berry was artistically, right at this turning point. And that shows even in the title of the record.

The name *After School Session* obviously refers to "School Day", and to the kids in the song going to listen to rock and roll after school ended, but it was also a tip of the hat to another song, one which may have inspired the lyrics to "School Day" in much the same way that Meade "Lux" Lewis had inspired the music, Louis Jordan's "After School Swing Session (Swinging With Symphony Sid)". Even at his most up-to-date, Chuck Berry was still paying homage to Louis Jordan.

"School Day" was the point where Chuck Berry went from middling rhythm and blues star to major rock and roll star, and his next twelve records would all make the Billboard pop charts. 1957 was going to be Chuck Berry's year, and we'll pick up on his story in the next volume, when we look at another Louis Jordan influenced song, about a kid who played the guitar. . .

"Goodnight My Love"

Jesse Belvin is a name that not many people recognise these days – he's a footnote in the biographies of people like Sam Cooke or the Penguins, someone whose contribution to music history is usually summed up in a line or two in a book about someone else – "and there was Jesse Belvin, the co-writer of 'Earth Angel'".

The problem is that Jesse Belvin was simply too good, and too prolific, to have a normal career. He put out a truly astonishing number of records as a songwriter, performer, and group leader, under so many different names that it's impossible to figure out the true extent of his career. And people like that, whose names don't get put on all of the records, don't end up having scholarly books written about them.

And when you do find something that actually talks about Belvin himself, you find wild inaccuracies. For example, in researching this chapter, I found over and over again that people claimed that Barry White played piano on Belvin's "Goodnight My Love". Now, White lived in the same neighbourhood as Belvin, and they attended the same school, so on the face of it that seems plausible. It seems plausible, at least, until you realise that Barry White was eleven when "Goodnight My Love" came out.

Even so, on the offchance, I tracked down an interview with White where he confirmed that no, he was not playing piano on doo wop classics before he hit puberty. But that kind of misinformation is all over everything to do with Jesse Belvin.

The end result of this is that Jesse Belvin is someone who exists in the gaps of other people's histories, and this chapter is an attempt to create a picture out of what you find when looking at the stories of other musicians. As a result, it will almost certainly contain some inaccuracies. There's so little information about Belvin that if you didn't know anything about him, you'd assume he was some unimportant, minor, figure.

But in 1950s R&B – among musicians, especially those on the West Coast – there was no bigger name than Jesse Belvin. He had the potential to be bigger than anyone, and he would have been, had he lived. He was Stevie Wonder's favourite singer of all time, and Etta James argued to her dying day that it was a travesty that she was in the rock and roll hall of fame while he wasn't. Sam Cooke explicitly tried to model his career after Belvin, to the extent that after Cooke's death, his widow kept all of Cooke's records separate from her other albums – except Belvin's, which she kept with Cooke's.

Marv Goldberg, who is by far the pre-eminent expert on forties and fifties black vocal group music, refers to Belvin as the genre's "most revered stylist". And at the time he died, he was on the verge of finally becoming as well known as he deserved to be.

Like so many greats of R&B and jazz, Belvin attended Jefferson High School and studied music under the great teacher Samuel Browne. One of the other people that Browne had taught was the great rhythm and blues saxophone player Big Jay McNeely. McNeely was one of the all-time great saxophone honkers, inspired mostly by Illinois Jacquet, and he had become the lead tenor saxophone player with Johnny Otis' band at the Barrelhouse Club.

As with many of the musicians Otis worked with, McNeely soon went on to a solo career of his own, and he formed a vocal group, Three Dots and a Dash, named after a popular drink which was, in turn, named after the Morse code sign for "V", used in wartime radio broadcasts as shorthand for "victory". Three Dots and a Dash backed McNeely's saxophone on a number of records, and McNeely invited Belvin to join them as lead singer. Belvin's first recording with the group was on "All That Wine is Gone", an answer record to "Drinking Wine Spo-De-O-Dee".

After recording two singles with McNeely, Belvin went off to make his own records, signing to Specialty. His first solo single, "Baby Don't Go", was not especially successful, so he teamed up with the songwriter

Marvin Phillips in a duo called Jesse and Marvin. The two of them had a hit with the song "Dream Girl".

"Dream Girl" went to number two on the R&B charts, and it looked like Jesse and Marvin were about to have a massive career. But shortly afterwards, Belvin was drafted.

It was while he was in the armed forces that "Earth Angel", which he co-wrote, became a hit. Like many of the songs Belvin wrote, he ended up not getting credit for that one – but unlike most of the others, he went to court over it and got some royalties in the end.

Marvin decided to continue the duo without Jesse, renaming it Marvin and Johnny, and moved over to Modern Records, but he didn't stick with a single "Johnny". Instead "Johnny" would be whoever was around, sometimes Marvin himself double-tracked. He had several hit singles under that name, including "Cherry Pie", on which the role of Johnny was played by Emory Perry.

"Cherry Pie" was a massive hit, but none of Marvin and Johnny's other records matched its success. However, on some of the follow-ups, Jesse Belvin returned as one of the Johnnies, notably on a cover version of "Ko Ko Mo", which didn't manage to outsell either the original or Perry Como's version.

Meanwhile, his time in the armed forces had set Belvin's career back, and when he came out he started recording for every label, and under every band name, he could. Most of the time, he would also be writing the songs, but he didn't get label credit on most of them, because he would just sell all his rights to the songs for a hundred dollars. Why not? There was always another song.

As well as recording as Marvin and Johnny for Modern Records, he also sang with the Californians and the Sheiks on Federal, the Gassers, on Cash, and under his own name on both Specialty and on John Dolphin's Hollywood Records.

But his big project at the time was the Cliques, a duo he formed with Eugene Church, who recorded for Modern. Their track, "The Girl in My Dreams" was the closest thing he'd had to a big success since the similarly-named "Dream Girl" several years earlier. That went to number forty-five on the pop chart – not a massive hit, but a clear commercial success.

And so, of course, at this point Belvin ditched the Cliques name, rather than follow up on the minor hit, and started making records as a solo artist instead. He signed to Modern Records as a solo artist, and went into the studio to record a new song.

Now, I am going to be careful how I phrase this, because John Marascalco, who is credited as the co-writer of "Goodnight My Love", is still alive. And I want to stress that Marascalco is, by all accounts, an actual songwriter who has written songs for people like Little Richard and Harry Nilsson.

But there have also been accusations that at least some of his song-writing credits were not deserved – in particular the song "Bertha Lou" by Johnny Faire, which Faire, whose real name was Donnie Brooks, recorded with the Burnette brothers.

Faire always said that that song was written, not by Marascalco, but by Johnny Burnette, who sold his rights to the song to Marascalco for fifty dollars – Burnette's son Rocky backs up the claim.

Now, in the case of "Goodnight My Love", the credited writers are George Motola and Marascalco, but the story as it's normally told goes as follows – Motola had written the bulk of the song several years earlier, but had never completed it. He brought it into the studio, and Jesse Belvin came up with the bridge – but he said that rather than take credit, he just wanted Motola to give him four hundred dollars. Motola didn't have four hundred dollars on him, but Marascalco, who was also at the session and is the credited producer, said he could get it for Belvin, and took the credit himself.

That's the story, and it would fit with both the rumour that Maras-calco had bought an entire song from Johnny Burnette and with Belvin's cavalier attitude towards credit. On the other hand, Marascalco was also apparently particularly good at rewriting and finishing other peo-ple's half-finished songs, and so it's entirely plausible that he could have done the finishing-up job himself.

Either way, the finished song became one of the most well-known songs of the fifties. Belvin's version of the song went to number seven in the R&B charts, but its impact went beyond its immediate chart success. Alan Freed started to use the song as the outro music for his radio show, making it familiar to an entire generation of American music lovers. The result was that the song became a standard, recorded by everyone from James Brown Harry Connick Jr. If John Marascalco did buy Jesse Belvin's share of the songwriting, that was about the best four hundred dollars he could possibly have spent.

Over the next year, Belvin recorded a host of other singles as a solo artist, none of which matched the level of success he'd seen with "Goodnight My Love", but which are the artistic foundation on which his reputation now rests. The stylistic range of these records is quite astonishing, from Latin pop like "Señorita", to doo wop novelty songs like "My Satellite", a song whose melody owes something to "Hound Dog", credited to Jesse Belvin and the Space Riders, and released to cash in on the space craze that had started with the launch of the Russian satellite Sputnik.

"My Satellite" featured Alex Hodge of the Platters on backing vocals. Hodge's brother Gaynel, who like Belvin would form groups at the drop of a hat, joined Jesse in yet another of the many groups he formed. The Saxons consisted of Belvin, Gaynel Hodge, Eugene Church (who had been in the Cliques with Belvin) and another former Jefferson High student, Belvin's friend Johnny "Guitar" Watson.

Watson would later become well known for his seventies "gangster of love" persona and funk records, but at this point he was mostly making hard electric blues records like "Three Hours Past Midnight". But when he worked with Belvin in the Saxons and other groups, he recorded much more straightforward doo wop and rock and roll.

The Saxons also recorded as the Capris (though with Alex Hodge rather than Gaynel in that lineup of the group) and, just to annoy everyone who cares about this stuff and drive us all into nervous breakdowns, there was another group, also called the Saxons, who also recorded as the Capris, on the same label – at least one single actually came out with one of the groups on one side and the other on the other. Indeed, the side featuring our Saxons had previously been released as a Jesse Belvin solo record.

Anyway, I hope in this first half of the story I've given some idea of just how many different groups Jesse Belvin recorded with, and under how many different names, though I haven't listed even half of them. This is someone who seemed to form a new group every time he crossed the street, and make records with most of them, and a surprising number of them had become hits – and "Goodnight My Love" and "Earth Angel" had become the kind of monster perennial standard that most musicians dream of ever writing.

And, of course, Belvin had become the kind of musician that most record companies and publishers dream of finding – the kind who will happily make hit records and sell the rights for a handful of dollars.

That was soon to change. Belvin was married; I haven't been able to find out exactly when he married, but his wife also became his songwriting partner and his manager, and in 1958 she seemed to finally take control of his career for him. But before she did, there was one last pickup group hit to make.

Frankie Ervin had been Charles Brown's replacement in Johnny Moore's Three Blazers, and had also sung briefly with Johnny Otis and Preston Love. While with Moore's group, he'd developed a reputation for being able to perform novelty cash-in records – he'd made "Dragnet Blues", which had resulted in a lawsuit from the makers of the TV show *Dragnet*, and he'd also done his Johnny Ace impression on "Johnny Ace's Last Letter", a single that had been rush-released by the Blazers after Ace's death.

Ervin was looking for a solo career after leaving the Blazers, and he was put in touch with George Motola, who had a suggestion for him. A white group from Texas called the Slades had recorded a track called "You Cheated", which looked like it could possibly be a big hit – except that the label it was on wasn't willing to come to terms with some of the big distributors over how much they were charging per record.

Motola wanted to record a soundalike version of the song with Jesse Belvin as the lead singer, but Belvin had just signed a record contract with RCA, and didn't want to put out lead vocals on another label. Would Ervin like to put out the song as a solo record?

Ervin hated the song – he didn't like doo wop generally, and he thought the song was a particularly bad example of the genre – but a gig was a gig, and it'd be a solo record under his own name. Ervin agreed to do it, and Motola got Jesse Belvin to put together a scratch vocal group for the session. Belvin found Johnny "Guitar" Watson and Tommy "Buster" Williams at a local ballroom and got them to come along, and on the way to the session they ran into "Handsome" Mel Williams and pulled him in.

They were just going to be the uncredited backing vocalists on a Frankie Ervin record, and didn't spend much time thinking about what was clearly a soundalike cash-in, but when it came out it was credited as "The Shields" rather than Frankie Ervin.

Ervin was naturally annoyed that he wasn't given the label credit for the record. The recording was made as an independent production but leased to Dot Records, and somewhere along the line someone decided that it was better to have a generic group name rather than promote it as by a solo singer who might get ideas about wanting money.

In a nice bit of irony, the Shields managed to reverse the normal course of the music industry – this time a soundalike record by a black group managed to outsell the original by a white group. "You Cheated" ended up making number twelve on the pop charts – a massive hit for an unknown doo wop group at the time.

Ervin started touring and making TV appearances as the Shields, backed by some random singers the record label had pulled together – the rest of the vocalists on the record had been people who were under contract to other labels, and so couldn't make TV appearances.

But the original Shields members reunited for the followup single, "Nature Boy", where they were joined by the members of the Turks, who were yet another group that Belvin was recording with, and who included both Hodge brothers.

That, according to Ervin, also sold a million copies, but it was nothing like as successful as "You Cheated". The record label were getting sick of Ervin wanting credit and royalties and other things they didn't like singers, especially black ones, asking for, so the third Shields record only featured Belvin out of the original lineup, and subsequent recordings didn't even feature him.

But while Belvin had accidentally put together yet another million-selling group, he had also moved on to bigger things. His wife had now firmly taken control of his career, and they had a plan. Belvin had signed to a major label – RCA, the same label that Elvis Presley was on – and he was going to make a play for the big time.

He could still keep making doo wop records with Johnny "Guitar" Watson and Eugene Church and the Hodge brothers and whoever else, if he felt like it, but his solo career was going to be something else. He was going to go for the same market as Nat "King" Cole, and become a smooth ballad singer, keeping enough soul in his voice to keep his black audience, and rocking just enough to keep the teenagers on side, but also getting white Middle America to buy his records.

He was going to be a huge star, and he actually got to record an album, *Just Jesse Belvin.* The first single off that album was "Guess Who?", a song written by his wife Jo Anne, based on a love letter she had written to him.

That made the top forty – hitting number thirty-three on the pop chart – and managed to reach number seven on the R&B charts, confirming the hypothesis that Belvin could keep his old R&B audience while going pop. More importantly, it gained Grammy nominations for both best R&B performance and best male vocal performance. He lost to Dinah Washington and Frank Sinatra, respectively, but just that kind of nomination should have been enough to make a career, and it's not as if losing to Dinah Washington or Frank Sinatra would have been an embarrassment.

But by the time he lost those Grammies, Jesse was already dead, and so was Jo Anne.

And here we get into the murkiest part of the story. There are a lot of rumours floating around about Jesse Belvin's death, and a lot of misinformation is out there, and frankly I've not been able to get to the bottom of exactly what happened. When someone you love dies young, especially if that someone is a public figure, there's a tendency to look for complex explanations, and there's also a tendency to exaggerate stories in the telling. That's just human nature. And in some cases, that tendency is exploited by people out to make money.

And Jesse and Jo Anne Belvin were both black people who died in the deep South, and so no real investigation was ever carried out. That means that by now, with almost everyone who was involved dead, it's impossible to tell what really happened.

Almost every single sentence of what follows may be false. It's my best guess as to the order of events and what happened, based on the limited information out there.

On February the sixth, 1960, there was a concert in Little Rock, Arkansas, at the Robinson Auditorium. Billed as "the first rock and roll show of 1960", the headliner was Jackie Wilson, a friend of Belvin's. As with many shows at that period, it had many acts on it, and this one included Belvin, Motown singer Marv Johnson, Bobby Freeman, who'd just had a hit with "Do You Wanna Dance?", Nappy Brown, who'd had a big hit with "Don't Be Angry" a few years earlier, and others. Jesse had just recorded his second album, *Mr Easy*, which would be coming out soon, and while he was still relatively low on the bill, he was a rising star.

It was an all-black lineup on stage, but according to some reports it was an integrated audience. In fact some reports go so far as to say it was the first integrated audience ever in Little Rock.

Little Rock was not a place where the white people were fans of integration – in fact they were so against it that the National Guard had had to be called in only two years earlier to protect black children when the first school in Little Rock had been integrated. And so apparently there was some racial abuse shouted by members of the audience. But it was nothing that the musicians hadn't dealt with before.

After the show they all drove on towards Dallas. Jackie Wilson had some car problems on the way, and got to their stop in Dallas later than he was expecting to. The Belvins hadn't arrived yet, and so Wilson called Jesse's mother in LA, asking if she'd heard from them.

She hadn't, and she never would again. Shortly after setting off, the car with Jesse and Jo Anne in had been in a crash. Jesse and the drivers of both cars had been killed instantly. Kirk Davis, Belvin's guitarist on that tour, who had apparently been asleep in the back seat, was seriously injured but eventually came out of his coma, though he was in pain and disfigured. And Jesse had apparently reacted fast enough to shield his wife from the worst of the accident. But she was still unconscious, and seriously injured.

The survivors were rushed to the hospital, where, according to Etta James, who heard the story from Jackie Wilson, they refused to treat Jo

Anne Belvin until they knew that they would get money. She remained untreated until someone got in touch with Wilson, who drove down from Dallas Texas to Hope, Arkansas, where the hospital was, with the cash. But she died of her injuries a few days later.

Now, here's the thing – within a fortnight of the accident, there were rumours circulating widely enough to have been picked up by the newspapers that Belvin's car had had its tyres slashed, apparently confirmed by a state trooper who attended the accident scene. There were also stories, never confirmed, that Belvin had received death threats before the show. And Jackie Wilson had also had car trouble that night – and according to some sources so had at least one other musician on the bill. So it's possible that the car was sabotaged.

On the other hand, Belvin's driver, Charles Shackleford, had got the job with Belvin after being fired by Ray Charles. He was fired, according to Charles, because he kept staying awake watching the late-night shows, not getting enough sleep, and driving dangerously enough to scare Ray Charles – who was fearless enough that he used to ride motorbikes despite being totally blind.

So when Jesse and Jo Anne Belvin died, they could have been the victims of a racist murder, or they could just have been horribly unlucky. But we'll never know for sure, because the institutional racism at the time meant that there was no investigation.

When they died, they left behind two children under the age of five, who were brought up by Jesse's mother. The oldest, Jesse Belvin Jr, became a singer himself, often performing material written or made famous by his father. Jesse Jr. devoted his life to finding out what actually happened to his parents, but never found any answers.

"Rock With the Caveman"

Let's talk a little bit about the Piltdown Man.

Piltdown Man was an early example of a hominid – a missing link between the apes and humans. Its skull was discovered in 1912 in Piltdown, East Sussex, by the eminent archaeologist Charles Dawson, and for years was considered one of the most important pieces of evidence in the story of human evolution.

And then, in 1953, it was discovered that the whole thing was a hoax, and not even a particularly good one. Someone had just taken the jaw of an orang-utan and the top part of a human skull, and filed down the orang-utan teeth, and then stained the bones to make them look old. It was almost certainly the work of Dawson himself, who seems to have spent his entire life making fraudulent discoveries. Dawson had died decades earlier, and the full extent of his fraud wasn't even confirmed until 2003.

Sometimes researching the history of rock and roll can be a lot like that. You can find a story repeated in numerous apparently reliable books, and then find out that it's all based on the inaccurate testimony of a single individual. The story never happened. It was just something someone made up.

Now, there's an important thing to note about the first wave of British rock and roll, and that is that it was, essentially, a music that had no roots in the culture. It was an imitation of American music, without any of the ties to social issues that made the American music so interesting.

Britain in the 1950s was a very different place to the one it is today, or to America. It was ethnically extremely homogeneous, as the waves of immigration that have so improved the country had only just started.

And while few people travelled much outside their own immediate areas, it was culturally more homogeneous as well, as Britain, unlike America, had a national media rather than a local one. In Britain, someone could become known throughout the country before they'd played their second gig, if they got the right media exposure.

And so British rock and roll started out at the point that American rock and roll was only just starting to get to – a clean-cut version of the music, with little black influence or sexuality left in it, designed from the outset to be a part of mainstream showbusiness aimed at teenagers, not music for an underclass or a racial or sexual minority.

Britain's first rock and roll star put out his first record in November 1956, and by November 1957 he was appearing on the Royal Variety Show, with Mario Lanza, Bob Monkhouse, and Vera Lynn. That is, fundamentally, what early British rock and roll was. Keep that in mind for the rest of the story, as we look at how a young sailor from a dirt-poor family became Britain's first teen idol.

To tell that story, we first have to discuss the career of the Vipers Skiffle Group. That was the group's full name, and they were just about the most important British group of the mid-fifties, even though they were never as commercially successful as some of the acts we've looked at.

The name of the Vipers Skiffle Group was actually the first drug reference in British pop music. They took the name from the auto-biography of the American jazz clarinettist Mezz Mezzrow – a man who was better known in the jazz community as a dope dealer than as a musician; so much so that "Mezz" itself became slang for marijuana. In Mezzrow's autobiography, he uses "viper" as the name for dope smokers, and that became a common term in the jazz community. For example in Stuff Smith's "You'se a Viper", he sings that he

Dreamed about a reefer five foot long

Mighty Mezz but not too strong

You'll be high, but not for long

If you're a viper

So when Wally Whyton, Johnny Booker, and Jean van den Bosch formed a guitar trio, they chose that name, even though as it turned out none of them actually smoked dope. They just thought it sounded cool.

They started performing at a cafe called the 2is, and started to build up something of a reputation – to the point that Lonnie Donegan started nicking their material. Whyton had taken an old sea shanty, "Sail Away Ladies", popularised by the country banjo player Uncle Dave Macon, and rewritten it substantially, turning it into "Don't You Rock Me Daddy-O". Donegan copyrighted Whyton's song as soon as he heard it, and rushed out his version of it, but the Vipers put out their own version too, and the two chased each other up the charts. Donegan's charted higher, but the Vipers ended up at a respectable number ten.

The Vipers' recording was on Parlophone records, and was produced by a young producer who normally did comedy and novelty records, named George Martin. We'll be hearing more about him in volume two.

But at the time we're talking about, the Vipers had not yet gained a recording contract, and they were still playing the 2is. Occasionally, they would be joined on stage by a young acquaintance named Thomas Hicks. Hicks was a merchant seaman, and was away at sea most of the time, and so was never a full part of the group, but even though he didn't care much for skiffle – he was a country and western fan first and foremost – he played guitar, and in Britain in 1955 and 56, if you played guitar, you played skiffle.

Hicks had come from an absolutely dirt-poor background. Three of his siblings had died at cruelly young ages, and young Thomas himself had had several brushes with ill health, which meant that while he was a voracious reader he had lacked formal education.

He had wanted to be a performer from a very early age, and had developed a routine that he used to do around the pubs in his early teens, in which he would mime to a record by Danny Kaye, "Knock on Wood". But at age fifteen he had joined the Merchant Navy. This isn't the same thing as the Royal Navy, but rather is the group of commercial shipping companies that provide non-military shipping, and Hicks worked as wait staff on a cruise ship making regular trips to

America. On an early trip, he fell in love with the music of Hank Williams, who would remain a favourite of his for the rest of his life, and he particularly loved the song "Kaw-Liga".

Hicks replaced his old party piece of miming to Danny Kaye with a new one of singing "Kaw-Liga", with accompaniment from anyone he could persuade to play guitar for him. Eventually one of his crewmates taught him how to play the song himself, and he started performing with pick-up groups, singing Hank Williams songs, whenever he was on shore leave in the UK. And when he couldn't get a paid gig he'd head to the 2is and sing with the Vipers.

But then came the event that changed his life. Young Tommy Hicks, with his love of country music, was delighted when on shore leave in 1955 to see an advert for a touring show based on the Grand Ole Opry, in Norfolk Virginia, where he happened to be. Of course he went along, and there he saw something that made a huge impression. One of the acts in the middle of the bill was a young man who wore horn-rimmed glasses. Tommy still remembers the details to this day. The young man came out and did a three-song set. The first song was a standard country song, but the second one was something else; something that hit like a bolt of lightning.

That song was young Thomas Hicks' introduction to the new music called rock and roll, and nothing would ever be the same for him ever again after seeing Buddy Holly sing "Peggy Sue". By February 1956 he had finished working on the cruise ships, and was performing rock and roll in London, the very first British rock and roller.

Except...

There's a reason why we're covering Tommy Steele before Buddy Holly, the man who he claims as his inspiration.

Buddy Holly did perform with a Grand Ole Opry tour. But it didn't tour until May 1956, three months after Thomas Hicks quit his job on the cruise ships, and about a year after the time Tommy claims to have seen Holly. That tour only hit Oklahoma, which is landlocked, and didn't visit Norfolk Virginia. According to various timelines put together by people like the Buddy Holly Centre in Lubbock Texas, Holly didn't perform outside Lubbock until that tour, and that's the only time he did perform outside West Texas until 1957.

Also, Buddy Holly didn't meet Peggy Sue Gerron, the woman who gave the song its name, until 1956, and the song doesn't seem to have been written until 1957.

So whatever it was that introduced young Tommy Hicks to the wonders of rock and roll, it wasn't seeing Buddy Holly sing "Peggy Sue" in Norfolk Virginia in 1955. But that's the story that's in his autobiography, and that's the story that's in every other source I've seen on the subject, because they're all just repeating what he said, on the assumption that he'd remember something like that, something which was so important in his life and future career.

Remember what I said at the beginning, about rock and roll history being like dealing with Piltdown Man? Yeah.

There are a lot of inaccuracies in the life story of Thomas Hicks, who became famous under the name Tommy Steele. Anything I tell you about him is based on information he put out, and that information is not always the truth, so be warned. For example, when he started his career, he claimed he'd worked his way up on the cruise ships to being a gymnastics instructor – something that the shipping federation denied to the press. You find a lot of that kind of thing when you dig into Steele's stories.

In fact, by the time Hicks started performing, there had already been at least one British rock and roll record made. He wasn't bringing something new that he'd discovered in America at all. *Rock Around the Clock*, the Bill Haley film, had played in UK cinemas at around the time of Hicks' supposed epiphany, and it had inspired a modern jazz drummer, Tony Crombie, to form Tony Crombie and the Rockets and record a Bill Haley soundalike called "Teach You to Rock".

However, Crombie was not teen idol material – a serious jazz drummer in his thirties, he soon went back to playing bebop, and has largely been written out of British rock history since, in favour of Tommy Steele as the first British rock and roller.

Thomas Hicks the merchant seaman became Tommy Steele the pop idol as a result of a chance meeting. Hicks went to a party with a friend, and the host was a man called Lionel Bart, who was celebrating because he'd just sold his first song, to the bandleader Bill Cotton.

No recording of that song seems to exist, but the lyrics to the song – a lament about the way that old-style cafes were being replaced by upscale coffee bars – are quoted in a biography of Bart:

Oh for a cup of tea, instead of a cuppuchini

What would it mean to me, just one little cup so teeny!

You ask for some char and they reckon you're barmy

Ask for a banger, they'll give you salami

Oh for the liquid they served in the Army

Just a cup of tea!

Heartrending stuff, I'm sure you'll agree. But Bart was proud of the twenty-five guineas the song had earned him, and so he was having a party.

Bart was at the centre of a Bohemian crowd in Soho, and the party was held at a squat where Bart, a card-carrying member of the Communist Party, spent most of his time. At that squat at various times around this period lived, among others, the playwright John Antrobus, the actor Shirley Eaton, who would later become famous as the woman painted gold in the beginning of *Goldfinger*, and the great folk guitarist Davey Graham.

Another inhabitant of the squat was Mike Pratt, a guitarist and pianist who would later turn to acting and become famous as Jeff Randall in the fantasy detective series *Randall and Hopkirk (Deceased)*. Hicks, Bart, and Pratt started collaborating on songs together – Hicks would bring in a basic idea, and then Bart would write the lyrics and Pratt the music. They also performed as The Cavemen, though Bart soon tired of playing washboard and stuck to writing. The Cavemen became a floating group of musicians, centred around Hicks and Pratt, and with various Vipers and other skifflers pulled in as and when they were available.

The various skiffle musicians looked down on Hicks, because of his tendency to want to play "Heartbreak Hotel" or "Blue Suede Shoes" rather than "Bring a Little Water Sylvie" or "Rock Island Line", but a gig was a gig, and they had to admit that Hicks seemed to go down well with the young women in the audience.

Two minor music industry people, Bill Varley and Roy Tuvey, agreed to manage Hicks, but they decided that they needed someone involved who would be able to publicise Hicks, so they invited John Kennedy, a PR man from New Zealand, to come to the 2is to see him. Hicks wasn't actually playing the 2is the night in question – it was the Vipers, who were just on the verge of getting signed and recording their first single.

While Hicks wasn't scheduled to play, at the request of Varley and Tuvey he jumped on stage when the Vipers took a break, and sang a song that he, Bart, and Pratt had written, called "Rock With the Caveman", with lyrics like

Piltdown Poppa sings this song

"Archaeology's done me wrong"

The British Museum's got my head

Most unfortunate 'cause I ain't dead

Kennedy was impressed. He was impressed enough, in fact, that he brought in a friend, Larry Parnes, who would go on to become the most important manager in British rock and roll in the fifties and early sixties. Kennedy, Parnes, and Hicks cut Varley and Tuvey out altogether – to the extent that neither of them are even mentioned in the version of this story in Tommy Steele's autobiography.

Hicks was renamed Tommy Steele, in a nod to his paternal grand-father Thomas Stil-Hicks (the Stil in that name is spelled either Stil or Stijl, depending on which source you believe) and Parnes would go on to name a whole host of further rock stars in a similar manner – Duffy Power, Johnny Gentle, Billy Fury, Marty Wilde. They had everything except a record contract, but that was why Kennedy was there.

Kennedy rented a big house, and hired a load of showgirls, models, and sex workers to turn up for a party and bring their boyfriends. They were to dress nicely, talk in fake posh accents, and if anyone asked who they were they were to give fake double-barrelled names. He then called the press and said it was "the first high society rock and roll show" and that the girls were all debutantes. The story made the newspapers, and got Steele national attention.

Steele was signed by Decca records, where Hugh Mendl, the producer of "Rock Island Line", was so eager to sign him that he didn't check if any studios were free for his audition, and so Britain's first homegrown rock idol auditioned for his record contract in the gents' toilets.

A bunch of slumming jazz musicians, including Dave Lee, the pianist with the Dankworth band, and the legendary saxophone player Ronnie Scott, were brought in to record "Rock With the Caveman". The single went to number thirteen. Tommy Steele was now a *bona fide* rock and roll star, at least in the UK. The next record, "Elevator Rock", didn't do so well, however.

That failed to chart, so Steele's producers went for the well-worn trick in British record making of simply copying a US hit. Guy Mitchell had just released "Singing the Blues", which was actually a cover version of a recording by Marty Robbins from earlier in the year, but Mitchell's version was the one that became the big hit. Steele was brought into the studio to record a soundalike version, and hopefully get it out before Mitchell's version hit the charts. Steele's version has an identical arrangement and sound to Mitchell's, except that Steele sings it in an incredibly mannered Elvis impression.

To twenty-first century ears, Steele's version is clearly inferior. But here was the birth of something particularly English – and indeed something particularly London – in rock and roll music: the overly mannered, music-hall inspired, Cockneyfied impression of an American singing style. On Steele's subsequent tour, a nine-year old kid called David Jones, who would later change his name to Bowie, went to see him and came away inspired to become a rock and roll star. And we can hear in Steele's performance the roots of Bowie's own London take on Elvis, as we can also hear a style that would be taken up by Anthony Newley, Ray Davies, and many more masters of Cockney archness.

I don't think "Singing the Blues" is a particularly good record compared to Mitchell's, but it is a prototype for something that would become good, and it deserves recognition for that.

Mitchell's version got out first, and went to the top of the charts, with Steele's following close behind, but then for one week Mitchell's record label had a minor distribution problem, and Steele took over the top spot, before Mitchell's record returned to number one the next week.

Tommy Steele had become the first British rock and roll singer to get to number one in the UK charts. It would be the only time he would do so, but it was enough. He was a real teen idol. He was so big, in fact, that even his brother, Colin Hicks, became a minor rock and roll star himself off the back of his brother's success.

Very soon, Tommy Steele moved on into light entertainment. First he moved into films – starting with *The Tommy Steele Story*, a film based on his life, for which he, Bart, and Pratt wrote all twelve of the songs in a week to meet the deadline, and then he went into stage musicals. Within a year, he had given up on rock and roll altogether.

But rock and roll hadn't quite given up on him. While Steele was appearing in stage musicals, one was also written about him – a hurtful parody of his life, which he claimed later he'd wanted to sue over. In *Expresso Bongo*, a satire of the British music industry, Steele was parodied as "Bongo Herbert", who rises to fame with no talent whatsoever.

That stage musical was then rewritten for a film version, with the satire taken out of it, so it was a straight rags-to-riches story. It was made into a vehicle for another singer who had been a regular at the 2is, and whose backing band was made up of former members of the Vipers Skiffle Group. We'll talk about both Cliff Richard and the Shadows in the next volume.

Tommy Steele would go on to become something of a national treasure, working on stage with Gene Kelly and on screen with Fred Astaire, writing several books, having a minor artistic career as a sculptor, and touring constantly in pantomimes and musicals. At age eighty-two he still tours every year, performing as Scrooge in a stage musical version of *A Christmas Carol*. His 1950s hits remain popular enough in the UK that a compilation of them went to number twenty-two in the charts in 2009.

He may not leave a large body of rock and roll work, but without him, there would be no British rock and roll industry as we know it, and the rest of this history would be very different.

"Love is Strange"

We've talked before, of course, about the great Bo Diddley, and his main contributions to rock and roll, but in this last chapter of this book, we're going to talk about a song he co-wrote which ended up, in a roundabout way, contributing to many other genres, in ways that we won't properly see until we reach the 1970s. A song that, for all that it is a classic that almost everyone knows, is still rarely treated as an important song in music history, but which offers a pointer to the future not only of rock and roll but of all popular music.

The story of this song starts with Billy Stewart. These days, Billy Stewart is a largely unknown figure – a minor blues man on Chess who was too close to soul music for the Chess Chicago blues fans to take him to heart.

Stewart, like so many black singers of the fifties, started out in the gospel field, but moved over to vocal group R&B. In his case, he did so by occasionally filling in for a group called the Rainbows, which featured Don Covay, who would later go on to become a very well-known soul singer.

Through his work with the group, Stewart got to know Bo Diddley, whose band he joined as a piano player. Through Diddley, Stewart signed with Chess, and his first record, "Billy's Blues", featured both Diddley and Diddley's guitarist Jody Williams on guitar.

Williams came up with the guitar part on that record, and that part would lead to a lot of trouble in the future, thanks to another guitarist, Mickey Baker.

Mickey Baker's birth name was McHouston Baker. Baker had a rough, impoverished, upbringing. He didn't know the identity of his father, and his mother was in and out of prison. He started out as a serious jazz musician, playing bebop, up until the point he saw the great blues musician Pee Wee Crayton.

Or, more precisely, when he saw Crayton's Cadillac. Baker was playing difficult, complex, music that required a great amount of skill and precision. What Crayton was doing was technically far, far, easier than anything Baker was doing, and he was making far more money. So, as Baker put it, "I started bending strings. I was starving to death, and the blues was just a financial thing for me then."

Baker became part of an informal group of people around Atlantic Records, centred around the blues songwriter Doc Pomus, Big Joe Turner and the saxophone player King Curtis. They were playing sophisticated city blues and R&B, and rather looked down on the country bluesmen who are now much better known, as being comparatively unsophisticated musicians. Baker's comments about "bending strings" come from this attitude, that real good music involved horns and pianos and rhythmic sophistication, and that what the Delta bluesmen were doing was something anyone can do.

Baker became one of the most sought-after studio guitarists in the R&B field. It's him on guitar on Ruth Brown's "Mama, He Treats Your Daughter Mean", Big Joe Turner's "Shake, Rattle, and Roll", and the Drifters' "Money Honey", among many others.

Baker was also a guitar teacher, and one of his students was a young woman named Sylvia Vanterpool. Sylvia was, at the time, a singer who was just starting out in her career, having recorded several unsuccessful tracks on Savoy and Jubilee records. She was only thirteen when she started her career, using the name "Little Sylvia" – inspired by Little Esther, who like her was making records for Savoy records – and her early recordings are a strange mix of different styles. For every syrupy ballad like "I Went to Your Wedding" there was a hard R&B number, more in the Little Esther style, like "Drive, Daddy, Drive".

While she had some vocal talent, she was not keeping to a coherent enough, distinctive enough, style to make her into a star, and by the time she was twenty, Sylvia was holding down a day job as a typist, trying and failing to earn enough money to live on as a singer. But she'd been taking guitar lessons from Mickey Baker and had got pretty good.

But then Sylvia started dating a man named Joe Robinson.

Joe Robinson was involved in some way with gangsters – nobody has written enough detail for me to get an exact sense of what it was he did with the mob, but he had connections. And he decided he was going to become Sylvia's manager.

While Sylvia's career was floundering, Joe thought he could beef it up. All that was needed was a gimmick.

Different sources tell different stories about who thought of the idea, but eventually it was decided that Sylvia should join with her guitar teacher and form a duo. Some sources say that the duo was Joe Robinson's idea, and that it was inspired by the success of Gene and Eunice, Shirley and Lee, and the other vocal duos around the time. Other sources, on the other hand, talk about how Mickey Baker, who had started out as a jazz guitarist very much in the Les Paul mode, had wanted to form his own version of Les Paul and Mary Ford.

Either way, the gimmick was a solid one – a male/female duo, both of whom could sing and play the guitar, but playing that string-bending music that Mickey was making money from.

And the two of them had chemistry – at least on stage and on recordings. Off stage, they soon began to grate on each other. Mickey was a man who had no interest in stardom or financial success – he was a rather studious, private, man who just wanted to make music and get better at his instrument, while Sylvia had a razor-sharp business mind, a huge amount of ambition, and a desire for stardom. But they worked well as a musical team, even if they were never going to be the best of friends.

Originally, they signed with a label called Rainbow Records, a medium-sized indie label in New York, where they put out their first single, "I'm So Glad". It's not an especially good record, and it does seem to have a bit of Gene and Eunice to it, and almost none of the distinctive guitar that would characterise their later work – just some stabbing punctuation on the middle eight and a rather perfunctory solo. The B-side, though, "Se De Boom Run Dun", while it's also far from a wonderful song, does have the semi-calypso rhythm that would later make them famous.

Unsurprisingly, it didn't sell, and nor did the follow-ups. But the records did get some airplay in New York, if nowhere else, and that brought them to the attention of Bob Rolontz at Groove Records.

Groove Records was a subsidiary of RCA, set up in 1953, as an attempt at solving a problem we've talked about before, which is that since the major labels had spent years ignoring R&B, while the small labels that did put out R&B had been locked out of the distribution networks that the major labels dominated, the independent network of shops – usually black-owned businesses selling to black customers – that only sold R&B records had no interest in selling the records put out by the major labels.

But, of course, the major labels still wanted to sell to those customers. After all, there was money out there in the pockets of people who weren't shareholders in RCA or Columbia, and in the eyes of those shareholders that was the greatest injustice in the world, and one that needed to be rectified forthwith.

And so those labels set up their own mini-divisions, to sell to those shops. They had different labels, because the shops wouldn't buy from the majors, but they were wholly-owned subsidiaries. Fake indie labels. And Groove was one of them.

Groove Records had had a minor hit in 1955 with the piano player Piano Red, and his "Jump Man Jump", but hadn't had a huge amount of commercial success since, and Rolontz thought that Mickey and Sylvia could be the ones to bring him that success. Rolontz put them together with the saxophonist and arranger King Curtis, who Mickey already knew from his work with Doc Pomus, and Curtis put together a team of the best R&B musicians in New York, many of them the same people who would play on most of Atlantic's sessions.

Mickey and Sylvia's first single on Groove, "Walking in the Rain", had the potential to be a big hit in the eyes of the record company. But unfortunately for them, Johnnie Ray put out "Just Walking in the Rain" at almost the exact same time. That's a totally different song, of course – it's a cover version of one of the first records ever released on Sun Records, a few years earlier, originally by a vocal group called the Prisonaires. But customers were understandably confused by the presence of two songs with almost identical titles in the market, and so

Mickey and Sylvia's song tanked. They still didn't have that hit they needed.

But at that point, fate intervened in the form of Bo Diddley.

In May 1956, Diddley had written and recorded a song called "Love is Strange", and not got round to releasing it. Jody Williams, who was in Diddley's band at the time, had played the lead guitar on the session, and he'd reused the licks he had used for "Billy's Blues" on the song.

At the time, Diddley was friendly with Mickey Baker, and was using Baker as a session guitarist on outside recordings he was producing for other artists. As a result, Mickey and Sylvia ended up playing a few shows on the same bill as Diddley, and at one of the shows, Williams, who was attracted to Sylvia, decided to play "Love is Strange" for her. Sylvia liked the song, and Mickey and Sylvia decided to record it.

Now, Diddley claimed that what he told the song's publishers was that Jody Williams wrote the music, while he wrote the lyrics, but he asked that the credit for the lyrics be put in the name of his wife Ethel Smith. While Smith's name made the credits, Williams' didn't, and Williams blamed Diddley for the omission, while Diddley just said (with some evidence) that most of the people he signed contracts with were liars and thieves, and that it didn't surprise him that they'd missed Williams' name off.

We'll never know for sure what was actually in Diddley's contracts because, again according to Diddley, just before he and Smith divorced she burned all his papers so she could claim that he never gave her any money and he couldn't prove otherwise.

Williams never believed him, and the two didn't speak for decades.

Meanwhile, two other people were credited as writers on the song – Mickey and Sylvia themselves. This is presumably for the changes that were made between Diddley's demo and the finished song, which mostly amount to Baker's lead guitar part and to the famous spoken-word section of the song in the middle.

According to Diddley, he also later sold his own share in the song to Sylvia, some time in the early sixties. This may well be the case, because Sylvia Vanterpool went on to become a very, very successful businesswoman, who made a lot of very wise business decisions.

Either way, "Love is Strange" was a big hit. It went to number eleven in the pop charts and number one on the R&B chart. It's one of those records that everyone knows, and it went on to be covered by dozens upon dozens of performers, including the Maddox Brothers and Rose, the Everly Brothers, and Paul McCartney and Wings. And Jody Williams never saw a penny from it.

But after Groove Records had had this breakthrough big hit, RCA decided to close the label down, and move the acts on the label, and their producer Rolontz, to another subsidiary, Vik. Vik Records had, according to Rolontz, "probably the worst collection of talent in the history of the world", and was severely in debt. All the momentum for Mickey and Sylvia's career was gone.

Mickey and Sylvia would release many more records, but they would have diminishing returns. Their next record went top ten R&B, but only number forty-seven on the pop charts, and the record after that, "Dearest", did even worse, only reaching number eighty-five in the hot one hundred, even though it was another Bo Diddley ballad very much in the same vein as "Love is Strange".

But even though that wasn't a big hit record, it was a favourite of Buddy Holly – a singer who at this time was just starting out in his own career. You can tell how much Holly liked Mickey and Sylvia just by comparing the way he sings the word "baby" on many of his records to the way Sylvia sings it in "Love is Strange", and he recorded his own home demos of both "Love is Strange" and "Dearest" – demos which were released on singles after his death.

But "Dearest" was so obscure that when Holly's single came out, the song was titled "Umm Oh Yeah", and credited to "unknown" for many years, because no-one at the record label had heard the earlier record.

Mickey and Sylvia would have several more records in the hot one hundred, but the highest would only reach number forty-six. But while they had no more hits under their own names, they did have another hit. . .as Ike Turner.

After Mickey and Sylvia were dropped along with the rest of the Vik artists, they split up temporarily, but then got back together to start their own company, Willow Records, to release their material. Ike

Turner played on some of their records, and to return the favour they agreed to produce a record for Ike and Tina Turner.

The song chosen was called "It's Gonna Work Out Fine", and it was co-written by the great R&B songwriter Rose Marie McCoy. The other credited co-writer is one Sylvia McKinney, who some sources suggest is the same person as Sylvia Vanterpool – who had by this point married Joe Robinson and changed her name to Sylvia Robinson.

Whether Vanterpool was the other co-writer or not, Mickey and Sylvia had recorded a version of the song for Vik Records, but it hadn't been released, and so they suggested to Ike that the song would work as an Ike and Tina Turner record – and they would produce and arrange it for them.

Indeed they did more than that. They *were* Ike Turner on the record – Sylvia played the lead guitar part, while Mickey did the spoken vocals, which Ike would do live. Sylvia also joined the Ikettes on backing vocals, and while Mickey and Sylvia aren't the credited producers, the end result is essentially a Mickey and Sylvia record with guest vocals from Tina Turner. It sold over a million copies, and got a Grammy nomination.

However, Mickey and Sylvia's recordings under their own name were still having no success, and Mickey was also having problems because his then-wife was white, and with the particularly virulent form of racism the US was suffering through at the time, he didn't want to be in the country any more.

He was also becoming more and more interested in the academic side of music. He had already, in 1955, written a book, *The Complete Course in Jazz Guitar*, which is still available today and highly regarded. So he moved to Europe, and went back into jazz, performing with people like Coleman Hawkins.

But he did more than just jazz. He studied composition with Iannis Xennakis and started writing fugues and a concerto for guitar and orchestra, "The Blues Suite". Possibly his most interesting work is from the mid-1970s, an album called *Mississippi Delta Dues*, released under his birth name McHouston Baker, where he paid tribute to the country bluesmen he'd looked down on early on by performing their songs, along with some of his own in a similar style. It's an odd album, in which sometimes he does a straight soundalike, while on other songs he uses strings. Sometimes this is just as a standard pop-style string section, but sometimes he's using them in ways he learned from Xenakkis, like on a version of J.B. Lenoir's "Alabama Blues", rewritten as "Alabama March", which ends up sounding like nothing as much as Scott Walker.

Baker carried on performing music of all kinds around Europe until his death in 2011. He died massively respected for his contributions to blues, jazz, R&B, and the technical proficiency of generations of guitarists.

Sylvia Robinson made even more of a contribution. After a few years off to have kids after the duo split up, she set up her own record label, All Platinum. For All Platinum she wrote and produced a number of proto-disco hits for other people in the late sixties and early seventies. Those included "Shame Shame Shame" for Shirley and Company, the song that inspired David Bowie, John Lennon, and Carlos Alomar to rework a song Bowie and Alomar had been working on, called "Footstompin'", into "Fame".

Sylvia also had a hit of her own, with a song called "Pillow Talk" that she'd written for Al Green, but which he'd turned down due to its blatant sexuality conflicting with his newfound religion. But I'm afraid we're going to have to wait until volume five before we find out more about Sylvia's biggest contribution to music, because Sylvia Robinson, who had been Little Sylvia and the woman calling her lover-boy, became to hip-hop what Sam Phillips was to rock and roll, and when we get to 1979 we will be looking at how, with financing from her husband's gangster friend Morris Levy, someone from the first wave of rock and roll stars was more responsible than anyone for seeing commercial potential in the music that eventually took rock's cultural place.

Bibliography

A project such as this requires the kind of deep dive into music history books and websites that it's impossible to recommend to any but the most devoted of researchers. Half the time, a sentence in one chapter will be the vital clue to unlock a whole episode, but the entire rest of the book will be an irrelevance. I would not wish on my worst enemies, let alone my readers and listeners, the task of wading through the reams of self-published autobiographies by members of vocal groups, or badly laid-out PDFs by people who are not writing in their first language and often paste their paragraphs in out of order, just to get this kind of information.

It's also surprising how many highly-regarded books on the subject of music are truly terrible. For example, one writer, who wrote what I have seen described in a reputable source as the best music biography ever, routinely manufactures events out of whole cloth and puts words – usually racial slurs – into the mouths of people who never said them, for dramatic effect. I have read some of his books, and discovered some useful information in them which I then confirmed in more reliable sources, but I won't suggest that anyone else read them.

But on the other hand, there are many books and websites that I have used for this project which are absolutely wonderful – works which show a respect to the music, books which are the results of lifetimes of research, and books which are so well written that anyone could take pleasure from reading them, even if they were unfamiliar with the musicians under discussion.

So here, I will list not every book I used, but a small selection of them which I think will actually be useful. I will also list a selection of

CDs which between them will allow you to obtain a fair chunk of the music I have discussed for a relatively low price.

Books

The most important book for my researches, but one which I can only recommend with caveats, is Larry Birnbaum's *Before Elvis*. This is the single most information-dense, highly-researched, music book I have ever read in my life, and Birnbaum appears to know literally every piece of American popular music from the early nineteenth century to the mid-twentieth. But it is so dense that it is not a book for light reading at all.

In the same way that Cecil B. DeMille was said to have once claimed that he could have made a film out of any two pages of the Bible, I could make an episode of the podcast out of any random half page of Birnbaum's book. But in the same way that one doesn't read the lists of begats in the book of Chronicles as one does a blockbuster novel, Birnbaum's work requires attention, and is best read in small doses, with a notepad by one's side, and with an Internet connection to track down copies of the many records he cites. It is a wonderful work of scholarship, and arguably the most important book in the whole field, but it's *dense*.

Another book which was essential for almost every song I looked at in the early stages of this project was *Honkers and Stompers* by Arnold Shaw. Shaw was someone who worked in music publishing in the 1950s, and so he knew many of the people he was writing about. His book is a mammoth history of 1950s rhythm and blues, covering everyone from Louis Jordan to Johnny Otis, Ruth Brown to LaVern Baker, and with interviews with many of the pivotal figures -- including, in some cases, their last interviews ever.

Roots, Radicals, and Rockers: How Skiffle Changed the World, by Billy Bragg, is an absolutely wonderful book about the social, political, and musical scene around skiffle in the 1950s. I came to Bragg's book not expecting it to be especially good – musicians are not generally regarded as particularly good writers, and I read it mostly because it was a new book that had had some publicity, and so if I didn't know what it had to say I would have been asked questions about it.

As it turned out, Bragg's book is absolutely indispensable for anyone who wants to know about Britain in the fifties, and especially about the intersections between skiffle, the folk revival scene, and early British rock and roll, and is extraordinarily well written. One of the best books I've read in the course of researching this project. There are some slight problems with some of the research when he strays outside the areas he knows the best (a short explanation of the origins of the Cajun people is horribly incorrect, for example) but when writing about folk music and British fifties culture, Bragg is astonishingly good.

Another book by a musician that I definitely recommend is Bob Stanley's *Yeah Yeah Yeah! The Story of Modern Pop*. Stanley's book is an attempt to cover similar ground to this series, though in far fewer words – it's "only" around nine hundred pages, covering the story of music that made the British charts from their inception to the early 2000s. I noticed a handful of minor factual errors in the book, but only a handful, and Stanley is an insightful critic and analyst of the music. It's not the book I would have written, but it's a very good one indeed for getting an understanding of the broad sweep of post-war popular music.

Every book by Peter Guralnick is, more or less by definition, worth reading. But in particular, two books by him have been invaluable to this project. *Last Train to Memphis*, the first volume of his two-volume look at Elvis Presley, manages to give a wonderful understanding of the background from which he came, and of the other musicians with whom he worked and interacted. It also paints a very different picture of Elvis' character from anything else I've read on the man – a picture which unlocked a lot of understanding for me. "My" Elvis – the take on Elvis' personality and behaviour in this series – is drawn more from Guralnick than from anyone else. The second volume of his two-volume biography is not quite as good – there are a couple of errors in there that should never have made it through the editorial process – but it's still better than anything else I've read on the latter half of Elvis' life.

The other book by Guralnick that shaped this book, and the pod-casts on which it was based, is *Sam Phillips: The Man Who Invented*

Rock 'n' Roll. As with all Guralnick's biographies, this one gives a rounded look at its subject, showing exactly why he was admirable and important – and Guralnick clearly had a great deal of personal affection for Phillips – without shying away from his myriad personality flaws and how he caused hurt to people around him.

When it comes to websites, one has proved more invaluable than the entire rest of the Internet – Marv Goldberg's site http://uncamarvey. com. Goldberg is an expert on rhythm and blues, especially 1950s vocal groups, and he provides detailed, exhaustive, biographies of almost every vocal group to make a record in the fifties.

And the final book I can recommend with almost no caveats is *Upside Your Head* by Johnny Otis. This is part oral history of the Central Avenue music scene in LA in the 1940s and 50s, with Otis interviewing other then-surviving participants in that scene; part Otis' opinions on racism and politics in the US from the forties through to the nineties (the title is, among other things, a reference to the Rodney King beating), and part Otis' own memories and impressions of musicians – usually people from the generation above him, like Count Basie and Lester Young, but also people of his own generation.

It's only a short book, and it's definitely one man's opinions rather than anything more organised or comprehensive, but it's the opinions of one man who, more than anyone else, defined R&B in the years that it was turning into rock and roll. Otis' personality shines through every word, and it's definitely worth your attention.

Music

Now we come to the music. Again, I will not list here every recording to which I have referred when writing this book. All the music I have talked about here is out of copyright in the EU, and so there are innumerable cheap compilations containing some or all the tracks I have discussed here.

Rather than name where you can find every track I have discussed – especially given that compilations come into and go out of print with astonishing rapidity, and in some cases I've talked about people who have only had one hit and who it probably wouldn't be worth getting a compilation by – the following is a short list of compilations that are, at the time of writing, in print, and which will allow you to get a broad overview of the music covered here, as well as introduce you to more.

If you just want to hear the songs I discuss, then my page at Mixcloud, http://mixcloud.com/AndrewHickey, has streaming mixes I put together for almost every episode of the podcast on which this book is based, containing every song I excerpted in those episodes. However, not all of these mixes are available in every country, due to differing licensing laws, and I would always recommend to anyone who can afford to that they purchase their own copies of music rather than streaming it, as streaming sites can disappear at any time.

For sheer value, and number of songs in this book (and one song that will turn up in the next volume) it's very hard to beat *That's Your Last Boogie*, a three-CD set of Johnny Otis-produced or performed material from Fantastic Voyage records. That box set features "Double-Crossing Blues", "Hound Dog", "Pledging My Love", "The Wallflower", and "Ko Ko Mo", plus tracks by Big Joe Turner, Wynonie Harris, Johnny Moore's Three Blazers, Little Richard and more. If you want a complete overview of 50s West Coast R&B, there's no better place to look than that set.

Similarly cheap and essential is the four-CD set *The Willie Dixon Story*, on Proper. That only contains "Maybellene" and "Sincerely" of the tracks covered here, but Willie Dixon was basically synonymous with Chess Records, and this box showcases him as writer, bass player, and producer, and will give you the best possible introduction to the output of that label.

And finally, when it comes to multi-artist compilations, the other cheap essential is *The Memphis Recordings: From the Legendary Sun Studios Vol. 1*. This ten-disc set from Documents has the A- and B-sides of ninety of the very first Sun singles, in chronological order. It has all the Carl Perkins, Johnny Cash, and Roy Orbison material covered here, as well as all of Elvis' Sun singles, and other relevant songs like Rufus Thomas' "Bear Cat", along with a ton of great classic rockabilly and blues and a few interesting misfires.

Those three sets -- seventeen CDs in all, for around thirty pounds -- will between them give you the perfect broad overview of at least the

R&B and Memphis rockabilly sides of rock and roll between the late forties and the mid fifties.

There are many, many, compilations covering doo wop, but most of these include later white acts like Dion and the Belmonts, or even the Four Seasons or Jan and Dean, interchangeably with the black acts discussed here, and they go in and out of print almost all the time. Most of these compilations are perfectly fine if you want fifties or early sixties nostalgia, but are much less useful if you want to understand the music in its historical context.

As of the time of writing, the box set I would recommend most is *Doo-Wop: The R&B Vocal Group Sound 1950-1960* from Crazy Warthog Media. This box contains almost all the doo-wop records discussed in this book, plus a few that make the next, in roughly chronological order. Its eighty-nine tracks cover essentially all the black vocal groups who had hits in the fifties, and it has liner notes by Marv Goldberg.

We now come on to the sets based around individual artists. I'll only list here those artists who have more than one entry in the book, as those artists tend to be the ones who have reasonable archival collections available. Almost all the others, though, will have decent cheap compilations in print – at the time of writing, I would recommend Real Gone Music's "Four Classic Albums" (or similarly-titled) sets, which generally collect all of an artist's work up to 1962 (the year at which things have currently stopped falling into the public domain in the EU).

First, and most obvious, is *Elvis: The King of Rock 'n' Roll – The Complete 50s Masters*, from Sony. This does exactly what you would expect from the title – it contains every single completed master recording he made in the 1950s (but not outtakes, live versions, and so on). Along with this, it's worth buying the box set *A Boy From Tupelo: The Complete 1953-55 Recordings*, also from Sony, which contains every surviving scrap of recording from Elvis before he signed with RCA.

Then there's *They Call Me The Fat Man: The Legendary Imperial Recordings*, on EMI. This four-CD box set covers Fats Domino's work from his first single through to his departure from Imperial, and contains all the essential tracks.

There are many, many, many compilations of Chuck Berry's 50s and early 60s recordings. *The Chess Box* is the one to get if you want something comprehensive, otherwise a compilation called *The Great Twenty-Eight* has Berry's most important recordings on it.

And finally, for Bill Haley I would recommend *From Western Swing to Rock*, from Proper Box, which contains recordings by Haley with the Four Aces of Western Swing, the Saddlemen, and the Comets, as well as recordings by the Jodimars, the group formed by several ex-members of the Comets.

Acknowledgements

This book would not exist without the podcast on which it is based, at http://500songs.com. I would like to thank every single listener to that podcast, especially those who have shared or reviewed it.

And the podcast itself would not exist without my backers on Patreon. I will not list them all here, because some of them, for legal reasons, back me under names they no longer use, and I would not feel right thanking some but not all of them for their backing. But thanks are due not only to the hundred and eighty-three people backing the Patreon at the moment, but to all those who have backed it in the past but are currently unable to. Your support is hugely appreciated, and I am grateful to every single one of you. If you would like to become a backer, visit http://patreon.com/join/andrewhickey .

Thanks to my fellow bloggers at Mindless Ones, the comic blog which has hosted much of my writing, and who have also provided me with a huge amount of emotional support over the years -- Dan, Fraser, David, Scott, Adam, Mark, Duncan, Spare5, and Bobsy. Thanks too to the wider community of which the Mindless Ones are a part -- Dan and John of Hitsville, Paul Jon Milne, Fiona Keery, Ruan, Ben DST, Al Kennedy, Al Ewing, Kelly Kanayama, Thal, Jesz, and the rest.

Thanks to everyone in the Awkward Squad for trying to give me some faith in humanity.

Thanks to Holly Boson, Tilt Araiza, Gary Rodger, and the TCBCast for inviting me to guest on their podcasts and talk about music with them.

Thanks should also go to all those who have encouraged me in my writing in the past, including, but not limited to (and in no particular order), Bill Ritchie, Jennie Rigg, Steve Hickey, Stuart Douglas, Elizabeth

Sandifer, Jack Graham, Christian Lipski, Shawn Taylor, Sean Dillon, Steven Hinkle, Richard Jones, Leonard Pierce, Matt Rossi, Omorka, Lawrence Burton, David Gerard, Simon Bucher-Jones, Philip Purser-Hallard, Paul Magrs, Al Ewing, Emily Wright, Dave Page, Eve Friday, Andrew Ducker, Socketwench, Andrew Rilstone, Gavin Burrows, Alex Wilcock, Richard Flowers, Wesley Osam, Iain Lee, James Brough, Aditya Bidakar, Ian Alexander-Barnes, Penny Goodman, Penny Andrews, Jo Coleman, Fred Langridge, Chad Nevett, Debi Linton, Mat Bowles, and Gavin Robinson. There are many more than I can possibly list here, and I have undoubtedly missed out dozens of people who deserve acknowledgement.

Special thanks should go to my parents, who encouraged my interest in music and music history from a very early age, and to my wife Holly Matthies, who has tolerated an immense amount of disruption over the last year and a half as I wrote this material.

This book was typeset in the Free Software text editing program LyX (http://lyx.org), so thanks go to the creators of that software, as well as to the creators of LATEX, and, ultimately, Donald Knuth, whose typesetting language TEX is the ultimate basis of all those programs. It was created on a machine running the Debian GNU/Linux distribution, so thanks to all the many thousands of people who gave their work freely to that system.

The book was mostly written in the online writing game 4thewords (http://4thewords.com), which I would recommend to anyone wanting to increase their writing productivity.

Song index

Index

Made in United States
Troutdale, OR
05/22/2024

20055636R00333